Perceptions of security

Public opinion and
expert assessments in
Europe's new democracies

edited by
Richard Smoke

Manchester University Press
Manchester and New York
distributed exclusively in the USA and Canada by St. Martin's Press

Copyright © Center for Foreign Policy Development
Thomas J. Watson Jr. Institute of International Studies
Brown University 1996

Published by Manchester University Press
Oxford Road, Manchester M13 9NR, UK
and Room 400, 175 Fifth Avenue,
New York, NY 10010, USA

Distributed exclusively in the USA and Canada
by St. Martin's Press, Inc.,
175 Fifth Avenue, New York NY 10010, USA

British Library Cataloguing-in-Publication Data
A catalogue record for this book is available from the British Library

Library of Congress Cataloging-in-Publication Data
Perceptions of security: public opinion and expert assessments in Europe's new democracies
  / edited by Richard Smoke
      p.   cm.
    ISBN 0-7190-4812-5 (hardback: alk, paper), – ISBN 0-7190-4813-3 (pbk.: alk, paper)
    1. Security, International.   2. Security, International – Public opinion.
3. Europe,   Eastern – Politics and government – 1989–   4. Europe, Eastern – Politics
and government – 1989–   – Public opinion.   5. Public opinion – Europe, Eastern. I.
Smoke, Richard.
JX1963.P426   1996
327.1′72′091717–dc20   95–16866
                                                                          CIP

ISBN   0 7190 4812 5 hardback
       0 7190 4813 3 paperback

First published in 1996

99 98 97 96 95   10 9 8 7 6 5 4 3 2 1

Typeset in Hong Kong by Best-set Typesetter Ltd.

Printed in Great Britain by Redwood Books Ltd, Trowbridge

Contents

Analytical table of contents

Contents

Abbreviations

CFE	Conventional Forces in Europe (treaty)
CIS	Commonwealth of Independent States
CSCE	Conference on Security and Cooperation in Europe (before December 1994)
CSFR	Czech and Slovak Federal Republic (before January 1993)
EC	European Community (before November 1993)
EU	European Union (since November 1993)
NACC	North Atlantic Cooperation Council
NATO	North Atlantic Treaty Organization
OSCE	Organization for Security and Cooperation in Europe (since December 1994)
PfP	Partnership for Peace
US	United States
USSR	Union of Soviet Socialist Republics
WEU	Western European Union
WTO	Warsaw Treaty Organization

The staff of the Center for Foreign Policy Development at Brown University's Watson Institute for International Studies, and all of the contributors to this volume, would like to dedicate this book to the memory of our colleague and friend, Richard Smoke, who died as this book was nearing completion. As co-director of the Security for Europe project, Professor Smoke was responsible for organizing and coordinating the entire project involving scholars from seven countries of Central and Eastern Europe. Throughout his career, he dedicated his work to the goals of enhancing world peace and security for all. For Richard Smoke, security could be realized only when all were secure. Security for one individual, group, state, or nation was not genuine if it came at the expense of a loss of security for others. This central principle guided his work on this project and in this, his last book. We all miss him immensely, but we also dedicate this book as well as our own future efforts to enhancing the cause of peace and security for which he devoted his entire professional life.

Preface

This book surveys and explores, in a broad way, how security is perceived in the major new democracies of Central and Eastern Europe. "Security" is used primarily in its standard sense in international affairs, namely political and military security, but other aspects of security are discussed as well. The book explores perceptions of security in six countries: Russia, Ukraine, and the four Central European countries of Poland, the Czech Republic, Slovakia and Hungary. Thirteen of the book's seventeen chapters are written by authors from those countries. These chapters and the book as a whole book examine the security of Central and Eastern Europe as an entire region, as well as the security issues facing each of the countries individually.

The book is the product of a collaboration that was unusual in not one but two ways. It involved research organizations from all the countries just named plus the United States and Germany. And it involved specialists from two quite different kinds of research organizations: ones that study international security, and ones that study public opinion. The need for both kinds is explained shortly. Thirteen research organizations in Europe participated in the collaboration. The European authors represented in this book are senior researchers in these organizations. (They are identified specifically in the contributors' listing at the end of the book.)

The effort that brought all these organizations together was called the "Security for Europe Project." It was led by the Watson Institute's Center for Foreign Policy Development, of Brown University in the USA. The research agenda was agreed jointly by all the collaborating organizations, as further described in chapter 2. More information about the organization and history of the Security for Europe Project is found in appendix 3.

This book, and the Project from which it derives, were conceived in response to the profound changes that have occurred in Europe. Through more than forty years of Cold War the political landscape of Europe had been frozen. Then in 1989 a torrent of changes began. The countries of

Central Europe regained their independence, and immediately faced wholly new questions of what their situation in Europe now was, and of how to find security. Then in late 1991 the Soviet Union collapsed. Countries emerged from the rubble, like Russia and Ukraine, that were both new and also very old lands. For these states too, new questions arose of how to relate to their region and to Europe generally, and how to find security. In short, the old landscape had vanished and a completely new one was appearing.

As it did, ancient conflicts began rising to the surface. Previously the Soviet empire had quashed any tensions among nationalities and ethnic groups under its control. The end of the empire left a vacuum in which old hostilities could reappear. In Yugoslavia, tensions that had been long growing erupted into open warfare. Through much of the eastern half of Europe other tensions, though not yet nearly so violent, began emerging that posed new questions for security.

Early in the 1990s, therefore, it was evident that the fresh landscape required an equally fresh exploration. The panaroma was so new that no familiar signposts could be assumed. It was from this starting point that this book, and the Security for Europe Project, were born. A fresh inquiry would be launched, making none of the old familiar assumptions. The exploration would begin from a completely blank slate and would survey the terrain in a broad way to capture its fresh features.

Two decisions were made at the outset. One was that this exploration would focus on security in the eastern half of Europe, as it was perceived and being thought about by people in that region themselves. Although the research effort was led by an American research center, the effort would not be chiefly shaped by the points of view and ideas held by Americans or Westerners. Instead, the research would identify the concerns, hopes, anxieties and expectations about security and peace felt by people in the region. The fact that nearly all of this book comprises chapters by authors from the region reflects that commitment.

While it might have been desirable to include researchers and research organizations from every one of the new democracies of Central and Eastern Europe, there are so many that this was not feasible. For practical reasons the effort was limited to the two most important of the post-Soviet countries, Russia and Ukraine, and to three of the most important Central European states, Poland, Hungary and Czechoslovakia. During the time research was underway, Czechoslovakia split into two states, the Czech and Slovak Republics, and work naturally continued in both. Wars in Yugoslavia and in the Caucasus region were deliberately excluded as topics in themselves, but their important implications were considered.

The other basic decision made at the outset was to examine the viewpoint of the public in each of these countries, as well as the thinking of experts on foreign and security policy. A truly fresh look at a completely new landscape should not be confined to the thinking of specialists. The perspective of the general population in these countries needs to be considered also. The hopes, fears and anticipations of the public are important. People in each of these lands have their own point of view on their country's situation in the region and in Europe, and their own point of view on how their country can become secure. Both the public's ideas *and* specialists' ideas need careful examination, particularly when a new international situation has appeared.

The viewpoint of the public was doubly important at this time because these countries, so long ruled by central authorities, were now making transitions toward democracy. In the early 1990s, every one of the countries represented in this book was in some stage of becoming democratic. Some were further along in the process than others, but even those where democracy was least developed had adopted democracy as a goal. For countries that had not previously been democratic, but now were trying to be, an examination of the public's views clearly was especially important, because policy would now have to take public attitudes into account. (More is said about the public opinion research in chapter 2.)

Central and Eastern Europe: the central area

For these reasons, the book gives approximately equal attention to the perceptions of policy specialists and the perspective of the public. Separate chapters, two from each country, present each perspective. The perspective of policy specialists – and of governments – is assessed by leading policy experts from the six countries. The viewpoint of the public is described by leading public opinion specialists from the countries.

Part I of the book gives the reader a factual introduction to the subject matter and, in a second chapter, a brief statement of the research methods and assumptions that were used in developing this book. The next four parts contain the chapters by the European authors. A single concluding chapter, in Part VI, offers some overall observations that may be derived from the preceding discussions viewed as a whole.

There are three appendices. One assesses public attitudes in eastern and western Germany, a country of enormous importance to Central and Eastern Europe. One gives a synopsis of the major East–West arms control agreements of the late 1980s and early 1990s. The third appendix gives information about the Security for Europe Project, including acknowledgements of the contributions to it and to this book made by many people and organizations.

This book is intended primarily for scholars and students in Europe and North America. For the benefit of students, the work presupposes no prior knowledge of the subject; the first chapter begins in simple terms that lay the groundwork for the more complicated assessments that follow in later chapters. The book is intended also for policy specialists inside and outside governments, and for general readers interested in world and European affairs.

Part I

Introduction

1

Background: the new and old Europe

Jan Kalicki

Security in Europe today is a subject profoundly different from what it was only a few years ago. For decades prior to 1989, Europe differed greatly from what it is today. The profound changes, which in some ways are still unfolding, have enormous significance not only for Europeans but also for Americans and many others. Certain dangers that used to exist have vanished. Other dangers have appeared that could lead to crises with potentially great consequences for Europeans, Americans and indeed for the whole world. Most of this book describes the changes that have been occurring and assesses today's new dangers, as they are seen by Europeans themselves. This introductory chapter sets the stage for those assessments, by providing the reader with a background of basic facts and events needed to understand today's challenges. This background will be especially useful for students, who may not be familiar with all the events summarized here; scholars and other experts may also find a brief résumé of essential facts and history useful.

Among the most central features of the security situation in Europe today are the rapid pace at which it changes, its relative unfamiliarity and the high uncertainty it presents. These features cannot be appreciated fully without first appreciating how opposite was the situation before 1989. For decades, the landscape in Europe had remained relatively fixed, was quite familiar, and (especially since the late 1960s) presented relatively few uncertainties. Let us begin this background review with a glance at that earlier Europe.

The fixed landscape before 1989

For more than forty years until 1989, Europe was divided sharply in half. An "iron curtain" down its middle separated the continent into western and eastern parts of radically different kinds. The western group of countries had market economies; all its chief nations and most of its lesser ones were stable democracies. The eastern group was, in essence, an empire ruled by

Moscow – militarily, politically and economically. These profoundly different kinds of social systems meant that Europe's separation into two halves could hardly have been more thorough. The sharpness and gravity of the division may be illustrated by, for instance, the fact that people were shot attempting to flee from the eastern to the western part.

The standing military confrontation between the two systems created the deepest chasm of all and, at certain moments at least, created a real danger of war. The western group formed a military alliance, the North Atlantic Treaty Organization (NATO). The United States was its most powerful member; the Treaty itself was signed in Washington and is called the Washington Treaty. The Soviet Union created an "alliance" of the eastern countries, which Moscow wholly directed through extensive and elaborate mechanisms of control. To bolster the idea that this military organization was a genuine alliance, the Soviets had the Treaty signed in Warsaw, not Moscow, and named it the Warsaw Treaty Organization (WTO). In the West it was generally called the Warsaw Pact. For decades the two military systems confronted each other across the middle of Europe. Only a small number of European countries, mainly Austria, Finland, Sweden, Switzerland, Ireland and Yugoslavia, were not part of either military bloc.

The period from the late 1940s to the early 1960s witnessed several sharp crises between the alliances which in the opinion of most historians, and most analysts at the time, could have escalated into a general European war and hence almost certainly into World War III. All the crises were focused on a single point, the city of Berlin.[1] All were caused by the fact that, as part of the World War II settlement, the western part of Berlin became part of West Germany and hence of the West, even though the city was located deep in East Germany and thus well inside the eastern bloc. A Western enclave there was an almost intolerable irritant to the Soviet system, because until 1961 people from the east could cross freely into the western part of the city and thus into the West. That year the Berlin Wall was erected, thereby completing and sealing the iron curtain. Thereafter, there were no more serious crises in Berlin, and by 1970 some East–West agreements made it clear that there would not be any more.

At no other place in Europe was there any clash between the two alliances that might have escalated into war, not even in the harshest days of the Cold War in the 1950s. The removal of Berlin as a crisis point helped usher in a milder period later. Efforts toward "detente" created, in the late 1960s and thereafter, a quite stable relationship between the two sides. Although the Soviet Union and United States carried their Cold War to other parts of the world, including Vietnam and Afghanistan, Europe now became a relatively stable and predictable region. NATO and the WTO continued to add new weapons to the arsenals they pointed at each other, but from this time on, war never seemed likely in Europe.

By the 1990s, many of the leaders on both sides during the harsh days of the 1950s and early 1960s were dead or retired. When thinking of the Cold

War, the generation now in power and younger generations in Europe remember mainly the mild decades that followed. And of course, everyone knows how peacefully the confrontation came to an end. With these memories in mind and with the advantage of hindsight, many Europeans now look back on the Cold War as a time of relative stability.

In particular, people interested in security in Europe tend to remember those decades for some positive qualities that more recently have turned into their opposites. The European landscape of the later Cold War decades was a fixed landscape where little of significance changed with respect to security. The long continuity of the two great blocs created a situation that remained reassuringly familiar, year after year. National leaders and also the public were able to feel that this essentially fixed and familiar situation presented few uncertainties. A tacit understanding between East and West that neither side really wanted to upset Europe's stability meant that people could feel considerable confidence that there would be no great surprises. How these features have lately turned into their opposites is one of the subjects of this book.

Of course the standing confrontation between the two Cold War military blocs produced some periods of political stress. One such period was the early 1980s, when a strong public dispute developed in several Western European countries over whether NATO should deploy some new nuclear weapons in answer to some new Soviet weapons. But these and other events took place within a larger European framework that fundamentally was familiar and almost unchanging, and which presented few uncertainties. Let us briefly review the situation in the eastern half of Europe prior to 1989, before turning to the changes that began then.

Eastern Europe before 1989

In the final years of World War II, the Soviet Army (also called the Red Army) had swept westwards toward Germany, steadily pushing back the Nazi German Army, called the Wehrmacht. By the time of the victory over Nazi Germany, the Red Army occupied a substantial portion of Germany itself and nearly all the lands to Germany's east and southeast. Following the war, the Red Army withdrew for several years from Czechoslovakia, but it remained in Poland, Hungary, East Germany and elsewhere. In 1948, Soviet forces returned to Czechoslovakia following a communist coup, described in a later chapter.

In these countries, and also in Bulgaria and Romania, the Soviets set up "puppet" governments, entirely controlled by local communists loyal to Moscow. These governments enforced their rule by all methods, including secret police, also ultimately controlled by Moscow. The external as well as internal affairs of these countries was fully controlled by the Soviets in all significant respects, although the propaganda claimed that these countries were merely "fraternal socialist" states acting together voluntarily. The

WTO was created in 1955, in response to West Germany joining NATO the year before. Later in the Cold War, several of these countries, including Hungary, Poland and Romania, were able to achieve some degree of autonomy in some aspects of their policy, but only within overall adherence to the "socialist camp."

On two occasions, Eastern European peoples attempted revolts against the Soviet regime.[2] Both were crushed. In Hungary in 1956, a popular uprising against the puppet government was forcibly put down in two weeks. In Czechoslovakia in 1968, a more liberal regime tried to introduce some humane reforms and limited freedoms. This "Prague Spring" was crushed in August. Both countries were invaded not only by large Soviet Army forces but also by WTO armies. Hungarians, Czechs and Slovaks remember well that the only invasions their countries have suffered since World War II were invasions not by the official "enemy," NATO, but by the official "allies," the WTO.

As early as 1949, the Soviets created an economic organization to manage the economic relations of these countries with the USSR. The organization was the "Council for Mutual Economic Assistance," called COMECON or, alternatively, the CMEA.[3] Later, as the European Community (EC) began to develop, the propaganda claimed that COMECON would be something similar for Eastern Europe. In fact it was very different from the European Community, and consisted essentially of a series of government-to-government trade and other economic relationships, designed and carried out in the communist style of central planning. In important ways it strengthened Moscow's economic control over its satellites. However, COMECON was not entirely disadvantageous to the satellites, as it provided them both with large guaranteed markets and with raw materials at prices below world levels.

After the iron curtain split the continent, no middle ground or Central Europe could exist. For the four Cold War decades the traditional idea of a "Central Europe" practically vanished from European and American thought, except in its strictly geographical sense. Yet for centuries "Central Europe" had represented a recognized cultural zone. The German word *Mitteleuropa* in particular designated this area (with a further connotation of German cultural influence in it). But with the Cold War, such traditional capitals of European culture as Prague, Budapest and Warsaw had fallen on the eastern side of the curtain. Everything that was "behind" (from the Western viewpoint) the curtain came to be called "Eastern Europe," a terminology that sometimes still lingers today.

The "glorious revolutions" of 1989

After Mikhail Gorbachev came to power in the Soviet Union in 1985, he and his Foreign Minister, Eduard Shevardnadze, were determined to bring the Cold War to an end.[4] Unlike their predecessors in the Kremlin, they believed the Cold War was too dangerous, and that the economic and other costs to the Soviet Union of continuing it outweighed any possible gains. Those costs, which had been high for a long time, were rising further due to a determined challenge by the Reagan administration in the United States. By early 1989 Moscow was giving hints to the WTO countries that they now had much greater freedom to make their own decisions.

The Gorbachev government did not anticipate what was to follow. Moscow did not expect its European "allies" to break away completely, but to form voluntarily a somewhat looser relationship. Instead, events began moving rapidly in a quite different direction. In Czechoslovakia and Hungary, new political movements formed that were genuinely supported by the people. In Poland, a similar broad-based movement, Solidarity, had been in existence since the 1980s. As everyone began to realize that this time Moscow would not enforce its rule, communist governments that had had no other ultimate basis crumbled away. (The same occurred in East Germany; on November 9, 1989 the world watched as eager citizens tore down the Berlin Wall.) Almost entirely peacefully, and with remarkable ease, the political movements that had the support of the people formed new governments, and wrote new, democratic constitutions. These "glorious revolutions," as they came to be called, are discussed further in chapter 8. (A sweeping change in regime came before long to Bulgaria also. In Romania, however, reform came only later, less completely, and with violence. Bulgaria and Romania are not further discussed in this book.)[5]

In the late 1980s, the Soviet Union under Gorbachev and Shevardnadze also reached a series of arms control agreements with the West involving military forces in Europe. These agreements, and some related ones involving strategic nuclear forces, are too technical to be discussed here and are described in appendix 2.

Europe at the beginning of the 1990s

By early in 1990 it was clear that an era had ended in Europe. Everyone understood that the WTO was collapsing, and that the WTO countries of "Eastern Europe" were reorienting themselves toward the West. By the summer of 1990 it also became clear that Germany would be reunified on Western terms. Reluctantly, Gorbachev agreed that the former East Germany could join the Federal Republic of Germany (which formerly had been the name of West Germany). Germany formally became one country on October 3, 1990.[6]

However, the Soviet Union remained, and was still a superpower far stronger than any country on earth but the United States. Looking back from later years, there is some tendency for people to remember the end of the Eastern European empire and the later collapse of the USSR itself almost as a single cascade of events. In fact some two years separated them. Through 1990 and 1991, Europe continued to live with an immensely powerful Soviet Union looming in the east, and through much of 1991 at least, people expected that the Soviet Union would continue indefinitely as the unified and huge state it was.

At the beginning of the 1990s, then, the overall image that Europe presented was more complicated than before, but was not yet as complicated as it would soon become. In the West was the powerful and prosperous group of democratic states, unified by NATO and the European Community. In the East was the Soviet Union, still the strongest single country in Europe by far. Caught between them were a group of countries, now enjoying freedom and self-determination, whose new status was ambiguous and whose future was uncertain. By 1991 these lands were sometimes being referred to as "East Central Europe," to distinguish them from the single monolithic bloc ruled from Moscow that previously had been called "Eastern Europe."

During 1990 and much of 1991, a novel discussion flowered among people interested in security about how security in Europe might now be fashioned. What should the relationship be among the USSR, the West and the ambiguous region between them? How could security and peace be preserved under these unprecedented circumstances? As these questions were being considered, a hot war erupted in Europe for the first time since 1945.

Yugoslavia

Yugoslavia had been created at the end of World War I as a state for several ethnic groups, some of which were riven by ancient enmities. Near the end of World War II, Yugoslavia was liberated from Nazi occupation by native partisans, not by the Soviet Army; thus it escaped Moscow's control. Marshall Josip Tito, who ruled the country with an iron hand through the following decades, followed a "non-aligned" policy, joining neither NATO nor the WTO. After Tito's death in 1980, the complex federal structure began to unravel. Ethnic tensions rose.

After 1989, as the static order in the eastern half of Europe dissolved and as the Hungarians, Poles and others achieved national self-determination, the various national groups within Yugoslavia insisted on their national self-determination too.[7] In 1991, the Slovenes and Croats declared their independence from the Serb-dominated federal government. The Serbs made a brief unsuccessful attempt to suppress Slovenia's secession by force, but soon decided to leave Slovenia alone in order to concentrate their efforts on Croatia. Fighting soon escalated into full-scale war. The next year, a ceasefire was reached after the Serbs achieved many of their objectives; later there were some violations and it remains to be seen whether a stable peace will result.

Soon another part of Yugoslavia, Bosnia-Herzegovina, likewise declared its independence. Here three ethnic groups lived intermingled – Croats, Serbs and a large group (originally also Slavic like the others) whose ancestors had converted to the Muslim religion centuries before, when the whole Balkan area had been ruled by Turkey. War in Bosnia began in February 1992 and devastation continued to an extent unseen since World War II.

Numerous efforts were made, mainly by the United Nations and the EC, to broker a peace settlement. But these efforts failed and the war in Bosnia continued. At the beginning of 1995, a shaky ceasefire was agreed, but earlier ones had soon broken down, and it was not clear how long this one would last. Through most of the first half of the 1990s, then, Europeans find themselves watching scenes of fighting in Europe almost every evening on their television screens, when there had been no war in Europe for almost half a century.

East–West security relations

After the "glorious revolutions" of 1989, the states of Central Europe who formerly had been WTO members immediately began negotiating with the USSR for the withdrawal of Soviet troops from their territories. Clearly the WTO had lost its meaning, and in 1991 this organization, which had defined security relations in the eastern half of Europe for forty years, came to an end.

Besides NATO in the West, one other structure related to security existed in Europe, the CSCE. Only occasionally referred to by its full name – the Conference on Security and Cooperation in Europe – CSCE had been one of the instruments for reducing tensions and advancing arms control in the late Cold War years (for details see appendix 2). What role it might play in the new Europe now appearing was one of the questions widely discussed at the beginning of the 1990s. CSCE had the advantage that every nation in Europe, plus the United States and Canada, were members of it.[8] But it had no forces; in fact until 1991 it had no offices or permanent staff. Traditionally it had really been a series of conferences and negotiating forums, some of which had produced some East–West agreements. In November 1990, a grand CSCE conference was held in Paris, and the resulting "Paris Charter" included, among other things, mutual promises by all the member states to seek greater security in Europe. In the years immediately following, CSCE did not develop, as some specialists thought it might, into an overall European security system. Another conference, held in Budapest in December 1994, changed the name to the Organization for Security and

Cooperation in Europe (OSCE). Incidentally, in this book both abbreviations will be used, depending on whether reference is made to a time before or after this date.

Meanwhile NATO had been reaching out to the former adversary countries since soon after the end of the Cold War. A summit of the NATO heads of state, held in London in July 1990, issued a declaration that the East–West confrontation had ended, and invited the Eastern countries to open dialogue and diplomatic relations with NATO. Another formal statement, issued in Copenhagen in June 1991, announced that NATO would substantially enlarge its contacts with the Eastern countries. In November 1991, NATO held another summit at the head-of-state level, this time in Rome.[9] Here the NATO powers announced the creation of a new entity, the North Atlantic Cooperation Council, usually referred to as NACC (pronounced nak-see). Invitation to join NACC was extended both to the former WTO countries of East Central Europe, and to the new states that emerged following the break-up of the USSR (to be discussed in a moment). In the years following, NACC became a forum in which NATO held discussions among these states on numerous issues related to security and military affairs. For instance, NACC held seminars for officials from the Eastern countries on the Western concept of the proper relationship between the military and civilian authorities in a democratic government. NACC did not include any kind of guarantee by NATO of the security of any of these countries.

In the next few years, obtaining such a guarantee and, indeed, becoming full members of NATO, became a chief goal for the Central European countries. Partly in response to mounting pressure from the Central Europeans, NATO decided to offer another initiative, one that would go considerably beyond NACC. At a summit held at NATO's Brussels headquarters in January 1994, NATO announced a new "Partnership for Peace."[10] Any of the former WTO or former Soviet countries were invited to apply to join the Partnership, and in the following months many did. Under the Partnership (often referred to by specialists as "PfP"), each country could propose to NATO an individual plan for bilateral cooperation of various kinds. PfP definitely did not include any NATO security guarantee to any country. PfP and views of it held in various countries are discussed at several points in this book.

In the United States, the Clinton administration (which took office in January 1993) was initially sceptical about expanding NATO to include Central European countries or other new members; some of the European members of the Alliance, notably including Britain and France, were also sceptical. PfP was widely viewed as a compromise designed to give the Central Europeans a closer relationship to NATO but not membership. In the autumn of 1994, the Clinton administration shifted its position and won acceptance by the allies of a further step. At a December 1994 meeting,

NATO formally announced that it would develop, in one year, a plan for enlargement of its membership. The important topic of the possible expansion of NATO is discussed from various points of view in later chapters.[11]

The collapse of the Soviet Union

When Mikhail Gorbachev became head of the Communist Party of the Soviet Union, and thus of the country, in 1985, he was determined to launch a campaign of reform. The Soviet economy was stagnating and its political system was corrupt. The vast campaign of change that Gorbachev spearheaded through the following years included different policies at different times; the whole of it was intended to subject the Soviet system to a thoroughgoing "restructuring" (in Russian, *perestroika*). As earlier, simpler, steps failed, the *perestroika* campaign moved on to more radical measures. Gorbachev was a reformer, not a revolutionary, and he wanted to modernize, revitalize and humanize the Soviet system while preserving what he regarded as its fundamentals. He did lift the previously strict censorship and promoted the open discussion of public issues (called *glasnost*).

By 1990 it was becoming increasingly clear that even the later, more radical measures of *perestroika* were failing to produce the intended results. The economy, rather than improving as predicted, was actually declining. Living conditions for most citizens were growing visibly worse; at the same time most of the elite found that their long-standing privileges were threatened. Discontent, both popular and elite, was rapidly growing, and *glasnost* allowed it relatively free expression. Gorbachev's government grew more and more deeply unpopular.

Another trend gathering pace during 1990 and 1991 was a gradual weakening of the central Soviet government, as the fifteen republics that made up the USSR, including Russia, gained in power.[12] Crucial questions of the country's future came more and more to be settled by negotiation between Gorbachev and the leaders of the republics, including Boris Yeltsin, the President of Russia. Gorbachev also hoped to achieve a new "Union Treaty" that would create a renewed Soviet federation on terms that the republics would accept.

On August 19, 1991, a group of high-ranking civilian and military figures attempted to seize power with a view to "restoring order" in the USSR and reversing the dissolution of the Union. Gorbachev, who was vacationing in the Crimea at the time, was held prisoner in his vacation home; he refused to endorse the new regime. An attempt to arrest Yeltsin in Moscow failed. Claiming legitimate authority as the President of Russia, Yeltsin established his headquarters in the Russian Parliament building and organized a campaign of non-violent resistance that contributed to the collapse of the coup in less than three days.

The coup plotters brought about the opposite of what they had hoped for. They gave Yeltsin a pretext for dismantling the Communist Party apparatus. Instead of saving the Soviet Union, they fatally weakened the central Soviet regime. Ukraine and other republics declared independence. Gorbachev, who returned to Moscow, formally remained President of the USSR, but in the next months real power passed increasingly into the hands of Yeltsin.

The Commonwealth of Independent States

On December 8, 1991, President Yeltsin of Russia, President Kravchuk of Ukraine and Chairman of the Belorussian Parliament Shushkevich met near Minsk. They declared that the USSR ceased to exist and that they were founding in its place a Commonwealth of Independent States (CIS). At a follow-up meeting on December 21, the membership of the CIS expanded to include eleven of the fifteen former Soviet republics. (The three Baltic states and Georgia remained outside the new organization; in 1994 Georgia agreed to join.) Gorbachev was left stranded; the country of which he was President no longer existed. The USSR formally came to an end at midnight on December 31.

Unlike the USSR, the CIS was not intended to constitute a government standing over and above the republics. Instead it was intended to provide the post-Soviet countries with a forum for consultation and negotiation, and a structure to coordinate cooperation in various fields. In the eyes of some, especially in Ukraine, the CIS was no more than a temporary instrument for achieving a "civilized divorce." However, the CIS has survived and a number of cooperative agreements have been reached in the CIS framework.

The Soviet armed forces, both nuclear and conventional, were initially relabeled the "Unified Armed Forces of the CIS" with a Commander-in-Chief who was, formally at least, responsible to the heads of state of *all* the CIS member states. But as the newly independent states[13] organized their own armed forces, the forces remaining to the CIS commander shrank, until by now they comprise only some "peacekeeping forces." The conventional (i.e. non-nuclear) forces were divided up, sometimes by agreement, sometimes simply by *fait accompli*. In general, each country simply took over the conventional military assets and forces that were located on its territory at the time the USSR collapsed. (The issue of the Black Sea Fleet is discussed later.)

It was agreed in principle that the former Soviet nuclear arsenal would be transferred to Russia. In fact, all the tactical (short-range) nuclear weapons were quickly moved to Russian territory. Moving the strategic (long-range) weapons is much more difficult and time-consuming. There was little question about the removal of those weapons from Belarus or Kazakhstan, a process carried out over the following years.[14] The other new country where Soviet strategic weapons were located was Ukraine, and this posed a more complicated and controversial issue, discussed later.

In May 1992 a meeting on security affairs was held in Tashkent (Uzbekistan). On May 15, six of the post-Soviet states – Russia, Armenia, Kazakhstan, Kyrgyzhstan, Tajikistan and Uzbekistan – signed a collective security treaty, generally referred to as the Tashkent Treaty. Later Belarus also conditionally joined. In general the Tashkent Treaty, discussed again in chapter 16, signaled which post-Soviet states were ready to cooperate closely with Russia in military affairs (and which not).

Over the next couple of years the real significance of the CIS remained ambiguous, as did Russia's role across the territories of the former Soviet Union. On the one hand, Russia completed the withdrawal of its military forces from the Baltic states (Estonia, Latvia and Lithuania) in August 1994, and these states have succeeded, as they have desired, in remaining outside the CIS. On the other hand, Russian military forces intervened, usually in what was said to be "peacekeeping," in Georgia, Tajikistan and elsewhere on former Soviet territories. As discussed further later, what role Russia could now play, and would want to try to play, in the former Soviet region and in Europe is a great question mark hanging over European security affairs.

In December 1994, Russian military forces intervened violently in Chechnya. Again scenes of fighting and destruction filled European television screens. Chechnya was a constituent unit inside the Russian Federation, not an independent country, so legally Moscow's military action involved internal, not international, affairs. However, the fact that it was precisely a bid for independence and sovereignty that Chechnya was making and that Moscow intervened to prevent, as well as the violence of the intervention and other factors, gave this event great importance on the international stage. The Chechnya action is mentioned at several points in later chapters. (In general the internal affairs of Russia, and all affairs involving the post-Soviet states other than Russia and Ukraine, cannot be discussed in this book.)

1992 and after: Europe in disarray

By the beginning of 1992, Europe found itself in a situation different from that of the previous couple of years, and of course profoundly different from long-frozen decades earlier. Not only was the WTO gone and its members turning westward; not only were hot wars raging in Yugoslavia and the Caucasus; now the Soviet Union itself had collapsed. The superpower that had seemed for such a long time to be so mighty, so threatening and so permanent had vanished with astonishing suddenness. The shock of this was so great that it took some time for the reality of it to sink in for most

Europeans, and perhaps even longer for people in the former Soviet lands themselves.

Throughout the whole eastern half of Europe, history now seemed to be producing a profound trend toward disintegration. The WTO and COMECON had disintegrated; Yugoslavia had disintegrated; and now the Soviet Union had disintegrated. (Within twelve more months Czechoslovakia also fragmented, although peacefully, into its two main constituent parts, the Czech Republic and Slovakia, as described later.) Beyond all this, there seemed to be a possibility that the Russian Federation too might begin to collapse. In 1992 and the years following, an idea became common throughout Europe, not only among specialists but also among the general public, that Russia might break up before long, perhaps violently. Around the same time a countervailing idea also arose, that Russia might seek hegemony over some, at least, of the new countries of the former Soviet Union. The two ideas were related, since a desire to stave off disintegration could be one motive for a new Russian bid for hegemony.

The trend toward disintegration produced a landscape in the eastern half of Europe largely devoid of structures that could define the security relationships among countries. What might be the relations, in security and other ways, among the many countries, many of them new, that now were operating freely? Furthermore, none of these collapses or wars had been predicted before they occurred. What further collapses, wars or other dramatic upsets might the future hold? Europe now lived in a state of immense uncertainty. The situation in the eastern half of the continent was so fluid, and the possibilities so many, that the future now seemed highly unpredictable. The pre-1989 Europe that had been so fixed, familiar and relatively certain had now become very fluid, quite unfamiliar and highly uncertain.

During this period another idea became widely accepted, namely that the trend toward disintegration in the East was being paralleled by a trend toward integration in the West. During the same years, Western Europe took major steps toward binding itself together more fully. The EC agreed on establishing a "single market," as of January 1, 1993, in which nearly all economic activities could be pursued throughout the Community with practically no regard to national boundaries.

In December 1991 the EC countries signed in Maastricht, a small city in the Netherlands, a new treaty committing themselves to far-reaching steps toward further political, as well as economic, integration. The Maastricht Treaty included a security component among many other important provisions. It named the Western European Union (WEU), previously an unimportant consultative body, to be the security and military arm of the Community. While it was clear to everyone that the WEU would, in practice, remain far less important than NATO for a considerable time at least, its more distant potential might be great. The Maastricht Treaty proved controversial in Western Europe, and just barely passed in referendum votes held in several countries. But the Treaty was finally approved by all the member states and came into force on November 1, 1993. Also as of that date, and as provided by the Treaty, the European Community (EC) became the European Union (EU). Again both abbreviations will be used in this book depending on whether reference is made to a time before or after this date.

By 1995 further evidence had appeared suggesting that both the disintegrative and integrative trends were continuing. The attempt by Chechnya to secede from the Russian Federation and become an independent country, and Moscow's strong military intervention to prevent it, suggested long-standing fears about disintegrative tendencies in the Russian Federation. Meanwhile the EU was expanding, through orderly legal and democratic processes, to admit Austria, Finland and Sweden as new members. It was widely felt that trends toward integration in the West and disintegration in the East might well persist. By the mid-1990s, the countries discussed in this book had also made some progress in fashioning a conception of their security position and some elements of their security policy. But a great many questions and uncertainties remained. And every one of these countries found its overall situation, and definitely its security situation, unsatisfactory. Every one of them was seeking further changes and developments.

During the first half of the 1990s, most of these countries were also going through profound internal transformations. With the end of communism, all of them had set democracy and market economies as goals. The social changes needed to move toward these goals were wrenching, and some countries made much faster progress than others. These internal transformations could not be entirely separated from the subject of security. Internal dislocations that became too extreme could lead to social collapse; on the other hand, too little progress might set the stage for new, undemocratic regimes appearing. The relevance of the agonizing internal transformations for security is discussed at several points later.

Such, briefly summarized, is the context for the assessments in this book. Parts II through V of the book survey perceptions of security in six of the most important countries of Central and Eastern Europe. Before turning to those assessments, a short description must be offered, in the next chapter, of the purposes of this book and of the way in which the research represented here was shaped.

Notes

1 There were other crises in other parts of the world, especially the Cuban Missile Crisis of 1962. The Soviet invasions of Hungary in 1956 and Czechoslovakia

in 1968 represented crises for those countries but did not escalate into major
East–West crises.

2 Some disorders in East Germany in the early 1950s also expressed popular
resistance to the communist regime, but these did not grow into a full-scale
revolt. The program of non-violent resistance led by Solidarity in Poland in the
1980s will be mentioned later.

3 Later Mongolia and Vietnam also joined the CMEA.

4 They were joined by like-minded others, notably Alexander Yakovlev.

5 For a useful chronological summary, in which events are arrayed next to each
other by country and by month, see Sarah Humphry, "A comparative chron-
ology of revolution, 1988–1990," in Gwyn Prins (ed.), *Spring in Winter: The
1989 Revolutions* (Manchester: Manchester University Press, 1990).

6 From the Soviet viewpoint this was a great concession, since it meant that a
former ally immediately became incorporated into a Western country, and
furthermore a country that was an important member of NATO, the previously
"enemy" alliance. In return, the Soviets received from the West the minor
concession that NATO forces would not be stationed on the territory of the
former East Germany. The major negotiations leading to this outcome were
called the "two-plus-four" talks because they comprised the two Germanies
and the four principal victors of World War II who at one time had occupied
defeated Germany – the Soviet Union, the United States, Britain and France.

7 Readers, perhaps especially American readers, should notice a potential confusion in the English language about the meaning of the words "nation" and
"national." Particularly in the United States, the word "nation" is often used as
synonymous with "country," and all English speakers refer to relations among
countries as "international relations." A second meaning of "nation" is "ethnic
group," a sense of the words that Americans know first-hand from the names
of Native American tribes, for instance the Iroquois Nation. Relations among
ethnic groups are extremely important now in Central and Eastern Europe. To
make more clear what sense is meant, the term "nationality" is often used for
ethnic groups.

8 After the breakup of the USSR at the end of 1991, CSCE also came to include
all the new states that formerly had been Soviet republics.

9 The formal NATO Declarations issued at the end of these conferences were as
follows: "London Declaration on a Transformed North Atlantic Alliance,"
Issued by the NATO Heads of State, London, July 5–6, 1990; "Partnership
With the Countries of Central and Eastern Europe," Issued by the North
Atlantic Council, Copenhagen, June 6–7, 1991; "Rome Declaration on Peace
and Cooperation," Issued by the NATO Heads of State, Rome, November 7–
8, 1991.

10 The NATO Declaration is as follows: "Partnership for Peace: Invitation,"
Issued by the Heads of State and Government Participating in the Meeting of
the North Atlantic Council held at NATO Headquarters, Brussels, on January
10–11, 1994.

11 Of the countries discussed in this book, the four Central European states and
Ukraine all joined PfP promptly. After considerable internal debate, Russia
agreed in July 1994 to join the program. In December 1994, Russia angrily
reversed its decision when NATO announced that it would develop a plan for

expansion in Central Europe. Russia's perceptions and decisions are discussed in chapter 16.

Until the Clinton administration's shift in position, Germany was the principal NATO ally advocating extending – under some conditions – NATO membership to the Central European states that were ardently seeking it.

The NATO Declaration of its intent to expand is stated in the "Communiqué Issued By the Ministerial Meeting of the North Atlantic Council," held at NATO headquarters at Brussels, December 1, 1994.

12 Unless otherwise specified, this book will use the term "Russia" to mean the Russian Federation. The word "Russia" can be used in several senses. The Russian Federation includes many autonomous republics and other units, although it functions largely as a single unit in foreign and security affairs.

13 The phrase "newly independent states" (NIS) subsequently became the terminology in Washington for these countries.

14 By the beginning of 1995, the removal was already complete from Belarus and was well underway from Kazakhstan. The difference is explained mainly by the fact that some of the weapons in Kazakhstan are SS-18s, which are extremely large and heavy.

2

The research design of this study

Richard Smoke

This short chapter describes the research design of this study. That is, it explains why the research was structured in the way it was and explains the goals that this study sought to achieve. This chapter also briefly explains the structure of the book.

Because this book is a product of a specific research project, its chapters naturally reflect, both individually and collectively, the design of that project. Not much need be said here about how the Security for Europe Project was carried out. Readers interested in the Project will find it described in appendix 3. But the overall viewpoint and purposes of both the Project and the book need to be briefly explained here.

The viewpoint: perspectives from the region

As mentioned in the preface, a basic purpose of the Project was to uncover ideas and viewpoints about security held in major countries of Central and Eastern Europe. Because such a new landscape was emerging in the eastern half of Europe in the early 1990s, a completely fresh exploration was needed. The main research goal therefore was to explore systematically the perceptions of security that were then appearing in the region.

Fundamental to the project, and thus to the book, was a focus on ideas and viewpoints held in the region itself, *not* on American or other Western viewpoints about the region. The focus was on the view from the "inside," not from the outside. Thus the basic research goal was an exploration of these countries' security situations as people in those countries see them. The book's title communicates this basic goal.

The book aims to offer an objective and unbiased presentation of the security issues of Central and Eastern Europe, as seen from the perspective of people in six major countries of the region. Four of these are major countries of Central Europe: Poland, the Czech and Slovak Republics and Hungary. The other two are the most important countries of the former

Soviet Union: Ukraine and Russia. (In addition, appendix 1 provides some information about another country, Germany, that has great importance for Central and Eastern Europe.) While it naturally would have been desirable to include in the study all the newly emerging democracies in the eastern half of Europe, research and practical considerations required limiting the investigation to these seven countries.

The aim of the book is to be "objective and unbiased" in the sense that the book aims to avoid introducing any American or Western "slant." Naturally the authors from each country cannot be unbiased about their own country. The book deliberately does not include any American or Western analysis of security in the region.[1] While the viewpoints of some authors here naturally disagree with the others in some respects, the book also passes no judgements on who is right or wrong. Each chapter is allowed to speak for itself and to present its own point of view without being subjected to a judgement afterwards. Readers may easily observe the differences in viewpoints for themselves.

An analytical and systematic approach

A second basic aim of the book is to present its exploration of security in the region in an analytical and systematic fashion. All the chapters present their material in an organized structure; where feasible the structure is similar from one chapter to another. More important, each chapter's discussion attempts to dissect issues in an analytical and systematic fashion. Ideas are developed and analyzed and, where feasible, their current consequences or their likely consequences in the future are traced.

The European authors represented here did not write their chapters entirely in isolation from each other, nor were they assembled as a group just to prepare this book. To show how their work is linked, it is necessary to say another word about the Security for Europe Project. The authors met together several times during the lifetime of the Project.[2] At the beginning of the research effort, they met to develop the Project's research agenda. The agenda was collectively agreed upon before work began. Near the end of the first year of work they met again to review the results of research done so far and to plan further research. Another general conference of all authors was held at the end of the second year, and other meetings of authors were held at various times. Joint research documents were prepared at intervals, and were reviewed and evaluated at later stages. In sum, an organized research program was carried out over a lengthy period in an integrated fashion by all authors working in partnership.[3] The specific chapters themselves were written separately by each author or team of authors, as the final stage of the project. In order to give all authors maximum discretion to express their views freely and fully, no author was allowed to raise objections to any statement in any other author's chapter.

Research design: comprehensive and exploratory

Two concrete objectives for the design of the research were determined by the overall research goal of producing a fresh systematic examination of people's thinking about security in Central and Eastern Europe. One was that the research aimed to be comprehensive. That is, the research aimed to uncover all the major ideas and perceptions about security held by people in these countries. Of course, many minor questions of interest only to a few people could be left aside. But the research intended to identify all of the security issues that are important for any of these six countries, or for Central and Eastern Europe as a whole.[4] Naturally this goal of comprehensiveness is carried over into the book. (Several specific topics were deliberately excluded, as explained in a moment. The meaning here of "security" is also discussed below.)

The other concrete objective for the design of the research is obvious. The research aimed to be exploratory. The research and the resulting book aim to explore the territory without preconceptions and without making assumptions ahead of time about what might or might not be important.

This goal carries an implication that may not be obvious and that is significant for scholars and students. A research effort of this kind must not engage in "hypothesis testing." Unlike much scholarly work in the field of international relations, this research was not designed to begin from one or more hypotheses or ideas, and test those ideas against some body of facts. Exploratory research is research of a different kind. It deliberately does not start from one set of hypotheses or ideas because to do so would run the risk of leaving out others. There would be a strong risk that the results might not be comprehensive. Thus in this kind of research, the goal of being comprehensive and the goal of being exploratory interconnect and mutually imply each other. If the research is to succeed at being comprehensive, it must be exploratory, adopting no hypotheses or ideas (or assumptions) at the start.[5]

Research design: scope

A topic as broad as perceptions of security in Central and Eastern Europe could, if interpreted completely comprehensively, raise issues that go beyond Europe itself, or in other ways could go too far afield. Therefore certain restrictions and exclusions were placed on the scope of this study at the outset.

Threats that might arise in the future from outside Europe were excluded. For example, there may be implications for Europe in the potential spread to Middle Eastern countries of nuclear weapons or the technology for making them, or of long-range ballistic missiles and their technology. These, and any other hypothetical threats that might come from outside Europe in the future were excluded from this research. The study was limited to threats that exist or may arise within Europe itself.

In general studies of Europe like this one, "Europe" is normally defined geographically as stretching from the Atlantic Ocean eastward as far as the Ural Mountains and Ural River. This conventional definition was used here. Whether all the peoples living west of the Urals are now, or will come to be, thought of as fully "Europeans" in a political sense is a separate question.[6]

In this book the chapters on Russia are concerned with Russia only as it relates to Europe. Of course Russia is also an Asian country. Russian perceptions and policies with respect to Central Asia, other parts of Asia and the Pacific region are excluded.

The time span of the research presented in this book was not limited arbitrarily, but looking too far ahead becomes unduly speculative. This book emphasizes security issues that are current or seem likely to arise by the year 2000. Since that year is so close, authors were also invited to consider problems of the following years that they believe can sensibly be discussed now.

Research design: the treatment of small wars

During the period that this research was under way, several small but significant wars raged in Europe. For Americans and for Central and Western Europeans, the most important of these was the war in the former Yugoslavia. That war also received by far the most attention from the international media. At least equally significant for Russians and Ukrainians were several small wars in the Caucasus region. The war already ongoing between Armenia and Azerbaijan also continued during this period. At one point during this time there also was some fighting in Moldova. The war in the former Yugoslavia and some of the fighting in the Caucasus were characterized by great brutality and by hideous atrocities and human rights violations. In the Yugoslav case these aspects received a significant degree of international attention.[7]

Wars like these pose a research problem for a study that aims to examine security in a way that is "comprehensive" in a broad sense, but for practical reasons cannot analyze any single event in great depth. Such wars are small in geographical scope but have considerable importance. These wars, especially the one in the former Yugoslavia, are also extremely complicated. A book longer than this one could easily be written about that war alone. Yet the main subject here is the overall security situation of the whole of Central and Eastern Europe. Furthermore, the research was conducted in six other European countries but not in any of the warring states themselves.

The decision was reached by the participating researchers to handle these small wars in this fashion: no attempt would be made to study these wars in their own terms, because any such attempt would either be superficial or would make this book far too long. Instead, the *implications* of these wars for larger security issues would be addressed. Thus various chapters here take up the implications and consequences of these wars, chiefly the Yugoslav war, both for specific neighboring countries (such as Hungary) and for Central and Eastern Europe as a whole.

There were no other restrictions placed on the scope of this book's research beyond those just discussed.[8] Within these constraints, no subject or idea involving security was precluded ahead of time from being a candidate for exploration. Needless to say, the chapter authors have made their own judgements about which subjects deserve more attention and which less.[9]

Research design: the conception of security

This study gives primary emphasis to "security" in its traditional sense in studies of international affairs, namely politico-military security. There is no danger to security more fundamental for a country than the danger of war. However, other and wider kinds of security or insecurity are also considered here. A study that aims to be, in a basic sense, comprehensive cannot properly exclude other aspects of security, such as environmental or economic security. And a research project that aimed to explore the perceptions of people in the Central and Eastern European region naturally should give them the freedom to define for themselves what "security" means. Any such research will quickly find that non-military insecurities loom large in the region, a conclusion that is emphasized repeatedly in the chapters that follow.

However, all forms of insecurity cannot receive equal attention. A lengthy study could be made just of environmental hazards in the region, to say nothing of economic insecurities. A decision was therefore made at the outset. Any conclusion could be reached that the research indicated to be valid, stating the overall importance of any form of insecurity. But only politico-military insecurities would be assessed in depth. In addition, the authors in this book were free to discuss in their own way various other forms of insecurity, including their impact on politico-military security.

The research on attitudes held by the public in the six countries began with no a priori limitations. People were invited to tell researchers, without restrictions, what they believe security means to their country (and the results are reported here). But only public attitudes involving politico-military aspects of security were researched in depth, and those attitudes receive most of the attention of the relevant chapters here.

The policy specialists represented in this book are experts on foreign policy and national security policy as these policies are usually defined, and they naturally write about security mainly in this sense.

Research design: the views of both experts and the public

A comprehensive exploration of people's thinking about security – in these six countries or any other – will be much stronger if it examines the views both of policy experts and of the public. Policy specialists and the public each have their own point of view, which may not be the same. Clearly it is important to know the views of each if one wishes to gain a comprehensive view of what people are thinking about security and foreign affairs in a country, or group of countries. Therefore this book presents two chapters about each of the six countries, one (which comes first) reporting the views of the public and one presenting the viewpoint of policy experts. A word is needed here about both kinds of chapters.

All the authors of chapters about the viewpoint of the public are specialists, in their own countries, on the research and analysis of public opinion. Needless to say, these authors do not offer their own ideas in their chapters here. Rather their chapters represent their analysis of public attitudes in their countries about security issues.

The chapters about the viewpoint of policy experts in the various countries are written by one or more policy experts in each country. These authors were asked to "report" the general perceptions and viewpoints held by the community of policy specialists in each country. Where there are markedly divergent viewpoints held by different groups of policy experts in a country, the author was asked to describe the various competing viewpoints. (Among these six countries, markedly divergent viewpoints among policy specialists are found mainly in Russia.) Naturally "the community of policy specialists" includes both specialists who currently occupy official positions inside governments and independent specialists outside the governments. Of course the authors of these chapters, being themselves leading specialists on foreign and security policy, write also from their own point of view; to a considerable extent they present their own assessment of their country's situation and policies.[10]

Changes in perceptions and attitudes that developed during the first half of the 1990s are discussed in both kinds of chapters.

The importance of the public's viewpoint

The importance of studying the viewpoint of the general public requires emphasis. The decision to give approximately equal attention to the public's viewpoint and to that of the policy experts was a deliberate and fundamental decision in the creation of this book, and in the design of the research project from which the book derived. The public in any country has its own point of view on what factors are making the country less secure or more secure, and on the foreign affairs of the country generally.

Most published works in international affairs do not include systematic attention to the public's viewpoint, for various reasons. If oriented toward academic political science, such works usually are interested in testing or developing theoretical hypotheses about relations among nation-states or other entities. If oriented toward policy issues, such works usually aim to analyze a specific policy problem. Only in certain cases is the public's viewpoint important for theoretical hypotheses or for a specific policy analysis. However, this study's purpose in conducting a comprehensive exploration requires great attention to public as well as to expert viewpoints. Public attitudes are so significant for a study of this kind, in fact, that more must be said about them at this point.

The perspective of the public on issues of foreign and security affairs is of some significance even in countries that are not democracies. There is one basic and elementary sense in which a country is made up of its people, whatever the nature of the regime. In this basic sense, what the people of a country feel – for example what makes them insecure – must be important. If the public feels, say, a threat from a certain direction and not from another direction, these are primary facts of a certain political kind about that country. This is still true even if most foreign policy specialists, inside and outside the government, have a different perception. Even many dictatorships find it prudent to pay attention to what the public thinks on many issues, including security issues.

Obviously the importance of the public's viewpoint is much greater in democratic countries and in countries that are in the process of becoming democratic. In such countries, the public has ways, to a greater or lesser degree, of ensuring that the government pays attention to their views. Certainly this includes views about security. If the public feels a threat of a certain kind, or does not feel a threat of another kind, these feelings must be taken into account by a democratic government. Even if the government, and the specialists it consults, have different perceptions about threats, nonetheless the government must respond to the public in some way, if only to try to reshape the public's opinion. Usually a complicated, two-way political process will develop in which, over time, public attitudes partly influence government decisions – including foreign policy actions – while political leaders and policy experts are simultaneously influencing what the public thinks.

During the early 1990s, every one of the countries discussed in this book was in some stage of becoming democratic. Some of these countries were further along the process of democratization than others, but every one of them had set democracy as a goal. Every one of them had a Parliament which exerted substantial influence over policy.[11] In every one of these countries, public attitudes did influence policy.

There is a further reason why attention to public attitudes is important to this particular study. In the early 1990s all of these countries were *new* democracies. The Central European countries discussed in this book had not been democratic before 1989, and Russia and Ukraine had not been democratic before the collapse of the Soviet Union in late 1991. Clearly, there is a special need to study public attitudes in newly democratic states. The public is free to express its views openly for the first time. And the public is able strongly to influence governments for the first time (with whatever opinions and attitudes the public may hold). The years immediately following the arrival of democracy, therefore, is a time when assessment of public attitudes is both newly possible and especially significant.[12]

Public opinion and public attitudes

It is important to distinguish, especially in a study of this kind, between public *opinion* and public *attitudes*. The two are not the same. Public opinion refers to the immediate, "surface" opinions that the public holds, usually on current affairs. Opinion may shift quickly and rather easily in response to events. Attitudes are feelings and viewpoints held more deeply. Attitudes usually change only slowly over time, or in response to great historical changes. The distinction is not absolute, however. For example, a public response that starts out as an opinion may solidify over time, gradually deepening into an attitude. But the difference is important, not only for researchers but also for policy-makers. For instance, the leaders of a country may find that some public opinions can be changed if the leaders make an effort to change them. Public attitudes are harder to change.

This book contains only a modest amount of information on public opinion in the countries it studies. Opinion is not excluded entirely, but it is de-emphasized. The chapters on public attitudes in the six countries report mainly on, precisely, attitudes. The authors of these chapters mainly describe and assess viewpoints and feelings held by the public in their countries that are not highly volatile, but have lasted for years and are likely to continue for some time.[13] As will be clear from the chapters, "attitudes" in the sphere of foreign and security affairs are intimately intertwined with "perceptions." The public has perceptions about what questions are and are not significant, and about why they are significant; the public in one country has various perceptions about a certain foreign country, and so forth. In the public mind, attitudes of these kinds are practically indistinguishable from the public's perceptions.

Research on public attitudes

As mentioned, the chapters of this book written by policy experts reflect the authors' own views, but the chapters written by specialists on public attitudes naturally do not present these specialists' own views. Instead they report on the public's views in each country. Those chapters are based on two kinds of research. Partly they are based on research programs carried out regularly by the various organizations to which these authors belong. And partly these chapters are based on research done by these organizations specifically for the Security for Europe Project. A word is necessary here about the method used in that research.[14]

The most common method of "public opinion" research, namely quantitative survey research (polling), is not as appropriate as a different method for *exploratory* research. Of course the goal of this study was to conduct an exploration. A qualitative research approach, specifically the focus group method, is more appropriate for exploratory research. The focus group method is now well established and widely used, especially in commercial and political research.

A focus group is a small group of citizens (usually about ten) who are gathered to hold an organized, lengthy discussion that is "focused" on one topic. In the type of focus group used in this study, citizens were chosen to reflect the whole public: equal numbers of men and women, a distribution of ages, a distribution of levels of education, etc. A "moderator" asks questions and keeps the discussion to the topic; after citizens express their initial views the moderator probes more deeply into their feelings about a question. For reliable results, separate focus groups (that is, with different citizens each time) are held repeatedly with the same agenda of questions. The Security for Europe Project conducted a total of sixty-six focus groups in the participating countries over a span of two years.[15]

The focus group method has several advantages and one disadvantage compared to survey research. The disadvantage is that it cannot give quantitative results, such as 37 percent in favor of something and 28 percent opposed. Obviously the number of citizens participating (the "n") is much too small for useful statistical results to be possible. However, a series of focus groups can identify areas where the public is generally in agreement about something – public consensus – and areas where there are important public disagreements.

The advantages of the method are valuable specifically for exploratory research, and especially for exploratory research that seeks, as here, to explore its topic comprehensively. First, citizens are not limited to answering the specific questions they are asked, but can express their own ideas and feelings freely. Secondly, the method allows citizens to address a subject in a broad and basic way. For example, the first question asked in some of the project's focus groups was this: "What does security for the country mean to you?" The citizens participating can interpret this question in their own way, answer in their own words, and express ideas and feelings on all aspects of the question that they think are relevant. A third advantage of the method lies in the ability of the moderator to probe what citizens say. For instance, after a certain viewpoint is expressed, the moderator can ask "Why do you think so?" The ample time available makes it possible to probe in this fashion repeatedly, thus uncovering deeper feelings and attitudes. In several ways, then, the focus group method is highly advantageous for a research effort that aims to be exploratory and to investigate its topic comprehensively.[16]

Since the chapters in this book that discuss public attitudes are drawn largely from the focus group research conducted by the Project, these chapters present their conclusions mainly in qualitative (that is, non-numerical) terms.[17] As mentioned, however, these chapters also draw upon other research done by the authors' research organizations, including survey research (polling). That other research, being largely quantitative, generated numerical findings. Hence these chapters also contain a few percentage figures. Footnotes in these chapters present a considerable amount of numerical data relevant to the topics discussed.[18]

The structure of this book

For ease of reading and comparison, the chapters on public attitudes in the four Central European countries are grouped together in this book, in part II, as are the chapters presenting Central European policy specialists' analyses, in part III. Part IV presents the two chapters on Ukraine and part V presents the two on Russia. A single chapter of "Concluding observations" follows in part VI. Because of Germany's importance to the overall subject of the book, appendix 1 discusses public attitudes in eastern and western Germany on foreign and security policy matters.

There is no political or other significance to the order of parts here – first Central Europe, then Ukraine, then Russia. From the viewpoint of the map, this sequence reads from left to right. There is also no significance to the order of countries discussed within the Central European region, namely Poland, the Czech Republic, Slovakia, and Hungary. This order is roughly their order from north to south.

Because a large part of the public attitudes in the four Central European countries are similar to one another, these attitudes are discussed in a single chapter (chapter 3). The four chapters following, which are all short, discuss attitudes that are particular to each country. Part III, on policy specialists' assessment of security in the Central European region, includes an introductory chapter of historical background. The pre-1945 history of these four countries has considerable and immediate importance for their situation today. (The pre-1917 histories of Russia and Ukraine are not as directly and richly relevant for European security today and do not require a separate chapter here. Relevant points from those histories are included in the chapters on Russia and Ukraine.) Because Russia is so important a country for the security situation of all the others, the chapter assessing its foreign and security policy is slightly longer than nearly all other chapters.

Some information about European arms control that is too technical for the main body of this book is offered in appendix 2. And finally, the Security for Europe Project is briefly described in appendix 3.

Notes

1 It may be impossible for the Western authors of the final chapter to avoid some Western bias in their analysis. However, the purpose of that chapter is not to present a Western analysis.

2 There is one exception. The Ukrainian policy specialists who are the authors of chapter 14 were not able to participate in the Security for Europe Project. That chapter was written separately, using the same guidelines. For more about Ukrainian participation in the project, see appendix 3.

3 For more about the organization of the research that yielded this book, see the project description in appendix 3.

4 Note the paragraph below that discusses the restriction on research on Russia to Russia's European affairs.

5 Scholars will note that of course there are methodological assumptions built into this approach from the start. In addition there is one unavoidable assumption that is partly substantive, namely that the general subject matter is significant. Some deliberate restrictions on scope, discussed below, also represent (or are based on) assumptions of other kinds.

6 Some peoples of the Trans-Caucasus region, such as the Azeris, live to the west of the Urals but may not be thought of as entirely "European" by many Europeans. Since the countries of the Trans-Caucasus region are not represented among the countries of this study, this question had little practical significance in this research.

7 In December 1994, the Russian Federation intervened militarily in Chechnya, a region inside the Federation. While not itself an action in foreign affairs, this intervention attracted much attention in Europe. Although this book had been largely completed before this event, some authors were able to include comments about the Chechnya events of December 1994 in their final, revised chapters.

8 It is obvious that a constraint of another kind is introduced by the limitation of the study to six countries of Central and Eastern Europe (plus Germany in part). It is self-evident that the inclusion of researchers from other countries, such as Romania, Bulgaria, Moldova or any of the Baltic countries, would automatically bring into the book the perspectives and policies of those countries, which would include specific security issues for those countries that are not addressed here.

9 As discussed above, all authors worked, in the Security for Europe Project, from a jointly agreed research agenda, which they had collectively generated and agreed upon. In writing their chapters, however, they were free (within broad limits) to add topics and to make their own judgements about what topics to emphasize or de-emphasize. The authors were asked to base their chapters not only on the research done as part of the Project, but also upon other work done

by their respective research organizations, as well as upon their overall expertise.

10   In addition, the Security for Europe Project included extensive interviews and other research with numerous other specialists in every country during 1992 and 1993. A summary assessment of the results of all those interviews is presented in part III of the *Final Report* of the Security for Europe Project. That information is not reproduced in any one place in this book because such information obsolesces much faster than the kinds of assessments this book contains. Instead, the policy specialist authors were asked to weave appropriate conclusions from that research into their chapters here.

All chapters in this book present the views of their individual authors only. None are meant to be, nor should be taken as, statements of the viewpoint or position of the organizations to which the authors belong. This disclaimer is especially noteworthy regarding the chapters authored by policy specialists, since some of the organizations to which they belong are government-supported and/or have some semi-official status.

11   In the case of every country represented in this book except Russia, the Parliament had been elected democratically prior to 1992, the time when research in this project was begun. Through most of 1993 the legislature in Moscow was made up of people who had been "elected" in the Soviet time, but a new Parliament was democratically elected in December 1993 in Russia, prior to the time that all the chapters in this book were written.

12   There was yet another reason, less applicable to this book, why the original Security for Europe Project paid great attention to public attitudes in the countries studied. Because the governments in those countries were only in the process of becoming democratic, officials were not yet fully familiar with the relevance of public attitudes for policy-making. Here "relevance" has a complex meaning that includes, for instance, an understanding of how to identify and conceptualize those elements of public attitudes that are most applicable to the development of policy. Partly to make a contribution toward governments' familiarity with these matters, as well as for other reasons, the *Final Report* of the Security for Europe Project was translated into the local languages and widely distributed in government circles in these countries. The *Final Report* is discussed further in appendix 3.

13   In the course of its research, the two-year Security for Europe Project had an opportunity to examine change over time in public views. Findings from near the beginning of the project could be compared with findings near the end. Authors of the chapters in this book were asked to focus mainly on stable attitudes and attitudes that were changing in a steady fashion over time. They were asked to de-emphasize volatile, "surface" opinion, which may change quickly even in a short time. Of course these specialists on public attitudes were also familiar with attitudes in their countries from other research conducted by their organizations. A few public responses to specific events and situations, reported at various points here, are so labeled.

14   The chapters by policy specialists are also based in part on research conducted as part of the Security for Europe Project, as well as other research conducted by the authors' research institutions. For more on the research program of the Security for Europe Project, see appendix 3.

15   The total of sixty-six includes nine groups held in eastern and western Germany, which form part of the basis for appendix 1 of this book. Needless to say, the focus groups conducted in each country represented here were conducted in the local languages. The focus group method was part of the standard research repertoire of all the professional public opinion research organizations participating in this study. As mentioned earlier, the questions posed had been previously agreed upon collectively by all the European (and American) researchers participating in the Security for Europe Project. (As noted in appendix 3, focus group research for the project was conducted in Ukraine only during one year, 1993. Chapter 13, on public attitudes in Ukraine, draws on other research as well.)

16   Naturally the moderator remains neutral during the group discussion, saying nothing that might "lead" the citizens participating to respond in one direction or another. Moderators are trained for this role. In addition, it is often possible for trained, experienced researchers to find "interpretive" results by observing things that citizens are saying "between the lines" or by implication, not in so many words.

17   It is important for scholars especially to observe that the notes that follow each of the chapters on public attitudes do *not*, in general, represent sources for the assessments and conclusions presented in those chapters. In general, those assessments and conclusions are based upon primary research carried out as part of the Security for Europe Project, and reported here. To some extent, these assessments and conclusions are also based upon other research done by the authors' institutions.

  In general, the notes in all the chapters on public attitudes present *additional* information and supporting data. The sources for this additional information are given in the notes. A few notes also provide elaborations of ideas.

18   Many of these footnotes cite survey research findings from other organizations. Such data is relatively scarce; thorough and extensive quantitative survey research did not exist in the first half of the 1990s in these six countries on many of the topics addressed by this book. While certain specific matters were investigated by various organizations at certain times and places, most of the topics assessed here were not systematically investigated by survey researchers during this period. This reflects the fact that these former communist states were so newly free that broad, thorough survey research on sensitive topics of foreign and security affairs was barely beginning at this time. (Much more survey research was done on internal questions.)

Part II

Public attitudes on security in Central Europe

3

Public attitudes in four Central European countries

Magda Boguszakova, Ivan Gabal, Endre Hann, Piotr Starzynski and Eva Taracova

Introduction

The peoples of Poland, Hungary and the Czech and Slovak Republics have experienced some important events of recent years in similar ways. They are also living in situations now that are similar in major respects. The result, not surprisingly, is that these peoples hold a number of similar attitudes about the situation of their countries in Europe. Similar does not mean identical; and of course it is not to be imagined that the same percentages of the population, from one country to another, hold any particular attitude. Nonetheless a number of attitudes are strikingly similar among these peoples. This chapter describes these attitudes held in common. Chapters to follow in this part will discuss other attitudes held in each country alone. All these chapters describe public *attitudes*, and not (except where specifically stated) short-term public *opinion*; the distinction was explained earlier.[1]

Some basic common elements in these countries' recent and current situation, which go far toward accounting for the common attitudes, are so obvious that they can be mentioned only briefly. Incidentally, we will not refer to these countries as "the Visegrad countries," even though some specialists in international affairs do, because this label is *not* part of the public's sense of who these countries are. Although substantial parts of the public in all four countries would understand this term if they heard it, it is not a term that most people think of as part of their image of themselves.

Czechoslovakia, Hungary and Poland were, of course, members of the Soviet bloc of countries for decades until 1989. All were involuntary members. At one time or another and in one way or another, all three tried to rebel against their Soviet overlords. (Historical events are discussed further later in this book.) During 1989, these countries unexpectedly and rather suddenly found themselves able to choose their own governments and to set their own courses. All chose to become parliamentary democracies and all chose, though in different ways, to move toward market economies. As described earlier, Czechoslovakia subsequently divided into two countries, the Czech Republic and Slovakia. It scarcely need be said that these choices reflected the public's attitudes and desires. All four peoples find themselves now in the midst of extremely difficult transformations, of which more will be said in a moment.

Meanwhile, the military alliance to which these countries had belonged for decades first became a formality and then vanished entirely. Very soon thereafter, the USSR itself vanished, disintegrating into its constituent "republics" which became independent countries. For people in the four Central European countries, the sudden break-up of the USSR was a stunning event. The public had been taught all their lives not only that the Soviet Union was the greatest and most permanent of countries, but also that the forces of history predetermined that the Soviet Union would become the chief country on earth and in time, the world's capital.[2]

Instead, the Central Europeans have seen the large lands to their east sinking into political instability and economic malaise. They also have seen the former Yugoslavia collapse (not unexpectedly), and then become inflamed in a civil war whose horrors can be seen nightly on their television screens. For Hungarians this war is right next door. On the positive side, there have been no direct military threats, and of course no attacks, on any of the four Central European countries themselves, and people do not feel that any military threats are imminent.

With this brief background, we now discuss a variety of attitudes that are held in roughly similar forms among the Czech, Slovak, Hungarian and Polish peoples.

The public's leading insecurity

In all four countries, people's chief insecurity is the economic and political crisis that they are living through daily. In the absence of any direct external military threat, the internal crisis of each country is, by far, the dominant source of anxiety.

In a book of this kind, it is essential to emphasize that for the public in Central Europe, the internal crisis is a *security* issue. There is a tendency in Western countries, which by Central European (and world) standards are politically stable and economically prosperous, for the idea of security to be separated from internal political and economic affairs. Security is thought to be one thing, and domestic political and economic problems to be another. This is not the way the public in Central Europe think. Of course people know that external threats are obviously different in kind. But the internal difficulties, actual and potential, are so severe that they are a deep source of insecurity for the public. In research done for this book, a number of representative groups of the public in all four countries were asked "What does security mean for your country?" The groups responded by naming the internal crisis, first and emphatically, *every time.*[3]

The scope of this book does not permit any detailed description of the internal crises of these countries, which anyway differ in their particulars from one country to another. A brief and general overview of the public's perceptions will suffice. (This passage applies less to the Czech Republic after about the middle of 1993; thereafter Czechs felt increasing confidence that the worst of the transformational crisis was behind them.)

People experience in many aspects of their own lives the difficult and painful transformation that all four countries are attempting. Almost the whole social fabric, including practically all economic and political, and many social and cultural, sides of life, is in the process of being torn apart and rewoven. People experience change, sometimes radical change, coming into their lives from many directions and creating many difficulties.

For most people, the most pervasive and immediate insecurity is the profound and never-ending economic crisis of their country. The exact shape of the crisis varies from one time to another, as the transition to a market economy proceeds in stages; it also varies from one country to another. Many people have either lost their jobs, or fear they will lose their jobs shortly when another stage comes. Many people have been forced into bad jobs far below their level of education; many are working two jobs. Meanwhile prices have risen, in some countries sharply. In these years following the end of communism, which supposedly was a bad economic system, people's standard of living has generally been falling, not rising.

People are highly aware that the economic crisis intersects with social disorders – existing disorders and worse ones feared for the future. The most immediate and visible disorder is crime. Societies that were accustomed, for decades, to strict order are shocked by crime that seems to be rising fast everywhere. People also sense, under the surface, possibilities for other kinds of social disorders that they may not be able to describe clearly but that make them feel unsettled.[4]

These insecurities about social order are inseparable from people's fears about their country's political future. Anxiety, often combined with cynicism, about one's own government is almost universal in Hungary, Poland and Slovakia (not, by now, in the Czech Republic.)[5] People in these countries also are uncertain about the democratic "rules of the game," in two important senses. People feel that they themselves are unsure what the democratic rules of the game should be. This is scarcely surprising, after decades of dictatorship and, in Poland and Hungary, little earlier democratic tradition to draw on. Secondly, the public feel unsure whether the new political parties, and most of the political leaders, understand the democratic rules of the game, and will act within those rules. The public's anxiety is not eased by watching the political parties' continual fighting among themselves, including constant attacks on each other in newspapers and on television. The public are not sure what the rules should be about what is legitimate and not legitimate in political competition, and are concerned that political fighting could escalate into ways that might damage democracy itself. These anxieties are much less now, but not entirely absent, in the Czech Republic. In the other countries especially, the public does *not* assume – although they would greatly like to be able to assume – that a democratic order is here to stay. Rather, the feeling is that democracy is fragile and could be lost.[6]

These political anxieties and the anxieties about possible social disorder are interwoven in these countries with the pains and fears of the economic crisis.[7] The public are quite aware that there must be profound links among all these areas. Ordinary citizens do not know just what the links might be, but they feel sure that deep links exist, and that sudden negative developments in one area could quickly produce a disaster in another. Hence the anxieties in each area magnify the others. The overall result is a general fear for their country's future (and their own), in which economic, social and political fears swirl around, intersecting and mingling.

These insecurities cannot be discussed more deeply in a book that is devoted, as this one is, to security in its external sense. But it can hardly be overemphasized that in the first half of the 1990s, the greatest insecurity felt by the Polish, Slovak and Hungarian peoples, by far, and for some time also the Czechs, is their insecurity about each country's ability to come through the profound crisis of transition without some kind of collapse, and to become economically well-functioning, stable and democratic societies. These peoples want their countries to become "normal European" countries, but are not at all sure that they will succeed in this.[8]

External non-military insecurities

The public in all four countries do not feel, in the early 1990s, any imminent military threat from any direction. One partial exception is a degree of danger, felt by some Hungarians for part of this time, about some possible threat from Serbia. That exception is discussed in chapter 7. Throughout these Central European countries, people recognize dangerous possibilities for the future, as discussed below. Much of the public also feel, in a vague way, that their countries are living in a kind of security vacuum, also discussed below. But people feel no present military threat. (A sense, especially after December 1993, of a potential future military threat from Russia, which may or may not materialize, is discussed shortly.)

The public in each of the four Central European countries do feel, and feel keenly, some *non-military* threats from outside their own country. Three external dangers are felt especially, and there is a fourth that is external in a sense. It was not possible to measure the order of importance, for the public, of these threats using the methods employed in this study, and any measurement by other methods would be questionable anyway because the order of importance probably changes as time passes. It might be noted here that the first two dangers are also felt by the public in Russia and Ukraine.

Danger from nuclear power stations has been on the public's mind, throughout Eastern and Central Europe, ever since the Chernobyl disaster of 1986. People fear another such disaster and fear that next time it may be even worse. People in all these countries are keenly aware that many nuclear power stations built in Soviet times, and located in neighboring (and in some cases their own) countries are unsafe. They fear that what happened once may easily happen again.[9]

A danger of other environmental disasters is also on the public's mind. Factories and other things built during the Soviet era operated with almost no attention at all to environmental consequences. Sizeable areas have been badly polluted, and the public is highly aware of it. People throughout Central Europe fear there could be a new environmental disaster, perhaps chemical in nature, that could begin in a nearby country and spread environmental damage to their own country.

Migrants arriving from abroad are feared in all the Central European countries. The public hold an image of hordes of migrants pouring in from the east (the former Soviet Union) or southeast (the Balkans). Central Europeans understand that there are various possible causes why huge numbers of people might arrive. They might be refugees from wars or political chaos, from any of various countries. Or migrants could arrive in large numbers simply for economic reasons, especially in the wake of a complete economic collapse in their home countries. The Hungarian, Slovak, Czech and Polish people all feel that their own countries have neither the economic resources nor the political stability to cope with hordes of foreigners arriving and living in their countries.[10]

Crime, including "mafias," is a mounting public anxiety. This fourth danger felt by the public is external in one way, and has been mentioned already. People feel that "mafias" are operating internationally, hardly hindered by national borders. The public in the Central European countries also feel that the police forces are not trained or equipped for fighting international crime and have little experience in it. While international "mafias" are only part of the soaring crime problem that raises public anxiety, they are an especially visible and worrisome part of it.

These four non-military dangers are "on the public's mind" in these countries. Many of the focus groups of citizens (described earlier) were given an opportunity to speak freely about what they felt security for their country meant, before any specific question was asked. In the Central European countries, the citizens named these insecurities more quickly, and with a stronger emotional sense of anxiety, than any military danger of any kind.

Chaos and possible dictatorships to the east

In addition to these four specific anxieties, the peoples of Central Europe also feel a much more general and diffuse anxiety. They fear that the lands to the east (and southeast) may be descending into chaos. A general trend toward chaos would include, of course, the specific dangers just named, and could include many other things as well. As Central Europeans see it, all aspects of life in the former Soviet Union, and also in the Balkans, may be drawn into deepening chaos: political, economic, social, environmental and military.[11]

The public feeling of a danger of chaos to the southeast and east has two consequences for other attitudes. With respect to the Balkans, it reinforces the already strong wish for effective peacekeeping, discussed later in this chapter. With respect to the former Soviet countries, it produces a certain modification of attitudes about democracy, among many (not all) Central Europeans. This response was visible as early as 1992.[12]

Many Central Europeans who strongly support the development of democracy in their own countries at a fast pace, also feel that the former Soviet states may not be ready for a fast transition to democracy. These people feel that the economic and other problems the former Soviet societies face are so immense that only "strong" governments, undemocratic but competent and resolute, would be able to push through the enormous steps needed to achieve working economies. Once a functioning economy and society is achieved, there would then be enough stability to move toward democracy. Central Europeans holding this viewpoint fear that governments that are temporarily more democratic, but weak and wavering, will result in ever-worsening disorder in the former Soviet countries, which in turn will lead either to complete chaos and collapse, or to harsh (and perhaps aggressive) tyrannies that would step in to "restore order." It is noteworthy that this idea about the former Soviet lands was common among the public in Central Europe long before the autumn 1993 struggle in Moscow between Parliament and president, and the destruction of the Russian White House.

Elections were held in Russia in December 1993, which brought Vladimir Zhirinovsky to prominence. Polls and other research done in Central Europe in the weeks and months following showed a distinct rise in public anxiety that ultranationalist elements in Russia may come to power in Moscow. Zhirinovsky's ideas for expansion of Russian power are seen by Central Europeans as aggressive in the extreme, and if he or people who think similarly take charge in Moscow, Russia may become a real threat.[13] This feeling, developing after the December 1993 Russian elections, represents a modification of the more general attitude, discussed above, that Central Europeans see no military threats. In the early 1990s, they felt none from the Russia of Boris Yeltsin. In the same years, however, the public in these countries also were well aware of a possibility that a future Russia, under a different government, could be expansionist.[14]

A distinction just used should be explained. In the early 1990s, most of the public in the four Central European countries held a view about non-democratic regimes that, from the American viewpoint at least, seems relatively subtle. It does not seem subtle to Central Europeans, whose history has included examples of many kinds of non-democratic governments. (It should be emphasized again that nearly all the public strongly desire democracy for themselves in all these countries.) The Central Europeans distinguish readily between degrees of "dictatorship." It is clear to them that some undemocratic, highly centralized regimes are harsher and more tyrannical than others, and also that highly centralized regimes vary greatly in how aggressively they act toward other countries. People in the Central European countries are aware that a new regime could appear in, say, Moscow that might be anti-democratic in Russian internal affairs, but might not pose any serious threat to Central Europe. Many Central Europeans make a distinction, too, between an undemocratic government in Moscow being aggressive inside the territory of the former Soviet Union, and making threats or taking aggressive action outside it. Naturally, Central Europeans also have long been aware that a different sort of harsh, anti-democratic government in Moscow could indeed be threatening even beyond the former Soviet boundaries – that is, to themselves. After December 1993, public anxiety rose that a Zhirinovsky government would be of that kind.[15]

The rise of nationalist feeling

The Slovak, Czech, Polish and Hungarian public are highly aware of rising nationalist feelings among many nationalities in the eastern half of Europe, and they are quite concerned about it. The general public are neither ignorant nor indifferent toward this phenomenon; people see it and are worried by it.

The public in all four of these countries do not believe that nationalist feeling rises spontaneously from the general population. Instead, people in all these countries say repeatedly and strongly that nationalist feelings are deliberately enflamed and manipulated by politicians. This is one of the most striking findings of the public opinion research undertaken for this study. This finding deserves emphasis because the opposite idea is widely believed among writers and commentators in the West, and indeed in Central and Eastern Europe also.

According to the public, rising nationalism is not, as that widespread idea suggests, some kind of spontaneous phenomenon that grows on its own among the general population. On the contrary, the public emphasize that rising nationalism is a result of political manipulation. According to the public, political leaders and other leaders throughout the region deliberately arouse nationalist and ethnic feelings, and hostile feelings toward other ethnic groups and nationalities, as part of these leaders' constant struggles to gain and keep power. These manipulations can be found in many countries, and at all levels, down to local and neighborhood levels. Manipulations can also be of many kinds; naturally the things that clan chieftains in the Caucasus mountains do differ in particulars from the things ambitious politicians in Central European democracies do. But the differing details are variations on one basic pattern. To arouse nationalist feelings is a political tool.

This research finding is all the more striking because citizens constantly raised this point themselves, without being asked. In this study, the public were *not* asked "do you believe this?". Of course, if they had been asked, it would have been easy for them just to say "yes." But they were not asked this question. Instead, groups of citizens were invited, in general terms, to discuss nationalism and its rise, and to say whatever they thought important about it. Citizens advanced this conclusion on their own. They did this repeatedly, and often strongly, in all four countries. (Incidentally they also did so in Ukraine and in Germany.)[16]

In fact no other idea about nationalism, other than its danger, was raised nearly as often by the public. In response to the general invitation to discuss nationalism, usually the public's first response was to say how dangerous it is, and the second response was to say that it is not spontaneous but is aroused from political motives. In most cases, other ideas were offered later and with less emphasis. An earlier chapter mentioned that points of public consensus can be identified with the focus group method. The conviction that rising nationalism is being deliberately enflamed by politicians for political motives is a point of public consensus in all four countries.[17]

This finding is important enough that a possible misunderstanding should be clarified. A sceptic might ask this question: We know that nationalist feelings are rising, among the *general* population, so how can these groups, drawn from the general population, say that it is not people like themselves who are feeling more nationalistic? The answer is that the citizens' groups do not deny that. They agree that people like themselves are feeling more nationalistic, and that nationalist feelings are growing among the general population. But citizens say that the feelings grow in *response* to actions by leaders that arouse such feelings. That is, political and other leaders take actions that enflame nationalist feelings among the people. Once those actions are taken, nationalist feelings are indeed aroused among the general population, and people in general do indeed feel them more than previously. But the general public are not the original source, and the process is not a spontaneous one.

Naturally, a large number of political actions are involved. While a few of them may, for instance, be nationalistic statements made in the capital city by national leaders and printed in newspapers, a much larger number of them are small actions, taken in small cities, towns and villages around the countryside, by local leaders. Many of these things may be known to only a relatively few people in the capital, and hardly known at all outside the country.

One other idea about nationalism was also advanced often by the citizens' groups. Many said that a distinction should be made between "nationalism" in an aggressive or hostile sense, and honest pride in one's own culture and people. A reasonable pride in one's own nation or ethnic group, and its culture and achievements, is only natural. It becomes dangerous at the point where it turns into hostility against other ethnic groups or nations. Again this idea was raised by the citizens' groups without being asked, and was raised so often that it probably is a point of public consensus.

Borders

Throughout the eastern half of Europe, the topic of borders is closely intertwined with the topic of nationalities. In many countries there is public concern about ethnic groups living as minorities inside one's own borders, or large populations of their own nationality living on the other side of borders. For clarity, we will first discuss attitudes about the borders themselves and then turn to attitudes about national minorities.

To a degree, Poles feel a concern that Germany someday might seek to change the Polish–German border. And the public in Slovakia feels some concern that Hungarians might seek a change in the Slovakia–Hungary border. Both these concerns are relatively mild; they are discussed later, in the chapters on Polish and Slovak attitudes, respectively. There are no other public concerns, in these four countries, that any of these countries, or Germany, might seek to change the borders. This finding is noteworthy, considering how often and how greatly borders in Central Europe have been changed, even in this century, and how often the desire for territory has been a fuel for wars.

One further attitude about borders should be mentioned, because there is a possible paradox that is easily resolved. In addition to what has just been said, it is also true that many people in these countries want "the borderless Europe." There is no contradiction. A large part of the public in all four of these countries want their country to join the European Union, and most people understand that after this occurs, their border with other EU countries will become almost a formality. Indeed, many want this "borderless" situation in the Europe of the EU, which their country will be inside, as they hope, in the future. Naturally this is a quite different question from people's simultaneous desire that there be no change in the borders – that is, no change made by any country unilaterally.[18]

National minorities and borders

Two of the four Central European countries discussed in this study, the Czech Republic and Poland, enjoy a fortunate situation regarding national- ity groups and borders. The borders of these countries correspond closely enough to where the Czech and Polish peoples live, and there are sufficiently few other peoples living in these countries as minorities, that no question involving borders is likely to arise for this reason. (The chapter on Poland discusses the topic of ethnic Poles who live in neighboring Lithuania.)

Hungary and Slovakia are less fortunate in the relationship between where borders are located and where people live. There is a small Slovak minority group living inside Hungary. A far larger number of Hungarians live in Slovakia, and also in the other countries neighboring Hungary: Romania, Serbia and Ukraine. The Hungarians living abroad are a subject of keen concern for Hungarians in Hungary, as discussed below in the chapter on Hungarian public attitudes. The Slovak public in Slovakia feels that the Hungarian minority there poses significant problems, including a possibility of troubling implications for the border between Slovakia and Hungary. These feelings in Slovakia are discussed later in the chapter on public attitudes in Slovakia.

The public feels that a mismatch between where peoples live and where borders are located is potentially one of the gravest issues throughout many parts of Eastern Europe. (This issue is further discussed elsewhere in this book.)

Peacekeeping

In all of the four Central European countries, the public strongly desire that adequate mechanisms be found to halt existing wars in Europe, and to prevent any new ones. The obvious fact that a war can occur in Europe, without effective measures being taken by the international community to prevent it or halt it, provokes anxiety in these countries.

The wars in the former Yugoslavia deeply concern the public in these countries because fighting continues endlessly. Month after month, year after year, the Central European public watch the slaughter on their tele- vision sets, and no international body acts to stop it.[19] For Central Europe- ans, it is bad enough that the West and the world do not halt this violence and all its terrible human consequences. These feelings are similar to those felt by many Western Europeans, Americans and others. In addition, the Central Europeans feel something further. Unlike Western Europeans, the Central Europeans feel they are living in an unstable region. Hence the Central Europeans, and especially Czechs, Hungarians and Slovaks, are disturbed by what the failure to stop this war may mean for their own future. If the West and the world cannot stop the war in the former Yugoslavia, perhaps they also could not stop other wars that might break out in the Balkans, or in the eastern half of Europe generally. The public in Central Europe fears that in that case, there could be great danger in their own future. This possible implication of the fighting in the former Yugoslavia disturbs the Central Europeans perhaps most of all.

Among the Hungarian, Slovak and Czech people especially, and to some extent also among Poles, a marked undercurrent of disillusionment with the West has been growing as the Yugoslav fighting has continued. People are increasingly disturbed that the West apparently is either unable or unwilling to halt the bloodshed, a feeling to which we return in the following section on NATO.

The clear need for effective peacekeeping in Europe is one strong feeling held by the Central European public. Equally clear is a second attitude involving legitimacy. In all four Central European countries, a consensus of the public holds clearly a belief that legitimacy for peacekeeping operations flows from one source, the United Nations (UN). Just *how* a peacekeeping operation is carried out – for example by the UN directly or by NATO acting for the UN – is something about which the public do not much care and are not much interested. From the public's viewpoint, the choice of how such operations are done is a detail. What is central and essential is that the United Nations must authorize, and in some basic sense control, any peacekeeping operation. (Later chapters will show that Ukrainian attitudes are similar, while Russian attitudes are quite different.)

There is a third public attitude about peacekeeping, held not only among the public of all four Central European countries, but also among the Russian and Ukrainian public. This attitude, too, represents a public consensus.[20] Soldiers assigned to peacekeeping duties must be volunteers. This attitude was advanced clearly and consistently in all the countries studied. In fact this principle was advocated strongly, and with general support from all present, in every group that was invited to discuss the topic of peacekeeping. Across a number of countries where people disagree about peacekeeping in other ways, people agree strongly about this. It is definitely not legitimate, in the eyes of the public in these countries, to put conscript soldiers (draftees) in danger by making them take up peacekeeping duties in foreign lands. The only soldiers who may be legitimately assigned to peacekeeping duties abroad are those soldiers who volunteer for it.

NATO and the US role in Europe

The public in the Central European countries hold a favorable – in some respects strongly favorable – image of the US role in Europe in economic, in political, and for the most part also in military, terms. The Central Europeans want these forms of American influence in Europe to continue.

American cultural influence is another matter, as we shall see. The US military role should be discussed first.

The public in three of the countries, the Czech Republic, Hungary and Poland, not only accept but actively favor the continuation, at least for a considerable time, of a significant US military presence in Europe. (Attitudes in Slovakia are shifting and will be taken up in a moment.) A consensus or near-consensus of the public, in the three countries, holds this attitude about the American military presence.[21]

The clarity with which the public hold this view in these countries is indicated by the fact that large numbers of people are able to say why they feel so. Consistently, they volunteer, as their chief reason for their feeling, the idea that the American military presence makes Europe a more stable and predictable place. Without necessarily mentioning Russia, Germany or any other country by name, people in the three countries feel that in the absence of American forces, negative behavior would become possible in Europe that is not possible or unlikely with American forces present.[22]

In these three countries, large numbers of people know what NATO is and know that the United States is a member of NATO and its most powerful member. Of these people, the great majority clearly approve of NATO's continued existence. There is far larger public awareness of NATO than of the WEU or OSCE. For Hungarian, Polish and Czech citizens, their approval of NATO's continuation is, of course, a quite different question from the issue whether their own countries should join NATO.[23]

Public attitudes in Slovakia on these questions have been changing. In 1992, the main perception of NATO by the public in Slovakia was that NATO was a Cold War organization, parallel to the Warsaw Treaty Organization (WTO), and after the end of the Cold War both organizations were unneeded and both should dissolve. Since the WTO had already come to an end, so should NATO. The American troops who had been in Europe as part of NATO should therefore go home. Incidentally this attitude was a common one in former WTO countries, and even more common in the former Soviet lands, in the years just following the end of the Cold War, although by 1992 it was already a minority view in Poland, Hungary and the Czech part of Czechoslovakia. During 1993, feelings changed noticeably in Slovakia. The public in Slovakia moved a considerable distance toward the attitudes held in the other Central European countries. By 1994, Slovak public attitudes more nearly resembled the attitudes about NATO and the US troops held by Czechs, Hungarians and Poles.[24]

The impact of the seemingly never-ending war in Bosnia has had an impact on the overall feelings about NATO and the US presence in Europe. The growing disenchantment with the West's failure to halt that war is affecting attitudes about NATO specifically. The public in these four countries (in Hungary the most, in Poland the least) become increasingly frustrated and disappointed, as NATO continues to fail to take any kind of effective action in Bosnia. A feeling is growing among the public in Central Europe that if NATO cannot solve the problem of this relatively small war, then perhaps it is not as powerful and effective an organization as people had thought. This feeling is introducing a note of ambivalence in the public's perceptions of NATO in Central Europe, and if the feeling continues to grow it may undermine the public's overall respect for NATO.

An additional complication is being introduced by recent developments in Russia. The violent intervention in Chechnya, beginning at the end of 1994, has reinforced the public perception of instability, and potentially chaos, in Russia.[25] This perception, in turn, tends to lead Central Europeans to wish that NATO could be a reliable source of security.[26] The cross-currents in public feeling are making Central Europeans' attitudes about NATO increasingly complicated as time passes.

The public in all the Central European countries are aware, in a general way, that the United States has and will have some degree of political influence in European affairs, as a result of the continuation of NATO, as a result of keeping some troops in Europe and as a result more generally of strong transatlantic links. In the research done for this study, almost no negative feelings were voiced in these countries about this American political influence in Europe. The public feel that this influence does not represent a problem, and many feel that it could be positive. Some people in these countries, especially in Hungary (as discussed in chapter 7), would like the USA to play a stronger politico-military role in Europe.

Not surprisingly, the public in all four countries desire private investment by American companies. People feel this partly for the obvious reason of economic self-interest. Investment by American firms provides jobs, income and economic growth. People desire American investment also for another reason. It helps counterbalance the German economic presence. This motive is felt more in some of these countries than others, as discussed in a moment. In Poland people also have other feelings, which make Polish attitudes on the topic of investments more complicated, as described in the chapter on Polish public attitudes.

In these four countries there are a few people who still hold the view of American (and other Western) business that was the official view in the communist era, namely that American "capitalists" exploit the people and serve American "economic imperialism." As the Central European countries proceed through their vast transformations, including their own transitions to market economies, this idea is held by a shrinking part of the population, mainly by older people who find it too difficult to change the beliefs they were taught and have held all their lives.[27]

Although it is not directly related to security, one other attitude in the Central European countries about the US role in Europe is so striking and is so strongly held that it cannot be omitted here. The public in these countries feel increasing revulsion against American pop culture, which is seen as a tidal wave now coming in. This public reaction is selective and thoughtful; it is not undiscriminating and is not anti-American *per se*. In these countries the public have no objection, for instance, to Coca-Cola or to McDonald's. But there is strong revulsion against what the public see as extreme violence and other kinds of human degradation, in American films and television, and to some extent on MTV. The public in these countries are increasingly concerned about the effect of this influence on their own cultures. There is also some concern about a trend toward the commercialization of nearly all aspects of life.[28]

Germany

There is no anxiety about any future military danger from Germany among the public in the four Central European countries, with the partial exception of Poland, as discussed in chapter 4. Elsewhere any military risk from Germany is dismissed.

Germany is almost universally seen not only as a rich country but as a peaceful, stable democracy. In spite of concerns about right-wing extremist incidents there, the Central European public (the Poles less) admire Germany. Indeed, in the minds of many Central Europeans, Germany enjoys today the image that the United States enjoyed earlier: the most desirable place on earth to live.

The public in the Central European countries, definitely including the Poles, do however feel one concern about Germany in relation to their own countries. That is anxiety about Germany's growing economic power. The strength of this feeling varies considerably from one country to another. It is highest in Poland, moderate in the Czech Republic and less (but present) in Slovakia and Hungary.

Not only business people but ordinary citizens also feel that the German economic presence is already quite visible (especially in the Czech Republic) and feel that that presence is likely to grow further. People are aware of investments in their countries by German firms, they see German business people in their cities, and they notice other signs of growing German business activity in their homelands. In all four countries, the public hold conflicting feelings about this perception. On the one hand, most people recognize that there are economic benefits from German investment. The benefit most visible to the public is the creation of jobs. People also hope for greater growth in their country's economy as a result of German investment. On the other hand, the extent and depth of the German penetration – especially in the absence of strong investment from other countries[29] – creates public anxiety. In considerably varying degrees, as noted, Central Europeans are anxious about whether German economic power may come to dominate their countries' economies and, in time, perhaps also dominate their countries in broader ways.[30]

Information

In all the Central European countries, the public are dissatisfied with the quantity of the information they receive about foreign and security affairs, and even more dissatisfied with the quality of this information. The strength of this feeling is less in the Czech Republic, where people feel the available information is not terribly deficient. Dissatisfaction is more pronounced in the other three countries. (However in Poland before September 1993, this attitude was combined with a high level of trust in the Foreign Minister personally.)[31]

The public's discontent applies both to the amount of information received, and especially to the kinds of information that are received and not received. People feel that they are not being told enough about their country's foreign and security affairs. More strikingly, they feel that what they are told is not adequate for them to understand these affairs as well as they would like to, and could, understand them.[32]

The exact ways that citizens express these dissatisfactions naturally vary from one group of citizens to the next. The remarks offered by people in many focus groups may be synthesized into the following conclusions. First, the public feel that they are given a fairly large number of isolated facts. People say "we know that the Foreign Minister traveled to country X last week" or "we know that the Foreign Minister recently made a speech condemning such-and-such." Secondly, the public also feel that they know one or two of the most basic foreign policy goals of the country, such as the goal to join the EU, but do not have adequate information about other goals. Thirdly, the public feel that generally they have not been given the reasons why the foreign and security policy is what it is. And finally, they feel that generally there is not enough information about possible alternative goals for foreign and security policy, or reasons for alternative goals. To sum up: the public feel that they have enough short-term facts, but not enough information about goals nor about the reasons for goals or their alternatives.

Although dissatisfaction is less in the Czech Republic, far more striking is the consistency with which this dissatisfaction was expressed, in all the countries and at various times. Indeed, the extraordinary consistency of this finding is one of the most striking conclusions of our research. During 1993 many focus groups were invited to discuss the topic of information. Group after group, in country after country, expressed these dissatisfactions every time the topic was raised. (A similar dissatisfaction was expressed, although not as strongly, in Ukraine also, as discussed in a later chapter.)

The public in the Central European countries offer several reasons for the inadequacy of their information. People say that basically it is a symptom of their country being not yet entirely democratic. They say, more specifically, that neither the government nor the media in their countries are familiar yet with the public's need for information about foreign and security affairs. The governmental ministries are providing immediate facts but are not providing much of the other information that the public would like to have about foreign and security affairs. The newspapers, television and radio are relaying the facts that the ministries announce, but are not doing enough to inquire into, and report, the broader information about goals, the reasons for them and alternatives.

Some readers may wonder how the public dissatisfaction with information, discussed here, may be reconciled with the common observation that most of the public in these (and perhaps all) countries do not seem to express great interest in foreign affairs. It is true that if people are simply asked at random how interested they are in foreign affairs, most will say "not very." But when citizens in these countries are assembled in small groups and asked to discuss foreign affairs, and then are asked about information, they consistently say, often strongly, that information available to the public is inadequate. There is no contradiction. The difference is one of context. If people are comparing their interest in foreign affairs with, say, their own economic or personal worries, then naturally the latter are greater. People respond this way particularly if individuals are asked one by one. If people are in a situation where their attention is focused on their country's affairs, then they consider the adequacy or inadequacy of their information for thinking about them. To exaggerate somewhat for the sake of clarity: when asked at random, people respond as individuals, but when asked in the context of a discussion of the country's affairs, they respond as citizens.

The importance of history

A chapter written mainly for Western audiences about public attitudes in Central Europe cannot omit a fundamental feature of the public's viewpoint, a feature that underlies and colors many other attitudes. That is the importance and "presence" of history. Events of the first half of the twentieth century, of the nineteenth century and, indeed, of earlier centuries, are more emotionally real and relevant for Central Europeans than similar events are for Western Europeans, and enormously more real and relevant than they are for Americans. Even events and situations of the Middle Ages may have a relevance to the present in the feelings of Central Europeans (and also Eastern Europeans) in a way that Westerners rarely feel. This different relationship to time is found not only among the intelligentsia but also among the whole public. It represents a basic cultural difference between Central and Eastern Europeans on the one hand, and Westerners – and especially Americans – on the other.

This concludes this study's findings of those public attitudes about foreign and security affairs that are similar among the Polish, Czech, Slovak and

Hungarian peoples. The next four chapters examine public attitudes and opinion specific to each country.[33]

Notes

1   Readers are reminded that in this chapter, and in all chapters devoted to public attitudes, notes do not, in general, give sources for the assessments offered in the text, which are based mainly upon primary research that was carried out by the Security for Europe Project and is being reported here. In this chapter and all chapters devoted to public attitudes, notes provide additional information, with sources indicated.

2   However, in the preceding years Central Europeans were more familiar than Western Europeans or Americans with the internal weaknesses of the USSR and of the Soviet empire. Despite the propaganda, some kind of disintegration of the empire and even of the USSR in time was not unexpected among Central Europeans. But almost nobody expected events to unfold as rapidly as they did in 1989. After 1989, some kind of disintegrative crisis in the USSR was also widely anticipated in Central Europe. But again, for the USSR to collapse so suddenly and so completely was unexpected.

3   This continued to be true in the Czech Republic through 1993 and 1994, in spite of the growing confidence mentioned just below, in part because of the nearly complete absence of any external danger.

   The remarkably low level of public concern in Central Europe with certain issues of external security that are taken seriously in the West is demonstrated, for instance, by a series of surveys conducted in the Czech and Slovak Republics in early 1993. These found that only 1–2 percent or fewer of Czechs or Slovaks regard the problem of nuclear weapons in the former Soviet Union as "a pressing matter." *Lidove noviny*, May 1, 5 and 11, 1993, pp. 1, 2 and 3 respectively.

   Most Poles' focus on domestic concerns was demonstrated in a survey conducted in Warsaw by "Poll-Media" in the autumn of 1992. 61 percent of respondents considered the economic situation one of "the most pressing issues" facing Poland, whereas only 12.4 percent said that protection of the country's external security was such an issue. *Trybuna*, September 23, 1992, p. 1.

   53 percent of citizens of Russia polled by ROMIR in December 1991 and 54 percent of those polled in December 1992 and January 1993 thought that the greatest threat to the security of Russia came from problems inside Russia; only 19 percent and 16 percent respectively thought that the greatest threat came from some other country (n = 1,804). *USIA Opinion Research Memorandum*, March 31, 1993, p. 8.

4   Any set of specific possibilities may be misleading because any one, by itself, may not seem likely. A few possibilities include riots, large public demonstrations that suddenly go out of control, and growing groups of skinheads or other anti-social elements that might become increasingly uncontrollable. Such possibilities are less significant for themselves than for the way they hint at the

depth and wide range of social disorders that people feel cannot be excluded, and hence are anxious about.

5 This statement applies also to Czechoslovakia prior to the division of the country and to the Czech Republic in its early months. Thereafter anxiety and cynicism declined in the Czech Republic.

6 One facet of political discontent has been widespread dissatisfaction over the rate at which democracy has been developing. According to the Eurobarometer surveys of the Commission of the European Community, only 28 percent of Czechs and Slovaks, 30 percent of Hungarians, and 27 percent of Poles were satisfied with the development of democracy in October 1991. The corresponding figures for November 1992 were: 38 percent of Czechs, 22 percent of Hungarians, 32 percent of Poles, and 23 percent of Slovaks (n = 1,076, 987, 1,000, 977 and 924, 1,000, 999, 734). The corresponding figures for November 1993 were: 48 percent of Czechs, 20 percent of Hungarians, 35 percent of Poles and 19 percent of Slovaks. *Central and Eastern Eurobarometer*, nos. 2, 3 and 3, 1992, 1993 and 1994. It appears that a process of differentiation is under way, with the Czech Republic standing out from the other countries of the region in the steady growth in the confidence of its public in democracy.

   A poll conducted in Poland by CBOS in May 1993 found that only 22 percent of Poles believed that the country's political system was democratic; 39 percent believed it was undemocratic and 24 percent believed it was partly democratic. "Polska po czterech latach reform," *CBOS Serwis Informacyjny*, (May 1993), p. 3.

   The Eurobarometer survey of November 1992 found that 10 percent of Czechs, 15 percent of Hungarians, 22 percent of Poles, and 19 percent of Slovaks thought it "likely" or "quite likely" that a dictatorship would exist in their country within the next twelve months (n = 924, 1,000, 999, 734). *Central and Eastern Eurobarometer*, no. 3, fig. 12.

7 For example, in December 1993 90 percent of Hungarians called the current economic situation "bad" and 74 percent said it was worse than under communism. *USIA Opinion Research Memorandum* (January 12, 1994).

   The European Commission's Eurobarometer survey found in November 1993 that 46 percent of Hungarians expected the financial situation of their household to deteriorate over the next twelve months, while only 17 percent expected it to improve. The corresponding figures for Slovaks were 43 percent and 27 percent, for Poles 23 percent and 24 percent, and for Czechs 28 percent and 31 percent. *Central and Eastern Eurobarometer*, no. 4 (March 1994), fig. 3. As in the case of confidence in democracy, some differentiation may be observed among these countries.

8 Czechs grew increasingly confident in 1993 and 1994 that their new Czech Republic was succeeding and would succeed in this.

9 The public in all these countries, including Ukraine and to some degree even Russia, feel also that this is one area where the West should give assistance on a large scale, even if the West is not willing to give much other aid. People say that it is in the West's own interest to do so since radioactive fallout could easily spread westward, as it did in the Chernobyl disaster. The public in all the countries are largely unaware of the quite modest, but useful, help that some

Western countries have provided to improve safeguards at a few of the nuclear power stations.

Many people in Central Europe distrust not nuclear power stations *per se*, but Soviet-built nuclear power stations, or for that matter any Soviet technology. For example, the general public in the Czech Republic (unlike Czech environmental activists) have no objection to the completion of a nuclear power station at Temelin, using American technology.

10 In Poland, concern about the flow of refugees from the east was strikingly evident in a CBOS survey in the spring of 1993, which showed that substantial majorities of Poles wanted to restrict the rights of Ukrainians (63 percent), Russians (62 percent), Belorussians (60 percent) and Baltic people (57 percent) to enter Poland. By contrast, only 41 percent wanted to restrict the right of Germans to enter, and only small minorities wanted to restrict the rights of French, Britons and Americans. "Spoleczenstwo polskie wobec otwartych granic – problem azylantow i wix," *CBOS Serwis Informacyjny*, no. 3 (March 1993), p. 12.

11 As early as September 1991, for example, 30 percent of Poles interviewed by Central Europe Market, when asked which of seven specified problems they thought posed the greatest threat to the security of Poland, chose "instability in the USSR"; a further 16 percent chose "mass immigration from the USSR" (n = 1,002). *USIA Research Memorandum* (October 31, 1991).

12 The public in the Central European countries feel there may be a possibility of fighting, and conceivably a war, between Russia and Ukraine. This sense of this possibility is another element in the Central Europeans' general feeling of chaos to the east. A possibility of serious fighting between Russia and Ukraine was generally rejected by the public in Russia and Ukraine themselves in the research done for this study, as discussed in later chapters.

13 Polls commissioned by the USIA showed that in Prague, the proportion of respondents who voiced concern that another country might "attack in the next few years" increased from 30 percent to 44 percent between October 1993 and January 1994. In Warsaw, the proportion who expressed this fear was the same in both months (37 percent). *USIA Opinion Research Memorandum* (January 19, 1994). However, other research shows rising anxiety in Poland during 1994; see chapter 4.

14 For many Central Europeans, Russia poses a genuine intellectual dilemma. On the one hand, many doubt that democracy is suitable for Russia and believe that some form of authoritarian regime is needed to prevent a slide into chaos. On the other hand, almost any authoritarian regime in Russia is likely to evoke, and pursue, Russian nationalism and traditional Russian expansionist dreams, which inevitably will be dangerous for Central Europe.

15 Feelings of insecurity in Central Europe are deepened by a sense that Russia's future is highly unpredictable. An impression that Russia could lurch in almost any political direction at any time leaves people feeling unsettled.

16 Here is one of the advantages of the focus group method used in this study. It gives citizens an opportunity to present their own thinking, without an idea being suggested to them in the act of asking a question.

17 This idea is also widely believed in Ukraine.

18 The wish to be part of a "borderless" Europe may be strongest in the Czech

Republic and weakest in Poland. As discussed in a later chapter, many Poles are concerned to maintain the clarity of their western border.

19 At the very end of 1994, a ceasefire was agreed upon among the warring parties in Bosnia. Whether this ceasefire will be continued, or will collapse like many previous ones, is not yet clear.

20 The discussion of the focus group method in chapter 2 pointed out that, although the method does not yield percentage results, a substantial number of focus groups can reliably show points on which there is a public consensus.

21 For example 60 percent of Poles interviewed by Demoskop in January–February 1993 agreed that the US military presence in Europe was necessary for the security of their country (n = 919). *USIA Opinion Research Memorandum* (April 2, 1993). In November–December 1992, 38 percent of Czechs and Slovaks interviewed by the Association for Independent Social Analysis (AISA) agreed with this view (n = 1,033). *USIA Opinion Research Memorandum* (February 8, 1993).

22 Here, as in other key points in the public attitude research reported here, people were not asked any "stability" question; rather, citizens volunteered this idea. If people were asked explicitly whether "stability" was a motive for them, it might be easy for them just to say "yes." The fact that they are able to volunteer a motive without one being suggested is significant.

23 Survey data is mixed about attitudes in Central Europe regarding NATO. Results vary considerably depending on how the question is worded, when it was asked, and in which country. For example, a survey by the Institute for Public Opinion Research in the spring of 1993 found that 58 percent of Czechs believe the Czech Republic should join NATO; only 18 percent were opposed. (*Ceske a moravskoslezske zemedelske noviny* April 20, 1993), p. 2. Other poll data suggests that many people in these countries do not have very much confidence in NATO. Thus 42 percent of Czechs and Slovaks interviewed by AISA in November–December 1992 said they had "a great deal" or a "fair amount" of confidence in NATO, as against 35 percent who said they had "not very much" or "no" confidence in it (n = 1,033). *USIA Opinion Research Memorandum* (February 8, 1993). Corresponding figures for Hungary, given by the Median poll of January 1992, were 39 percent and 24 percent (n = 919). *USIA Research Memorandum* (April 13, 1992). Corresponding figures for Poland, given by the Demoskop poll of January–February 1993, were 38 percent and 33 percent (n = 919). *USIA Opinion Research Memorandum* (April 2, 1993).

In June 1993, a survey was conducted in Poland by CBOS, examining any change in public opinion since May 1992. Those saying "Poland should seek membership in NATO" increased in that time period from 35 percent to 57 percent. In the same period, those saying that "Poland should stay out of any military alliances and remain neutral" fell from 35 percent to 14 percent (n = 1,015). *Polish Public Opinion*, CBOS (September 1993).

There appears to be a strong trend in at least the capitals of the Czech Republic and Poland in favor of their countries joining NATO. A telephone USIA survey in January 1994 found that 84 percent of respondents in Prague and 86 percent of respondents in Warsaw believed that full NATO membership is important for their countries. *USIA Opinion Research Memorandum*

(January 19, 1994). See also the discussion of attitudes about Poland and NATO in chapter 4.

24 By September 1994, according to a survey commissioned by the USIA, 60 percent of Slovaks favored and only 20 percent opposed strengthening Slovakia's ties with NATO. Full membership in NATO was favored by 48 percent and opposed by 22 percent. *Opinion Analysis*, USIA Office of Research and Media Reaction (November 23, 1994).

25 For example, consider a survey taken in Poland shortly after the beginning of the Russian military intervention in Chechnya. 92 percent of respondents had heard about the Chechnya conflict. 67 percent expressed sympathy to Chechnya and only 1 percent to Russia; 26 percent were indifferent in their sympathies. More than half of respondents said that events in Chechnya can create threats for Poland (58 percent), for peace in Europe (63 percent) and for peace in the world (51 percent). *Polish Public Opinion*, CBOS, Warsaw (January 1995).

26 See, for instance, evidence discussed in the next chapter of Poles' increasing wish (even before the Chechnya intervention) for Poland to be able to rely on the West for security, and increasing interest in Poland joining NATO.

27 In Central Europe, attitudes (positive or negative) toward Western investment correlate strongly with attitudes (supportive or opposing) toward the transformational process. For those who oppose the political and economic changes, foreign investment represents a threat. For those who support the changes, foreign investment is valuable for promoting economic reform, and also improves links with the West.

28 For example, a USIA commissioned survey conducted in October 1993 showed that while 85 percent of Czechs voice a favorable overall opinion of the United States, the proportion perceiving American culture as a threat to Czech culture had increased, in just one year, from 36 percent to 47 percent. *USIA Opinion Research Memorandum* (January 18, 1994). Similarly, another USIA commissioned survey conducted in May 1994 showed that while 84 percent of Poles voice a favorable overall opinion of the United States, only 52 percent did not perceive American culture as a threat to Polish culture (and 39 percent did so perceive it). *USIA Opinion Research Memorandum* (July 1, 1994).

29 In Hungary in 1992 and 1993, investment by American firms exceeded German investment. In the other three countries, German investment exceeds all others; in the Czech Republic it considerably exceeds all other countries' investments combined. In Slovakia, German investment was not great during these years, but investment from other countries was even less.

30 In Central Europe at this time there is a well-known joke about the foreign languages people decide to learn: "The pessimists are learning Russian, the optimists are learning English, and the realists are learning German."

31 The September 1993 elections in Poland brought a new coalition of parties to power and Foreign Minister Krzysztof Skubiszewski left office.

32 Particularly in Hungary, this attitude is connected to a larger public dissatisfaction with the media. A long struggle in Hungary over control of television and radio, called "the media war," has reduced public respect for these media.

33 Portions of the material in this chapter were first published in part II of the *Final Report* of the Security for Europe Project. The authors of this chapter express

appreciation to the book editor for his contributions toward synthesizing and formulating the assessments presented here.

For an interesting comparative review of public opinion in many Central and Eastern European countries on a variety of *internal* issues, see Richard Rose and Christian Haerpfer, "Mass response to transformation in post-communist societies," *Europe-Asia Studies*, 46 (1) (1994), pp. 3–28.

4

Poland

Piotr Starzynski WARSAW

The preceding chapter has already discussed attitudes held by the public in Poland that are similar to those held throughout Central Europe, and they need not be reviewed here. It might be emphasized that the chief security anxieties of the Polish people involve internal, not external, affairs. This chapter describes other attitudes and feelings that are specific to Poles and have not been discussed already.

Anxiety about Germany

Poles are the one people in Europe who feel some fear that Germany might again seek to enlarge its borders. Many Poles are familiar with the German phrase *Drang nach Osten*, and do not believe that the German people have abandoned a desire that they have shown repeatedly over centuries.[1] There is little concern about any military action at any time soon, although a small number of Poles think even this possible someday. A far larger number are concerned that as time passes, Germany could expand its territory at Poland's expense in non-military ways.[2]

One possibility mentioned often is the issue of buying up land. The Polish public are keenly aware of purchases of Polish land by German individuals and companies. There is some Polish feeling that a continual buying of land, especially in western Poland, could gradually achieve a kind of *de facto* German annexation. So keen is the anxiety that the actual extent and significance of purchases are exaggerated in the public's imagination. In actuality, there is a law in force that rigorosly restricts the amount of land that foreigners can buy. Even so, any purchase of land by Germans strikes an extremely sensitive chord for Poles. Even minor purchases, for instance, may be trumpeted in local newspapers. Of course, a public perception that is "actually" exaggerated is as emotionally real for the public as an accurate perception.

Another way that the public fear that Germany could expand eastward at

Poland's expense would be by way of Germany exploiting its immense economic power and the political influence that flows from it. Perhaps Poland could be compelled sometime to yield some territories to Germany through extreme political and economic pressure.[3]

This notion is just one form of a much more general anxiety about Germany. The overall effect of German wealth and power on the Polish mind produces a pervasive anxiety that Poland may become dominated by the colossus to its west. Future German domination could take many forms. Naturally the public are unsure about the particular mechanisms through which German economic and political power would be exerted. But anxiety that domination is coming is pronounced and widespread.

An entirely different attitude about Germany can also be found among the public in Poland. Some Poles feel that a moderately strong German presence, even including some German purchase of land, would not be a threat to Poland so long as the German influence does not extend to changing Polish culture or the national character. These people, who often are inclined toward a pragmatic view, feel that German investment helps the Polish economy. Some also say that Germany, as a stable, well-functioning democracy, provides a political model that Poland can emulate. In addition, some feel that German economic power and political influence help bring stability to the whole region.[4]

The Polish people as a whole thus feel great ambivalence about Germany. Anxiety about domination mingles with hope for positive influences. To a considerable extent, this ambivalence within the public as a whole is reflected in differences of opinion between one person and another, where some people feel mainly the anxiety and some feel mainly the hope. But the ambivalence can often be found even within a single individual.

The West and the European Union

Polish attitudes about the European Union and the West generally are mingled with feelings about Germany. Each set of feelings colors the other. Here one must not forget the importance of geography. Germany is not only the strongest member of the EU in fact; it is also the EU country that looms immediately on the western border. All other EU countries are further away, geographically and also psychologically.

The fact that Germany is a member of the EU gives a more positive color to Polish feelings about Germany. People feel that the eastward ambitions that Germany has, or would otherwise have, are restrained by the EU structures and by the influences on Germany of the other members. Poles expect that France and Britain especially can restrain Germany. More subtly, Germany's membership in the EU has the effect of "Europeanizing" Germany and thus taming it. A Germany that was not Europeanized might be more dangerous. But so long as Germany is a good member of the EU, Poland may have less to fear.

At the same time, Polish perceptions of the EU cannot escape being colored by Germany's presence in it. When Poles visualize their own future membership in the EU, which will include almost dissolving the national border, the most important border that will be affected will be the border with Germany. Some people fear that in the EU of the future the general language will not be English but German. The fact that this possibility is considered, and is feared, indicates the depth of the fear of Germany and of the way it is linked to the EU.

Meanwhile many Poles feel that the EU, and the West as a whole including the United States, is taking an economic stance toward Poland today that is not much different from that of Germany. Poles are anxious that the West is treating Poland as a second-class country to be used and exploited for the West's convenience. People feel that Western countries sell in Poland their inferior products, which would not be competitive in the West, and that the West puts Poland in a subordinate position in international finance. Any Polish industry that is valuable is in danger of being bought up by Western firms. People think the West is already taking advantage of Polish labor being inexpensive, and they fear that in the future Poland may be assigned the role in the European economy of a cheap manpower reservoir.

These attitudes do not mean that the public rejects membership in the EU as a goal for Poland.[5] People also realize that Western investment helps Polish economic growth. Many people feel that Poland can learn from Western models of production and business, and then perhaps improve upon them in ways uniquely Polish. There is a common attitude that the quicker Poland enters the EU the better, and that the thing to worry about is whether the West will allow Poland in. Membership in the EU is also seen favorably for other, non-economic reasons. A large number of Poles want their country to be inside, and not excluded from, the community of stable, democratic European states. The public thus feel ambivalent about the EU, simultaneously wanting the advantages it offers and fearing subordination.

There also is another level of feelings about the EU among Poles. Beyond whatever the pros and cons may be, the Polish public generally feel that it is inevitable that Poland will be drawn into the EU. The growing integration, in countless ways, of Poland with the West is seen as an irresistible historical force. People feel that it is Poland's fate to be pulled into the EU whether or not it is to Poland's benefit and regardless of Poland's own will. It is only a question of time. This sense of fate is colored by Poles' strong feelings about their history, in which basic turning points often resulted from great external forces beyond Poland's control. People feel that Poland, now as so often in the past, will do best if it learns to adapt to circumstances that once again are beyond its control.

Russia

Important parts of the public's attitude toward Russia resemble attitudes held elsewhere in Central Europe and these have already been discussed in the previous chapter. Historically, Poles have suffered under Russian domination far longer than other Central Europeans, and a fear of Russia is ingrained in the Polish mind. The possibility of an attack from Russia was easily imaginable for Poles long before Zhirinovsky appeared. Should he come to power in Moscow, Poles will be alarmed.[6]

The public in Poland were also sceptical, even before Zhirinovsky, that democracy will take root in Russia. Poles tend to feel that Russia is not entirely a European country and that the Asian part of the Russian character makes the country inclined to strong centralized rule. People expect that such a government in Moscow would strengthen the Russian Army and revive Russian great-power ambitions. Concern about developments in Russia increased somewhat in late 1993 and 1994, as discussed further below.

However, Poles are reluctant to make predictions about what will actually occur in Russia. They feel that in Russia almost anything is possible. Any kind of regime may appear, including a new quasi-communism, a turn toward authoritarian nationalism, actual progress toward democracy or almost anything else.

The eastern border

Another element in the public perceptions of Russia involves Poland's eastern border. People see many Russians in Poland and know that many of them are present illegally. Poles are concerned that the eastern border is not being controlled.[7]

A loose border presents a number of problems. Because of poor customs control there is an enormous inflow of smuggled goods, which lure customers who otherwise would buy Polish products. Criminal gangs and "mafias" move across the border into Poland easily. People feel that Polish cities are full of Russian mafias. In addition, Russian laborers will work for cheaper wages than Poles and many come illegally into Poland for work. Many of them eventually return to Russia, but people feel that in the meantime they take jobs that Poles might otherwise have. In the big cities, one often finds peddlers of cheap wares, and also beggars, who turn out to be Russians, Ukrainians, Romanians, or gypsies. The Polish public are keenly aware of all these problems and want the eastern frontier to be much more strictly controlled. Generally people are even willing to use the Army, if it is necessary to get firm control of the border. Some people add that the problems should be halted now, before an accumulation of bad experiences begins to reawaken old grievances and hostile feelings with their eastern neighbors.

Beyond these existing problems, Poles, like other Central Europeans, are worried (as discussed earlier) about waves of migrants arriving from the east in the future, fleeing turmoil, conflict and disasters.

Retaining the borders

There is a consensus among the public in Poland that the country's borders should not be changed. This attitude, which Poles share with other Central Europeans, is noteworthy because Poland had very different borders as recently as 1945. Many Poles still living lost their own land when the Polish border was shifted westward at that time. And it is only natural that there is a certain nostalgia among the public for territories, now lost, that were part of Poland for a long time. For instance the beautiful and important city of Lvov, now in Ukraine, was a Polish city for centuries.

In spite of this, there is almost no public support for any new change in Poland's borders. On the contrary, there is almost a consensus that any serious discussion in the Polish government of any border change would be foolish and dangerous. There is an important difference between people's nostalgia, which is felt, and any serious wish to regain territories, which generally is not felt. Even citizens who express warm feelings about the lost lands and cities usually say that they do not seriously want to recover them, and even say that any serious talk in government circles of regaining them would be a mistake.

Lithuania

A significant number of Poles, about 260,000, live in Lithuania and Poles have lived there for a very long time. Poland and Lithuania have a long and complicated mutual history, as briefly discussed in a later chapter. The Polish minority in Lithuania feels strongly that it is discriminated against. While the public in Poland naturally feel strongly supportive of the Poles across the border, attitudes differ about what this should mean.

Some people feel that Poland should exert pressure, perhaps strong pressure, on the Lithuanian government to improve the treatment of the Polish minority. Some of these people feel considerable hostility against the Lithuanian authorities and complain, for example, against their giving Lithuanian names to streets in the Polish districts. These people often emphasize that the chief city, "Vilnius" in Lithuanian, was traditionally an old Polish city, pronounced "Vilno" in Polish.[8]

Other people in Poland emphasize the importance of maintaining good relations between the two countries. These people want to see help given to the Poles in Lithuania mainly in the form of material assistance. They say that Lithuanians tend to feel an anxiety about Poland similar to that which Poles feel about Germany, and that this needs to be understood in Poland. These people point out that, as a practical matter, relations between the peoples in the immediate border areas are good, and that this should be the model for Polish–Lithuanian relations generally.

Ukraine

The public in Poland want Poland and Ukraine to have good relations, and there is a consensus that old historical grudges are best forgotten. Poles feel no military or political fear of Ukraine at present, although there is an undercurrent of anxiety that if strong nationalists come to power in Ukraine they might try to exert pressures on Poland. Most Poles do not expect that the strong nationalists in Ukraine will come to power there, however. In general, Poles feel warmer feelings toward Ukraine than they do toward Russia, and many Poles hope for growing economic relations with Ukraine that would benefit both Poland and Ukraine.[9] People feel that Poland should not take sides in any conflicts between Ukraine and Russia, but rather seek to mediate and help make peace between them where possible.

Attitudes toward NATO and Poland

Support for Poland joining NATO has been increasing among the public, primarily as a result of growing concern about developments in Russia. The attack on the White House in Moscow in October 1993, the ominous vote for Zhirinovsky in the Russian elections in December 1993 and the strong Russian objection (often repeated during 1993 and 1994) to any expansion of NATO have had a cumulative impact on Poles. The view is growing, for instance, that Russia will seek to rebuild an empire.[10]

Concurrently, the Polish attitude toward Poland's integration into NATO is growing warmer. In June 1994 a full 75 percent of Poles surveyed declared that if a referendum were held on Poland joining NATO, they would vote in favor.[11] Opinion is also growing that the post-socialist countries joining would increase peace and stability not only for them but for Europe as a whole.[12] At the same time, Poles are concerned that the United States may be more interested in good relations with Russia than in guaranteeing the security of Central Europe.[13]

Conclusion: two patterns in Polish attitudes

The public's thinking about Poland's present situation and past experience tends to fall into two patterns or viewpoints. One might be called "patriotic-romantic"; the other might be called "liberal-pragmatic." Naturally these are not pure types and any one person may reflect elements of both. Nonetheless these two general patterns are quite noticeable in many issues.

The patriotic-romantic viewpoint sees Poland's past, present and future in a way that glorifies and celebrates Poland. For centuries this has been a traditional way of thinking among Poles. This viewpoint cherishes and strongly desires to protect Poland's independence, freedom of action, and territorial integrity. It reveres the Polish tradition of uprisings, including armed uprisings, against oppressors. This viewpoint tends to glorify fighting. It is people who hold predominantly this viewpoint who are most worried about Germans buying Polish land, and about the West incorporating Poland into the EU as a way to make Poland a dependent, subordinate country. Also it is usually people holding this viewpoint who want to protect the Poles in Lithuania by pressuring the Lithuanian authorities.

The liberal-pragmatic viewpoint is a more familiar one to Western Europeans and Americans, and it resembles a "Western" way of thinking. From this viewpoint, the important economic issue is modernizing the Polish economy. The productivity of a firm is more important than whether or not it is "Polish." For the Polish economy to grow as fast as possible, Poland should shift to a market economy in a far-reaching way, and should open itself to the inflow of Western capital and the modern technology that comes with it. It is people who hold predominantly this viewpoint who desire Poland to join the EU for the political benefits and for the sake of "joining Europe," even to the point of eventually almost dissolving Poland's borders with the rest of the EU. People holding this viewpoint prefer to give material assistance to the Poles in Lithuania over pressuring the Lithuanian government.

Both points of view have deep roots in Polish culture, and we may expect both to remain, side by side, in Polish thinking for a long time to come. These two sets of attitudes may not need to clash sharply, if Poland's current transformation into a market economy develops well and Poland's economy proves both successful and Polish. However, if the public comes to feel that "modernization" is making Poland into a poor backwater of the West, a clash of values may follow, with unpredictable consequences.

Notes

1 *Drang nach Osten* means literally "drive to the east" in German. For a long time in German culture, this has been the traditional phrase for German eastward ambitions. In focus groups held by the Security for Europe Project, Polish citizens frequently used this phrase in German.

2 Although more than 60 percent of respondents polled believed that Poland's independence is not threatened, Germany was cited as the state which Poland should be most wary of, by 41 percent of respondents. *Polish Public Opinion*, published by CBOS, Warsaw (September 1993).

3   Also relevant here is a trend today, in parts of Poland that used to be German territory, to give the old German street names to the streets again. Poles who fear advancing German influence see this trend as more evidence for their fears. Other Poles see this trend as merely satisfying the rights of a minority (just as Poles living in Lithuania want to use Polish names for the streets in their districts).

4   People who feel this way often point to Holland as an example of a country that is greatly under the influence of Germany, yet benefits from it, enjoys its own stable democracy and its own culture, and is in no danger from Germany.

5   As of May 1994, a strong majority of Poles, 70 percent, support Poland's full membership in the EU. In 1992 and 1993, the equivalent figures were 80 percent and 75 percent respectively. The number opposed has remained constant at 7 percent; the proportion who respond "difficult to say" has grown. *Polish Public Opinion*, CBOS, Warsaw (May 1994).

6   After the battle over the White House in Moscow in October 1993 and the electoral success of Zhirinovsky's party in December 1993, the percentage of respondents polled who believe that Poland's independence is threatened grew from 22 percent (in June 1993) to nearly 40 percent. *Polish Public Opinion*, CBOS, Warsaw (February 1994).

   Early in 1994, 65 percent of Poles expressed dislike of Zhirinovsky, and more than half opposed his visiting Poland. He was perceived by 75 percent as a politician who "may be of some danger not only to Poland but also to the world." *Polish Public Opinion*, CBOS, Warsaw (February 1994).

7   A strong majority, 62 percent, of respondents polled said that citizens of Russia should have their right of entry into Poland restricted. *Polish Public Opinion*, CBOS, Warsaw (February 1994).

8   In Polish the spelling of the city is "Wilno." In Polish, the letter "w" is pronounced "v." The Polish name of Poland's capital city should also be mentioned. In Polish, the letters "sz" are pronounced "sh." The city called "Warsaw" in English is called "Warszawa" in Polish, which is pronounced "Var-SHA-va." Relevant chapters of this book also give the pronunciation of the country's name in its own language. In the Polish language the name of the country is "Polska."

9   The different attitudes toward Russia and Ukraine have much of their roots in history. Russia ruled part of Poland for a long time but Ukraine never did. Rather, Poland ruled most of Ukraine for a long time.

10 In January 1994, 59 percent of those polled believed that Russia will try to rebuild its empire. The corresponding figure in June 1993 was 39 percent. *Polish Public Opinion*, CBOS, Warsaw (February 1994).

11 *Polish Public Opinion*, CBOS, Warsaw (July 1994).

12 That view was supported by 59 percent of those surveyed in January 1994 and by 70 percent in June 1994. *Polish Public Opinion*, CBOS, Warsaw (July 1994). Here "post-socialist countries" means the former Warsaw Pact countries, not the former republics of the USSR.

13 In February 1994, close to 70 percent of those polled said that the United States is more interested in good relations with Russia than in guaranteeing the security of Poland and the post-socialist countries of Central Europe. Less than half of people polled believe that Poland can count on the help of the West in

case of a direct threat to Polish sovereignty; however, the percentage who believe that Poland can count on it grew from 29 percent in November 1993 to 40 percent in June 1994. *Polish Public Opinion*, CBOS, Warsaw (February 1994 and July 1994).

5

The Czech Republic

Magda Boguszakova and Ivan Gabal PRAGUE

Public attitudes in the Czech lands changed rather rapidly in the period from 1992 through 1994, mainly as a result of the division of Czechoslovakia. The creation of an independent Czech Republic at the beginning of 1993 led to a rapid evolution of Czech attitudes, as people became convinced that the new Republic could follow a different and better path than was possible for the old federal state. Although the main topic of this book is security in its international sense, this shift in Czechs' feelings about their country is important enough to demand brief attention first.

The generalizations presented in chapter 3 about internal insecurities being much greater for citizens than any external insecurities remained true for the Czech lands throughout this period. During 1993 and especially 1994, however, the public's sense of internal insecurity diminished steadily. People felt a growing sense of confidence in the political and economic stability of the new Czech Republic and its favorable prospects for the future. Internal uncertainties did remain greater than external ones, because external insecurities were quite low.

Czechs generally felt in 1993 and especially 1994 that their new country was progressing economically as rapidly as could be expected, and that the future would bring further economic growth. They also came to feel confidence that the new Republic was and would remain politically stable, and that its democratic institutions were becoming well-established. During this period the sense of being in a profound "transition" to a new economic, political and social system began to fade, as people came to feel that some of the most critical parts of the transition were now safely behind them. This does not mean, however, that the majority of citizens felt that either they or the country had achieved a satisfactory life. The Czech Republic was still a relatively poor country, and many people were still experiencing great economic strain. Raising the standards of living and, more generally, completing the transition to becoming "a normal European country" continued to be the public's main concern.

With this basic observation about the internal situation, we devote the remainder of this chapter to Czech attitudes about external affairs. Many important Czech attitudes have been described earlier; here we describe others that are specific to Czechs.[1] The division of Czechoslovakia was by far the most dramatic, and for the Czech public the most riveting, topic during these two years, although for Czechs and Slovaks the topic was "external" only in a sense.

The division of Czechoslovakia

For most Czechs, as for many Slovaks, the division of Czechoslovakia was painful. After all, the country had existed in its unified state (except briefly during the Nazi occupation years) throughout the lifetimes of everyone alive. The division was also a surprise. At the beginning of 1992, hardly any Czechs expected such a thing. By sometime in the autumn it was felt to be inevitable.

The intervening months were a time not only of pain but also of confusion for most Czechs. It became clear to the public that strong pressures were developing that were leading toward the country's division, but it was less clear just where those pressures were coming from. The most widespread idea in the Czech lands was that the pressure toward division was coming from Slovakia. Yet many Czechs also knew that poll after poll showed that a majority of Slovaks did not want a complete rupture. The polls also showed repeatedly that a majority of Czechs did not want it either.

For the public, the question was complicated by the fact that during much of this time, people believed that the issue would be settled by a referendum. A general referendum, to be held throughout Czechoslovakia, was promised several times, and these promises generated public expectations that one would be held. Yet it never was. In its absence, a feeling gradually grew, and by the end of the summer was becoming strong, that there was something inevitable about the split. As this feeling took hold, a new attitude began to appear in addition to the pain and sadness. A sentiment developed among many Czechs that "if it's to be done, it's best done quickly." During the autumn, opinion among Czechs shifted around to support for the creation of a new Czech Republic.

The Czech public were determined that the "divorce" be accomplished in a completely fair and civilized manner. This attitude was strong and nearly universal. Above all, Czechs were determined that it should be peaceful. A common feeling in the Czech lands in the autumn of 1992 was a sense that might be put this way: "we and the Slovaks will show Europe and the world how this can be done in a civilized fashion." Afterwards there was a general feeling that the split had been a success in this sense.

The birth of the new Czech Republic on January 1, 1993 was a moment of mixed feelings for the Czech people. As most had really wanted the preservation of a united Czechoslovakia, it was partly a moment of sadness and nostalgia. Warm feelings toward Czechoslovakia and (despite a few unpleasant incidents) toward the Slovaks naturally continued. At the same time, most Czechs viewed their new Republic in a positive light. They felt that a Czech Republic would have certain advantages compared to Czechoslovakia. Thus on January 1 they felt a measure of confidence as they contemplated the prospects for their new state. This sense of confidence grew in 1993 and 1994 as various economic and political indications suggested that the Republic was indeed progressing, in spite of the difficulties of the transformation.

Slovakia

The basic feeling of Czechs for Slovakia and the Slovaks continues to be, and is likely to remain, warm. The depth of this feeling is indicated by, for instance, the fact that many Czechs hope that the "divorce" will be only a historical phase, and that eventually the two countries will reunite in some fashion. However, even Czechs who feel this also usually feel that no reunion is likely to come soon. There is a widespread feeling in the Czech Republic that the two countries will move apart, before they (perhaps) eventually reapproach each other. By 1994, a majority of Czechs did not want any reunion soon.[2]

Czechs generally feel that Slovakia is burdened with more problems than the Czech Republic has, and has fewer economic and social resources for dealing with its problems. Czechs have also been sceptical about the competence of the first governments in independent Slovakia, and somewhat sceptical about the ability of Slovakia to form any competent government, at least in the near future. There is a consensus among Czechs that Slovakia faces a more difficult future than the Czech Republic does. At the same time, Czechs generally believe that in the long run, the economic and political situation in Slovakia will improve, even if at a slower pace than in the Czech Republic.

Almost universally, the Czech public want close and very friendly relations, now and into the future, between the Czech Republic and Slovakia. However, Czechs are not sure this can be attained in a continuing way. While nobody doubts the basic good feelings of the Slovaks toward Czechs, there is widespread doubt whether the government in Slovakia will behave well. There is also a common opinion among Czechs that the Slovaks, "having made their own bed, should now lie in it." That is, Slovaks will now have to learn from hard experience how difficult it is to run a country, and they will have to learn for themselves how to do it.

"Europe"

A consensus of the Czech public agrees that the future of the Czech Republic lies with the European Union. That is, if the Republic is to have the kind of positive future of economic growth, and of development in all aspects of society, that Czechs want for their country, it can only be achieved as part of the EU. Only a small minority of Czechs feels any doubt that this is the direction the country must go. This consensus among Czechs was already visible in early 1993, soon after the Czech Republic was created, and despite minor fluctuations, a basic consensus on this has continued since.

The fact that there is a consensus on the goal does not mean, however, that Czechs have exclusively positive feelings about joining the European Union. On the contrary, many feel that there are certain risks in doing so. They merely feel that the risks are much outweighed by the probable benefits and that no alternative course is attractive.

In general, the risks seen by Czechs are those that a small country faces in opening itself to a huge grouping of states, some of which, even by themselves, are much larger and more powerful. Different individuals naturally emphasize different specific risks. For instance, business people are aware of competitive dangers in giving completely free access to the Czech market to powerful foreign firms, even while many of the same business people are eager to have access to the tremendous EU market themselves. A broader segment of the population feels an anxiety that Czech culture, so recently freed from one kind of foreign domination, may be about to be swamped by another kind of foreign domination. Almost inseparable from this are specific anxieties about Germany and German influence, discussed below. Since Germany is both huge and right on the border, it is especially difficult for Czechs to feel a distinction between opening the Czech Republic to the EU and opening it to Germany, the most powerful EU member. In spite of these concerns, Czechs have centuries of experience of being a small unit in some big entity, and feel a certain degree of confidence that they can find a more or less satisfactory place for themselves in the future in another big entity, the EU.

In a book for an international audience, another point must be added. For Czechs, perhaps more than for any people not presently members of the EU, there is a great paradox contained in any phrase like "joining Europe." In a sense this is an impossible phrase for Czechs, because all Czechs feel that their land is already, and inescapably, part of Europe. For centuries all Czech children have been taught that their country lies, geographically, in the exact center of Europe. Not just geographically but also in other ways, Czechs feel in their bones that they are at the heart of Europe. How can you "join" what you already are at the heart of? This feeling also lies uneasily and paradoxically next to another, namely a keen sense among Czechs of having been cut off (through no fault of their own) from Europe and European culture for more than four decades. Czechs intend to make up that lost time quickly.

In-migration

The prospect of membership in the EU raises another concern that is specifically Czech. The Europe of the EU will be a "borderless Europe" which citizens of all member states can cross at will. This fact creates ambivalent feelings for Czechs. They like, in principle, the idea of a "borderless Europe." At the same time they feel a concrete concern that this might mean, for the Czech Republic, an unwanted inflow of people from *Western* European countries. This concern about in-migration from the west and north is felt in addition to the (greater) anxiety, discussed in the previous chapter, about in-migration from the east and south. To some extent the two feelings merge.

Czechs are concerned that rich Western Europeans may buy up choice bits of the Czech countryside, where land is cheap by Western standards. And Czechs are concerned that a considerable number of Western Europeans could move to Prague. Already flooded by huge numbers of Western tourists, Prague is regarded by Europeans as a highly attractive city. If Westerners are allowed to rent or buy apartments and houses in Prague, they will bid up prices. For most Czechs, the cost of being able to live in their own capital city could soar out of reach.

Perceptions of Germany

Czech feelings about Germany, and about German culture and language, are complex. Over the centuries, layer after layer of feelings and associations have built up in the Czech mind about the intimate links with German culture, in several directions. Not only do the Czech lands border directly on Germany, but for centuries they were part of the Austrian empire. The empire had its capital in German-speaking Vienna, not far away, and gave pre-eminence to German culture. For Czechs therefore, the German cultural influence came even more from the south than from the northwest. On top of this, a substantial group of Germans, the Sudeten Germans, lived as a national minority within the Czech lands for centuries until 1945. And now today, Czechs find enormous German influences returning.

A book longer than this one could be written about the complicated interplay of all these influences, and reactions to them in the Czech mind, down through the centuries and now. Here all that need be said is that Czechs feel a deep and highly nuanced ambivalence about the German influence. On the negative side there is no other influence (certainly not the Soviet one of recent decades) that could be so overwhelming, and thus perhaps so threatening to Czech culture. At the same time, no external influence could be so familiar, and Czechs feel they understand the Germanic mind well, in both its Austrian and German variations.

At present there is a distinct generational difference among Czechs, depending on whether or not they can personally remember the dreadful years of Nazi domination. Those who are old enough to remember that time often feel frightened by today's fresh surge of German influence in the Czech Republic. Younger Czechs who do not remember that time feel little or none of this fear. Czechs of all ages do feel a sense of caution about a specific danger of the coming years. German businesses and banks might come either to own outright, or otherwise to gain control of, many key sectors of the Czech economy.

Memories and fears of Western betrayal

One further element in Czech attitudes must be mentioned in a book of this kind. There is a memory of not only one, but repeated, betrayals by the West, and hence there is fear of another. These feelings are felt also by Slovaks. Incidentally, here is another area, like many others, where Central Europeans are keenly aware of history. It is worth emphasizing again that feelings and memories from the past have a strong presence and immediacy in Central European cultures; the public as well as elites quickly recall past situations as a way of understanding present ones.

The betrayal of Czechoslovakia at Munich in 1938 was so great a disaster in the life of the country that feelings about it remain strong even now. Czechs and Slovaks cannot forget that when Hitler demanded that he be allowed to take over Czechoslovakia, the West simply yielded. Czechoslovakia had pinned its destiny on its military alliance with France and Britain. At the crucial moment, the West walked away.

As Czechs and Slovaks see it, the West betrayed Czechoslovakia a second time only a few years later. Under the terms of the Yalta Agreement, signed in February 1945, the Western Allies agreed to an arrangement by which the Soviet Union, not the West, would liberate Czechoslovakia from the Nazis. Although an American Army reached western Czechoslovakia in May 1945, it was required to halt, and it was Soviet troops who marched into Prague.

Similarly, in the minds of Czechs and Slovaks, the West betrayed Czechoslovakia yet again in 1968. Czechoslovakia defied the USSR by turning away from the harsh, Soviet form of communism to try to create a more humane society. In August, the Soviets crushed the "Prague Spring" with a massive military invasion. Then and now, Czechs and Slovaks feel that the West could have prevented that invasion and simply did not, but it could have told Moscow that it would not tolerate such a thing, but it did not even try to do so, and Czechoslovakia was occupied by the Soviet Army for more than two more decades.

Czechoslovakia only came into existence in 1920, and in the short time since, the West has betrayed it three times.[3] It is not surprising that Czechs and Slovaks now fear another such event. Many feel that a comparable event would be a Western refusal to admit their countries into NATO.[4] Such a decision would not be seen by Czechs and Slovaks as just one more diplomatic or political occurrence, but rather as yet another Western betrayal, which Czechs and Slovaks would compare directly and explicitly to the events of 1938, 1945 and 1968. This possibility needs emphasis here, because many in the West are contemplating the possibility of admitting the countries to NATO from their own, Western, point of view. Czechs and Slovaks would have a quite different point of view on any negative decision. President Vaclav Havel has pointed out publicly that such a decision would be seen by Czechs and Slovaks as a "betrayal."[5] His use of this term may have been seen in the West as mere rhetorical exaggeration. It was not; it was an accurate observation of what the reaction of many Czechs and Slovaks will probably be if the West refuses to admit their countries into NATO.[6]

Notes

1 Conclusions presented in this chapter are based partly on research conducted specifically for the Security for Europe Project and partly on other information available to the authors. Since notes to other chapters in this book give the pronunciation of the country and capital city in the native language, this information is provided here also. In the Czech language the name of the country is pronouced "cheska republika," and the name of the capital city is not Prague but Praha.

2 Asked in January 1994 "would you vote for a reunion this year?" 65 percent of respondents said "no" while 35 percent said "yes." From "Attitudes toward the split of the CSFR in the Czech Republic," STEM Research Agency, Prague (January 1994).

3 Some Czechs and Slovaks count the events of 1948 as a fourth Western betrayal. When Moscow rigged a coup in Czechoslovakia that year, the West could have intervened to reverse it, or so many Czechs and Slovaks believe. However, this event is not felt so deeply as a Western betrayal because the coup itself was actually carried out by the communist element in Czechoslovakia, in other words by Czechs and Slovaks.

4 In May 1994, a poll asked Czech respondents about their preferred security strategy for the Czech Republic. A total of 62 percent chose either "a security guarantee by NATO" or "a quick entry by the four Visegrad countries into NATO." By contrast, only 19 percent chose a strategy of the four Visegrad countries forming an alliance by themselves, and only 12 percent favored an

alliance among the Visegrad countries, Ukraine and Russia. "Selected attitudes toward the security situation of the Czech Republic," STEM Research Agency, Prague (May 1994).

5 Perhaps Havel's best-known statement to this effect was made during a visit to Warsaw in October 1993. See "Politycy przepowiadaja dlugi marsz do NATO," *Rzeczpospolita* (Warsaw, October 23–24, 1993). See also "Droga wstecz nie istnieje," *Rzeczpospolita* (Warsaw), October 22, 1993; and "Havel w Warszawie: NATO nie jest wrogiem Rosji," *Rzeczpospolita* (Warsaw, October 22, 1993).

6 In focus groups assembled by the Security for Europe Project, citizens were asked about the NATO question. Repeatedly, citizens spontaneously used the word "betrayal" to describe a negative decision by the West, *without* this word having been suggested to them by the way the question was asked.

6

Slovakia

Eva Taracova and Stanislava Chmelikova BRATISLAVA

The birth of Slovakia as a new country is, of course, by far the most important recent event in the life of the Slovak people. This chapter will give its first attention to this subject, and then turn briefly to topics involving Slovaks' views of their external affairs. Two prefatory remarks should be offered first.

Chapter 3 has summarized attitudes that Slovaks feel in common with other Central Europeans on various topics. That chapter's emphasis on internal insecurities applies strongly to Slovakia, where anxieties about internal matters are dominant. This chapter will describe other attitudes, ones that are specific to the public in Slovakia, without further reiteration of the central place of internal affairs.

National elections were held in Slovakia in September 1994. There was also a change of government in March 1994. At that time the Parliament removed the Prime Minister, Vladimir Meciar, and other ministers and replaced them with a caretaker government.[1] In the elections that followed, Meciar received more votes than any other candidate but not enough to form a government immediately. In December 1994, a new government was formed consisting of a somewhat unexpected coalition between Meciar's group and the far-left Labor party. None of these political changes materially changed Slovak public opinion regarding *foreign* affairs, nor did foreign affairs play an important role in the elections. For the purposes of this book, these things do not need to be discussed further.

The birth of Slovakia and the division of Czechoslovakia

Slovaks have a distinctly different viewpoint from Czechs about what occurred on January 1, 1993. The Slovak view is important enough for a book of this kind to require some emphasis and explanation.

Legally, the old Czechoslovakia was replaced on that day by two new states, the Czech Republic and Slovakia, *both* of which are officially "successor states" to Czechoslovakia. Of course the public in each of the two understand and support this legal reality. However, the emotional reality is different. Both Slovaks and Czechs, in different ways, feel that the Czech Republic is more nearly the continuation of the previous state and that Slovakia is more nearly a new country.

Hence January 1, 1993 had, and still has, a different feeling and a different meaning for Slovaks and for Czechs. Czechs tend to feel that since that date they have been living in a state that has been greatly restructured, and has a different name and much less territory, but in a basic way is not so different from the former country. In many ways the new state functions in ways similar to the old one. And of course the new one retains the same capital, Prague, which remains, as it has always been, the great lodestar around which all things Czech revolve. For Slovaks, January 1, 1993 was something more profound. For Slovaks it was the birth of a truly new country, *their* country. For the first time in history, the Slovak people have a country that belongs to them and that they control. (The entity called Slovakia from 1939–45, while technically a separate country, was in fact dominated by Nazi Germany.) Hardly anything can be more profound for a people than, for the first time, to have their own country.[2]

This difference in attitude between Slovaks and Czechs follows closely from the feeling, which in different ways both peoples have had for a long time, that in the previous Czechoslovakia the Czechs enjoyed the dominant position. This was partly a reflection of the facts that the Czechs outnumbered the Slovaks, by a ratio of about two to one, and that Prague was located deep in the Czech region and was populated mainly by Czechs. In addition, Slovaks felt that Czech influences tended to dominate policy-making in the capital.[3] Slovaks usually regarded this with resentment; Czechs tended to see it as natural. In any case, this disparity meant that when Czechoslovakia ended and two new countries were formed, Slovaks perceived their new situation as a liberation. The Czechs had no reason to see their new situation so.

Slovaks' feelings of resentment about their inferior position in Czechoslovakia should not be exaggerated. During 1992, poll after poll showed that a majority (though at times not a large majority) of Slovaks preferred that the country not be divided. Many Slovaks did not feel the resentment very strongly, and many felt that there would be practical advantages in having a unified Czechoslovakia continue. But these considerations did not change the fact that the birth of an independent Slovakia was felt by many Slovaks as a liberation.[4]

In the latter part of 1992, Slovaks felt just as much as Czechs that the "divorce" should be carried out in a completely fair and civilized way and, above all, peacefully. Since the division of the country, Slovaks feel, as Czechs do, that they deserve credit from Europe and the world for the way it was carried out so peacefully (in such marked contrast to the split of Yugoslavia).

The basic difference in how Slovaks and Czechs saw the meaning of January 1, 1993 also explains other things. For instance it explains why Slovaks were more emotional than Czechs at the time, as some foreign observers noticed. This reaction was natural; for Slovaks the event had a much greater meaning.[5]

For the same basic reason, the Slovak people tended, in the period after January 1993, to show a certain patience with their new government even though many felt that it made some blunders. Some patience was only sensible. Slovaks felt that their new country was like a newborn infant; naturally it could not be expected to perform well right away. In the same period Czechs certainly did not see their government as being like a newborn infant, and they expected it to perform well immediately.

Slovaks also noticed, in the weeks following January 1, 1993 that the birth of their new state did not seem to receive a warm reception in Europe. (Czechs, not seeing their state as really new, had no reason to expect any particular European welcome for it.) Of course European governments acted correctly by promptly recognizing Slovakia and establishing normal diplomatic relations, but the birth of Slovakia received little attention in the press or on television around Europe. Thus Slovaks felt with disappointment that when their new country leapt on to the European stage, there was no general applause and praise. That absence was all the more significant because one of the motives for the split of Czechoslovakia in the first place was precisely to make Slovakia more visible.

The Czech Republic

Slovaks, like Czechs, now want relations between the two new countries to be warm and close, and want relations to continue so in the future. Even after both countries are members of the EU, Slovaks hope for especially close relations with the Czechs. In a more basic way, Slovaks trust that they will always have a close relationship with the Czechs. Not only did the two peoples live together in the same country for nearly a century, they are ethnic cousins who have been linked for 1,500 years.[6]

At the same time, the idea sometimes found among Czechs that a "Czechoslovakia" might be reunified someday is not often voiced by Slovaks at present. Naturally the achievement of independence produced a quite different mood. Even many Slovaks who did not want the separation now feel that since an independent Slovakia has been created, it must find its own place in the world. Indeed, at this point there is hardly any choice. Even Slovaks who are pessimistic about the country's future, and especially about its serious economic situation, usually feel that now there is no alternative but to cope with the problems as well as possible.

Attitudes about external affairs

In the period following Slovakia's independence, attitudes about external affairs formed only gradually among the public in Slovakia. For a time, people continued to hold the views they had held as citizens of Czechoslovakia; to some degree they still do. Public attitudes of Slovaks *as citizens of Slovakia* have been in the process of formation.

This is not surprising in a new state. Naturally it does not suggest any deficiency on the part of the Slovak public. On the contrary, this is a reasonable product of an awareness that on issues basic to the country it would be foolish to leap to hasty judgements. It is not to be expected that the public of a new country should make its mind up quickly on many questions facing the country. While a superficial and potentially volatile public *opinion* could naturally be found on many questions even in early 1993, well-defined, deeper *attitudes* take longer to develop.

Attitudes, developed to the point of being clear and stable, can be identified regarding certain topics in foreign affairs. The remainder of this chapter discusses those.

The European Union

The original Czechoslovakia had applied to join the EU and at the time that the country split, this was rather widely supported. During 1993, shortly following the split, a noticeable difference appeared in the public's feelings in the two successor states. In the Czech Republic, a strong consensus formed rather rapidly that joining the EU is a highly desirable goal, and indeed the goal that the Republic definitely must choose for its future. In Slovakia in the early months of its existence, the goal of Slovakia joining the EU had a somewhat less firm status in the public mind. There was a tendency to favor it, but this inclination was not as broadly or strongly felt. Certainly there was more inclination in favor of joining the EU than in favor of any other path, but a real consensus had not yet formed.

As time passed, Slovak's desire for their country to join the EU grew stronger and deeper.[7] A public consensus took shape that this definitely should be a main goal for the country. We may conclude that in less than two years of national independence, a firm public attitude developed, one that almost certainly will now remain stable. By late 1994, the question among Slovaks was no longer whether their country should join the EU (or that the public had now made up its mind), but rather, what terms the EU would give Slovakia for admittance, and when.

Germany

Germany does not occupy as large a place in the minds of Slovaks as it does in the minds of other Central Europeans, especially Czechs and Poles.

Among the public in Slovakia, impressions (of any kind) about Germany and about its relationship to Slovakia are not as strongly or as widely felt as in the other countries. Partly this reflects the fact that the German economic and other presence in Slovakia is not, in actuality, as great as it is in the other three. The predominant feeling about Germany that does exist among Slovaks is a desire for greater German investment. This is not surprising, since Slovakia has the most severe economic difficulties of any of the four Central European countries discussed in this book.

NATO

Chapter 3 described how the public attitude in Slovakia toward NATO shifted in 1993. Earlier the predominant feeling had been, in essence, a residue from the Soviet era, when NATO and the Warsaw Treaty Organization were seen as parallel organizations, and people felt that after the WTO dissolved, NATO should dissolve also. In 1993, the Slovak public began to develop an attitude toward NATO similar to the attitude held in the other Central European countries. It is no coincidence that this shift began *after* Slovakia became an independent country. Only then did Slovaks feel a need to rethink the security situation in Europe.[8] A moderate trend of increasing public support for Slovakia joining NATO continued in 1994.[9]

Hungary and the Hungarians

An area in which Slovak public attitudes are well developed is the topic of Hungary and the Hungarians. This is a single topic, in which the external question of relations with Hungary is completely intertwined with the internal matter of the Hungarian minority living inside Slovakia. More than half a million Hungarians, a little more than 10 percent of the total population, live in Slovakia (and have for centuries, as discussed in another chapter). They are not distributed evenly around the country but live almost entirely in the south, near the Hungarian border. In the last several years, the Hungarian districts have been both complaining about infringements on their rights and seeking a form of autonomy.

Slovaks see the Hungarian minority as vocal and demanding. Slovaks are especially concerned about the demand for autonomy. A group of autonomous Hungarian provinces, situated right on the border, could in time have the effect of making the border "invisible" and meaningless. Slovaks fear that those districts would come to operate *de facto* practically as if they were part of Hungary.

Slovaks also feel strongly that Hungarians who are living in, and legally are citizens of, Slovakia should learn the Slovak language. Some Hungarians speak it badly or not at all. Regarding the claims of the Hungarian minority for better protection of their rights, Slovaks point out that there is also a

Slovak minority living inside Hungary, and say that those Slovaks should receive the same rights that the Hungarians in Slovakia receive.

The Slovak public are rather strongly concerned about the Hungarian minority and the possibility that Hungary could try to back the Hungarians' demands in various ways.[10] However, the Slovaks' anxiety is not as sharp as some peoples' anxieties in the eastern part of Europe about minority groups (for instance, the anxiety of Ukrainians, discussed in a later chapter). One reason may be that many Slovaks know that both Slovakia and Hungary are on the road toward joining the European Union, and believe that this factor may limit the difficulties.[11]

In the period since Slovakia has been an independent country, there have been various "standard earthquakes" (a phrase in the Slovak language) with the Hungarian minority. But these have not become deeper or stronger than Slovaks had expected. Of course the public in Slovakia hopes that they will not increase. At one point during 1994, the Hungarians sent a communication of complaint to the EU in Brussels, but in response, the EU declined to declare that their rights had been violated.

Notes

1 The elections were originally scheduled for October 1994, and subsequently moved forward to September.
2 In the time, more than a thousand years ago, before the Hungarians arrived and conquered them, the Slovak people, like other European peoples, had self-ruling local bodies but did not have a "country" in anything like the modern sense.
3 The government of Czechoslovakia had various rules designed to protect both groups' interests. One house of Parliament was proportional; the other was divided 50–50 between Slovaks and Czechs. Positions in the federal administration were assigned proportionally. However, all federal institutions were headquartered in Prague, and there was a strong tendency for Slovaks working in the capital to lose legitimacy in the eyes of people in Slovakia. There was a disparaging nickname, "federal Slovak," for these people who, it was felt, soon took on the perspective and thinking of Prague, a Czech city.
4 A feeling of liberation was not the only feeling to be found in Slovakia around January 1, 1993. There were also feelings of uncertainty about the future and, to some extent, surprise that independence had actually come, and so quickly. Some Slovaks also felt to some extent that they and Slovakia had been abandoned by the Czechoslovak state.
5 We will leave aside here the observation, often made, that Slovaks are a more emotional people than Czechs, as a matter of national temperament.
6 The Slovak people also are distantly related ethnically to the Slovene people, but for historical and geographical reasons the bond is not nearly as close.
7 Even by October 1993 more than 80 percent of Slovaks agreed, or were inclined toward agreeing, that Slovakia should aim for membership in the EU. Of

respondents, 45 percent agreed "definitely" and a further 42 percent "more agreed than disagreed." Only 5 percent more disagreed than agreed, only 4 percent disagreed definitely, and only 7 percent responded "don't know." "Actual problems in Slovakia after the split of the CSFR." FOCUS Research, Bratislava (October 1993).

8 The shift in mood toward NATO may have begun in late 1992 when it became definite that Slovakia would soon be an independent country. Survey data from FOCUS Research shows a marked growth in positive feelings toward NATO in 1993. Asked whether they feel trust in NATO (regarding its relationship to Slovakia), 28 percent said "yes" in March 1993 compared to 21 percent a year earlier; by October 1993 those responding "yes" grew to 44 percent. Interestingly, the number responding "no" remained roughly constant at all three times (34–38 percent). The increase in people responding "yes" came from people who previously responded "don't know" (45 percent in April 1992; 34 percent in March 1993; 18 percent in October 1993). "Actual problems in Slovakia after the split of the CSFR." FOCUS Research, Bratislava (October 1993).

9 Asked how they would vote if asked in a national referendum whether Slovakia should join NATO, 48.4 percent responded "yes" in July 1994, up from 44.7 percent a year earlier. Those responding "no" declined from 35.1 percent to 33.2 percent. The rest responded "don't know." Perhaps equally significant, 51.1 percent of respondents in July 1994 said that Slovakia's participation in the Partnership for Peace is "very important," while only 14.6 percent said it is "less important" or "not important." From a poll conducted by the MVK Institute (Metodicko vyskumny kabinet Slovensko razhlasu), and reported in *Narodna Obroda* (Bratislava, October 10, 1994). In general, support for ties with NATO is stronger among people of higher educational levels; it is weakest among retired people.

 A poll commissioned by the USIA in September 1994 showed that 48 percent of respondents expressed confidence in NATO while 33 percent did not. USIA Office of Research and Media Reaction, *Opinion Analysis* (November 23, 1994).

10 According to a USIA-commissioned survey conducted in September 1994, 86 percent of Slovaks see Hungary as a threat to the peace and security of Slovakia, while 88 percent see internal Hungarian–Slovak conflict as such a threat. USIA Office of Research and Media Reaction, *Opinion Analysis* (November 23, 1994).

11 In addition, elections held in May 1994 in Hungary brought a new government to power in Budapest which, in the view of Slovaks, may not push Hungarian ambitions as strongly as the previous Hungarian government did.

7

Hungary

Endre Hann BUDAPEST

Introduction

Many attitudes held by the public in Hungary are similar to attitudes held elsewhere in Central Europe, discussed in chapter 3. Some differing attitudes are discussed in this chapter, along with certain viewpoints that are specific to Hungarians.

The Hungarian public are much more concerned about internal problems than about any external threat or any international issue. When asked to talk generally about their security and insecurity, Hungarians almost always raise internal concerns, and usually raise economic issues first. In general, the dangers perceived by the public as threats to the security of Hungary can be placed into four groups, roughly in this order: economic problems, political problems, a complex of problems that are simultaneously psychological, social and moral, and international problems. It is clear that insecurities about economic threats come first and insecurities about international issues come last; the other two groups of issues may be roughly equal in significance.[1]

Economic problems: in recent years Hungarians have experienced a general decrease in the standard of living, together with growing unemployment and inflation. These are new phenomena for the public in a former socialist country, which had behind it decades of full employment, as well as little inflation and a slowly growing economy. Lately there has been an impoverishment of the middle class and of Hungarian society generally. Also new and disturbing for Hungarians is the growing economic inequality. Egalitarian values play a central role in Hungarian attitudes; this is another legacy of the forty years of the socialist system.

People feel that behind these economic difficulties lie political issues, particularly the sluggishness with which legislation about economic and business affairs has been passed by Parliament, and uncertainties connected with privatization. A conservative, mildly nationalist government was elected in the spring of 1990 and governed Hungary for four years. That government tried to defuse popular criticism by alluding often to the grave heritage of communism which had to be overcome. However, the average citizen was inclined to hold the new elite responsible for the economic difficulties. In the elections of spring 1994, the conservative government was voted out by a landslide vote, and was replaced by an alliance of two parties of the left, the Hungarian Socialist Party and the Alliance of Free Democrats. These parties stressed the urgency of the economic situation in their campaign and continued to give it their primary attention after gaining office.[2]

The public also perceive two international aspects of the economic difficulties worth mentioning. One is the collapse of markets in the east for Hungarian goods. The other is the absence of Western aid that the public expected after 1989.

Political problems: Hungary's political situation in recent years has been perceived as turbulent. During the four years following the 1990 elections, the public came to feel that there were loud discussions in Parliament and the media, mostly about secondary issues. There was a feeling that attempts were made to divert attention from the grave economic problems by over-emphasizing ideological themes. People felt too that incompetent politicians who started out as democrats increasingly demonstrated autocratic tendencies. The growing public dissatisfaction contributed to the landslide shift in government in the 1994 elections, which expressed a desire for a change, both in policies and in political tone. The election result can also be interpreted as an expression of people's need for some continuity with the pre-1989 past. A reasonable continuity was promised by the winners of the 1990 elections, but people felt the promise was broken.

Psychological, social and moral problems: people feel anxious about another change since 1989 which is at once psychological, social and moral. Not only do the public feel that Hungary's situation overall has been unstable and sometimes even chaotic, but worse, people feel a general loss of values. There is a sense of exaggerated dominance of material wishes and material ambitions now, with an accompanying loss of moral and social values. Society is becoming preoccupied with money and things, at the expense of human and humane feelings, and of social warmth and solidarity.

Furthermore, feelings of indifference and hopelessness have been growing. Many people worry that the youth in Hungary are responding with indifference or anxiety to a sense that their future is very uncertain. This is a source of concern, both because people worry that there may be some real basis for such feelings, and because such a mood among any country's youth is itself a sign of a lack of social health.[3]

International problems: these are least pressing for the public, but are not insignificant.[4] Because such problems are the subject of this book, the remainder of this chapter is devoted to them.

Hungary's international situation in general

The public in Hungary has several worries about the country's external affairs and its situation in Europe. Several basic concerns should be mentioned at the outset, before turning to some specific current issues. Among these are a general anxiety about the overall insecure situation among most of Hungary's immediate neighbors, and the insecure position of Central Europe generally. The break-up of the Soviet Union has led to conditions in the east that also inspire anxiety. Looking eastward, Hungarians tend to think first of the possible danger of a great wave of refugees arriving. There also are concerns about some environmental disaster.

These attitudes are responses to basic features in Hungary's situation. People cannot easily imagine Hungary's neighborhood, or Central Europe generally, becoming a region of stability and secure peace in the near future. Neither can they easily imagine a way in which the regions to the east might soon be stable, and safe from various upheavals and dangers. In these fundamental ways, Hungarians' sense of insecurity about their situation is not something likely to change soon.

From other points of view, Hungarians evaluate their country's situation with a certain ambivalence. On the one hand, they see Hungary as an insignificant, small country that does not play an important role in the world or even in Europe, and which does not have a major place in the thinking of Western countries. On the other hand, they see Hungary as a relatively stable country that potentially could play a valuable role for Europe in bringing stability to the region. To do so, people feel, Hungary would need a little assistance and the West's willingness to make Hungary an important partner.

A second ambivalence can be found in the image that Hungarians hold of themselves. In one way, Hungarians are quite confident of their identity as a people who have been basically Western in culture in recent centuries, and who most certainly have made significant contributions to European civilization. At the same time, Hungarians remember that they were the last of the peoples to come into Europe from Central Asia and that their language, which is not Indo-European, seems different and strange to most Europeans.[5] A sense of Hungary's history and uniqueness is very strong in the Hungarian mind.

These general observations made, we turn now to various specific attitudes regarding foreign affairs held by the Hungarian public today and in recent years.

The fighting beyond the border

For every other country represented in this book, the fighting in the former Yugoslavia is located at some remove – at least the distance of one intervening country. For Hungarians there is nothing in between. The war is right over the border. This gives the war a painful immediacy and urgency.

The fighting is so close and so much in danger of expanding that Hungarians are of two minds about whether it could reach Hungary itself. A clear majority is anxious that Hungary could get drawn into the maelstrom at some point; only about one-third exclude this possibility.[6]

Hungarians are the only Central European people discussed in this book who can readily imagine their country becoming somehow involved in a war soon. This naturally produces an ongoing sense of insecurity and anxiety, and this sensation is an important element in the life of the Hungarian people in these years. At the same time, most Hungarians do not believe that there is an immediate danger of a direct attack on Hungary.

Hungary and the Balkans

The endless fighting in the former Yugoslavia has other important meanings for Hungarians besides the possibility of direct danger. One is a disillusionment with the West, discussed later. Another concerns Hungary's geographical position bordering on the Balkan region.

The war is a constant and vivid reminder of a basic truth that Hungarians have known for centuries. The Balkan area has always been chaotic, violent and dangerous. The current war is only the latest of innumerable wars that have been fought in the Balkans down through the centuries. Hungarians see the Balkans as a viper's pit of endless hostilities and hatreds. This casts a certain light on the unchangeable geographical fact that Hungary itself lies immediately next to the Balkans.

Hungarians can always imagine two possibilities for the future of their land, which they naturally see as a very civilized country. They would prefer to see Hungary attached securely to "Europe," that is, to the stable Europe that lies to the west and north. They hope for a future in which Hungary is raised to the level of the safe, stable Europe. But the opposite possibility cannot be entirely dismissed. If events in Hungary and in the region unfold badly, Hungary's future might be grim. Instead of Hungary being sharply *distinct from* the Balkans, as one of the stable, civilized European countries, Hungary might come to be seen as *part of* the Balkans. Or at least, perceptions of the country might move enough in this direction that Hungary might take on the appearance of a semi-Balkan, unstable place that civilized Europe would not wish to embrace. While these two futures for Hungary are not part of people's everyday awareness and conversation, they represent an undercurrent in Hungarians' feelings, an undercurrent that affects other attitudes.

Slovakia, Romania and the Hungarian minorities

Not only is there a war beyond the southern border but, in addition, Hungarians feel that relations with two other neighboring countries, Slovakia and Romania, are uncomfortably tense. As the public see it, the chief reason is the very unsatisfactory situation of Hungarians living in these countries. For historical reasons discussed in later chapters, about 600,000 ethnic Hungarians live in Slovakia and more than two million in Romania. The Hungarians living in each of those countries feel that they are discriminated against as a minority group.

In Hungary itself, the public feel strong concern for the Hungarians living in the neighboring countries. The public in Hungary are concerned for their security, for the protection of their human rights generally and for the preservation of their cultural and linguistic identity. That the Hungarians abroad deserve the support of the Hungarians living in the homeland goes without saying. Official relations between states raises other questions. The extent to which Hungary as a country should seek to exert influence or pressure on the neighboring countries, for the sake of the Hungarian minorities there, is controversial in Hungary. The bulk of the public in Hungary does not want the government to take "strong" action on behalf of the cross-border Hungarians. Many citizens even disapprove of "too strong" statements on this topic by Hungarian political leaders. Such statements might be seen in the neighboring countries as aggressive, and therefore might actually provoke a worsening of the situation of the cross-border Hungarians. Anything that might raise any possibility of borders between countries being changed at Hungary's initiative is even more delicate. There is a consensus among most of the Hungarian public, except for some marginal right-wing radicals, that even any talk in official circles about changing the borders is undesirable.

The Hungarians abroad are a difficult, painful and complicated subject for the public in Hungary. There are, and almost certainly will continue to be, different points of view about how restrained or how vigorous Hungary as a country should be about the cross-border Hungarians.

Disillusionment with the West

Hungarians' sense of disillusionment with the West, and with the United States in particular, goes far beyond their disappointment that substantial aid has not been received. People feel that the West is basically indifferent to Hungary and to the region. They also feel that the complicated situation in Russia is distracting the West's attention from the small countries of Central Europe, including Hungary.

The sense of Western indifference is intertwined with a loss of trust in any sort of effective peacekeeping in Europe, either by the United Nations or by the West. Here the war in the former Yugoslavia is naturally foremost in the public's mind.[7] But disillusionment about the West's failure to halt that war is merely the sharpest edge, as it were, of a larger disillusionment about the West's ability or willingness to keep the peace in Europe. Many Hungarians still remember keenly the failure of the West to provide any help at all, at the time of the great popular uprising against the Soviets in 1956. For Hungarians, this was both a failure by the West, and especially the United States, on the one hand, and a failure by the United Nations on the other. The tragedy of 1956 is not seen as significant only by itself. When it is followed by the tragedy now unfolding in the Balkans, these failures come to be seen as part of a more general pattern of Western failure. At the same time, many people also notice that the West did intervene, quickly and very forcefully, in Kuwait. The result is a kind of cynicism. People feel that the great powers of the West are not willing to mobilize their military forces except in a case of a direct threat to their own, most immediate interests. The West acted in Kuwait, Hungarians feel, because the West needs oil from the Persian Gulf.

For the Hungarian public, the West's failure in the Balkans is certainly a failure by the United States specifically. In a November 1992 poll, two-thirds of the public expressed dissatisfaction with the American role in the Balkans; only about one-quarter said that the US either was doing its best or should not intervene.[8] During 1993 and 1994, Hungarians continued to feel that the West generally, and definitely including the United States, was continuing to fail, month in and month out, to bring the Balkan bloodshed to an end.

However, there is not a complete public consensus in judging the West badly. Some people, including some who are disappointed, still feel that the stability of Western Europe and the democratic character of the West is the best available guarantee for peace and stability in the region. However, others object that the West is so ill-informed about Central and Eastern Europe, and operates with such a short-range vision, that it fails to recognize how dangerous the problems of the region really are.

Partly because of the disillusionment with the West, Hungarians are greatly divided about the best way for the country to find security. A survey conducted in March 1994 showed that only one-third of the public is in favor of Hungary joining NATO or being associated with it. This figure is strikingly low, considering that exactly that has been proclaimed officially for years as a main goal of the country's foreign policy. Another one-third would prefer some kind of common defense system with the neighboring countries. Slightly more than one-quarter would prefer that Hungary stands alone with a security system of its own.[9]

Hungarians' opinions about the West go beyond just security and military affairs. Some feel that the West tries to transfer its ideas and techniques of democracy too mechanically into Central Europe, again because the West has too shallow an understanding of the region. A simple transfer of democracy worked successfully in Spain and Portugal, but that does not mean that the transfer can be equally straightforward in Central Europe.

At a simpler level, many Hungarians feel like throwing up their hands at the West's sheer ignorance, and its lack of interest, in the region. At the same time, people feel anxiously that Hungary's destiny is now being controlled by the decisions – or more probably the lack of decisions – being made by the West. There is a feeling of frustration, at a basic level, that Hungary's future is in the hands of people who understand little and care little.

Notes

1   The overall pessimism of the Hungarian public, regarding the country's problems as a whole, is noteworthy. A poll conducted in fifty countries around the world by Gallup International showed that 63 percent of the public expects 1995 to be a worse year than 1994, and 53 percent expect a rise in international tensions in 1995. Both figures are the highest of any of the fifty countries. *Magyar Hirlap* (January 3, 1995).

2   At the end of 1994, public support for the new governing coalition was approximately the same as it had been at the time of the May 1994 elections. An analysis by Median, reaching this conclusion, was published in *Heti Vilaggazdasag* on January 7, 1995.

3   No less than 66 percent of Hungarians polled in a Eurobarometer survey in November 1993 thought that "things [in Hungary] are going in the wrong direction." Of the countries discussed in this book, only in Ukraine was the proportion expressing this view higher (75 percent). European Commission, *Central and Eastern Eurobarometer*, no. 4 (March 1994).

4   A survey conducted near the end of 1994 showed the public's evaluation of the performance of the twelve ministries of the Hungarian government. The public indicated it was "most satisfied" with the Ministry of Foreign Affairs, and put the Ministry of Defense in second place. From a survey by the Szonda Ipsos institute, published in the *Magyar Hirlap* of December 21, 1994.

5   The arrival of the Hungarian people in Europe is briefly described in a later chapter. In Hungarian the name "Budapest" is pronounced as if the word were spelled, in English, Budapesht. In the Hungarian language the word for "Hungary" is Magyarozag.

6   A Median poll of March 1994 asked this question: "In your opinion, how likely is it that Hungary may get involved in a military conflict, because of the civil war in Yugoslavia?" 11 percent responded "very likely" and 50 percent responded "a little likely," a total of 61 percent. 34 percent said "not at all likely." The remaining 5 percent responded "don't know."

7   Of Hungarians questioned in a Eurobarometer survey in November 1992, 20 percent said that the UN had been effective in trying to resolve the Yugoslav conflict, while 54 percent said it had been ineffective. The corresponding figures for the efforts of the EC were 17 percent and 49 percent, and for those of NATO

9 percent and 51 percent. European Commission, *Central and Eastern Eurobarometer,* no. 3 (February 1993).

8   In a Median poll of November 1992, the question was asked "what is your opinion about the United States' efforts to end the fighting in the former Yugoslavia?" and three possible answers were offered. Responses to them broke down as follows: 65 percent agreed with the statement "US efforts are insufficient"; 12 percent agreed with the statement "the US is doing its best"; and 12 percent agreed with the statement "the US should not intervene." The other 11 percent responded "do not know."

9   From a Median survey of March 1994. The small remaining portion responded "don't know." There is a striking difference between the attitudes of different age groups. Only about one-quarter of people age 50 or older favor Hungary joining NATO. Among people aged 30–50, support is around 40 percent, while among people aged 18–29, support is 36 percent, close to the national mean.

Part III

Expert assessments of security in Central Europe

8

The security situation of the Central European countries: historical background

Richard Smoke

The four chapters that follow this one present asssessments of the security and foreign policies of Poland, the Czech Republic, Slovakia and Hungary, written by policy specialists from each of these countries. For Western readers, some introduction and background to the security situation of the countries is needed for a full appreciation of these chapters. In particular, the security problems facing these countries today cannot be adequately understood without a little basic knowledge of their history. This chapter begins with a brief sketch of elements of history that are relevant today, and then provides an introduction to some major developments of the first years following the Cold War.

1 Historical background

The earlier history of Poland

In the late Middle Ages, Poland ruled a vast domain to the east and especially southeast, including most of what is now Ukraine and Belarus. This realm was ruled jointly with Lithuania. Poland and Lithuania had formed a union in 1385, which was confirmed and formalized in 1569 to create the Republic of Poland–Lithuania.[1] The term "republic" should not, of course, be understood in a modern sense; it was an empire ruled by the nobility.[2] At its height, this empire reached to the Black Sea.

During the seventeenth and eighteenth centuries, the territories controlled by Poland–Lithuania progressively shrank, primarily as a result of uprisings and wars with the Ukrainians and Russians. Poland became weaker and weaker in a period when both the Russian empire and the kingdom of Prussia were growing stronger. The Austrian empire was also consolidating its position. All three neighboring lands sought to expand at Poland's expense. After various diplomatic maneuverings and lost wars, Poland found itself, in the eighteenth century, unable to preserve even its traditional core territory or its identity as an independent country.

Poland was partitioned by these three neighbors and its territory was divided among them. The key steps in this process were taken in 1773, 1793 and 1795. The eastern part of the country became part of the Russian empire, the western and northwestern part became part of Prussia and an area in the southwest became part of the Austrian empire. (Later, in the nineteenth century, Prussia became the core of the German empire.) The three empires continued to rule these regions until all three were destroyed by World War I. Although the Polish people continued to live in these territories, no country called "Poland" existed on the maps of Europe for well over a century.[3]

Poland in the twentieth century

Poland was recreated by the Great Powers that redrew the map of Europe at the conclusion of World War I. An independent, self-governing Poland was established with its capital in Warsaw. It was immediately menaced by aggression from the Soviet Union. The Battle of the Vistula in August 1920 crushed the Soviet forces and secured Polish independence. The hero of this battle, Marshall Josef Pilsudski, initially withdrew from public life. But when the democratic government proved unable to cope with the great problems of a brand new country, Pilsudski took power in an almost bloodless coup in May 1926. The regime he established ruled Poland until 1939.

Then Poland vanished from the map again. Hitler and Stalin made a secret agreement to divide the country between them. On September 1, 1939, Nazi Germany attacked and some days later Soviet forces occupied eastern Poland. Later, when the Nazis attacked the USSR, they overran and occupied all of Poland.

During the occupation years there were not one but two uprisings in Warsaw, the first by the Jews of the city, the second by the whole population. Both were ruthlessly crushed by the Nazis. After the second, Hitler ordered that, as punishment, Warsaw be demolished down to the ground. In the closing period of the war, the Soviet Army pushed the Nazis westward through Poland toward Germany.[4] As elsewhere in Central Europe, the arrival of the Red Army brought both genuine liberation and new tyranny. After the war Poland remained occupied by the Soviet troops and a communist government chosen by Stalin was installed. Moscow remained fundamentally in control until 1989.

At the end of World War II, a number of the borders in eastern Europe, notably including Poland's, were redrawn by agreement among the victorious Allies. A substantial swathe of territory in what had been eastern Poland was transferred to the Soviet Union, specifically to the Soviet republics of

Belarus and Ukraine. To compensate the Poles, a substantial swathe of territory in what had been eastern Germany was transferred to Poland (and the Germans who had been living there were ejected). Thus both the eastern and western borders of Poland were shifted westward. The new borders remain Poland's borders today.

During the 1970s, the failures of the communist government in Poland led to increasing popular discontent. In 1980 strikes erupted, led by a shipyard worker, Lech Walesa; a nationwide workers' movement, Solidarity, developed. In response to Solidarity's growing power, the government, headed by General Wojciech Jaruzelski, imposed martial law and declared Solidarity illegal. Jaruzelski claimed, both at the time and afterward, that if he had not clamped down, the WTO powers led by the USSR would have invaded Poland, as they had invaded Hungary in 1956 and Czechoslovakia in 1968, and that he acted as a patriot to save Poland from this fate. Through the 1980s Solidarity, though illegal and underground, was able to carry on a continuing struggle. Jaruzelski later decided to make Solidarity a legal organization to help add legitimacy to his regime, and he called new elections for June 1989, held under conditions that were partly free. To Jaruzelski's surprise, the Solidarity representatives won almost every contested seat. The government had no choice but to admit the new deputies to power, and a transition to a non-communist government began. Initially Lech Walesa declined an official position, though he later accepted the presidency.

The Austrian and Austro-Hungarian empires

The Austrian empire, ruled by the Hapsburg dynasty, took shape during the Middle Ages. Through the centuries since, until World War I, the empire included the lands that are now the Czech Republic, Slovakia and Hungary, as well as other lands. Vienna was the imperial capital. For centuries the subject peoples of these three lands (and others) looked to Vienna and to the emperor there as the final ruler of their destinies.

Throughout this time the Hungarians were the militarily strongest of these peoples. Hundreds of years earlier, before the rise of the empire, the Hungarians had created a powerful kingdom of Hungary. The Hungarians, also called the Magyars, had been the last major people to arrive in Europe from Central Asia, arriving only during the 900s, centuries after all the other major European peoples had arrived. The Magyars soon conquered most of the Carpathian basin. In the year 1000 the Magyar king, later dubbed St Stephen, received his crown from the pope. Later the Hungarians formed an uneasy and shifting relationship with the Austrians. The kingdom became a part of the empire, and thus subordinate to Vienna, in some respects; simultaneously it retained a measure of autonomy, especially in internal affairs, in other respects. Over the centuries the exact relationship between the Austrians and Hungarians, and the freedom of action of the latter, changed often, but at nearly all times the Hungarians enjoyed substantial authority within their own kingdom, whose capital in recent centuries has been Budapest.

For various reasons that need not be discussed here, the Austrians decided in the 1860s that they needed the Hungarians' help in maintaining the empire as a whole. A new arrangement was worked out, by which the empire became the Austro-Hungarian empire in 1867. Budapest was elevated to be equal to Vienna (at least in principle) as a second capital, and the emperor and chief government officials spent about half their time in Budapest and half in Vienna. However, the emperor was the young Franz Joseph II, a Hapsburg and of course an Austrian, who remained on the throne until the empire was destroyed by World War I. The twentieth-century history of Hungary is sketched below.

The Czech and Slovak lands

Although both the Czech and Slovak portions of what became Czechoslovakia had been parts of the empire, the two were ruled in very different ways. It is crucial, for understanding contemporary affairs as well as recent history, to grasp the significance of this.

The Czech lands, consisting of Bohemia and Moravia, were ruled directly from Vienna. But the region that now is Slovakia was part of the kingdom of Hungary (which in turn was, of course, a unit of the empire). The Slovak people were ruled not from Vienna, but by the Hungarians. In general, Vienna regarded this part and other parts of the kingdom of Hungary as fiefdoms subservient to Hungary, and Vienna cared little about how Hungary went about exercising its rule.

The result was that, over a span of many centuries, the Czech and Slovak peoples had very different historical experiences, which shaped them quite differently. Vienna's rule over the Czechs was relatively light, at least for considerable periods. Holding Prague and its high culture in esteem, the emperors in Vienna allowed the Czechs a significant degree of control in their internal affairs. (However, the emperors never gave the Czech people the same autonomy they allowed the Hungarians.) Over the centuries, Vienna also gave many Czechs positions of authority throughout the empire. In strong contrast, the Hungarians' rule over the Slovaks was harsh. For the Hungarian lords, the Slovaks were simply serfs. Century after century the Slovaks had no chance to develop their own culture, nor even much sense of identity. For example, while Czech literature dates from the thirteenth century, Slovak literature began only in the nineteenth century.

When the cataclysm of World War I destroyed the Austro-Hungarian empire, the victors – chiefly the Western Allies, Britain, France and the United States – had the opportunity to completely redesign the map of

Central Europe. Partly as a result of President Woodrow Wilson's deep belief in every people's right to self-determination, the victors created new countries for the previously subservient peoples. Because nationalities were intermingled to some degree, it was impossible to draw national boundaries that corresponded exactly to where each people lived. The best the victors could do was to create countries where the great majority would be made up of a single nationality (and the victors also paid some attention to traditional dividing lines). The territories for the new countries were taken, as necessary, from the territories of the Austrians and Hungarians, who were considered responsible for the world war and who had been the main rulers and beneficiaries of the empire for centuries.

The South Slav peoples who had previously ruled by the empire were given a new country, called Yugoslavia, which simply means "South Slavia" in the Slavic languages. The Czechs and Slovaks were also given a new country. Some Slovaks wanted their own country. But many Czechs and also some Slovaks felt that the extremely close ethnic and cultural bonds, and very similar language, between the two peoples made it more sensible to create a single country for them both. Thomas Masaryk and other leaders convinced the victorious Allies of the desirability of this solution, and the result was the creation of a new country called Czechoslovakia. The country was conceived as a democratic and national state, based upon an idea of a single, common "Czechoslovak nation." However, the concept of a Czechoslovak nation was not entirely accepted by the Slovaks, nor by other nationalities including a substantial population of Germans.

Czechoslovakia in the twentieth century

Between the wars, Czechoslovakia was economically prosperous; industrially and technologically it was one of the advanced countries of Europe. It was the only democratic country of Central Europe. Masaryk and its other founders had a deep commitment to democracy and they created a stable, constitutional state that held regular elections throughout the interwar period.

In September 1938 occurred one of the most important diplomatic events of the twentieth century. Hitler demanded that Czechoslovakia be dismembered and that the portion where the Germans were concentrated (the Sudetenland) be incorporated into Germany. One of the most famous international conferences ever held now took place in Munich, and the French and British yielded to this demand.[5] Shortly, other pieces were taken by Poland and Hungary.

In March 1939, Czechoslovakia was extinguished entirely. Hitler split the country up to make it easier to rule. A quasi-fascist regime was put in power in Slovakia, which formed an alliance with the Germans. The Czech lands were transferred directly into the Third Reich and were renamed the Protectorate of Bohemia and Moravia. This renaming was part of the Nazis' general ethnic strategy of divide-and-rule. They adopted a policy of trying to abolish the "Czech" idea and of encouraging people to think of themselves as Bohemians or Moravians.

Liberated in 1945, Czechoslovakia reestablished itself as a democracy, which lasted until 1948. It was the one country of the region from which the Soviet Army withdrew. However, as the Cold War began and Europe began dividing into East and West, the Soviet Union felt that it could not allow Czechoslovakia to continue free. The Communist Party in Czechoslovakia was large, and after the war it was genuinely popular because of the leading role it had played in the wartime underground resistance. It was also essentially controlled by Moscow. It seized power in a bloodless coup in February 1948 and took Czechoslovakia into the Soviet camp.

Early in 1968 a reshuffling of the government brought new ministers to the fore. Essentially democratic-minded, they decided to test the limits of Moscow's tolerance. They suspended the repressive apparatus of communism and tried to create a much freer kind of society which they called "socialism with a human face." The result became generally known as the Prague Spring. In August, the Soviet Union crushed it with a massive invasion by the Red Army, joined by contingents from four other WTO armies. An orthodox communist regime was reestablished in Czechoslovakia under close Soviet supervision. Only in 1989 did communist rule end.

In November of that year, public protests erupted as they had in East Germany shortly before. A large public gathering on November 17 was brutally broken up by police. Two days later, leading dissidents, including Vaclav Havel, formed an umbrella opposition movement in the Czech lands called Civic Forum. A parallel organization, called Public Against Violence, sprang up in Slovakia. On November 20, 200,000 people demonstrated in Prague. On November 25, Havel spoke to another public demonstration, this one numbering 800,000. In a "velvet revolution," the communist regime melted away and the democrats took power. In December, Havel was elected president by the Parliament.

Czechoslovakia 1989–1992

The new democratic state began to make plans for many political and economic reforms needed to develop a stable constitutional democracy and a market economy. In the new free atmosphere, and after many decades of repression of all national feelings, the question of the relationship between the Czech and Slovak peoples arose again.

In legal terms, the new state was a federation, officially called the Czech and Slovak Federal Republic or CSFR, and composed of two republics, the Czech and Slovak republics. Its capital was in Prague. But no parties or movements formed that embraced the whole country. The new political parties that now formed were either Czech or Slovak. The next couple of years saw a gradual decline in the real power of the federal structures, most importantly the president, the Parliament and the government of the federation, primarily because of pressures from Slovakia.

A somewhat confused situation developed in 1991 and 1992. Although a Slovak nationalist party did arise, it did not gain support of the majority of Slovaks, and outside that party few political leaders of either nationality advocated a split of the country, at least not openly. Nonetheless an important difference now emerged between the Czechs and Slovaks. Most Czechs wanted a single, federative state in which the separate Czech and Slovak republics would have a defined but limited role and identity. Most Slovaks wanted something much looser, in which the Slovak Republic would have a larger role. In this situation, a clash of perceptions inevitably arose. The Czechs, who wanted political structures to be defined quickly and clearly, perceived the Slovaks as demanding a protracted bargaining process in which major political and social questions would remain unresolved for a long time. The Slovaks, who had not yet defined exactly what they wanted, perceived the Czechs as demanding quick conclusions, and conclusions that would define a structure so firmly that future changes in the Slovaks' favor would be precluded. As time passed, the gaps between these two perceptions grew wider. After general elections in June 1992, a point was reached where the preservation of the common federal state proved impossible. The parties that had gained the most votes – the Civic Democratic Party in the Czech Republic and the Movement for a Democratic Slovakia in Slovakia – held incompatible concepts. It became easier to decide on a peaceful division of the country than to continue trying to bridge the gaps.

It was agreed that Czechoslovakia would come to an end at midnight on December 31, 1992, to be succeeded by two separate states, Slovakia and the Czech Republic. The complicated process of dividing the country was determined through many negotiated agreements and was carried out remarkably peacefully. In this "velvet divorce," there was hardly any violence at any time.[6]

Hungary in the twentieth century

The peace treaty following World War I and actually signed in 1920, applying to the southern part of Central Europe, was called the Treaty of Trianon. For the Czechs, Slovaks and some others, Trianon was the birth of their national independence. For the Hungarians, Trianon was one of the greatest disasters in history.

The Treaty of Trianon cut down Hungary to about one-third of the territory of the previous kingdom of Hungary. A southern portion was handed over to Yugoslavia. A large portion in the east, including the area called Transylvania, was transferred to Romania. A large northern area, including Slovakia, was handed over to Czechoslovakia.

For Hungary, the disaster was not only one of territory, although the loss of two-thirds of one's territory is one of the largest territorial losses that has been suffered in modern times by any country that still exists at all.[7] Even worse was the fact that large numbers of Hungarians lived, naturally, in the parts of the kingdom that were now gone. At that time (and also today), about one third of the Hungarian people lived in the areas that were transferred to foreign flags. Of course the great majority of these people could not move to the new, shrunken Hungary. There were no economic resources for such mass movements, and in any case the Hungary that remained was (and still is now) too small to absorb so many people. A few moved, but the great majority of the Hungarians who suddenly found themselves in other countries had to remain where their homes were; their descendants still remain there today.

The shock of defeat in World War I brought briefly to power an extreme left, communist-style government. The "red terror" that it launched alienated the Hungarian people so deeply that after it was overthrown, governments of the right held power in Budapest for more than two decades. Admiral Miklos Horthy, who had helped lead the counter-revolutionary forces, remained head of state and presided over a series of governments that tried to cope with postwar reconstruction and the many difficult social consequences of Trianon.

Somehow to achieve some favorable change in that Treaty became Hungary's overriding objective in foreign affairs. Partly for that reason, Hungary in the 1930s developed friendly relations with Nazi Germany; Hitler represented the chief force in Europe seeking to upset the status quo. As World War II loomed, Budapest resisted becoming Hitler's ally fully, but by late 1940 had taken so many steps to assist him that there was little choice left but full alliance.[8]

When the Soviets overran Hungary on their westward drive toward Germany, they installed their communist puppets. For the next decade, Hungary was another of the subservient Eastern European countries that were part of the Soviet empire. In 1956, the Hungarian people revolted. Waiting anxiously for help from the West that never came, people battled Soviet tanks in the streets with molotov cocktails. Nearly 10,000 Hungarians were killed before the revolt was crushed. Moscow installed a strict new regime to enforce communist orthodoxy.

In the 1970s, a somewhat more liberal regime in Budapest began experimenting with tentative steps toward loosening centralized economic controls. Further steps toward market economics were tried in the 1980s, and in the last years of the Soviet empire the Hungarians could claim to have achieved more market-oriented economic reform than any other WTO country.

In 1989, Hungary was also the first WTO country to open its border with the West, by opening its frontier with Austria in May. During the summer, the communist regime began negotiations with opposition groups, and an agreement was reached in September to create a multi-party system and hold free elections. The next month the existing Parliament changed Hungary's constitution to one of a Western, democratic character.

Meanwhile the newly open frontier was playing an important role in unraveling the Soviet empire. Many East Germans traveled to Hungary, and thus escaped to Austria and on to West Germany. This new exit through the iron curtain, along with the revolutionary changes sweeping the region, made the position of the communist East German regime increasingly untenable. Huge public protests erupted in East Germany in October; a demonstration by half a million people in East Berlin on November 4 led to the tearing down of the Berlin Wall on November 9 and to the collapse of the regime.

2   The first years following the Cold War

Terminating the previous arrangements

As Poland, Czechoslovakia and Hungary began to be self-governing countries, basic questions about security and foreign affairs naturally arose. The most fundamental issues had to be addressed, and in a rapidly changing European environment. The security and foreign policy issues were also deeply connected to the profound internal transformations that these countries now began to launch. This section sketches some of the most important developments of the next years that affected these countries in approximately the same way.

In 1990 it rapidly became apparent to the governments and specialists of these countries that the Warsaw Treaty Organization had lost all meaning. Not only was there no threat from the West but, in addition, the WTO had been the final guarantee of Soviet control, now abandoned. Some Central Europeans thought that the WTO should be abolished at once.

For two reasons it was not. One was that Moscow, not surprisingly, saw the situation differently. For most of 1990 and into 1991, Moscow still expected the Soviet Union to be the chief influence on the international behavior of the Central European countries. The Gorbachev government proposed that the WTO be continued as a "political" organization rather than as a military alliance. The Central Europeans were not much interested in this, but discussions on this topic consumed some time.

The other reason was that arms control reasons made it convenient for the WTO to continue for a short time. In this period a major treaty, on Conventional Forces in Europe (CFE) was close to being completed (see appendix 2). The negotiation was "bloc to bloc," that is, between NATO

and the WTO. To abolish the WTO immediately would disrupt the negotiation and make impossible a rapid agreement, now in sight, on major arms
reductions in Europe. All parties therefore agreed to continue the WTO long
enough to complete that treaty, though increasingly the WTO had only a
formal existence with no real significance. The CFE Treaty was completed
and signed in November 1990.[9]

Seeing the end of the WTO approaching, Moscow tried a new policy
toward the member countries. During late 1990 and much of 1991 the
Soviet Union proposed new bilateral security treaties to be signed with each
country individually. From Moscow's viewpoint, success at this effort
would have meant that each of the former satellites would be linked in
individual security relationships with the Soviet Union. While not as desirable an arrangement as the collective WTO, a set of separate bilateral
treaties would be fairly satisfactory to Moscow.

The proposed treaties contained one clause that from Moscow's viewpoint was highly important and that for most of the Central Europeans was
highly undesirable. Romania did sign the treaty containing that clause.
Hungary, Czechoslovakia and Poland all refused so long as that clause
remained. The clause stated that neither party, in the bilateral treaty, would
enter any other multi-national organization or security link that *either* party
considered threatening. This meant that after such a treaty was in effect, the
Soviet Union could declare that the Central European countries could make
no security relationship with any Western organization that Moscow might
feel to be hostile, NATO for instance. Thus Moscow would have linked
each of these countries to itself with a veto over any other arrangements that
any of them might want.

Moscow's desire for this kind of relationship with the Central European
countries, and their desire to resist it, sprang from a fundamental difference
in perspectives. The Soviets felt that they had given the Central Europeans
their freedom, and that Moscow deserved to receive some loyalty in return.
The Central Europeans felt that their freedom was not a gift but simply a
restoration of the sovereignty that was rightly theirs; therefore they owed
Moscow nothing.

For a period, obtaining the Central Europeans' agreement to this kind of
treaty was Moscow's main foreign policy goal toward the region. But after
the abortive coup in Moscow in August 1991, the Soviet government was
much weakened. Negotiations were transferred to the Russian government
of Boris Yeltsin, which did not demand that clause. Thereafter, agreements
were reached quickly on bilateral treaties of a normal kind, ones that
contained nothing restricting the Central Europeans' freedom of action.

The "return to Europe"

Meanwhile the Central European countries were quickly turning their attention westward. They rapidly became interested in making links with the EC,

NATO and other European and Atlantic organizations. These specific interests reflected a more fundamental shift in orientation, away from the eastward focus and toward a redevelopment of these countries' historic bonds with the rest of Europe. In these countries, this broad shift in orientation was now sometimes called "the return to Europe."

In the military sphere, the interest of the Central Europeans in a connection to NATO was one of the reasons for NATO's creation of NACC in 1991. Before long, each of these countries had set, as a basic goal, joining NATO as full members. Steady pressure for membership from the Central European countries over the following years was also one of the reasons why NATO developed the Partnership for Peace (PfP) program, announced in January 1994. PfP provided a way for these and other European countries to form closer bonds to NATO, while postponing any basic decisions about admitting them to membership or extending a NATO security guarantee to them. (In December 1994, NATO announced that it would develop a "plan" for expansion within one more year.) The Central European countries' perceptions of, and relations with, NATO, and the question of NATO's expansion are discussed extensively in the following chapters and need not be described further here.

The Central European countries also soon decided to set membership in the European Community as another long-term goal. In the meantime, they reached "Association Agreements" with the EC, which formalized their relationship with it and promised membership as a goal for a future, unspecified time.

The European Community was hugely attractive to the four Central European countries (as the European Union is now) for reasons worth pausing on. Naturally the EC was the main symbol in Europe of enormously successful market economies. And the economies of the EC countries were working so smoothly with each other that increasingly the EC was becoming a single economy. Especially in the long run, to be included within it would be highly advantageous; conversely, to be excluded would be very disadvantageous.

For many Central Europeans, the EC was, and the EU is now, something else that is perhaps even more important and attractive. It is a family of stable democracies. Comprising countries, especially Germany and France, that not long ago had been fierce enemies, the Community is now a model of cooperation. Political, not just economic, links within the EC are now so numerous and so intimate that the members have become a "community" in the genuine sense of the word. By now, these relations among the EC member countries have rendered severe conflict among them essentially impossible, and their relations are now more than "international" relations in the traditional sense. For Central European countries whose histories have been torn by centuries of bitter struggles, any chance to join this new kind of community is enormously desirable. This *political* attractiveness of the EC to the Central European countries deserves emphasis, because their desire to join has sometimes been misunderstood as merely a wish to join a "rich people's club." While the Central Europeans naturally feel economic motives also, they are attracted perhaps even more deeply by a chance to join a realm that is democratic, politically stable, internally at peace and almost certain to remain a true community as far into the future as anyone can see.

NATO membership also has a political attractiveness for the Central Europeans, quite apart from the military benefits they perceive in it. They see NATO as an organization that has been able to nourish and sustain democratic values and institutions among its members. As many policy specialists in Central Europe see it, the important role that NATO played in bolstering democracy in Portugal, Spain and Greece after those countries emerged from dictatorships could be played again in Central Europe. To some specialists in Central Europe, this political value of NATO membership would be even more important than the military value.[10]

Regional groupings

At no time since 1989 have the Central European countries given serious consideration to forming a military alliance among themselves, alone or with a few others. Even combined, the military strength of these countries would be very small, compared either to NATO on the one side or to the USSR or Russia on the other. Perhaps more important, specialists in the Central European countries concluded quickly after 1989 that anything resembling an alliance might prove a hindrance to their entry into the EC, NATO and other Western European organizations. A local alliance could be too easily seen in the West as a substitute for admitting the countries into these organizations.

Even so, some degree of cooperation among the Central European countries on security affairs made obvious sense to all of them, at least for a while. In April 1990 they created an arrangement with strictly limited purposes, being careful to emphasize its limited purposes both to the West and to the USSR and Russia. Originally, this arrangement among Poland, Czechoslovakia and Hungary was called the Visegrad Triangle. After the division of Czechoslovakia, it was renamed the Visegrad Group. Hungary, Poland, Slovakia and the Czech Republic are often referred to by specialists as the "Visegrad countries" because no other countries are members of this arrangement and it is convenient to have a label for these four considered together.[11]

Military and civilian representatives of the Visegrad Triangle/Group met together periodically during the early 1990s, to discuss common security problems, to consult with each other on points of security and military doctrine, and for other consultations. The Visegrad arrangement also included plans for these countries to consult together in any time of crisis, and to some extent they did so, for instance, during the August 1991 coup in Moscow. In addition, the Visegrad countries signed an agreement establishing free trade among themselves.

After the division of Czechoslovakia, the new Czech Republic began developing its own foreign and security policy, which deemphasized the Visegrad Group, as discussed in later chapters. In a more modest way, the Visegrad arrangement continues and it retains some practical usefulness.

Another regional grouping formed after 1989 fell into disuse by 1994. This arrangement was formed for cooperation not mainly in security, but for economic and to a lesser degree environmental cooperation. Originally it was called the Pentagonale, for its five members, Austria, Czechoslovakia, Hungary, Italy and Yugoslavia. After the split of Czechoslovakia it was renamed the Hexagonale, and later the Central European Initiative. This grouping gradually came to be seen as impractical, partly because of the continuing war in the former Yugloslavia and partly because other arrangements, often involving other countries too, were made for dealing with many specific issues that earlier might have been considered in this forum.

Relations between the Central European countries and Russia

For all the Central European countries, the relationship with Russia has been a fundamental question throughout the years since the collapse of the Soviet Union, and inevitably will continue to be in the future. Russia's sheer size, and its geographical location close to Central Europe, mean that Russia will always have importance, and will always have influence, in Central Europe. However, the nature of that influence may vary tremendously depending upon the character and ambitions of the government in power in Moscow.

The Russia of Boris Yeltsin recognized the full independence and sovereignty of the Central European countries. However, it quickly became clear after the collapse of the USSR that most elements in Moscow, even most of the democratic reformers, wished to perpetuate the status quo in Central Europe. Specifically they wished to perpetuate a situation where the Central European countries belong to no defense system or alliance, and definitely not to NATO. Of course that Russian goal stood, and still stands, directly at odds with the desire of the Central European states to join NATO. Both Central European and Russian viewpoints on this question are discussed in later chapters. It is worth emphasizing that this conflict in goals exists already with the *democratically* oriented government of Yeltsin. Should a less democratic government emerge in Moscow in the future, presumably this conflict would become sharper. The final chapter of this book returns to this possibility.

The overall relationship between the Central European countries and Russia is made more complicated and ambiguous by their economic relations. Trade and other mutually beneficial economic relations between Central Europe and Russia are clearly in the interests of both. Here the history of recent decades is important.

For forty years prior to 1989, the Central European states, as members of the "socialist camp," were dependent on the Soviet Union economically as well as politically and militarily. The economic relationship, codified in CMEA, had important positive, as well as negative, implications for the Central Europeans. The USSR was their principal source of raw materials and energy (especially oil and gas), and also was a huge market for their manufactured goods. The raw materials and energy were received at prices cheaper than world market levels, and the Central Europeans' manufactured goods were bought even though their quality was below world levels. This situation simultaneously kept the Central Europeans in a state of economic dependency, yet also provided real and enormous trade, and helped make possible some economic growth.

With the collapse of CMEA and then the USSR itself, economic relations suffered large setbacks. Trade by no means ended, but encountered many and varied difficulties. In the 1990s the economic crisis of the Central European states has been made somewhat worse by the decline in economic relations with Russia, and could be made much worse still if those relations should deteriorate sharply.

Thus the Central European states have a strong interest in a stable, economically developing, Russia that can be an important economic partner. Russia will continue to be a huge potential market for the Central Europeans, who have some advantage over others because they are familiar with this market and make products that are already well known to Russians. At the same time, the Central European states clearly have a deep interest in Russia being non-aggressive in political and military relations. Thus the Russia that Central Europe needs is a Russia that is economically as well as politically stable, and that is growing economically but not "growing" in the territories it controls. Virtually all specialists in Central Europe agree that this means a Russia that is on a path toward success in its own transformation toward democracy and a market economy.

In the early 1990s there were considerable grounds for hope for the Russian reforms. But several events in late 1993 were disquieting for Central Europeans. First, President Boris Yeltsin employed the Russian Army to subdue a fractious Parliament, by means of a military attack on the Parliament building, called the White House. In addition to many and important internal implications, this action suggested to many Central Europeans that Yeltsin might subsequently be indebted to the military, and hence that the military might have greater influence in Russian foreign and security policy. Secondly, Russian elections in December 1993 for a new Parliament produced a vote much larger than expected for the Russian ultra-nationalists, led by Vladimir Zhirinovsky. This result caused great anxiety throughout

Central Europe. Zhirinovsky had made explicit and extreme statements about the restoration of the old Russian empire to its maximum extent, and about imperial ambitions beyond even that.

Two policy documents released in Moscow in November 1993 also contained grounds for concern for Central Europeans. One document was a new Russian military doctrine.[12] Because this document appeared so soon after Yeltsin had turned to the army to deal with the previous Parliament, its publication appeared to signal that the president was indeed giving increased attention to the army. The new military doctrine (discussed further in chapter 16) did not name any state as an enemy of Russia, and makes no claims for territory that was not presently part of the Russian Federation. However, the doctrine explicitly opposed the extension of any military blocs that could threaten Russia, an obvious reference to NATO. The document published in November 1993 thus elevated Russian opposition to the Central European states joining NATO into an element of Russia's official military doctrine.

The second document published that month is often called the Primakov Report, after its principal author and proponent, Yevgeny Primakov, who is the head of the Russian foreign intelligence service.[13] The Primakov Report explicitly named NATO as a potential threat to the security of Russia. Both the report and Primakov's public statements at the time of its release described NATO in harsh terms as a potentially aggressive organization, using language that did not differ greatly from the old Soviet anti-NATO rhetoric of the Cold War era. Central Europeans concluded that if elements holding this point of view gain greater influence in Moscow in the future, Russia presumably would seek even more strongly to block the Central European countries from attaining their goal of joining NATO.

Late 1994 brought further events that were disquieting for the Central Europeans. At the beginning of December, NATO announced that it would develop, within one year, a plan for its expansion. Several days later, the CSCE held a long-scheduled summit in Budapest. President Yeltsin used the occasion to deliver a strong speech emphatically reiterating Russia's objection and warning that a NATO expansion could plunge Europe into a "cold peace."

In late December, Moscow intervened violently in Chechnya to prevent it from declaring independence from the Russian Federation. Although this action formally was a matter of internal affairs, it included a military attack, sustained over a substantial time, on the city of Grozny with, inevitably, high civilian casualties. Many observers in Central Europe, and also in Ukraine, perceived this intervention as evidence that Russia was prepared to go to war, and pay the price of great international protest, to achieve its objectives. What other objectives might Moscow set in the future? Indeed, so drastic an action made the Chechnya intervention the most dramatic and most important event yet in the post-Soviet history of Russia. Its potential long-term and even short-term consequences, which cannot be predicted at the time of this writing, could come to have great implications for all Europe.

The triple transformation

Of all aspects of the situation of Poland, Hungary, Slovakia and the Czech Republic in the first half of the 1990s, none is more important than the fundamental transformation these countries were, and still are, undergoing. While differing greatly in many particulars, the overall thrust of this transformation is broadly similar among these countries.

While often discussed as "the" transformation, three transformations can be usefully distinguished.[14] Any one of the three by itself is a change of a magnitude that would be experienced as revolutionary by any Western nation. For a country to attempt all three at the same time represents a change so profound and so multifaceted that there are few precedents in history. All four of the Central European countries have been attempting this triple transformation since 1989; the outcomes are far from assured.

One of the three is the comprehensive reorientation of the foreign affairs of each country from one direction, the East, to the opposite direction. While revolutionary enough, this transformation may actually be the least profound of the three from the viewpoint of the government as a whole, not to mention the society as a whole. This reorientation is discussed in more detail in following chapters.

More farreaching are the internal transformations in the realms of politics and economics. Politically, each country is trying to transform itself into a stable democracy, that is, a country with well-functioning democratic institutions that can be counted upon in all circumstances. This is much more difficult than it may seem to Western societies, many of which have centuries of democratic experience behind them. It is one thing to write a democratic constitution and hold genuinely free elections, as the Central European countries all have. It is another for Parliaments, made up of brand new and fiercely competing political parties, to learn how to work constructively, and for the ministries of state to learn how to function in a democratic environment and under parliamentary control. It is a third, and still more difficult, thing for both the state and the whole society to learn the processes of democracy so thoroughly that everyone can be sure these processes will never collapse, even in a crisis.

The economic transformation is equally difficult.[15] All four countries are trying, in a rather short time, to reshape radically the whole structure and operation of their economies. Hardly any economic change could be more radical than to switch from a centrally planned economy to a true market economy. (For instance, a switch from communist to fascist models, or vice versa, would be easier, as both represent versions of central control by the state.) The four Central European countries are taking somewhat different routes to the destination; the differences are outside the scope of this book. But all routes are painful and difficult. All routes involve imposing changes, often great changes, on the lives of citizens. While the overwhelming majority of citizens support the economic transformation in principle, for many individuals the pain is great. And except perhaps in the Czech Republic, even now there is no certainty of a successful outcome. In the other countries, specialists as well as the public feel that there is still some question whether well-functioning, growing market economies, with rising incomes for most, will be successfully built.

With this background regarding earlier history and recent developments in these four countries, we may now turn to specialists' assessment in depth of these countries' perceptions and policies regarding security. The next four chapters present these assessments, as seen from the perspectives of Warsaw, Prague, Bratislava, and Budapest.[16]

Notes

1 The "Lithuania" of that time should not be confused with the modern idea of Lithuania. The "Lithuania" of the Middle Ages comprised a loose collection of tribes and princes, made up of various of today's ethnic groups, including many Belorussians.

2 The term "republic" was important in one sense. Even more than in the England of that day, the powers of the king were greatly limited by the Parliament (Sejm).

3 During the short-lived Napoleonic empire, the French emperor created a semi-autonomous "Warsaw Principality" in central Poland. After Napoleon's defeat the Congress of Vienna recreated approximately the same district, largely autonomous in internal affairs but formally ruled by the Russian czar as king. That district was popularly called "the Congress Kingdom" (Kongresowka). After a failed Polish revolt in 1830, the limited internal freedoms of the Congress Kingdom were abolished by Russia, which reasserted full control. After a second failed rebellion in 1863, the Congress Kingdom was abolished outright and the area again became a district of the Russian empire.

4 The second Warsaw uprising took place as the Red Army was approaching the city, when the populace expected its prompt aid. Instead the Red Army units halted, while the Nazis put down the revolt and destroyed the city. Polish and Western specialists believed that the Soviets halted deliberately; for decades the Soviet Union denied it. Now it is generally recognized that the Red Army did halt deliberately, so that no independent Polish authority could establish itself in Poland's traditional capital, an outcome that would have made Poland more difficult for the Soviets to rule later.

5 Hitler said, in one of his great lies, that Czechoslovakia would be the last territory he would seek. At the time Czechoslovakia, which naturally could not stand up to Germany on its own, had a military alliance with France and Britain. The alternative to accepting Hitler's demand was immediate war.

France and Britain acquiesced. The British Prime Minister, Neville Chamber-
lain, believed or hoped that Hitler would indeed seek nothing further, and
returned to London declaring that the decision to sacrifice Czechoslovakia
would ensure "peace in our time."

6 At the time of this writing, a few elements in the process of division have not yet
been agreed.

7 Naturally this statement does not apply to overseas empires, such as the British
or French empires, but to loss of territory of the homeland.

8 Even thereafter, Budapest resisted the most extreme Nazi demands. For
example it tried to protect the Jews living in Hungary for as long as possible;
however, the majority were eventually sent to the Nazi death camps.

9 At a conference held in March 1991, Moscow reluctantly acceded to the
demand of the Central Europeans that the Warsaw Treaty Organization be
abolished completely. Three months were allowed to complete all the practical
details, and the WTO formally ended at the end of June 1991.

10 See, for example, the interview with Czech Defense Minister Antonin Baudys in
"Cim driv budeme v. NATO, tim lepe," in *Lidove noviny* (Prague, October 12,
1993).

11 The word "Visegrad" is pronounced VISH-e-grad. It is the name of a castle
where the formal documents were signed (February 1991). The castle is located
on the Danube River, in Hungary not far from the border of Slovakia. The site
was selected because at one point in the Middle Ages, the lands that are now
these countries also made an arrangement for mutual cooperation, which was
agreed upon at Visegrad castle. Several other locations in Central or Eastern
Europe, also called Visegrad or Visehrad, including a castle and district in
Prague, should not be confused with this topic.

12 "The basic principles of the new Russian military doctrine," *Izvestia* (Moscow,
November 18, 1993).

13 "Perspectives on NATO expanding and Russia's interests," Summary of the
Report Prepared by the External Intelligence Service, *Nezavisimaya Gazeta*
(November 26, 1993).

14 The concept of the "triple transformation" has been advanced by many Central
European thinkers in the period since 1989. Grateful acknowledgement is made
to Janos Matus for assistance in formulating the brief statement of it here.

15 By late 1993 and certainly in 1994, the economic transition in the Czech
Republic was becoming less painful than in the other three countries, primarily
because much of the transition had been successfully accomplished.

16 It should be noted again that because this book went to press shortly after the
Russian intervention in Chechnya, the long-term and also short-term consequences of that action cannot be assessed in these chapters, nor in later chapters
of this book.

9

Poland

Janusz Stefanowicz WARSAW

1 Introduction

Like Rip van Winkle, Poland as a fully sovereign state was put to sleep for half a century, from 1939 to 1989, by goblins, first the Nazi kind, then the Soviet kind. It is true that during the World War II years there was a Polish "government in exile," which was housed in London. But that government had only the faintest ability to defend Poland's interests, as witness the Yalta Agreement which drastically changed Poland's borders, virtually as a "diktat" by the Great Powers that won the war. For the next forty-five years, the foreign policy of Poland was, generally speaking, made in Moscow. There were, however, noteworthy successes by two Polish communist leaders to gain a wider margin of freedom, which would serve Poland's interests (as they saw them) without any real prejudice to the Soviet imperium.[1]

The Polish Rip van Winkle not only woke up into a brand new, "post bipolar," world, as all the Central European countries did; in addition Poland found itself among new neighbors. By 1993, every one of Poland's previous three neighbors – the USSR, Czechoslovakia and the German Democratic Republic – had vanished. In the place of those three Poland found itself with seven new neighbors. In the east there are Lithuania, Russia (specifically the district of Kaliningrad), Belarus and Ukraine. In the south there are the Czech Republic and Slovakia. In the west there is united Germany. As Poles look around their horizon, only the Baltic Sea has stayed the same. This is an utterly extraordinary event in the history of nations. Even the African states, in the hour of their decolonizations, did not go through such an experience.

It is remarkable that within just four years – 1990 to 1994 – Poland has been able to sign treaties of reconciliation and good neighborly relations with every one of the seven. All these treaties contain the clause that frontiers will remain unchanged and inviolate. Where appropriate they also contain clauses on the rights of minorities.

Foreign, and especially American, readers might wonder why these two items are so crucial for Poland. The answer lies in Poland's unique history, in which borders have shifted often and drastically, and in which Poles have both often been ruled by other peoples, and have often been the rulers of other peoples. With a little literary license, we may say that in about a thousand years Poland has made a full circle, returning in the mid-twentieth century to approximately the boundaries drawn in the year 1000 by the first Polish king, Breslaw Chrobry. Across the centuries, Polish territory waxed and then waned toward the southeast, and the boundaries to the west and north also moved many times. Poland was partitioned for well over a century, and partitioned again between the Nazis and Soviets in 1939. Inevitably, Poland's national identity and self-consciousness, and Poles' feelings of security or its lack, depend more than most peoples' on the country's borders, and on whether Poles can feel that the borders are fixed and secure now.

Sensitivity on problems of minorities is also more a repercussion of the past than any reflection of the present. Poland today is almost entirely homogeneous ethnically, but it is so for almost the first time in Poland's history. Even in the period between the world wars, other nationalities made up about one-third of the population, and this was a cause of internal troubles and external turbulences. The lessons of the past make us vigilant, and our neighbors also.

For these reasons, the new network of treaties is a source of great satisfaction and it offers some guarantee for the future. However, as a famous saying of Charles de Gaulle puts it, treaties are like roses and virgins: they last as long as they last. Poland must stake its security, and develop its foreign policy, on more than these treaties, gratifying as they may be. The next section surveys Poland's perceptions of its real relations with its neighbors, and then examines how Polish policy for security is developing.

2   The security and foreign policy of Poland

Perceptions come before, and are a basis for, policy. What prospects and risks, and from which directions, does Poland perceive? Let us begin with Germany.

Germany

The treaty just mentioned with the Federal Republic of Germany, signed in June 1991, formally closed a period of uncertainty, especially regarding the final recognition of Poland's western border. Germany formally committed itself to respect the existing border, determined at the close of World

War II. Important and even historic as this commitment is, it cannot dissipate automatically all shadows from the past and all anxieties for the future. These anxieties do *not* include a fear that Germany might again resort to military aggression. On this, there is a consensus among policy specialists and among the political parties; the majority of public opinion agrees.

Nonetheless, memories remain. For obvious practical reasons, military cooperation with Germany is already more developed than with any other NATO member (for instance, common exercises in sea-rescue operations in the Baltic Sea). But much time passed before it was possible to take the step to joint army maneuvers. The image of German soldiers bearing weapons on Polish soil is seared in the Polish memory. Only in 1994 was it possible to conduct a joint military exercise in Poland that included some German troops.

Another and more serious example of the persistence of memory is the impossibility of large-scale cooperation in the border areas. It is normal in Europe for neighboring countries to create cooperative projects and enterprises of various kinds in border regions. Logically, this should be an important element in Polish–German relations. Yet it cannot be done. The pressure of some rightist, nationalistically flavored political parties in Poland and – perhaps more important – a general mistrust in Polish public opinion have all but blocked such endeavors on any substantial scale. Impossibilities such as this produce a jarring note of ambiguity in what is fundamentally a sound, positive and developing relationship with Germany.

If there are memories from the past, there also are anxieties for the future, although here too the great question has roots in the past. To put it bluntly: should Poland accept German predominance in Central Europe, including Poland? Many Poles foresee a predominance that, while fundamentally economic, might extend to political domination also.

In Poland the prevailing view among policy specialists, and for that matter the intelligentsia generally, may be summed up in five ideas that to a considerable extent depend on each other:

- The obvious discrepancy in economic and other power should be neither a reason for unwarranted expansion of political influence by the stronger, nor a source of fear for the weaker. Hence there is no need for any isolationist policy by Poland.
- It is in the interest of both countries (and of Central Europe generally) that Germany remain firmly anchored in the Western structures of integration and security.
- Poland deems it obvious and even desirable that Germany should play a leading role in the process of the enlargement eastward of the European Union and NATO.

- Germany should make sure that it does not raise even any appearance of wishing to establish a "special relationship" with Russia (or Ukraine) over the heads of Poland and Central Europe.
- In the bilateral relationship with Poland, Germany should avoid any appearance of possible duplicity, or even ambiguity, regarding two things particularly: the mutual frontier and the political status of the German minority in Poland.[2]

It should be clear how these ideas are connected, if only psychologically. Should Germany begin to arouse suspicions in one area, a mood of suspicion would begin to carry over into others. Equally, confidence built in one area will inspire confidence in others. And, of course, the positive view of German leadership in the expansion of the EU and NATO presupposes that Germany itself is firmly anchored in these institutions. At present the prevailing view is one of guarded optimism that the future will unfold positively in all these ways. A recent contribution that has furthered this view was German President Herzog's presence at the 50th anniversary of the Warsaw Uprising, and his memorable request for forgiveness for German crimes against the Polish nation.[3]

Poland's eastern neighbors

The resumption of a policy toward the east is a difficult task for Poland, for both internal and external reasons. In the first place, such a policy obviously did not and could not exist for the past half-century. Poland was on the receiving end of policy *from* the east. In today's era of peaceful but profound revolution, Polish resentments are much stronger toward the USSR than toward Germany. While Poland was scourged by both in the war, the experience of more than four more decades thereafter was embittered by the humiliations and wrongdoings of the Soviet imperium.

Now, of course, there is no USSR. In the days when the emancipation of some of the former Soviet republics first began, Poland attempted a "two track" diplomacy. Warsaw sought to continue relations with "the center," the superpower, and simultaneously to develop constructive bonds with the emerging new countries, especially the ones adjacent to Poland. During the important period after 1989 when the USSR still existed, Warsaw negotiated with it on two matters of particular importance. Of course, one was the withdrawal of the Red Army from Polish territory. The other was a new bilateral relationship, based on reciprocal recognition of full sovereignty and of the equality of independent states. On the second track, Poland established official contacts even in 1991 with Ukraine, Belarus and the three Baltic republics. Following the formal dissolution of the USSR at the end of that year, Poland recognized the independence of Russia. Recognition of the other new states that formerly were Soviet republics followed in a formal declaration on January 29, 1992. Since then, however, the "two track" policy has become obsolete; there has been no "center" in the old sense. So Warsaw has begun, not without difficulties, to carve separate, but necessarily interdependent, relations with the states that appeared from the rubble of the old superpower.

Russia

Relations with Russia are not only the most important, for obvious reasons; they are also the most intricate. The relationship has been and remains disquieting, because of two fundamental uncertainties about which Poland can do nothing. One is the future political and economic shape of Russia. For Poland, the success of democracy and of reasonable material progress in Russia is virtually an absolute prerequisite of Poland's security.[4] Yet Warsaw understands well that such a success in Russia is considerably less than certain. At the time of this writing the trends are, if anything, more worrisome than reassuring. A second uncertainty would remain even if they were otherwise. History teaches us that even democratic countries do not always resist the temptation of an imperialistic policy, if other great powers allow it.[5]

Poland has been concerned by certain tendencies visible in Russian foreign policy. One is the persisting ambiguity of Russia's idea of its "near abroad." Does this idea mean, as it seems to do most often, only the territory of the former Soviet Union? Or does it also embrace the former Warsaw Treaty states, as some voices in Moscow seem to imply at times? Another worrisome tendency involves Moscow's recognition of the independence of Ukraine, which was more than reluctant at first and carries a note of reluctance still. For Central Europe this is no light question, as Ukraine's independence is deeply important for Central European security.

Most important of all, of course, is Moscow's attitude toward Poland's future participation in NATO. On this vital question we continue to hear conflicting voices from Russia, with the predominant tone negative. In August 1993, President Yeltsin said, during a visit to Warsaw, that Russia would not object. Almost immediately thereafter Moscow withdrew this statement, and the following months witnessed many Russian demurrals. In June 1994, when Russian Foreign Minister Kozyrev visited NATO headquarters in Brussels, he seemed to say that Russia would permit a NATO enlargement, on condition that it be done discreetly and without isolating Russia. Again the following months witnessed many Russian statements to the contrary, and indeed a growing campaign of opposition. The future of this question, so basic for Poland, may hang upon the unfolding political drama in Moscow.

Kaliningrad, which borders Poland directly to the north and which is Russian territory, provides a special, further twist in Polish–Russian relations. Russian military units there are so huge that they nearly equal the whole Polish Army. Warsaw cannot exclude the possibility of some incursions across the border by some of these troops if they become undisciplined or simply hungry. However, it would be nonsense to imagine any organized invasion.

Ukraine and the other new states

It is difficult to speak with confidence about Poland's future relations with the other former Soviet countries, because so much depends upon their relationship with Moscow. Poland, for its part, desires their genuine independence. Poland has no territorial or other claims upon them and will certainly seek good relations with them, based on genuine goodwill for them. At the same time Warsaw certainly notices some disturbing trends.

Ukraine, the most important of the new countries for Poland and for Central Europe, shows signs of weakness. There is a danger that the country may break apart or be dismembered. Conflict over the status of Crimea, already significant, could become serious at almost any moment. Strong nationalist fervor in the western part of Ukraine could worsen the country's prospects.

In Belarus, on the other hand, Poland is concerned that the sense of national identity is too weak. There is a visible inclination to reintegrate with Russia.

Finally, in Lithuania, Warsaw observes with sorrow many signs of anti-Polish nationalism. It was for this reason that Lithuania was the last of the neighboring countries to sign a formal declaration of good relations with Poland. But Warsaw intends to approach this phenomenon with magnanimity, and certainly without anxiety.

Central Europe

Regarding the neighboring states of Central Europe, Poland has no concerns. Relations with the Czech Republic are perhaps only lukewarm, but they pose no difficulties. With the new state of Slovakia, relations understandably are not yet clearly formed. With both of its neighbors across the southern mountains, Poland anticipates no problems of any significance.

Relations with the other country of the Visegrad Group, Hungary, are also satisfactory. Poland's relationship with the Visegrad Group as a whole is discussed later.

Poland's basic perspective on its security

This *tour d'horizon* locates Poland in its international environment, certainly not one that is entirely favorable, but one that presents no threats, either presently or for the readily forseeable future. Policy specialists in Warsaw, like the public, perceive security risks to be more internal than external and more non-military than military. There is greater danger from "non-sovereign" actors – for example multinational corporations, migrating peoples and organized crime – than from any sovereign, state actor.

However, specialists, the ministries of government and for that matter the public, know well that the absence of any military threat is a felicity that may not endure. Security is forever a goal to be achieved, not a fate that is guaranteed. It is plain to Poles that a military threat from the east could arise in the future, should Russia – or just possibly, Ukraine – become an aggressive dictatorship.

Thus Poland, on regaining its independence in 1989, had to make a long-term, strategic choice. By what path could security be best sought? A new alliance with the Soviet Union, or its successor, Russia, was wholly excluded for obvious reasons. An alliance with the small Central European neighbors, even adding Hungary, could never provide enough strength to make Poland secure.

Neutrality was not a feasible option either. During the Cold War decades, neutrality had always seemed attractive, in Poland as in other Central European countries, to the dissident forces and other elements in opposition to the communist regime. In the era of the Soviet yoke, neutrality seemed like a realistic alternative. It was natural, and perhaps not completely fantastic, to dream of a condition like Finland's or Austria's. But in the wholly different circumstances of the post-Cold War era, neutrality became impractical and perhaps even dangerous for a country in Poland's geographical position. Finland's and Austria's neutrality had been sanctioned by the Great Powers. None of them would be ready to guarantee Poland's security as a neutral state now.

Hence the only true strategic option for Poland, after 1989 and today, is to participate in a larger European organization of collective self-defense. For the present and the foreseeable future, the only such organization in Europe that wields real power is NATO. For Poland, NATO is not merely a desirable choice for various reasons; in a basic sense it is the only choice.

Two formal documents adopted in November 1992 establish Poland's national security policy for the post-communist era. The documents are "The Principles of Polish Security Policy" and "The Security Policy and Defense Strategy of the Republic of Poland."[6] These policy documents say that, at present, no country poses any military threat to Poland. But they leave open the possibility that a threat could materialize in the future, and emphasize the need for political, economic and other cooperation with neighboring countries to help defuse any potential dangers. The documents also formally state that membership in NATO is Poland's long-term national security goal.

NATO and the Partnership for Peace

Poland began informally inquiring about a link with NATO even in 1990, and has been seeking membership in NATO perseveringly ever since. This goal remained unchanged when one government was discharged in the September 1993 national elections and another, quite different one, was installed.

Poland's rationale for joining NATO has been stated, officially and unofficially, many times. One succinct statement of it was offered by the Foreign Minister, Adrzej Olechowski, during a visit to Washington in December 1993.[7] Excerpts of his essential points may be quoted here:

1 An American presence in Europe is critically important for Polish security . . .
2 Central Europe is now a "security vacuum" . . .
3 Poland has to be anchored in Western institutions . . .
4 The Partnership for Peace needs to include the following five features, which would amount to a "road map" to NATO membership: *One:* the aims of the PfP should include a progressive extension of the Alliance. *Two:* the PfP should emphasize requirements and rules of conduct in the political and military sphere . . . *Three:* provisions based on Article 4 of the Washington Treaty should be expanded and stipulate . . . that in the event of a threat to the territorial integrity, political independence or security of partners, consultation could include a definition of joint actions . . . *Four:* bilateral agreements [in PfP] should allow for a diversification of the character and extent of cooperation according to each partner's interests . . . *Five:* cooperation should be offered to all partners with identical initial prerequisites. Progress by one country should not be obstructed by others.
5 Poland in NATO would be an asset and not a liability [for several reasons]. *One:* in the last four years we have made remarkable progress in our drive toward democracy and stability . . . *Two:* we are a "stability exporter" in the region, which is still far from being stable. *Three:* Poland in NATO would be an example and an incentive to other countries in the region, including Russia, that the world of the rich and secure is not an exclusive club . . . *Four:* Poland boasts of a big land army whose size is surpassed [among Western European forces] only by those of Germany and France.
6 No security system will be viable in the medium to long term without the presence of a democratic and strong Russia . . .
7 There is a need for this Russia to become party to a new Euro-Atlantic contract which should include the following: enlargement of the NATO-covered zone of stability . . . [and] NATO's new relationship with Russia embracing the issues of peace and security and closer economic contacts.

Poland, Russia and the West

As these last two points indicate, Warsaw does not desire a situation where Poland and Central Europe enter NATO and other Western institutions at Russia's expense. Poland does not hold a simplistic view of European security in which Russian concerns might be dismissed, and Poland certainly does not seek to antagonize Russia. In Warsaw's view, Russia should not be isolated from Europe, but rather connected to Europe in a way that helps ensure the security of both.

Poland thus has a double objective in its security policy. Poland emphatically seeks NATO's enlargement to include Polish membership, and also wants the enlarged NATO and Russia to have a mutually constructive relationship that neither finds threatening. Poland can be most secure if it is *neither* caught between NATO and Russia, as now, *nor* facing (even as a NATO member) a Russia that feels anxious, threatened and perhaps hostile, as might be possible in the future. The two aspects of Warsaw's diplomacy remind us of the origins of the word itself. In ancient Greek, a "diploma" was a formal letter folded into two parts.

This necessity to find a positive and mutually constructive relationship between the West and Russia also sheds light on the right role for NATO in European security. There is a popular saying that "everything is politics but politics is not everything." A paraphrase of this sums up Warsaw's view of NATO. Everything in European security is bound up with NATO, but NATO alone cannot be everything for European security. A constructive and mutually secure relationship between Europe, NATO and Russia will be essential.

In the autumn of 1994 several new factors emerged affecting Poland's participation in NATO. On the one hand, the Clinton administration in the United States displayed a more resolute attitude toward the enlargement of NATO. On the other hand, some influential American circles firmly opposed it.[8] Some of the main European members of the Alliance – France and Britain first and foremost, but also the "southern flank" countries – expressed unwillingness in the face of ever-growing Russian opposition. That resistance reached a climax at the December 1994 CSCE summit in Budapest, where President Yeltsin delivered his now-famous warning of a "cold peace" if NATO expands. Poland learned that Russia would make a strong statement, and President Lech Walesa's speech to the summit was modified at the last minute to warn that "states who want to join the victorious structures [i.e. NATO] cannot be hindered by others who do not share the principles [of international conduct]."[9]

The resoluteness of Poland's will to join NATO remains unchanged, regardless of Russian pressures. It must be noted, however, that the enthusiasm for joining NATO in Polish public opinion has been much tempered by the continuing failure of NATO to cope effectively with the war in Bosnia.

Poland and the European Union

Poland's leaders and the bulk of the Polish people do not conceive security for the nation in only the narrow, traditional sense of security. Naturally the survival of the nation, the preservation of the national identity, territorial integrity, and Poland's sovereignty remain fundamental. In the contemporary era, however, equal to this and under some circumstances perhaps even paramount is the development of Poland's life in all spheres – economic, social and cultural. We may sum up this goal in the idea of progress, both material and spiritual. In short, Poland does not seek physical security only. The progress of the Polish people must be secured as well.

Here Poland's choice is clear. Poland seeks to include itself in the broad progression of European integration, while doing so in a way that does not prejudice Poland's national identity and independence. The majority of the Polish political class is convinced that the vision of the European Union, as set forth in the Maastricht Treaty, can achieve this combination of transnational integration without loss of national identity.

On December 16, 1991, Poland signed the Association Agreement with the EC, which entered fully into force on February 1, 1994. Warsaw has made clear innumerable times its goal that Poland become a full member of the EU at the earliest feasible date.

Warsaw is fully aware of the EU's current internal debate as to whether enlarging itself or deepening the integration among its current members should take priority in the coming years. Warsaw also realizes fully that Poland is presently burdened with many economic problems which will have to be resolved on the road to membership.[10]

Poland's relations beyond the EU

Being realistic about the long road to full membership in the EU, governing circles in Poland are also interested in rebuilding, naturally on a new basis, the natural links with Poland's neighbors in Eastern and Central Europe. Speaking frankly, however, our success in these areas has been less than satisfactory so far. With the eastern neighbors, the road to renewed and healthy cooperative relationships is strewn with barriers: their internal chaos, their poverty, their lack of hard currency and enormous uncertainty regarding both their foreign policies and economic policies. Nonetheless, Poland will continue to seek economic and other cooperative relationships in so far as they may be possible.

Poland would also like to develop its economic and other relations with the Visegrad Group of Central European countries. Unfortunately, cooperation with the Visegrad Group is stigmatized by a kind of "original sin." For Poland, the original formation of the Visegrad Group was an attempt to begin to create a network of economic and political (including security) ties that would be valuable in their own right. However, the other members saw Visegrad almost exclusively as something that could speed their entry into the EU. Later even this aim evaporated, at least in the case of the Czechs, who now propel themselves toward Europe on their own and see little advantage and perhaps some disadvantage in linking themselves with their neighbors.

However, there has been one important success in the mutual relations among the Central European countries. That was the creation in 1993 of CEFTA, the Central European Free Trade Area. There is mutual benefit for all these countries in being able to trade among themselves, free of the tariff barriers that the EU, for instance, has erected.

One observation of a more global nature might be added. Poland's understandable focus on membership in the EU, combined with the fragility of the Polish economy, has yielded certain disadvantages. Ties have not been developed as rapidly as they might have been with other great dynamos of the world economy: the United States, East Asia, and the giant multinational corporations. In the longer run a better balance should be achieved.

3 European security

The security map

At this point, let us step back from Poland's perceptions of its situation and resulting policies, and consider the security of Europe in larger terms. At first glance, the "security map" of Europe might seem simple. There is one large, secure group in the West and there are many insecure countries in the East. In actuality, the map has two layers: an upper, more visible layer and a lower, less visible layer.

The upper layer, which is the basic division into a "West" and an "East," is much older than some people remember. This way of thinking about Europe is far older than the Cold War division and its "iron curtain." For centuries people spoke of a "Europe A" and a "Europe B." The line between them ran roughly from the western border of Poland in the north, southward to the Mediterranean at the top of the Adriatic Sea, where the city of Trieste is. "Europe A," to the west of this approximate line, was the Europe that was modernizing and was in the forefront of advancing civilization. "Europe B," on the eastern side of this line, was more backward and still had some medieval residues.[11]

It was one of the coincidences of history that when the Soviet Union created its zone of satellites after World War II, the great division thus created between "Eastern Europe" and "Western Europe" turned out roughly to match the older dividing line. Eastern Germany fell on the eastern side, Greece on the western; otherwise the line was almost the same. During the Cold War decades, the division became very sharp. In political terms it meant the cleavage between democracy and communist tyranny. In economic terms it meant the difference between free-market and state-directed economies. In military terms and security structures, it meant NATO and the Warsaw Treaty Organization.

In the years since the Cold War, the division has become only somewhat less sharp. We see now the contrast between mature, smoothly functioning democracies (except in Italy) and the thorny beginnings of democracy. We see the difference between the integrated single market of the European Union and scattered national economies. And we see the contrast between the secure NATO area and the territories eastward of it, most commonly called a "gray zone," a "no man's land," or a "security vacuum." These phrases may be too dramatic when, as presently, there are no direct external military threats to the security of Poland or to most other states on the eastern side of the line. But even if we use a softer term like "region of unsettled security," the realities remain as they are. The Partnership for Peace confirms it by doing nothing to change it.

The second layer of the security map, underneath the first and somewhat less visible, reveals several distinct zones on the eastern side of the line. From the viewpoint of security risks and threats, three can be usefully distinguished.

First, *Central Europe* embraces first of all the four countries discussed in this part of this book. To them may be added the three Baltic states to the north, and Slovenia to the south. All eight of these countries currently enjoy a fairly high degree of *de facto* security due to a combination of internal and external factors.[12]

Their internal conditions include solidly developing democracy, some economic growth with good prospects for more, and (except in two of the Baltics) not too serious ethnic problems. Their external situation includes the end of being pawns in the Cold War, a low probability of any direct military threat from any nearby great powers, and an absence of any reason for serious conflict among themselves. Their security situation can be described as a "gray zone" in its proper meaning. To these internal and external factors one might add that these eight countries identify emotionally with "Western" norms and ideas; they generally consider that they historically have been part of the mainstream of European civilization; and they are now building as rapidly as they can a web of business, cultural and other links with Western Europe and (in so far as possible) with the United States.

Secondly, *Eastern Europe*, as the term should be used now, refers to the countries of the former Soviet Union (except the Baltics), east to the Urals. These countries are in a quite different security, and general, situation. Their condition is stigmatized by political chaos, dim prospects for democracy and economic misery, all of which promote great social disorders, including huge organized crime. Against this troubling internal background, we observe a nearly infinite maneuvering among these countries, motivated by two great forces. One is Russia's seduction of the others into rebuilding a

Soviet Union, in which Russia will have the upper hand (above all in security matters). The second is the urge of the others to find real independence and their own identity. Presently we find Georgia and some of the Central Asian states almost submitting to the seduction. Oscillating somewhere around the opposite pole is Ukraine, from whom we sometimes hear that even nuclear weapons have value in protecting independence. In security affairs and in many other ways, Eastern Europe (in great contrast to Central Europe) has a future that is unpredictable in the extreme, virtually a black hole of invisibility.

Thirdly, *Southeastern Europe* is the Balkans as traditionally defined, except Slovenia. This region is scourged by intense ethnic problems, which have already caused Yugoslavia to fall apart and which can spill over more borders. Rivalries and tensions in Southeastern Europe involve Albania and Bulgaria as well as the former Yugoslav states, and on the "western" side, Greece and Turkey. Hungary may also become a party. There is a possibility of interventions by outside great powers, with potentially explosive results. Russia might intervene; Ukraine could; Western European powers might also; so possibly might the United States. A suitable image of Southeastern Europe is a kettle, boiling and perhaps about to boil over.

Building security in the eastern half of Europe

This second, underlying layer draws our attention to the complexity, to the point of obscurity, of the security map of Europe overall. Contrary to what is sometimes said, it is not true that the lack of strong interventions by the West in the eastern half is due to shortsightedness, egoism or cowardice. Frankly speaking, no organization or group of states can take clear-cut and prompt decisions in the face of such a mess. Time, and a variety of measures of different sorts, will be needed to clean it up; or in some cases wisdom may suggest leaving it alone. The real choice is to decide where and when to take limited, selective steps, and where and when to wait. Some quick, universal solution is not a possibility.

The productive approach to building European security is that of building and extending security structures gradually. Some specialists speak of creating "a new architecture of European security." But this phrase is misleading because it is inconsistent with the present and probable future realities. The phrase implies the existence of, if not an architect, at least a design, a blueprint or plan for some agreed project of construction. This imagery is too mechanical. What we see in the eastern half of Europe is more like a watercolor painting.

What we in Central Europe can achieve in the foreseeable future is a gradual development of several kinds of security relationships, mainly with the West. Some specialists use the term "variable geometry" for this approach, a more useful phrase if still a bit mechanical.[13] What is needed in the coming years is an evolution and mutual interconnection of security links, in a process that may have more in common with the life-processes of living organisms than with architecture or geometry. Let us probe more deeply into what this means.

The evolution of security relations

Several organizations should play a role in the development of security in the region. This discussion naturally addresses this topic from the point of view of Poland and Central Europe.

NATO is a unique organization. It is an existing military alliance, politically unified and militarily muscled. Understandably, NATO hesitates to involve itself in the uncertainties of Central Europe or Southeastern Europe, to say nothing of Eastern Europe. Perhaps NATO, which is led by the United States, still hears the voice of George Washington, who in his Farewell Address warned against "entangling alliances," and had the uncertainties and incessant wars of Europe specifically in mind. But this does not mean that NATO should, or even can, remain indifferent to developments in the eastern half of Europe.

For one thing, NATO members have become increasingly aware that NATO's original mission and goal have simply evaporated. In a sense the end of the great European confrontation of recent decades is unfortunate for NATO. The situation then actually was rather comfortable. One of the secrets of the Cold War was that NATO's "containment" of the other superpower posed little real risk, because in reality the USSR loved to be "contained" in its large and quite satisfactory external empire. The spectre of a superpower war, often captured by the image of "two scorpions in a bottle," was terrible but quite improbable. Now that the essentially static and not very troubled bipolar division of Europe has vanished, NATO risks becoming void and pointless. As has been rightly said, NATO now must "go out of area or go out of business."[14]

The new situation poses dangers that are smaller than the old bipolar confrontation, but more real. During the Cold War we did not see actual fighting in Europe on our televisions every evening; in the new Europe we do, in the former Yugoslavia. Some, albeit insufficient, signs are now appearing that NATO is adapting to the new realities and dangers. On the military side, the Cold War doctrines of "forward defense" and "flexible response" have been abandoned along with large army formations and a heavy reliance on nuclear weapons. Now we see the development of rapid deployment forces and mobility. Political counterparts to these changes are visible in NATO's London, Copenhagen, Rome and Brussels Declarations.[15]

Much as Poland wants to join NATO soon as a regular member, many Polish specialists anticipate a somewhat different development. NATO may continue to reach eastward more in a functional than in a structural manner. For some time that can be a middle-of-the-road approach between the extremes of "doing nothing" and a costly and complicated full-scale expansion. Many Polish specialists also anticipate that in the coming years NATO will be increasingly ready to react to situations to its east, but on a "case-by-case" basis. No automatic formula is to be expected. Instead, NATO can be expected to act pragmatically, and chiefly on the criterion of to what extent vital interests of the United States and/or the main Western European powers are at stake in a given situation. That "and/or" may be important for the next organization, and for its relationship with NATO.

The *Western European Union* (WEU) seems to be in rapid transition. Until recently it could have been called a phoney institution. But the Maastricht Treaty converts it into an arm of an extremely real institution, the European Union. It is not by chance that Mr Clinton is the first American president to find kind and even encouraging words for the WEU. As long as some modest efforts by European Union members to give the EU a security dimension coincide with the current aloofness of the United States toward European affairs, the chances grow that the WEU will gain real functions. Certainly it will never act contrary to American desires. But one can imagine situations in which the US would not like to engage itself openly (for instance because of Congressional reluctance or a lack of public support), yet Washington would give tacit approval and even official backing for action by the European allies. The WEU presumably will not become an operational military organization, and also does not need to be, for it can always borrow NATO forces and facilities.

The WEU may also have another useful role to play. The Russians say they want understandings about security arrangements for the whole of Europe. The WEU may be able to help build up a climate of mutual or cooperative security with Eastern Europe, perhaps including some tacit understandings.

Although Poland and the other Central European countries certainly would like to be part of the WEU, there is one important and obvious obstacle. They must first become full members of the European Union. Until they are, relations between the WEU and these countries must, again, be more functional than structural. Meanwhile Poland has applied for and has been promised the status of associate member of the WEU.

The *OSCE* (formerly the CSCE and still sometimes called that) may be able to play certain very useful roles for security in Europe. It can initiate political consultations in advance of an impeding crisis. Under some circumstances the OSCE might be able to prevent a crisis. (Here one should note two new offices in it, one for prevention of conflicts and another of High Commissioner for Minorities.) In some cases, the OSCE may be able to undertake small-scale peacekeeping actions, and in others can give moral legitimacy and formal authorization for peacekeeping or "peacemaking" actions undertaken by NATO and/or the WEU Above all, the OSCE can play a constructive role in furthering arms reductions and confidence- and security-building measures (csbm's).[16] Poland favors efforts to make the OSCE more effective.[17]

However, in many situations the real efficacy of the OSCE will be limited by two factors. One is its huge size. Fifty-three members make it nearly the size of the United Nations when it was first formed. The other is its members' political diversity and broad dispersion. It stretches from Uzbekistan to Portugal, indeed from the Russian Far East all the way around most of the globe to the North American West Coast.[18]

The constructive but limited role that Poland visualizes for the OSCE was expressed by Poland's ambassador to the organization, Jerzy Nowak, at the summit in Budapest in December 1994: "The change in name means that it ceases to be [only] a debating club . . . It should play the role of damper on Russian concerns . . . One should understand [these concerns and] they must have a place for discussing European security structures, but we saw to it that the stipulation on the initiation of the work on a common and comprehensive model of European security does not bring any prejudice to our endeavor to enter NATO."[19]

The *United Nations Security Council* has more opportunity in the post-Cold War era than ever before to be the supreme judge, and legitimating authority, for peacekeeping and even peacemaking actions in Europe and elsewhere. For a variety of reasons, Polish specialists do not expect the United Nations to create its own military committee and staff, even though the UN Charter includes provision for them.

This sketch of the main organizations suggests not only that none of them are able by themselves to provide security in the eastern half of Europe, but also that no pre-set architecture combining them can be designed that can meet all situations. Instead, a pragmatic "variable geometry" can employ one combination of them in one case and another combination in another. In the view of most Polish specialists, this approach is both the most desirable and the most probable general scenario for the evolution of European security affairs in the coming years.

However, this approach can succeed only if certain conditions are met. There must be some confidence in these organizations and a willingness to use them. Their application in shifting combinations requires an element of imagination. Many applications will not be entirely free of costs, which requires a willingness to bear those costs. If these prerequisites are not met, this general approach could falter, and could be abandoned. In that case, either of two other general scenarios, both undesirable, are possible.

Renationalization

One negative scenario is that interstate relations in Europe, especially in the eastern half of Europe, may come to be based again, as they were in earlier centuries, on the maneuverings of individual states to gain power and advantage. Such a development could plunge Europe down into a dangerous and complex game in which many countries would be jockeying among each other.

A milder form of renationalization is appearing already. It is the inevitable consequence of the end of the ugly but stable and coherent system of the Cold War blocs. Some renationalization is becoming visible in both halves of Europe, but with what a difference! In the West it expresses itself merely in the greater importance attached by governments to *raisons d'état*. But this stress on individual national interests is now, and will continue to be, encompassed by the developing structures of integration – econonic, political and military. More fundamentally, no Western European state has any intention at all to fight another. No territorial or other expansive ambitions are at stake and these states now see themselves as so mutually interdependent that armed conflict has become nearly inconceivable.

In the eastern half of Europe, the trend toward renationalization has already had grave consequences in the Balkans. If allowed to developed unchecked throughout the region, the trend could take a wholly different shape from anything occurring in the West. We may already be seeing the beginning of a competitive race to join Western structures. Much worse things are possible. Renationalization in the eastern part of Europe can grow into strong and even harsh forms of political and economic nationalism. It can lead to serious quarrels between neighboring countries. It can easily become envenomed with old ethnic hatreds.

A strong renationalization would have a negative impact on the whole of Europe, with consequences worse in the east than in the west. We could expect to see a revival of a classical European balance of power among "great powers." In all probability this would mean a balance between Russia in the east, and a western group consisting of Britain, France and (in the first position) Germany, with some form of backing from the United States. In the western half of Europe this reappearance of a classical balance of power would inflict only limited damage, probably only a slowing down of the Western European integration processes and some discomfort for the small countries. In the eastern half, this scenario would lead to the re-creation of "spheres of influence" and of "buffer states" in the classical senses. For Poland this scenario could be a disaster. It would reproduce the fatal geographical situation of the past, in which Poland was caught between East and West for centuries. For part of that time, Poland even lost its statehood, and was partitioned into pieces ruled by other powers.[20]

Could the worst possibilities in this scenario be headed off by creating regional groupings of various Central and Eastern European countries? Neither past experience nor current analysis suggests much hope for this. In the past, zonal security arrangements were invariably created by external forces, not by the countries of the region. Earlier we saw the Hapsburg and Ottoman empires in the southeast and the Prussian/German and Russian empires further north. Between the world wars, the "Little Entente" was created at the initiative of Western powers. And now in the current period, the Visegrad Group was again created at Western encouragement. Like the Little Entente, the Visegrad Group has proved useless, at least as a real security grouping which Poland hoped it would be. The three Baltic countries have now boldly decided to make a sort of security alliance, but its real value remains uncertain and it, too, has been forced on the Baltic countries by the combination of Russian pressure and Western indifference.

In the absence of reliable security structures, any strong trend to renationalization can be expected to lead, in the eastern half of Europe, to a revival of old, traditional friendships and antipathies. Estonia and Latvia will seek Finland's support to become linked to Scandinavia, and through it to the West. Lithuania will appeal to Germany to guarantee its security in the face of a disliked Poland, an uncertain Belarus and a hostile Russia. Poland would take up, once again, its all-too-familiar role of trying to be a "friendly balancer" between Germany and Russia, a role that history has rarely crowned with success. Ukraine will oscillate between Russia and Poland, and secondarily between Hungary and Slovakia as Slovakia seeks aid (perhaps also from Poland) against Hungarian expansionism. Hungary will become obsessed with its problem of Hungarian minorities abroad; Slovakia will become obsessed with the Hungarian danger. The Czech Republic, secondarily Hungary, and also Slovenia and Croatia, will (despite economic fears) be pulled toward a new German-speaking *Mitteleuropa* based on Germany and Austria. Moldova will naturally lean on Romania, even if formal unification remains impossible. Romania, the rest of the former Yugoslav states and Bulgaria, will pursue their Balkan maneuvers, variously seeking German or Russian support. In a larger sense the policies of every country will take, as their main points of reference, the policies and intentions of Germany and Russia, the two "great powers" of the region.

This scenario is a deeply pessimistic one for several reasons. The endless maneuvering for power and security that would follow would drain away resources desperately needed for economic development and the development of democracy. Worse, in past centuries this kind of maneuvering has repeatedly led to wars. There is no reason to think that it would not again. Furthermore, a Europe of this character would produce the maximum possible temptations to Russia to expand and strengthen its "sphere of interest." And if it is possible to tempt Germany away from building Western European integration and toward playing again its old games of power, the greatest temptation would be the appearance of just this kind of Eastern Europe.

The overall result of this kind of renationalization in the eastern half of Europe would be so much insecurity for so many that we certainly must choose to work instead toward the first scenario which, even if tortuous, promises enormously greater security.

Appeasement of Russia

There is one more general scenario possible for Europe. This one would be simply tragic for Poland and for the eastern half of Europe generally, for it would again deprive them of their independence. It is possible that the United States would allow and even encourage Russia to reestablish dominance in the region (without, of course, necessarily declaring openly that this was the American policy).

There are some indications in recent American behavior that could lead to extremely disturbing conclusions.[21] The United States may be scared of, or unable to come to grips with, what seemed only a few years ago to be the hour of its great triumph: the end of the only other superpower and hence a "unipolar moment" in world history. Possibly the United States is so caught up in its internal troubles that it is no longer able, or at any rate willing, to carry the responsibilities of being the world's sole superpower. It may be that Washington is quietly looking for a renewed balance of power with Russia at the global level, a kind of "partnership in bipolarity." Such an informal partnership with Russia could free Washington from responsibility for maintaining international "law and order" in certain troubled areas around the globe, notably including the eastern half of Europe. Washington could quietly give Moscow a "*droit de regard*" or sphere of influence there. This scenario bears disturbing resemblances to the appeasement of Hitler in the late 1930s. In the end this scenario would simply mean the reestablishment of Russian control in the region, which would overwhelm, and for practical purposes end, the freedom and sovereignty so recently won by so many countries there.

Not only every political leader in Poland but also every citizen of Poland would shrink from so terrible a prospect. After decades of tyranny by an outside power, Poland has only just recently gained its independence, its real national existence as a self-governing country. Poland now is making strides toward becoming a well-functioning democracy, and wants nothing more than simply to become a normal European country. Is all this to be snuffed out again?

A variation on this grim scenario is also possible, a variation that would be much better for Poland but not for some of its neighbors. One can interpret some American, and other Western, behavior as suggesting a somewhat different implication. The unspoken signal to Moscow may be, not that Moscow may regain control of the whole eastern half of Europe, but that Moscow may regain control of the territory of the former Soviet Union. If this is the intention – and for Poland this "if" is the gravest possible question of national destiny – then the outcome for the region will be different. A new "curtain" may appear, one that is not "iron" but decisive nonetheless. The former Soviet republics will fall again under Moscow's sway while the Central European countries, on the western side of this new line, retain their independence. While incomparably better for Poland, this variation could nonetheless place an imperial Russia right on Poland's long eastern border. For the Baltic countries and Ukraine, Poland's near neighbors, this scenario would still be tragic.

4 Concluding remarks

This review of three major possible scenarios for the future can end on a brighter note. The judgement of these three scenarios presented below would probably be shared by the great majority of Polish specialists.

The first general scenario is not only the most positive one, but also appears to be the most likely. The prospects appear moderately favorable for a gradual development of security links between Central Europe and the West. This scenario would not so much represent the deliberate creation of a planned "architecture" as a flexible, organic and only partly planned evolution of Western activities in the region. Security arrangements embracing all of Europe, including Eastern Europe, would gradually emerge as a result of various, perhaps mostly tacit, understandings, especially between the West and Russia.

If this evolution does not develop, then the second scenario is quite possible. A sharp renationalization of European affairs, especially in the eastern half of the continent, would be a discouraging outcome of the current transitional years. This outcome would surely impede the political (i.e. democratic) and economic development of the region. This scenario would be dangerous for peace, dangerous for many countries in the region, and dangerous for the West also in the long run.

The third scenario of Russia again reclaiming the region as its sphere is the grimmest of all, and the most awesome. There are few things in modern history that would match the drama and the tragedy of Russia, having lost its eastern European empire, regaining it in the years to come through the passivity or even the permission of the West. Fortunately this scenario appears the least likely of the three, at least for Central Europe.

If Europe and the West can find sufficient wisdom, confidence, imagination and perseverance in the years to come, we may look forward to the probability of the first scenario materializing, and to a gradual evolution toward improved security for many – and in the end, we may hope, for all – of the countries in the region.

Notes

1 One was the success of Wladislaw Gomulka (the Communist Party First Secretary from 1956–1970) in gaining recognition by the Federal Republic of Germany (West Germany) for the western Polish border established by the Great Powers in the Potsdam agreement of 1945. In this so-called "normalization," the FRG received full diplomatic relations with Poland. The other was the success by Edward Gierek (Gomulka's successor in the same position, 1970–1980) in gaining substantial economic aid from the West, in return for some change in climate in political relations between Poland and the West. These efforts were honest in motivation and gave Poles some apparent satisfaction, but of course they were not aimed at, nor could they possibly have achieved, Poland regaining its sovereignty. The Russians' reaction was, therefore, twofold. Fundamentally they remained confident of their control of Poland. At the same time they were irritated by the maneuvers of the Polish leaders, which Moscow saw as inconsistent with its policy and as threatening to disseminate a "turbulent spirit" among the other WTO countries.
2 In spite of the statement earlier that Poland is essentially homogeneous ethnically, there are a fairly small number of ethnic Germans, primarily in the southwest.
3 The Warsaw Uprising occurred in August 1944.
4 Foreign Minister Olechowski has observed that the Partnership for Peace with the West should be accompanied by a "Partnership for Transformation" between Poland and Russia. From the Minister's statement at the time of a meeting in Warsaw with the Russian Foreign Minister, Andrei Kozyrev, on February 23, 1993.
5 For example, Great Britain pursued an imperialistic policy through much of the nineteenth century. Recently in the West, the idea has been advanced that democracies very rarely make war on other democracies. This may be true of mature democracies, but even a Russia that is as successful as can be hoped will not be a mature democracy soon.
6 "Zalozenia polskiej polityki bezpieczenstwa," *Polska Zbrojna* (Warsaw, November 3, 1992); and "Polityka bezpieczenstwa i strategia obronna Rzeczypospolitej Polskiej," *Polska Zbrojna* (Warsaw, November 12, 1992).
7 The following extracts are from Minister Olechowski's address, entitled "Seven statements on Poland's security," delivered at the Center for Strategic and International Studies in Washington on December 14, 1993.
8 See for example, a series of editorials in the *New York Times* strongly opposing any NATO expansion and warning against the administration's shift in attitude.
9 Bulletin of the Polish Delegation to the CSCE summit, dated December 4, 1994. See also *Gazeta Wyborcza* (December 6, 1994).
10 Some of the most important are these: (1) Structural barriers in the economy. Much of Polish industry suffers from low productivity at high costs. The state sector, which still represents some 70 percent of GNP, has only limited adaptability to the new market conditions internally or to foreign markets. (2) There will be high costs in adapting to EU norms and standards. (3) Difficulties in adjusting Polish external trade, including customs policies, to the conditions

and requirements of the EU. This will arise, and arises already, especially in agriculture. (4) Poland has a poor transportation and communications infrastructure. (5) The environment in Poland is degraded to a substantial degree, with rather high soil, water and air pollution. (6) All of these problems will require time and considerable expenditure before Poland can meet the standards expected of an EU member.

11　See, for example, Francis Delaisi, *Les Deux Europes* (Paris: Payot Publishing Co, 1929).

12　In September 1994 the US Department of State abolished, in its own usage, the term "Eastern Europe" to refer to what had previously been "Eastern Europe" and substituted the term "Central Europe."

13　The term "variable geometry," with a political meaning, was first used by former French President Giscard d'Estaing in the late 1980s. In the context of European security it has recently been used by, for example, the German specialist M. Sturmer in his paper "Living in interesting times: the conceptual challenge," presented at an international conference on Institutes and the Security Dialogue, Zurich, April 26–28, 1994 (unpublished).

14　This phrase, since repeated countless times, was first coined by US Senator Richard Lugar in a speech given on June 24, 1993 to the Overseas Writers Club in Washington, DC.

　　To be more exact, the division of Europe was static and rather untroubled after about 1970. But even earlier, there was really only one dangerous hot spot: Berlin. The whole rest of the "iron curtain" was not even lukewarm. "Out of area" is NATO terminology for areas beyond the territory of the NATO states.

15　For the titles of these NATO Declarations see chapter 1, notes 2 and 3.

16　Csbm's are defined and described in appendix 2.

17　See, for example, the address of Foreign Minister Olechowski to the meeting of the CSCE Council of Ministers in Rome on November 30, 1993.

18　Since the United States includes Alaska, in a literal sense the CSCE goes around the whole globe.

19　Quoted in *Gazeta Wyboroza* (December 7, 1994).

20　Vladmir Zhirinovsky in Russia has released a map suggesting his designs for Europe, in which he takes this approach. His proposed map again partitions Poland, into a western piece to be ruled by Germany and an eastern piece to be ruled by Russia.

21　Here one might observe some aspects of President Clinton's January 1994 trip to Europe and to Moscow, seen against the background of various remarks by Deputy Secretary of State Strobe Talbott.

10

The Czech Republic

Miloslav Had and Vladimir Handl   PRAGUE

1   Introduction

The Czech Republic is a new state on the map of Europe, formed along with Slovakia on January 1, 1993 from the former Czechoslovakia. In many respects the security and foreign policy positions of the Czech Republic are continuations of the positions of the Czech and Slovak Federal Republic (CSFR) in the period 1989–1992; in some significant respects they are not. To understand Czech foreign and security policy now, a brief review of policy in the CSFR period is useful.

Czechoslovakia 1989–1992

After the "Velvet Revolution," a federal government was formed in early December 1989. Vaclav Havel, a leading dissident in the communist era, was elected president by the end of the same month. Czechoslovak society embarked on the great task of rebuilding a democratic society and a market economy. The first free general elections in forty years were held in June 1990.

The first objective in foreign and security affairs was to secure Czechoslovakia's sovereignty and independence, which in practical terms meant first of all achieving a rapid withdrawal of the Soviet troops in the country. All Soviet forces were gone by July 1991. The WTO and Comecon were dissolved in the same period.

A second basic objective became known as Czechoslovakia's "return to Europe." In practice this meant joining the political and economic structures of the Western European countries, along with reestablishing good relations with the United States and Canada. Czechoslovakia joined the Council of Europe in February 1991 and signed a European Association Agreement with the EC in December 1991.[1]

Czechoslovakia's concept of security initially gave much emphasis to the

CSCE, a mechanism in existence since 1975. In this period Prague hoped that the CSCE could evolve into a pan-European design for security, also including the US and Canada. At first, President Havel and some other leaders were inclined to see NATO as a Cold War institution whose future was in doubt. CSCE had the advantage of seeming capable of evolving into a genuine collective security structure for all Europe. Especially under Foreign Minister Jiri Dienstbier, Prague was one of the leading CSCE advocates in Europe.[2]

President Havel soon changed his view of NATO, primarily because of the unforeseen complexities and new risks stemming from the collapse of communism in Central and Eastern Europe. Signs of a reemergence of hardline policies in the then Soviet Union, ethnic war in the former Yugoslavia and other developments suggested that instability might grow in the eastern half of Europe. This in turn indicated the need for an existing, functioning and stable military security organization. As early as March 1991, President Havel began publicly advocating both the preservation of NATO and its expansion to include Czechoslovakia and the other Central European countries.[3] For a while, Prague pursued policies of promoting both NATO and the CSCE as two approaches, mutually consistent and mutually supporting, for improving security in Europe. In time it became increasingly clear that CSCE was not going to be able to develop soon into a real collective security system and did not enjoy strong support from many countries. Especially after the departure of Dienstbier as Foreign Minister after the June 1992 elections, Prague deemphasized CSCE.

After these elections it also became clear that Czechoslovakia would divide into two countries. Over the following months, much of the attention of the Foreign and Defense Ministries, as well as other parts of the government, was focused on analyzing and then carrying out a fair division of the country and its assets, including its military forces. Despite many complicated problems, the division was accomplished relatively smoothly and quite peacefully.

2 The security and foreign policy of the Czech Republic

Introduction

The situation of the Czech Republic is in some respects distinctly different from that of the former Czechoslovakia. Of course the Czech Republic is much smaller; it has only about 60 percent of the territory, and about two-thirds of the population, of the former Czechoslovakia. But in some other ways the new Republic enjoys a more favorable situation.

The new Republic, unlike Czechoslovakia, has no common border with the countries of the former Soviet Union. It is Slovakia that borders on the east with former Soviet territory, specifically Ukraine. This geographical change for the Czech Republic has several effects. Perhaps the most general and pervasive effect is that it moves the "center of gravity" of the new Republic westward. This is significant politically and psychologically as much as geographically. For example, in the new Czech Republic, even more than in the other former WTO countries, people are increasingly coming to think of themselves as Central Europeans, not as Eastern Europeans. Also, the shift westward tends to put more distance, psychologically as well as "really," between the Czech Republic and the turmoil of the Balkans. At the same time, the shift may place the Republic more completely within the German sphere of economic and other influence.

The absence of any common border with the former Soviet Union could have direct political and even military significance in the future, if a nationalist and imperialist Russia were to recapture, say, the formerly Soviet territories. In such a situation, Russian forces might be positioned on the eastern border of Slovakia. While this might be a dangerous situation for the Czech Republic, it would not be the same as if Russian troops were directly on the Czech border.

A second way in which the Czech Republic enjoys a more favorable situation than Czechoslovakia did involves minorities. There are no substantial minority groups in the new Republic, at least none of the kinds that could produce significant problems in external relations. The large Hungarian minority, previously a source of possible problems for Czechoslovakia, lives in Slovakia. There are no ethnic groups in the Czech Republic who have a nearby "homeland." (We will take up shortly the topic of the Sudeten Germans, which is a different kind of issue.) There are a significant number of "gypsies" (Romany) in the Republic, as there are throughout Central and Eastern Europe, but this ethnic group does not claim any homeland elsewhere.

Certain economic advantages that the Czech Republic enjoys, compared to the previous Czechoslovakia, are outside the scope of this book.[4] Naturally the Republic also inherited the city that was by far the greatest city of Czechoslovakia, Prague.

A question much debated in the new Republic is the Czech identity. Many citizens of the new Republic identified with the old Czechoslovakia, would have preferred that state to continue, and saw the impulse that caused its split as coming from someone else (the Slovaks). In a significant sense, then, many citizens of the new Republic find themselves living in a country that they did not want.

Furthermore the constitution of the new Republic is based on a civic, not a nationality, principle. When the Republic was formed it was not necessary to be Czech in order to be a citizen. For example, over 300,000 ethnic Slovaks living in the Republic chose to, and were allowed to, become citizens. Because of the way the Republic came into being, and because it is not a nationality-based state, it may take some time for a Czech political identity to become emotionally real to people. There is some concern, therefore, that the Czech state may be seen by many as a mere instrument, arousing little feeling. This could produce excessive pragmatism, perhaps even nihilism, in public behavior.

Czech foreign and security policy

The relatively favorable position of the Czech Republic among the countries of Central Europe is suggested by the relative absence in Czech foreign affairs of potentially significant security issues. On April 21, 1993, the lower chamber of the Parliament received and noted the principal guidelines for foreign policy, presented by the foreign minister. The guidelines stated the main Czech goals as the promotion and defense of the vital interests of the Czech people and the enhancement and consolidation of the stability, security and economic prosperity of the Czech Republic and its position in the community of European democratic states.[5] The guidelines went on to identify objectives, called "strategic tasks," that stem from these basic goals. There are three principal ones, which may be summarized as follows:

The first objective is to strive for balanced, unconflicting relations on a basis of partnership and cooperation with each of the neighboring states (Germany, Poland, Austria, Slovakia) as well as with nearby Hungary. Special attention will be paid to the relationship with Slovakia, enhancing that bilateral relationship in the context of good international relations generally.

The second is to create conditions that will favor the progressive engagement, and then membership, of the Czech Republic in the main political, economic and security organizations of Europe: the EU, NATO and the WEU.

The third is to maintain good relations with the former communist states, to seek opportunities with them for trade and economic cooperation, and to assist in so far as possible in their stabilization. It is in the interests of the Czech Republic that Russia and Ukraine, as well as the Balkan countries, evolve in an orderly and peaceful way toward democracy and toward prosperous market economies.

The guidelines also addressed Czech security affairs. Being a formal document, the guidelines say that the ultimate aim of Czech foreign policy is "to seek such arrangements and to enter such international treaties and organizations as would guarantee to the utmost the inviolability of the state's frontiers, consolidate the security of the state, and in case of need, enable its effective defense."[6] It is clear that the Czech Republic, as a small state, must enter into collective arrangements to ensure its defense. In case of any large-scale conflict, the Republic would be unable to defend itself with its own forces. Regional security is discussed later in this chapter.

Nonetheless the guidelines also state that, if attacked, the Czech Republic "is determined to fight with arms."

The guidelines observe that direct military threats to the Republic have receded greatly. But sources of conflict exist and in some ways the situation is becoming less "transparent," a term meaning that the situation in significant foreign countries is less visible and less predictable than before. Czech security may be endangered by factors less predictable than direct military threats, such as the growth of militant nationalism in the region, the appearance of ethnic/territorial disputes, the possibility of uncontrollable waves of refugees arriving and the possibility of a collapse in supplies of vital raw materials.[7]

Most of these dangers are discussed at several points in this book; the Republic's dependence on raw materials from the east should be explained here. The Czech Republic must import oil and gas, and many other raw materials. The dependence on oil and gas imports is especially critical because at present both come only through pipelines that pass through Slovakia and Ukraine, and originate in Russia. The other set of pipelines, up from the Mediterranean, has been cut by the civil war in the former Yugoslavia and does not seem likely to be restored soon.

It is obvious that supplies from the one remaining set of pipelines from the east could be cut off, either at the point of origin or along the way. Some worrisome signs have already arisen. The first Prime Minister of Slovakia, after Slovakia became independent, made pointed public remarks about the Czech Republic's dependence on pipelines that run through Slovakia.[8] In January 1994 there was a temporary halt in oil supplies due to administrative delays in Russia. Russia has already halted oil supplies to Estonia temporarily for political reasons.

To provide more security in the long term, new pipelines have been planned to bring oil and gas into the Czech Republic through Germany. For a while this plan was complicated by hints by the prime minister of Bavaria that Bavaria might make some linkage between the planned pipelines and the Sudeten German issue. In April 1994, however, the relevant treaty for the construction of the pipeline was concluded without any political precondition from either side. The Ingolstadt–Litvinov oil pipeline will be put into operation at the end of 1995 and will be able, if necessary, to meet the demand of the Czech economy (about 7 million tons of oil annually).

No overall policy paper on Czech security policy, comparable to the guidelines on foreign affairs, has yet been created. The ingredients of a basic security document are presently under discussion in Prague. However, some of the basic elements of security doctrine are already well known. It is axiomatic that security includes a goal of maintaining good relations with all neighbors. Czech membership in NATO is now fundamental in Czech thinking about the Republic's security, as discussed further below. Doubtless the Czech Republic will accept responsibility to participate in the peacekeeping operations of the United Nations, and presumably of the OSCE if any arise. The Republic is likely to adopt a strictly defensive military doctrine, insofar as a defensive doctrine and posture are consistent with NATO membership and participation in peacekeeping operations.

The Czech defense budget is less than 3 percent of GDP. This amount is sufficient to maintain the country's present military forces, but it is not enough to modernize the forces substantially nor to acquire significant new weapons.

Bilateral relations of special interest: Slovakia

Two bilateral relationships, with Slovakia and with Germany, are inevitably of particular interest to the Czech Republic. After discussing these relations, this section will briefly review several other particular policy concerns. The next section of this chapter will turn to regional and pan-European matters including NATO and OSCE.

Slovakia and the Czech Republic were one country for more than seventy years and have been intimately linked for more than a thousand years. Many Czechs wish that the two countries might again be reunited at some point in the future, within the wider European framework when both countries are members of the EU.[9] Under these conditions it goes without saying that relations between the two are of deep and special interest to Prague, and will continue to be so indefinitely. The foreign policy guidelines say that the Czech Republic "will pay special attention to relations with the Slovak Republic, and will endeavor to create conditions for their stability."[10]

At the same time, and for obvious benevolent reasons, Prague wishes to be careful not to seem to meddle in Slovakia's affairs. For this reason and others, the Czech Republic withdrew from a sharp controversy between Slovakia and Hungary, which stretches back many years, over a dam on the Danube River.

Following the division of Czechoslovakia, trade between the two parts has declined more than was originally expected. Slovakia's share in total Czech foreign trade turnover fell from approximately 25 percent in 1992 to 19.3 percent in 1993 and to 15.1 percent in the first ten months of 1994. Even so, Slovakia remains the Czech Republic's most important trading partner after Germany, and will almost certainly remain a major trading partner for the indefinite future.

As of this writing, a few issues pertaining to the division of assets of the former Czechoslovakia have not yet been resolved. It is hoped that these remaining questions will not become a stumbling block to good Czech–Slovak relations.

In Prague's view, relations between the Czech and Slovak Republics have a special character and this will continue. Both states acknowledge this.

There is the important legacy of the common state, and innumerable close ties in political, economic, cultural and human spheres. The two peoples have never fought each other. The Czech Republic is also deeply interested in a stable and democratic Slovakia for the obvious reason that such a Slovakia represents an important element in overall Czech security. The same applies in reverse for Slovakia.

Bilateral relations of special interest: Germany

Germany is, and will remain, a country of particular importance for the Czech Republic for economic as well as the obvious geographic reasons. The role that Germany plays in the Czech economy is huge and may well grow further. Germany has become the Czech Republic's most important trading partner. German capital has the leading role in some important branches of the Czech economy, including machinery, chemicals and banking.

Inevitably the almost overwhelming German presence in the Republic's economy has mixed effects. On the positive side, it has played a large role in the economy's relative success in the last several years, compared to the other Central European countries. On the other hand, Czechs have no illusions that German and Czech economic interests are the same. There is concern that the Czech Republic may, in economic affairs, gradually come under German dominance. For some Czechs this concern becomes linked to other feelings about Germany, discussed in chapter 5.

Close relations, including close economic relations, with Germany can have positive political effects for the Czech Republic. Within the EU, Germany has championed, and is expected to continue to champion, the Czech Republic becoming a full member sooner rather than later. Among the NATO countries, Germany has again been the chief advocate of Czech membership in NATO. However, it is obvious that Germany's main concern relates to Russia. Bonn is making it clear that an extension of NATO is not possible unless Russia's interests are embedded in a broader European security arrangement.

Relations between Czechoslovakia and Germany after 1989, and now between the Czech Republic and Germany, have developed favorably in political and economic spheres. The two countries share similar views on the main issues of security in Europe. The two have also concluded important bilateral treaties. In November 1991, treaties were signed on the Czech–German border (an issue of symbolic importance for the Czech public) and on the readmission of asylum-seekers. However, there have been two problematic issues as well.

One involves compensation for Czech victims of Nazi Germany, stemming from the time that Hitler incorporated the Czech lands into the Third Reich. About 14,000 elderly Czechs are still alive who were persecuted by the Nazis; most were prisoners in concentration camps. There has been no substantial progress on Prague's claim for compensation for these people. In this case no compensation has been received, unlike cases in other countries who suffered under Nazi German occupation or even, like Hungary, who were formal allies of Hitler.

The other issue involves the Sudeten Germans, a complicated question with deep historical roots. A German minority lived in the Czech lands (mainly in the border regions) since the twelfth century. In the era of growing German nationalism in the nineteenth century, these "Sudeten Germans" began to support pan-Germanic nationalist aims. Most of them opposed the creation of Czechoslovakia after World War I, and later a majority welcomed the Munich Agreement and supported the dismemberment of Czechoslovakia and the incorporation of the Czech lands into the Reich.

During World War II, Czech leaders (like leaders in Poland and elsewhere) gave thought to how any similar situation might be prevented in the future, after the victory over Hitler. Czech, Polish and other leaders concluded that the safest measure would be the transfer of ethnic Germans back into Germany, so there could never again be an excuse for a future Germany to claim, as Hitler had, that it should "protect" Germans abroad. This conclusion was shared by the victorious Allies – the United States, Britain and the Soviet Union – who included it in the Potsdam Agreement of 1945. Article XIII of that Agreement stated that German populations remaining in Czechoslovakia, Poland and Hungary at the end of the war would be transferred in an orderly and humane way to Germany. This Agreement was carried out in all three countries. About 2.9 million Germans were removed from Czechoslovakia and transferred to Germany, and their property in Czechoslovakia was confiscated. This action became an emotional and very sensitive issue in relations with Germany in the years and decades after World War II. During or after the transfer, thousands of Sudeten Germans died, and Bonn never accepted the Potsdam Agreement on this question as a just solution. However, many Czechs (as well as Poles) do.

After 1989, President Havel in one of his first official statements rejected the principle of "collective guilt" as immoral, and called the transfer a form of revenge.[11] However, this bold statement was not well received by many political parties and much of the public in Czechoslovakia, who continued to feel (as they still do today) that the transfer was a legitimate response to Nazi crimes and to the support, by the majority of the Sudeten Germans, of the dismemberment of Czechoslovakia. Since 1945, the Sudeten Germans and their descendants have created organizations in Germany that demand the right to return to the Czech lands – while retaining German citizenship – and the restitution of confiscated property. This delicate issue between Prague and Bonn has been further complicated by support given to the Sudeten Germans' demands by one of the major political parties in the

German state of Bavaria. Meanwhile, many Czechs perceive the demand that the Sudeten Germans be allowed to return as an attempt to revise the outcome of World War II. The sensitive issue of the Sudeten Germans has not yet been resolved.

The October 1994 elections in Germany resulted in a mixture of continuity and change. It proved once again the stability of German democracy, although further changes in its political constellation can be expected. One of the positive features of the election was the very low vote for nationalist and racist forces.[12] In spite of the two unresolved issues, Prague expects a continuation of the positive overall development in Czech–German relations.

Other questions in foreign and security affairs

No attempt by any country to make any forcible change in the Czech Republic's borders is thought to be even slightly probable. Potential efforts to change some borders of other countries to the east and southeast cannot be excluded, however. Such possibilities are worrisome, not least because such events could easily trigger an influx of refugees or migrants.

Migration, for this or other possible reasons, is seen by Czech specialists as an acute risk. The tightening of the asylum law in Germany increases the potential hazards for countries immediately to Germany's east, since migrants who might wish to enter Germany may be stopped at the German border. In addition, the Czech Republic is itself becoming attractive for migrants. Relative economic success, political stability and positive prospects for a future "within Europe" are beginning to make the Czech Republic desirable to potential migrants. Yet the Republic does not have resources remotely comparable to the resources of Western European countries, either to absorb immigrants or to manage its borders.

There are other non-military risks to security. One of these is international crime, including drug trafficking. About 85 percent of the drug consumption of Western Europe is supplied through a "Balkan route" that begins in Turkey and passes through the Balkans, Hungary, Slovakia and the Czech Republic. In addition, international "mafias" are increasingly active in the Czech Republic. Originating both in Italy and in Russia, they pose a serious threat to the peace and stability of society. Czech police and security forces have been unprepared for this new danger, and are not adequately equipped or funded.

Other problems in the region could pose difficulties for the Czech Republic even if they do not rise to the level of actual security threats. Ethnic tensions in close neighbors are uncomfortable even though they are unlikely to involve the Czech Republic directly. Prague hopes that the common interest of the Central European countries in joining Western economic and security structures, and in deepening the links already formed, will contribute to keeping any unfavorable tendencies in check.

3 European security

The Czech viewpoint on European security

Like other small Central European countries that are inherently unable to defend themselves against large countries in the region, the Czech Republic has no choice but to find its security in some larger structure. The Republic needs, in essence, a security guarantee from a powerful organization, alliance or entity that is genuinely able to provide it.[13]

In this respect Czech security policy represents a continuation of the policy of Czechoslovakia. Although some consideration was given to neutrality as an option for a time after 1989, it was never accepted as a basis for policy. Rather, the concept of the "return to Europe" led to a strategic aim for Czechoslovakia to seek membership in the EC and NATO, which were seen as stable economic and security structures. The Czech Republic has never considered neutrality as an option. There is a general consensus on this among the main political parties and the majority of the public. The only exceptions are the Communist and the (nationalist) Republican parties, whose influence is limited.

At least in the present era, the United Nations and the OSCE cannot provide the kind of security guarantee upon which a country can stake its existence. Among other reasons, several great powers including Russia can veto any security action by the United Nations; in the OSCE even two small countries can veto any effective action.

There is no willingness in Prague to seek, or to accept, any security guarantee from Russia. The main direction of Czech actions and policy since the "Velvet Revolution" of 1989 has been precisely to move away from any military dependence upon Russia. The worrisome results of the December 1993 parliamentary elections in Russia merely reemphasize the necessity for this movement.

The Czech Republic has no choice, then, but to seek its security with the West in some form. The existing security structures of the West are, first, NATO, which includes the United States, and secondly, the WEU, which under the Maastricht Treaty is the military arm of the EU. As the foreign policy guidelines state, "NATO and the WEU provide the only real alternatives for gaining security guarantees for the Czech Republic."[14]

The Czech viewpoint may be put in more general terms. Essentially all Czech specialists, and the overwhelming majority of informed Czech citizens, are convinced that the major responsibility for the evolution of the European security order, as well as the maintenance of such order as exists now, rests with the West. Specialists also believe that the West is or would be the chief manager of conflict on all levels of the "escalation ladder."[15] At least in Europe, the West is assumed to have the decisive role in crisis-prevention, crisis-management and crisis-resolution. Prague also expects that any military actions the West may take in Europe will be only those that are legitimated by the United Nations or OSCE.

NATO

Prague desires a strong continuing US military as well as political presence in Europe. That presence not only provides the strongest military protection but also helps maintain stability in international affairs in Europe. In addition, NATO is an effective military alliance now, whereas the WEU has only some of the features of a true alliance. While interested in the potential of the WEU as well, as discussed below, the Czech Republic's primary strategic goal is membership in NATO. Until membership is achieved, the Republic seeks the closest feasible relationship with NATO.

The Czech Republic's deep and unaltering interest in NATO membership is not based solely on security and military considerations. For many Czechs, membership is not even primarily a security matter. It would bring a whole spectrum of additional benefits. It would provide a powerful emblem of the Republic's respectability as a fully-fledged member of the Western community of democracies. It would thus be a signal of a major success along the country's difficult road of transformation. The enhanced international status would, in turn, yield important advantages in attracting foreign capital and in other aspects of international economic affairs. (Full membership in the EU would bring similar benefits but is not a matter for the forseeable future.) NATO membership would also work "the other way around," as a guarantee as well as an emblem of the Republic's transition into a stable, lasting democracy and market economy.

Although Czech specialists inside and outside the government are unanimous that NATO is the Republic's main security goal, several schools of thought can be distinguished about timing and methods. One viewpoint emphatically and powerfully urges membership at the earliest possible moment. President Vaclav Havel is the most prominent exponent of this viewpoint. He has warned the West that a failure to bring Central Europe into the Western community would amount to "a new Yalta." The implication is that it would be a naked and cynical carving-up of Europe into crude spheres of influence. President Havel also has publicly suggested that a failure to admit the Czech Republic would be a "betrayal," in a way that made a comparison to the West's infamous betrayal of Czechoslovakia at Munich in 1938.[16]

While sharing the President's goal, many in the Foreign and Defense ministries prefer a gradualist approach to NATO membership. Convinced that full membership is not possible in the near future, they recommend developing, in the meantime, all possible contacts and connections with NATO.

A third school of thought, known as "NATO sceptics," can be found among some Czech economists who approach the issue from the angle of economic costs and benefits. They emphasize the absence of any direct military threats, and the high money costs of modernizing and improving the Czech military up to NATO standards. They point out that the public does not support increased taxes. To this calculus they may also add a probability estimate, suggesting that membership soon is unlikely anyhow. On this basis, they do not advocate NATO membership now, and tend to support the gradualists.

The violent Russian intervention in Chechnya, which began late in 1994, has had the effect of Prague strengthening still further its effort to see the Czech Republic integrated into NATO. The previous perception of Moscow as a partner within a system of collective security was considerably damaged. Prague saw the excessive use of military force, especially against the Chechen civilian population, as disturbing. Of course Prague, like most other European governments, called for a political, negotiated settlement of the conflict.

NACC and the Partnership for Peace

Shortly after the formation of NACC, the Czech Republic became a member. While NACC's efforts to give useful forms of assistance to the unstable countries of the east is appreciated in Prague, the fact that NACC embraces all the former WTO and all former Soviet states makes the institution too loose and not sufficiently effective to meet Czech security interests. Such a loose organization cannot be a substitute for NATO membership. Furthermore, NACC's principle of "equal treatment" stops short of Czech interests. A perception of Europe prevails in Prague in which the different geographical and historical position of various countries, and their various stages of transformation, should be reflected in their status in Western institutions. For Prague, an individualization and differentiation of the Czech relationship with NATO is a priority. Meanwhile the strategic priority of NATO – to smooth the relationship with Russia as a way to prevent a new era of confrontation – seems to be underestimated in Prague.

The Partnership for Peace, formally announced by NATO in January 1994, found a generally positive response in Prague, even though it does not provide a definite security guarantee. It is seen as providing an opportunity for something Prague wanted anyway: to develop an individual relationship with NATO. Prague hopes to become the "best pupil" in the new "school," and thereby perhaps develop some form of special status with NATO. The Partnership for Peace is seen as providing another pathway by which the

Czech Republic can "define itself out." This is a new term in the *lingua politica* of Prague and means defining the Republic "out" of "the East."

At the same time, it is clear to Czech specialists that the Partnership for Peace can also be seen as a NATO device for postponing the basic decision about real membership. Those who most emphatically want a prompt positive decision on the basic question thus view the Partnership more negatively, and may see it as further evidence that NATO (and mainly the United States) is yielding to Russian demands.

The decision by the December 1994 NATO summit in Brussels to elaborate, by the end of 1995, a strategy for widening NATO was well received in Prague. In general, an optimistic perception prevails in Prague regarding the future of the Alliance and also of the American presence in Europe. However, there is not a clear perception regarding the positions of individual NATO member countries concerning the extension of NATO.

The growing attraction of the EU/WEU

In the period immediately following 1989, membership in the EC became the core idea of the "return to Europe." Prague's perception of the EC, however, tended to embrace economic matters only. The conservative politicians and also a part of the public perceived the EC primarily as a structure for economic integration. The political, security and social aspects of the integration process seemed to be secondary, and for some politicians even a burden. During the same period, contacts with the WEU evolved. The Czech Republic participates in the WEU Forum of Consultation. However, the Forum has remained only at the level of discussion and has not evolved into genuine cooperation, and therefore does not satisfy Prague's interests.

There are a significant number of Czech "Euro-sceptics" who view the Maastricht Treaty critically. This critical stance is reinforced by the growing supranational elements in the construction of the European Union, the increasing role of the "Eurobureaucracy" in Brussels and the declining role of the national state. There is evident unease in Prague about the competition between European and Atlantic security options, and the tensions that competition is producing in the Atlantic Alliance.

There has been a gradual change in Prague's evaluation of the EU. This has partly resulted from the enlargement of the EU in 1995, bringing in Austria, Finland and Sweden, and from the approach of the EU to the Central and Eastern European states, which took the form of a "pre-accession strategy" adopted by the European Council at its December 1994 meeting at Essen. In Prague's view, the January 1994 NATO summit (at which PfP was announced), and various transatlantic understandings including agreements about a "division of labor" and of financial burdens, were important developments demonstrating that Washington has communicated an overall acceptance of the EU developing a security and defense dimension. The transatlantic relationship was evidently strengthened by the successful completion of the GATT Uruguay Round agreement. All these developments have contributed to a shift in the Czech assessment of the EU and WEU from the security viewpoint. The Czech government has announced that it will apply for EU membership in 1996. The Czech Republic, along with other countries of Central and Eastern Europe, has also intensified its efforts to gain a closer relationship with the WEU. The "associate partnership" offered by the WEU in May 1994 is a long-awaited step in this direction.[17] But uncertainty remains about the outcome of the EU intergovernmental reform conference of 1996, and more basically, about the future shape of the Union.

Regional and collective security arrangements

Experience in recent years has shown that a number of important issues must be dealt with by collective security arrangements. These include arms control/reduction treaties, the verification activities supporting them, information exchange and monitoring, potential and actual peacekeeping missions, and some forms of preventive diplomacy. The role of the UN in the world is growing. In 1994 the Czech Republic was elected a non-permanent member of the UN Security Council.

The former CSCE was changed to the OSCE at its Budapest summit in December 1994. Prague perceives this step as demonstrating that the CSCE has been transformed into a genuine international institution. However, the character of the organization, especially its decision-making based on consensus, has not changed. Prague believes that the OSCE will be a useful forum for discussing significant international issues. In his address to the Budapest summit, President Havel called for a strengthening of OSCE's instruments of preventive diplomacy.[18]

The scope of UN and OSCE activities is far broader than the Visegrad arrangement, which was created among Czechoslovakia, Hungary and Poland in 1991, mainly for political cooperation and coordination. The Czech Republic has declined to institutionalize the Visegrad Group, partly to avoid creating any structure that might appear to parallel EU or NATO structures. As a result of the Czech policy there has been no joint meeting of the leading state representatives of the Visegrad Group since 1992. On the other hand, the Czech Republic has been very active in supporting cooperation on various practical issues, and especially in promoting free trade among the Central and Eastern European countries. In December 1992, the Czech Republic, Hungary, Poland and Slovakia signed a treaty that will create, within eight years, a Central European Free Trade Area (CEFTA). Since then, Czech policy has advocated both a speeding up of the free-trade process and an enlargement of the CEFTA area.

4 Concluding remarks

The foreign and security policy of the Czech Republic makes no major break with the policy of the former Czechoslovakia, but does change its focus somewhat. Two fundamentals are the westward shift in the "center of gravity" and the relative economic and political success of the Republic compared to its Central European neighbors. In practical terms these factors mutually reinforce each other.

There is a tendency in Czech policy and psychology to see Western structures, chiefly the EU and NATO, as organizations that the Czech Republic deserves to belong to, as a result of its smoothly working democracy and economy. Membership would not only be an emblem of success, but also would largely guarantee a successful completion of the remaining phases of a difficult transition. Membership would be the decisive symbol, not merely that one epoch has ended but that a new and favorable one has begun. Emphasis on membership is also attractive in domestic political terms to nearly all Czech political parties, because it enhances their image as truly Western (hence, genuinely democratic and modern) parties.

Presently there may be some tendency for Prague to overemphasize Western links and orientations and give less attention to Central Europe, to the countries to the east, and perhaps also to pan-European possibilities. Ironically, Czechoslovakia's emphasis in the years just after 1989 on what many thought a "visionary," idealistic emphasis on pan-European ideas, such as a grand and powerful CSCE, may have almost turned into the opposite in the new Czech Republic. Prague's pragmatism and pursuit of specifically Czech interests now may be almost too provincial. The appearance of an almost cold "realism" is suggested by hints that some politicians would accept a "new Yalta" carving up Europe into an "east" and a "west," on the absolutely fundamental condition that the four Visegrad countries were placed on the western side of the carving line.

Pragmatism and "realism," perhaps to an excessive degree, also seems to characterize Czech thinking about international institutions. Like many Western European capitals, Prague tends to perceive international institutions in terms of how they can be used to achieve the goals of national policy (a "realist" approach) more than in terms of the values the institutions have in themselves (a "liberal" approach). This seems to apply even to Prague's thinking about the most important institutions, those of European integration. At the same time, Prague may be underestimating the problems inherent in the expansion, and perhaps "overstretch," of Western European institutions.

In any case there are sharp limits on how much influence Prague can have. Most of the elements in the drama are beyond Czech control. A list of these is sobering: the evolution (or not) of the EU, the evolution (or not) of the WEU, developments in Russia, developments in Ukraine, potential changes in the relationship between NATO and Russia and possible changes in the overall European–American partnership. Although it is limited, there is room for active Czech engagement with this complex environment. A productive engagement depends on the great Czech transformation into a stable democracy and a sound market economy continuing to proceed well.

Notes

1   After the division of Czechoslovakia, both successor states had to rejoin the Council of Europe. The Czech Republic rejoined on June 30, 1993.

2   To be more exact, Minister Dienstbier advocated replacing the old system of two blocs with a new system that would evolve in three phases. First would come the establishment of a European Security Commission on the basis of the CSCE. Second would come the creation of an Organization of European States, based on an all-European treaty and building upon the CSCE process. Third and last would come the establishment of a Confederated Europe. See the address by Jiri Dienstbier, Minister of Foreign Affairs of Czechoslovakia, at Harvard University on May 16, 1990. In *Europe: a Czechoslovak View*; in the collection of documents, pp. 31–41, Institute of International Relations, Prague, 1990.

3   See President Havel's address on the occasion of his visit to NATO headquarters in Brussels on March 31, 1991. The text is found in *Czechoslovak Foreign Policy, 3/1991, Documents of the Ministry of Foreign Affairs* (Prague, 1991), pp. 179–86.

4   One economic advantage concerns the arms industry. The Czech Republic inherited predominantly the part that is both more advanced and more diversified. Slovakia inherited predominantly the large factories, which are not as up-to-date, for manufacturing heavy equipment such as tanks.

5   The "guidelines" document, as it is often known informally, is formally referenced as follows: "Address of the Minister of Foreign Affairs, Josef Zieleniec, Relating the Concept of Foreign Policy of the Czech Republic, to the 8th Session of the Lower Chamber of the Parliament of the Czech Republic." (*Czechoslovak Foreign Policy 4/1993, Documents, Ministry of Foreign Affairs of the Czech Republic*, pp. 308–24, Prague, 1993.)

6   See note 5.

7   In April 1994, the Minister of the Interior presented to Parliament a new report on the Czech Republic's security situation. The report is consistent with the description of Czech foreign and security policy being offered in this section. The report gives some emphasis to the problems of organized crime (including drugs), especially noting crime being controlled by immigrants and foreigners. Among its conclusions, the report emphasizes the need to improve the Czech Republic's control of its eastern border and to introduce greater controls on immigrants.

8   See "We won," an interview with Vladimir Meciar, the Prime Minister of the Slovak Republic, in *Der Spiegel* (May 17, 1993), p. 184.

9   A bilateral reunion of the Czech and Slovak Republics, not inside the EU, is now generally regarded by Czechs as highly improbable.

10 See note 5.

11 President Havel's statement was made on March 15, 1990, on the occasion of the visit to Prague of German President Richard von Weiszaeker. *Czechoslovak Foreign Policy 1–3/1990, Documents, Ministry of Foreign Affairs* (Prague, 1990), p. 184.

12 The principal far-right party, the Republican Party, received only 1.9 percent of the vote. See appendix 1.

13 For decades the Warsaw Treaty Organization played, officially, exactly this role for Czechoslovakia. In reality, the only time Czechoslovakia was attacked during these decades was an invasion by its Warsaw Treaty "allies."

14 See note 5.

15 This phrase means that the West has the responsibility to, and should be able to, manage, control and, if necessary, win, any conflict involving Europe from the smallest conflicts to the largest level of war.

16 For the citation, see chapter 5, note 5.

17 Associate partnership status was offered by the WEU to the Czech Republic and eight other countries in the Kirchberg Declaration of May 9, 1994.

18 Address by Vaclav Havel, President of the Czech Republic, at the Summit Meeting of CSCE (Budapest, December 5, 1994), *Foreign Policy of the Czech Republic, Documents 12/1994, Ministry of Foreign Affairs of the Czech Republic*, pp. 750–53, Prague 1994.

11

Slovakia

Svetoslav Bombik and Ivo Samson   BRATISLAVA

1   Introduction

The Slovak Republic came into existence on January 1, 1993 as one of the two successor states of the former Czech and Slovak Federal Republic (CSFR). The newly arisen Slovakia naturally became a legal successor to all international treaties and agreements that had been concluded by the former CSFR.

Those agreements, indeed, largely predestined the orientation of the Slovak foreign policy, even before Slovakia appeared on the map of Europe as an independent country. The decisive step was the Association Agreement made by the CSFR with the European Community. The agreement has various specific implications; more broadly it expressed clearly the overall Western orientation of the CSFR. After January 1993, that Association Agreement applied to both successor states.

It should be stressed at once that the Western orientation that Slovakia has chosen does not arise merely from the fact of having inherited the Association Agreement. Slovakia desires this Association as a choice of its own. The agreement and, more deeply, the basic Western orientation it embodies, correspond fully to the basic cultural character of Slovakia, and represents the historical path Slovakia wants to follow, as discussed further later.

Historical background

From the viewpoint of the Slovak people, the creation of Czechoslovakia at the end of World War I was not a satisfactory solution to the problem of dissolving the Austro-Hungarian empire. The population of the new country was ethnically diverse, but a single state was created and an idea arose of a "Czechoslovak nation." Practically speaking, the new state represented a new Austro-Hungary on a smaller scale, because the new state inherited all the ethnic problems of the former empire, and for similar reasons was not able to solve them well. The new state obliged all elements of the ethnically pluralist society to identify with the new "Czechoslovakia." But in practice the new country embodied mainly the historical experience, the culture and especially the political interests of one ethnic group, the Czechs. After the new state was established, the Czechs also proved reluctant to honor agreements that had been reached earlier, during the war, that were meant to guarantee an equal position for Slovakia in the new state. Even so, the Slovak people decided to participate in the new democratic state rather than try to challenge or disrupt the decision of the Great Powers at Versailles, which had created the new country.

In 1939, Nazi Germany went far toward destroying Czechoslovakia. Hitler divided the country and set up a puppet state, the Slovak Republic. He did it partly with the help of some chauvinist elements in Slovakia, and partly by making a threat that if the Slovak people did not comply, he would divide up Slovakia and give the pieces to Hungary and Poland. The real feelings of the people were shown by the Slovak National Uprising near the end of World War II. This armed resistance joined the anti-German Allies and aimed to overthrow the puppet regime and remove the Nazis from the country. The leaders of the Uprising stood for the restoration of a "Czecho-Slovakia," but on new terms. They rejected prewar centralism in which all things were focused on Prague, and rejected the fiction of a "Czechoslovak" nation. They wanted to build the postwar country as a federation of two equal ethnic groups, the Czechs and the Slovaks. Again, however, the Slovak leaders did not succeed in achieving their goals, and "Czechoslovakia" was recreated along roughly similar lines as before.

Soviet totalitarianism ruled from 1948 to 1989. One of its many ill consequences was that nationality questions were not solved, merely buried. In Western Europe, democracy allowed a harmonization of national and other interests, which could then be followed by true integration. But in the Eastern bloc, all questions were subordinated to the will of one totalitarian center. Only in 1989 could Central Europe become free.

The end of the Eastern bloc did not necessarily mean that Central Europe must return automatically and completely to the arrangements set up in 1919. The Versailles decisions had only marginally taken into account the authentic interests of the Central European peoples. After the disintegration in 1989, new possibilities were open. Almost immediately following the creation of the CSFR, negotiations began between Slovak and Czech leaders about the new state. However, those negotiations were not successful in developing a concept satisfactory to all parties for a genuine Czecho-Slovakia. It became inevitable that the country would be divided.

The division of the CSFR

In the West, the rise of an independent, sovereign state of Slovakia has often been misinterpreted as a product of extreme Slovak nationalism. Sometimes an analogy has been drawn to the ethnically intolerant, chauvinist and indeed totalitarian puppet state of the World War II years. Sometimes it has also been said that the Slovaks chose to go their own way because they were unwilling to continue to endure the painful transitions to a democratic, market-oriented country that the CSFR was undertaking. These ideas misunderstand the real reasons why Slovakia sought independence.

The new Slovakia is *also* undertaking the transition to a fully democratic, market-oriented system, and has clearly set that as its goal. Naturally Slovakia need not take just the same route as other countries but can define its own path. It should be obvious that the new, democratic Slovakia, in which the people have participated several times now in free elections, cannot possibly be compared to Hitler's puppet government. Nor was independence achieved by political forces in Slovakia reminiscent of that government. Such elements are found today only on the periphery of the political spectrum. There also was no striving, such as we have seen in the former Yugoslavia, to create an "ethnically pure state." In fact there was no ethnic conflict at all, at the time that the CSFR was quite peacefully divided.

The main goal of the division had other sources. After 1989, Czech society did not throw off the remainders of the old "Czechoslovak" ideology. At stake were the position and the rights of Slovakia. The state mechanisms of the CSFR did not, in fact, offer the opportunity for Slovakia to participate in the governing of the common state, or even of Slovakia itself, to the degree that was demanded by the majority of the Slovak people. That being the case, the remaining alternative was for Slovakia to become independent.

The thinking behind Slovakia's independence was more subtle than is sometimes appreciated, and indeed may seem to include an element of paradox. The Slovak Republic made itself independent, not to be cut off from its environment, but to become involved, as an independent state, with the process of European integration. This was deliberate and was a direct expression of contemporary Slovak thought. The process was, to be sure, one of disintegration in one way, but with the explicit purpose of developing a more authentic cooperation and integration in another way, namely with the larger Europe, which is in the process of unification.

The idea behind this seeming paradox has its roots in 150 years of Slovak political thinking, which has always had strong federalist or confederalist features. Slovaks have always tried to assess realistically the possibilities for their small country. Since the second half of the nineteenth century, Slovaks have been looking for a political situation that could accomplish two things at once. On the one hand, it must enable them to make independent decisions about matters of sovereignty and about their internal affairs. On the other, Slovakia must be incorporated into a larger entity that can guarantee security, naturally on condition that Slovakia can exert influence on that larger entity's decisions.

Thus, in the second half of the nineteenth century and early in the twentieth, the most significant Slovak political thinkers wanted the Austro-Hungarian empire converted into a federation, in which Slovakia would be one unit, autonomous in internal affairs.[1] In the twentieth century, Slovakia entered into the union with the Czechs, to form Czechoslovakia, with essentially the same idea. The Slovak and Czech parts of the larger body should have equal rights.[2] After this idea failed, Slovakia decided to try again in a new way. Slovakia declared its independence, specifically with the intention again of becoming a self-governing unit in a larger body, this time the European Union. Properly understood, then, Slovakia's independence is not something entirely new, but is really the third attempt to find the situation that Slovaks have always been seeking.

2   The security and foreign policy of Slovakia

The security context: the question of Central Europe

It is evident that the security of Slovakia is closely linked to the security of the central part of Europe. The security position of Central Europe, however, is very unclear. The boundaries of "Central Europe" have never been defined precisely and there is no consensus about Central Europe's situation.

World War II solved this question in a splendid way in one sense. It cut Europe into two well-defined parts that could be readily controlled, Western Europe and Eastern Europe. All the "trouble-making" problems of modern European history – the small Slavonic nations, the peoples of the Balkans, the "worse" half of Germany, the Prussians – ended up in the Russian sphere and became parts of Eastern Europe. Many of these had been primarily identified with the Eastern European culture even earlier.

Now, after the collapse of Soviet-controlled Eastern Europe and of the Soviet Union itself, many questions are open again. Central Europe reemerges, as a geographical zone with tremendous problems that cause fear, distrust and instability. Many countries, including Slovakia, have been left alone, unattached to any big partner. Geopolitically they have lost their previous link to the East, and meanwhile they had already been cut off, culturally, from contact with the dynamically evolving Western European civilization. Every country in this hard-to-define region therefore seeks to find some firm position. Many of them are doing it by trying to resurrect the once-famous concept of "Central Europe." But they may overestimate the importance for the Western European states of the middle part of Europe. The repeated efforts of some Central European countries to convince Western Europe that "Central Europe" is a basic, constituent part of Western civilization often takes quite undignified forms. Of course, it is understandable that they try, because the closer they seem to be to the East and the Southeast, the closer they seem to instability and perhaps to violent eruptions.

Sadly, the prospects for "Central Europe" as a distinct cultural and political entity are not promising. Meanwhile the former concept of "Eastern Europe" has now been replaced by the term "post-communist countries," which generally means the group of former communist states that are now seeking to join Western political and military institutions. Slovakia certainly is one of these countries. It is situated in what has classically been regarded as Central Europe and shares in the ambiguities that the region is heir to. Slovakia certainly seeks to join the Western institutions, as discussed later.

The security position of Slovakia

In Slovakia one finds various ideas and orientations regarding the security position of the country. Especially in the time since Slovakia has been independent, an orientation toward the security institutions of the West generally prevails; the political and security decision-makers prefer this option almost unanimously. However, some members of the intellectual elite seem to overestimate the position of Slovakia, and calculate as if Slovakia's position were a precious commodity marketable with advantage both in the East and in the West. This is a mistake; specifically it is a mistake of overestimating the value of Central Europe.

In today's political thinking in Slovakia there are several general ideas, or stereotypes, of the country's possible position and role. Three may be singled out.

One is the concept of Slovakia as a *bridge between East and West*.[3] This viewpoint originates in a belief that Central Europe is an indispensable part of Europe, and that Slovakia is a country of major importance in Central Europe. To this way of thinking, Slovakia has a mission to fulfill, bridging between Eastern Europe and Western Europe. This idea depends not only on the assumption that an "indispensable" Central Europe exists, but also that such a unit is fully acceptable to "the world" – that is, to Western Europe and North America. However, the real world consists of several generally accepted geopolitical zones and Central Europe is not really one of them. Furthermore, it is presumptuous to regard Europe as the center of "the world" and even more presumptuous to presume that something called "Central Europe" is indispensable.

It could be reasonably argued that the same bridging function could also be fulfilled by the Czech Republic, and for that matter by Austria, Hungary, indeed by the whole Carpathian region and even by Germany. Slovakia forms only a small area lying between the Czechs and the Ukrainians, whereas the Czech Republic forms a wedge reaching deeply into the Germanic world. And the Hungarians can argue more successfully than the Slovaks that they occupy a "unique" position among the Slavic, Germanic and Mediterranean worlds. They also have a historical role, which they can document, in playing a bridging role among these worlds. The same may be true for Austria.

The second general concept sometimes found in Slovakia today is a theory of Slovakia forming a *neutral zone*. In the time before January 1993 when Slovakia's independence was being formed, this idea appeared among some Slovak intellectuals.[4] This concept is another example of an attempt to solve the far larger problem of the whole Central European region, and solve it in such a way that Slovakia is supposed to play a key role. In 1989 and just after, when the former bipolar world was breaking down, the concept of neutrality was very appealing and vivid for many people. Later, there was an effort to revive this concept and apply it to independent Slovakia.

This effort was nothing more than an attempt to preserve an East–West division, even after the decline of the Eastern bloc. The concept suggested the forming of a Central Europe including Slovakia that would be "nuclear free" and demilitarized. In fact this was one of Moscow's dreams in the time when the Soviet bloc existed. Today, when the major Central European countries are exerting every effort to become incorporated into Western Europe, the idea of Slovakia being a neutral zone does not seem very relevant. It should be emphasized that this concept has been fully abandoned by security theorists in Slovakia, and has never played a serious part in the official thinking on which Slovakia's foreign policy is constructed. Since the first moment of independence, the orientation to the West has received the clear priority.

In the last several years, some Slovak theoreticians have given attention to a third idea, a concept of a *buffer zone*.[5] With regard to the two nuclear powers to the east, Russia and Ukraine, Slovakia has one great problem. It borders on Ukraine. Unfortunately, Slovakia is not the only post-communist Central European country that has a common frontier with this new nuclear power. Poland and Hungary also have such a frontier, and so does Romania. In Slovakia, an idea has appeared that Slovakia, at least, could play the extraordinary role of being a buffer zone for Western Europe. Indeed, in this conception the whole tier of post-communist countries bordering on Ukraine would fulfill the function of a buffer zone between the West and the incalculable two nuclear powers of the East. According to this thinking, such a zone could serve as a factor for stability, because it would prevent any direct contact between two political and military blocs that once were hostile. Furthermore, in some possible future conflict, Slovakia might serve as a first line of defense for the West. For these thinkers, that fact alone should mean that Slovakia should be seen, even today, as having increased importance.

The buffer zone concept has several difficulties. For one, this idea again tries to revive the great East–West division, although the East has collapsed as a cohesive bloc. This idea also assumes, once again, that "Central Europe" is a defined, accepted region in its own right, which it really is not. Furthermore a "buffer zone" can be an insecure and even dangerous place to be. There are many examples in history where a supposed "buffer zone" was sooner or later overrun by one side or the other. Finally, it is inconsistent for Slovakia to try both to be a "buffer zone" and to integrate into the West. Slovakia must do one or the other. It may be reiterated that the thinking of security specialists in Slovakia, and the official thinking that underlies the state's policy, has chosen to integrate Slovakia into the West.

Slovakia's independence

The founding of a sovereign and independent Slovak Republic created a new reality for the Slovak people, one that they have little or no experience of. Until January 1993, Slovakia had always been part of some larger state structure and had never had any sovereignty. There is absolutely no historical experience, of any kind, of Slovakia being an independent actor making its own decisions. Slovakia had first been part of Hungary (within the empire) and then part of Czechoslovakia. Hence independent thinking in security or foreign policy matters never had a chance to develop. In this area there is no tradition to refer to; instead, Slovakia must develop its policy absolutely from the beginning.

Slovakia is developing its security and foreign policy on the basis of its analysis of the European and world situation as a whole. Here we describe briefly the main elements of Slovakia's thinking.

Basic elements of security and foreign policy

After the breakdown of the bipolar global order, the world is undergoing a redistribution of power. We see the rise of a new international political system and of new institutional expressions of it. Naturally, Slovakia's security position can only be understood in the context of the security situation of Central Europe as a whole. From there, one must go on to consider the situation of all of Europe, and further, the system of global security. Slovakia must consider this entire context in order to comprehend and develop its own security and foreign policy interests.

The basic goals of Slovakia's security and foreign policy are two. One is that Slovakia seeks to become integrated into the Western political, economic, security and military structures. The other is, naturally, to build good relations with Slovakia's neighbors.

Slovakia seeks to find its natural place in the broader European framework. Together with the other three Visegrad countries, Slovakia aims to achieve its natural position in the European-Atlantic system. We have already explained how this goal is a natural one in the tradition of Slovak political thought. Slovakia's history and small size lead naturally to a defensive view of security affairs, and Slovakia naturally desires the protection that would be gained by being part of existing European structures. Slovakia's view of those structures is discussed later in this chapter.

Slovakia has favorable preconditions for friendly relations with its neighbors, and does not and cannot represent any threat to them. In population, Slovakia is the smallest country in its immediate region. The Slovak Republic has a population of about 5.3 million. The population of Austria is some 7 million, and of Hungary and the Czech Republic about 10 million each. Poland and Ukraine, of course, are much larger. Furthermore, Slovakia has no claim on any territory belonging to any neighbor. Slovakia has never been a hegemonic state, holding or claiming broader territories; on the contrary Slovakia historically has been a land held by others. Since achieving independence, Slovakia has in fact had no serious difficulties with any neighbor. Let us briefly consider the particular relationship with each of the neighbors in turn.

The Czech Republic

Slovakia has worked hard with the Czech Republic to ensure a peaceful and relatively easy division of the former Czechoslovakia. Numerous separate agreements have been developed and signed. Today some problems still exist of an economic character, resulting from the differing levels of the two economies in the former CSFR. Certain problems also remain in settling mutual claims and debts. These remaining questions are being worked on intensively, and there is a strong desire in both countries to reach agreements. Final solutions of all problems involving the division of property may be protracted. Fortunately, the two countries have agreed to isolate these negotiations from their overall relationship, a decision that should go far toward ensuring good relations.

Hungary and the Hungarians in Slovakia

The Hungarian minority in Slovakia is by far the largest minority group in the country. There are 600,000 Hungarians in Slovakia, about 11 percent of the country's total population.

Between Slovakia and Hungary there exist certain differences of opinion regarding the status of the Hungarian minority in Slovakia, and of the

Slovak minority in Hungary. The Slovak people feel serious apprehensions regarding Hungarian revisionism. One political segment of the Hungarian political leadership within Slovakia is advancing ideas that would significantly change the situation, ideas that seem reminiscent of old Hungarian dreams. Part of the political leadership within Hungary itself seems to share these ideas. Slovak concerns are regularly fed by such expressions. Naturally, Slovakia has a vital interest in the inviolability of its frontiers.

In particular, some representatives of the Hungarian minority in Slovakia want to create territorial "autonomy" for some districts located next to the Hungarian border. Slovakia does not accept such a claim, pointing out that the southern regions are not ethnically homogeneous, but a mixed area in which there are approximately equal numbers of Slovaks and Hungarians overall. Despite the concerns, it should be said that this question is considerably less controversial than some analogous problems in several of the European Union countries.

The Slovak and Hungarian sides also differ about the right "methodology" for dealing with the ethnic minority questions. The Hungarian side wants to take a "collective rights" approach. The Slovak side prefers that problems be solved on the basis of each citizen's individual rights.

Reaching a consensus with the Hungarian minority will have a decisive impact on the development of security for the whole region, and on overall stability from Slovakia to Hungary to Serbia. The resolution of the Hungarian minority question is of vital interest for all of Slovakia's neighbors.

In addition to the ethnic issues, there also remain unresolved issues with Hungary regarding the construction of a dam on the Danube River.[6] This controversy has its origins far back in the Soviet era. After 1989, the two new democratic governments agreed to take the issue to the International Court of Justice at The Hague, and are now awaiting its judgement.

Poland, Austria and Ukraine

If we may say that relations with the Czech Republic and Hungary do not contain conflict, but only problems as yet unresolved, then relations with the other three neighbors contain no problems at all. Bilateral cooperation with Poland and Austria is developing normally and positively in every respect. Slovakia's interest in cooperation with Austria will only increase as Austria joins the European Union. Austria will be the only neighbor that is a member of the EU. Austria's experience over the past several years in preparing to join can be a good source of lessons useful for Slovakia, which of course has the same goal.

Ukraine has great importance for Slovakia as an economic partner. Ukraine is the largest and most populous of Slovakia's neighbors. It is also a key intermediary in Slovakia's trade with Russia. Raw materials that are strategically important for Slovakia are imported from Russia through pipelines and other routes passing through Ukraine. If the reliability of these imports should deteriorate for any reason, the consequences for Slovakia could be serious, so Slovakia's interest in positive relations with Ukraine is clear.

Ukraine, in seeking allies, has expressed an interest in developing security relations with Slovakia and other Central European countries. Ukraine offered to Central Europe a security project often referred to as the "Kravchuk plan." The essence of that plan was to bring the Central European countries under the nuclear "umbrella" of Ukraine; its basic intention was to strengthen Ukraine's regional influence against Russia. Slovakia, like other Central European states, has refused this initiative. There is no desire in Bratislava to offend Moscow unnecessarily, and in any case Slovakia's goal is to achieve security guarantees only within the framework of the Western security structures.

Germany and Russia are not immediate neighbors of Slovakia, but for obvious reasons concerning their size and power, they will greatly influence the long-term evolution of security affairs in Central Europe. Hence Slovakia gives serious attention to these two powers.

Germany

Since the early Middle Ages, Germany has been the traditional hegemonic leader in Central Europe. On the positive side, Germany brought much to the region in culture and civilization. On the other side was a recurrent tendency toward military expansion to the east (*"drang nach Osten"*) and toward assimilation of non-German ethnic groups into the German culture. This history does not change the fact that Central Europeans highly appreciated German cultural contributions in the past, and even today nobody doubts their historical cultural mission. In today's Europe, German influence expresses itself primarily in the form of investment capital. In Slovakia and elsewhere in Central Europe, the preconditions are in place for economic integration with German capital. The hegemonic role that German capital would otherwise play is, however, hindered by apprehensions, born of history, that it could lead to another German political expansion.

Following the reunification of Germany, German foreign policy has several options at its disposal. The most probable is an orientation to Central Europe. Indeed, this was anticipated already in the *ostpolitik* that Germany began even in the 1960s. The *ostpolitik* reawakened again the traditional German identification with, and interest in, Central Europe. Today, because of its geographical location and its strong economy, Germany can exercise its Central European option, i.e. the economic penetration of its much weaker Central European neighbors.

In spite of its powerful position, Germany will have to reconcile itself with the knowledge that its cultural and other roles in Central Europe will never again reach the monopoly status that they had at times in the past. There are several reasons for this. One is contemporary worldwide communications. Another is the spread of modern industry to non-European parts of the world. A third is the widespread familiarity of elites in Central Europe with the English language and the cultural influences that are carried by the English language.

The real possibilities for integration between Germany and Central Europe primarily concern economics and security. The concept of former German Foreign Minister Genscher, that the goal is a "European Germany" rather than a "Germanized Europe," meets the requirements of Central Europe. In this context, Central Europeans also appreciate the fact that Germany seeks to develop the ties between the EU and the Central European countries in order to make easier the integration of these countries into the EU. Germany has been quite open about this goal, and also its goal of deepening the security cooperation between the Central European countries and the EU, primarily via the WEU. Naturally these goals support the Central European states' own goals of joining the Western economic and security structures.

Russia

Because of Central Europe's geographical position, its relationship to Russia and to the CIS as a whole is necessarily somewhat ambivalent. Slovakia perceives the reform efforts in Russia in very positive terms. However, the historical experience of the forty years before 1989 suggests a certain caution, which is deepened by the current situation on the Russian political and ideological scene. Future developments in the former Soviet Union generally, and in Russia especially, are somewhat inscrutable. Central Europe lives in a standing fear that neocommunist or nationalist–imperialist forces may prevail in Russia.

Although the Russian political mentality does not bear the brand of Soviet thinking any more, it is far from having accepted Moscow's loss of hegemony in the Central European region. Consider for example the words of Russia's new ambassador to Slovakia, who formerly was spokesman for the Russian foreign minister. After assuming his duties in Slovakia, Ambassador Sergei Yastrzembiyskiy emphasized the importance of Central Europe for Russia in this way: "Russia is still a superpower and has global interests concentrated on the adjacent area . . . on the Central European countries tied to Russia economically . . . We cannot be expected to let these countries go to Western Europe."[7]

Central European specialists agree that Russia will not support the goal of the Visegrad countries, to achieve membership in the Western security, political and economic structures, which can only mean a "Westernization" of Central Europe. Membership of these countries in Western security structures especially is evaluated in Russia as meaning at least the loss of a "security balance" in Europe as a whole, and perhaps an attempt to isolate Russia. It is beyond doubt that Russia does not want the Visegrad countries to become members of NATO or the WEU. Any statements to the contrary are nothing more than propagandistic rhetoric.

This means that, in the final analysis, Central Europe has only two options. Either it becomes an integral part of the West, or it must depend upon Russia (whatever the exact form that dependency may take). While respecting and admiring the reform efforts of the Yeltsin government in Moscow, Central Europeans recognize that Russia's imperial tendencies cannot be reversed by a single act of cultivation by the current state. A long-term, tenacious and patient process will most certainly be needed.

The situation of Russian society today suggests a very low and unstable psychological threshold between two tendencies in Russian thought that have competed with each other for a long time. One is "European–Western"; the other is traditional–authoritarian. If today the imposition of *some* form of "strong government" in Russia is more than sure, the chance that it will have an authoritarian inclination is more than probable. Indeed, it is debatable whether the establishment of Western-style democracy there might lead to the disintegration of Russia itself. The country can be seen as the product of two centuries of imperial policy made by the Russian czars. Can a country made this way last under democracy? To preserve its territorial integrity and to avoid disintegrative processes that already are strong, Russia obviously is in need of some form of authoritarian regime.

However, any shift toward authoritarianism in Russia will produce, sooner or later, a classical expansionist policy. It will be the more expansionist, in proportion to the degree that Russia is unable to cope with its heavy economic and political problems at home. Thus Slovakia and the other countries of the Visegrad Group have compelling reasons to seek security guarantees from the West. For obvious geographical and economic reasons, it is natural for the Visegrad countries, including Slovakia, to be vitally interested in mutually beneficial cooperation with Russia. However, from the political, economic and security point of view these countries want to belong to the West and to its integration structures.

3 European security

It hardly needs to be said that Slovakia is vitally interested in security and peace in Central Europe and in Europe as a whole. Here we discuss first the main regional arrangement, Visegrad, and then Slovakia's perceptions and policies regarding European integration, the Partnership for Peace, and the European Union and WEU.

Visegrad

The original *raison d'être* of the Visegrad arrangement should be remembered clearly. When it was established, the arrangement (then called the Visegrad Triangle or Visegrad Three) included Hungary, Poland and Czechoslovakia. The original reason for establishing it was to facilitate the transition of these "sovietized" countries to the political and economic standards of the West. In no way did any of the three countries regard the formal institutionalization of Visegrad as an alternative to integration into the West.

Today, the official Czech interpretation is different. That interpretation claims that Visegrad was a product of Western policy, from a Western wish that the Central European countries solve their problems themselves, and thus the West would not need to worry about the question of integration. In fact, however, it was actually the West that caused the first impulse to weaken the Visegrad arrangement. At a summit held in Copenhagen in the summer of 1993, the European Community offered expanded cooperation to six post-communist countries – the four plus Bulgaria and Romania. Because the Copenhagen communiqué named these countries individually and did not mention Visegrad at all, the impression was created that, for the West, Visegrad did not exist as a coherent, significant entity. Within the Visegrad Group itself, people who were already pessimistic were inclined thereafter to even greater pessimism about the prospects for mutual cooperation.

Another interpretation has also arisen, this one involving the fact that Slovakia has become an independent state. An idea has begun to take root that there are two groups of states. Poland, Hungary and the Czech Republic are alleged to form a more progressive first group, while Slovakia, together with Bulgaria and Romania, are said to represent a less prosperous group. It is significant that the term that was previously used – the Visegrad Three or Visegrad Triangle – was not automatically replaced, after Slovakia's independence, with the term "the Visegrad Four." An opinion has begun to grow up that Slovakia falls behind the other three countries.

This sense that the Visegrad countries are no longer so clearly a group has also led to another development. At least one capital is now interested in "going it alone." Prague has developed a conviction that the Czech Republic is capable of pursuing alone the road to European integration, and can even benefit by separating itself from the others. Since 1993 Prague has been consistently adhering to this approach. It should also be admitted that to some extent, this belief may be substantiated by developments in the Czech Republic.

European integration

As stated already, integration into the European structures is one of Slovakia's basic foreign policy goals. Slovak views on this question emerged clearly after the parliamentary elections of 1992 (at that time, still the CSFR). Following those elections, the new government of the CSFR was fairly cautious concerning NATO, because attention was soon concentrated on the division of the country. It became necessary to break with the past, symbolized by the single, institutionalized security structures of the CSFR such as the unified Czecho-Slovak Army. After the victory of the independence-oriented forces, it quickly became clear that the basic position that would be taken by the new Slovakia toward European integration would remain unchanged.

As of January 1, 1993, the Slovak Republic became a legal successor, as was the Czech Republic also, to all international treaties that the former CSFR had signed. Meanwhile it had also been decided, as part of the Czecho-Slovak "divorce," that all international agreements should subsequently be renegotiated by both successor states. Since January 1993, the official Slovak foreign policy has clearly been a pro-European one, in terms of security integration as well as other integration. Slovakia has not engaged itself in the controversies between Europe and the United States concerning the presence of American military forces in Western Europe. Slovakia has declared consistently its basic goal. In statements by the foreign minister, the president of the Republic, and the prime minister, Slovakia has stated repeatedly its goal of being incorporated into the European Union as an equal partner.

The same goal applies to NATO. The president of the Republic, as head of state, formally declared Slovakia's intention at NATO headquarters in Brussels in November 1993, and officially applied for the admission of Slovakia into the Alliance.

The Partnership for Peace

A quite new situation was created by the January 1994 NATO summit in Brussels and by the Partnership for Peace, adopted and announced at that time by the NATO heads of state. Although the summit final document reaffirmed that the Alliance is in principle open to membership by additional European states, as provided in Article 10 of the Washington Treaty, it became clear that a NATO expansion to the East cannot realistically be expected in the coming years. The post-communist countries will have to wait several years or more to warrant full membership. Furthermore, the provisions of the Partnership for Peace do not include any "hard" guarantee of security, which Slovakia needs urgently.

However, Slovakia has not hesitated to join in the Partnership, because Slovakia believes that even the inadequate guarantees provided by the Partnership are better than no guarantees at all. Furthermore, the PfP provides at least a common ground where the signatories can meet to discuss any burning security problems, hopefully in time to prevent any outbreak of open conflict. The Partnership also provides some opportunities that can facilitate security for countries that join in it. For example, after an appropriate agreement these countries may send permanent liaison officers to a separate Partnership Coordination Cell. Another, especially significant, example is guaranteed access to technical data regarding interoperability. For these reasons, Slovakia was one of the first countries to join the PfP, and has signed the PfP agreement at the head of government level.

The official Slovak view of the Partnership for Peace program can be summarized as follows. From the beginning, Slovakia has expressed cautious approval of the PfP program. Obviously, the outcome of the January 1994 Brussels NATO summit did not fully meet the expectations of Slovak foreign policy. Although the original goal of becoming a full member of NATO was not achieved, Slovakia accepted "the PfP solution." Naturally, Slovakia accepts PfP as a step toward eventual NATO membership, which remains the goal. Certainly the PfP does not correspond to the original intention and final goal. However, Slovakia understands fully the apprehensions of NATO that quick admission of the former communist states could cause problems. From the PfP framework document, Slovakia draws the conviction that stability and security in the Euro-Atlantic area can be achieved only through cooperation and common action.[8]

Slovakia also accepts the PfP program as a step toward the further deepening of relations between NATO member countries and Slovak society as a whole, including the opposition political elites. These elites also share the values of democracy, respect for human rights and the rule of law. Without any reservations, Slovakia committed itself to the democratic principles stipulated in the Partnership agreement.[9]

The European Union and the WEU

There are several basic reasons why Slovakia is committed to the conception of integration into Western Europe, that is, into the major existing Western European supranational institutions, the European Union and the WEU. First, Slovak foreign policy begins from the assumption that growing integration will be a long-term feature of European development. Second, by participating in this integration Slovakia can achieve, in general terms, the overall level of security that the country highly needs because of the geographical position it occupies. Third, and more specific, through participation in the major Western European institutions relevant to security – the WEU and European Union as well as NATO – Slovakia can expect to gain the explicit security guarantees it urgently needs.

Slovakia anticipates three levels of integration, which are graduated by specificity and geographical scope. The largest and most general level (also the most vague) is the level of pan-European integration. At this level we find the Council of Europe and the OSCE. Slovakia was engaged with these already, through the former CSFR, and has renewed its engagement as an independent country. The next level represents processes involving Western Europe, chiefly NATO, the WEU and the EU. The third level is that of bilateral relations with other countries. In addition to these three levels, Slovakia also remains involved in Central European regional affairs. The Visegrad conception may not have been the last impetus toward coordinating the actions of Central European states in foreign and security affairs. Nonetheless, it should be emphasized that Slovakia regards initiatives like Visegrad only as means to progress toward integration with the West.

The openness of the WEU toward the post-communist countries, as expressed in various declarations, has been welcomed by Slovakia. Of these, the most significant expression so far is the Kirchberg Declaration, issued in Luxembourg on May 9, 1994. In Slovakia's view, there is a straight line to this Declaration, beginning with the WEU Maastricht Declaration of December 10, 1991, and passing through the Petersberg Declaration of June 19, 1992. Each was another step in the progress toward the status of Association with the WEU, declared at Kirchberg, for Slovakia and eight other post-communist and post-Soviet countries.

This status does not bring, of course, any "hard" security guarantee. But there is no possible doubt that the process of integrating the former communist countries into Western Europe has started and is growing steadily. Slovakia's evaluation of the step taken at Kirchberg is very positive.

4   Concluding remarks

In the last decade of the twentieth century, the Slovak people have finally succeeded in taking decisive steps toward the goal they have been seeking for nearly 150 years. That goal is the subtle aim of achieving two things at once: the capacity to decide their own affairs in independence and freedom; and full participation, as an equal member, in a larger entity that can guarantee security. In different ways, earlier arrangements all proved unsatisfactory. Neither the Austro-Hungarian empire, nor the long experiment of a "Czechoslovakia," nor of course the Soviet empire, gave the Slovak people sufficient autonomy to determine their own affairs. The end of the Cold War and of Europe frozen in two blocs offered finally an opening for Slovakia to gain its freedom of action. Not only the Slovak people but also the Czech people deserve credit for the historic fact that, in the 1990s, Slovakia's independence was achieved without great difficulties and without much violence or loss of life.

An independent state is, however, only one of the two Slovak goals. The other now lies before us, waiting to be achieved. Slovakia is fortunate that there already is a large political entity in Europe, in which many free countries participate on an equal basis. Such a thing does not have to be invented; it exists. The European Union is precisely this. Slovakia, already an Associate in the Union, eagerly seeks full membership, which Slovakia is confident will secure the country's future. The military security of Europe is best guaranteed, as Slovakia knows well, through Europe's alliance with North America, the specific form of which is NATO. Slovakia seeks full membership in, and the protection of, NATO, which due to the country's geographical position in an unstable region is much needed.

Of course Slovakia is fully ready to fulfill the obligations of membership in the EU and NATO. It is recognized that, for various reasons, full membership may not be achieved immediately. In the meantime, Slovakia will welcome the various forms of tangible and intangible support and participation that the EU and NATO can provide. Slovakia naturally also seeks excellent bilateral relations with all its neighbors, and with all countries in its region, definitely including Russia and Germany. Slovakia desires, and will do its best to achieve, a full resolution of any and all questions with Hungary and the Hungarian people on a fair and equitable basis.

Slovakia is now well-positioned in its Central European environment, consistently seeking good relations with all neighbors. Slovakia seeks admission to the European economic and security groupings along with, and not separated from, the other countries of the Visegrad Four. Incidentally, Slovakia does not exclude the admission of Slovenia to the Visegrad Group. Any misunderstandings among the Central European countries in the future could be easily avoided by employing the common procedures of the Visegrad countries. Slovakia sees a common approach by the Visegrad countries to the transformation of post-communist Central Europe as the most promising approach.

Slovakia is a new country in Europe, but the Slovaks are certainly not a new people. The Slovak nation knows what place and position it desires in Europe. The country has set definite goals and will work to achieve them. Slovakia looks forward eagerly to the day when, as a full and equal member of the European Union, Slovakia can determine its destiny with security. On that day, it will have achieved both of the two great goals that Slovaks have sought for so long.

Notes

1 For example, Jan Palarik and Jozef Viktorin were members of the so-called "New Slovak School" which advocated this after 1867. In the period shortly before World War I, a group of Slovak intellectuals called the "Belvedere Workshop" argued that the Austro-Hungarian empire should be replaced by a "Danubian empire" which would be a federation of fifteen "semi-sovereign" states, Slovakia being one of the fifteen. Milan Hodza, mentioned in the next note, was a member of the Belvedere Workshop.

2 Milan Hodza, a Slovak who was the last prime minister of Czechoslovakia

(1935–38), subsequently advocated a "Danubian Federation" including Slovakia. See his book *Federation in Central Europe* (London: Jarrolds Publishing Co., 1942). Another prominent Slovak who thought along similar lines was Stefan Osusky. He was Secretary-General of the Czechoslovak delegation to the Paris Peace Conference after World War I, and one of the co-founders of the League of Nations. He too wrote during the World War II years of the need for a more independent Slovakia, more equal to the Czech lands.

3 This conception is vivid in some cultural journals before the split of the CSFR, notably *Literarny Tyzdennik*.

4 See, for example, the discussion in the quarterly journal *Medzinarodny Otazky* during 1992.

5 See, for instance, Pavol Zatlkaj, *Geopoliticke postavenie Slovenska*, especially section 1.3 (Bratislava: Military Pedagogical Academy, 1992).

6 The name of the dam is *Gabtchikovo* in Slovak and *Nagymaros* in Hungarian.

7 Quoted in *Rossiya* (Moscow, July 21–27, 1993).

8 See Article 2 of the *Partnership for Peace Framework Document*.

9 Again see Article 2 of the *Partnership for Peace Framework Document*. "Opposition political elites" refers to the elites of the political parties that were in opposition to the ruling government coalition at the time that Slovakia signed the PfP. No opposition parties opposed this document.

12

Hungary

Janos Matus BUDAPEST

1 Introduction

Background

Like other former members of the Warsaw Treaty Organization, Hungary found itself in a completely new strategic situation at the beginning of the post-Cold War era. Three elements of the new situation were fundamental. First and most basic of all, Hungary recovered its national sovereignty and its independence. Soviet troops began withdrawing from Hungary and their withdrawal was completed by the end of June 1991. Second, the principal international structures to which Hungary had belonged for more than forty years collapsed. Both the Warsaw Treaty Organization and the Council on Mutual Economic Assistance (CMEA) vanished. Third, Hungary's neighbors changed. Not one but three multinational countries on Hungary's borders soon disintegrated – the Soviet Union, Yugoslavia and Czechoslovakia. As a result, Hungary has found itself with no less than five new neighbors: Ukraine, Yugoslavia proper, Croatia, Slovenia and Slovakia.[1] The importance of Hungary regaining its sovereignty and independence cannot be overstated. Nothing is more fundamental to a state than whether it can make its own decisions. With the partial exception of the period between the world wars,[2] Hungary had not been an entirely independent and sovereign country for 500 years!

Options at the time of transition

When Hungary gained the ability to choose its own directions, most citizens agreed that, in internal affairs, Hungary should aim to become a democracy and to have a market economy. It was less obvious what to do about Hungary's international relations. Several choices were possible.

Discussion about the possibilities had begun even before the great changes of 1989 and 1990. As early as February 1989, Soviet leaders gave

signals suggesting that Hungary might leave the Warsaw Treaty Organization without posing a threat to the Soviet Union. An intense debate started
among specialists, officials and other Hungarians about Hungary adopting
neutrality. Many felt it to be an attractive option. At the beginning of the
1956 revolution the government, headed by Imre Nagy, had withdrawn
from the Warsaw Treaty and declared neutrality. To do something similar
again was an obvious possibility.[3]

People in favor of neutrality also raised attractive analogies. Austria,
located right next door and so closely part of Hungarian history for so long,
had been politically and militarily neutral for decades. Finland had also long
been a neutral country. The Finns are the only people who are ethnically
related to Hungarians, even if the relationship is distant. Hungarians'
special feelings about Austria and Finland for these historial and ethnic
reasons naturally drew people's attention to those countries' policies.
Furthermore, Austria and Finland had developed prosperous economies and
stable, democratic political systems during the decades of their neutrality.
They were also part of the Western world in non-political respects. For
Hungarians at this time, a deeper motive underlying the interest in neutrality was a desire to move cautiously away from Soviet domination and to get
closer to the West. Naturally this could not be said openly at the time.

However, the idea of neutrality was not welcomed by everyone. Particularly among the community of foreign affairs specialists, people raised three
arguments against any rapid movement toward neutrality. First, the talks
between the Warsaw Treaty Organization and NATO on the reduction of
conventional weapons in Europe (CFE) were beginning to show signs of
possible success. A number of specialists believed that if Hungary withdrew
unilaterally from the Warsaw Treaty, it could endanger the CFE talks.[4]
They also argued that the Warsaw Treaty Organization would collapse
soon anyway and there was no need for Hungary to hasten the process.
Some specialists also still believed that such a decision would anger the
Russians, although others were certain that people close to Gorbachev had
given clear signals that Hungary now had a choice.

The second major argument against neutrality, already embraced by a
few specialists, was that it might impede a much greater movement by
Hungary toward the West that might become possible soon. These specialists foresaw that possibility of Hungary joining the European Community,
and conceivably even NATO, sometime in the future, and feared that if
Hungary declared itself neutral it might then find these goals more difficult.
These specialists were informed about Western debates on European issues
such as the enlargement of the EC, in which a country's neutrality was a
specific concern. The barriers to entering the EC that Austria, Finland (and
Sweden) encountered soon after showed that this argument was correct.

Third, strong financial arguments were put forward by the specialists who
opposed Hungarian neutrality. In their view, neutral countries needed to

maintain a strong national defense, as for instance Sweden and Switzerland did. Hungary did not have the economic resources to sustain a strong military.

Discussion, both for and against, neutrality continued during 1989 and 1990. The position adopted by Hungary's last communist government was that Hungary should not make any unilateral move regarding the WTO. Any decision about its future should be made jointly by all its members.[5] This was also essentially the position taken in the spring of 1990 by the first democratically elected Hungarian government. That government, together with the other Central European countries, played an active role in the negotiated abolition of the WTO.

Moscow proposed a bilateral treaty with Hungary, as described in chapter 8. While Hungary naturally rejected any treaty that the USSR would dominate, some Hungarian specialists believed that neutral status for Hungary was desirable even in this context. They pointed out that much of Finland's economic prosperity was based on its strong trade with the USSR. And the Soviet-Finnish special relationship since World War II had not been oppressive to Finland. The Soviets had not intervened in Finland's internal affairs and had placed only moderate and bearable constraints on Finland's foreign policy.

By late 1990, however, neutrality as an option for Hungary was fading. A new general concept was developing for Hungarian foreign and security policy, a concept quite different from neutrality and inconsistent with it. This was the other main option for Hungary besides neutrality. Most basically, the concept was to join the West rather than to adopt some position between West and East. In policy terms, this meant setting, as a fundamental goal, Hungary joining the main Western institutions. Of course the most important of these were the European Community and NATO.

The program of the government elected democratically in the spring of 1990 adopted this goal. This goal was subsequently declared by Hungarian political leaders on many occasions, and official and unofficial consultations were undertaken with the West. Hungary joined the Council of Europe in November 1990, and in December 1991 signed the Treaty of Association with the European Community. That Treaty entered into full force on February 1, 1994 and on April 1, 1994 Hungary applied officially for full membership in what is now the European Union.

The government elected in the spring of 1990 also included membership in NATO on its agenda. The NATO summit meeting of November 1991 in Rome made it possible for this goal to be discussed seriously, and Hungarian leaders declared repeatedly thereafter that this was the country's goal. The crisis in Russia in the autumn of 1993 gave new impetus in Budapest to this intention, and for a while, high hopes were raised in government circles that NATO membership might be achieved in a relatively short time. However, by announcing the Partnership for Peace program in January 1994, NATO signaled that the time for the Alliance's enlargement had not yet come.

There is a general consensus among specialists in Hungary that integration into Western institutions is the only viable option for the country. For years, neutrality has not been discussed as a realistic option. The political parties in Hungary agree that full integration into Western institutions must be Hungary's principal strategic concept. Specialists' views diverge, not about the goal but about the speed and time frame for achieving it that can be expected.

2 The security and foreign policy of Hungary

Introduction

With the elections of spring 1990, a long and complicated period of transition began for Hungary. While some of this transition had already begun, it was the free election of an entire new government that determined definitely the directions of the transition and put it fully into motion. The "triple transformation," discussed in chapter 8, now got under way in earnest.

Meanwhile Hungary's international environment was also changing. The European world does not stand still while Hungary makes its difficult and painful transformations. New situations and problems arise. Fortunately no major, direct military threat to Hungary has arisen or has seemed imminent in the first half of the 1990s. Partly for this reason, the Hungarian public has tended to give its main attention to the acute internal economic and other problems of the country. Naturally, it is the role of specialists and government officials who are responsible for foreign affairs to pay close attention to Hungary's international environment, and to analyze any possible dangers carefully.

Doctrine

In the spring of 1993, Parliament voted to approve two formal documents, the National Security Policy and the Defense Principles of Hungary. The National Security Policy, which is the broader of the two documents, establishes Hungary's national security objectives. There are two principal ones. The first is to seek the full integration of Hungary into Western European institutions. Membership in the major European institutions is seen as the surest and most thorough way of protecting Hungary's security in the future. The second objective is to improve relations with the countries neighboring on Hungary. Good relations with neighbors obviously promotes security. In addition it is explicitly part of this objective that good relations should, as just mentioned, have the result that conditions for the Hungarian minorities in these countries improve. Both the National Security Policy and the narrower Defense Principles document state that Hungary does not consider any country to be an enemy, and the only goal of the Hungarian armed forces is to defend the territory and population of Hungary.

Hungary's armed forces, as everyone knows, are weak and will probably remain so, at least as long as the crisis of the transition to a market economy continues, and possibly longer. For this reason, there is a consensus among specialists and political leaders in Hungary that real security for the country can be found only by joining those international security organizations that can effectively defend Hungary.

The principal security problems of Hungary today

The remainder of this section discusses the three major problems, potential and actual, that have deeply engaged the attention of Hungarian specialists in the early 1990s. Naturally, specialists are well aware of various other potential dangers – for instance, environmental risks and possible migrations from the east – which are discussed elsewhere in this book. But the three topics to be assessed now have dominated Hungary's security agenda in the current period. The order in which they are discussed does not represent their order of importance, about which there might be some disagreement, and in any case their importance cannot be arranged in a precise order because the problems differ in kind. The three are: the civil war raging just over the border in the former Yugoslavia; developments in Russia; and the problem of the Hungarian minorities abroad. It might be noticed that only one of these three, Russia, is a major issue also for the other Central European countries. The other two are uniquely Hungarian problems.

The civil war in the former Yugoslavia

The most immediate external danger to the security of Hungary is posed by the civil war in the former Yugoslavia. The break-up of the former Federal Republic of Yugoslavia did not come as a surprise to most Hungarians (as it did to some Westerners), primarily because there are so many personal contacts, on many levels, between Hungarians and their neighbors to the south. For Hungarians it was clear before the war that differences and tensions, of economic, political and other kinds, were growing in the former Yugoslavia.

To specialists it also was clear that the overall withdrawal of Soviet power from Central Europe, and the huge political changes in the region that followed, were giving a strong impetus to forces of divergence first in

Slovenia and Croatia. More precisely, these changes were allowing the forces of divergence, which had always been latent, the opportunity to come to the surface. Simultaneously, growing nationalist feelings in Serbia aimed at strengthening Serb domination of the Federation, and thus further alienated the other nationalities. When US Secretary of State James Baker traveled to Belgrade in June 1991 and spoke about preserving the unity of Yugoslavia, most Hungarian experts found his remarks unhelpful and, indeed, misplaced. These remarks amounted to direct US encouragement to the Federal Yugoslav Army to use force in defense of the unity of the country. A couple of days later the Federal Army attacked Slovenia and later Croatia.

For Hungary, the first consequence of armed conflict over the border was an influx of refugees from Yugoslav territory. Most of the refugees coming to Hungary were ethnic Hungarians, part of the large Hungarian population living in Vojvodina. This district, part of the northern area of Yugoslavia since World War I, had formerly been part of the kingdom of Hungary. The Hungarian population of Vojvodina was approximately half a million. At the time refugees from Yugoslavia began arriving, other refugees, also ethnic Hungarians, were already arriving from Romania because of the oppressive policy of the Ceausescu regime then in power. The flood of refugees from Yugoslavia thus added to a burden already growing.

Between 1988 and 1992, a total of about 100,000 refugees arrived in Hungary, an immense burden on a small country that was in a deep economic crisis. Hungary did not have the social mechanisms needed to cope with refugees on such a scale, which meant that substantial money had to be found to create some way of receiving these people. This by itself produced a major problem for a state that, at the time, was in its most sensitive period of political change. In addition, any influx on a mass scale into a small country threatens political, economic and social stability. An influx of this magnitude therefore unavoidably becomes a security problem of a kind.

The problem of incoming refugees may persist for a long time, especially as the civil war in the former Yugoslavia drags on endlessly. Even an end to the fighting would not necessarily solve the problem soon. For several reasons, many of the refugees cannot return home. The houses of some families have been destroyed in the war, so there is no place for them to return to. Many other houses that belonged to, and legally are still owned by, Hungarians have been occupied by other refugees from elsewhere in the former Yugoslavia, such as Bosnia. Many of the Hungarians who are young men cannot return because they escaped to avoid being drafted into the Yugoslav Federal Army.

The civil war also creates a second security problem for Hungary. This problem has not proven too serious yet, but it could grow much greater, perhaps quickly. That is the danger of a military spillover of the fighting. In politico-military language it is a direct danger of "horizontal escalation."

In the first phase of the war, when the Yugoslav Federal Army – which in fact was a Serbian Army – carried out military operations in Croatia, its military aircraft violated Hungarian airspace on a number of occasions. Once, a bomb was even dropped on a small Hungarian town, Barcs, near the border. On several occasions, small groups of armed people crossed the border and came on to Hungarian territory. It is difficult for Hungary to judge whether such incidents are truly accidents and mistakes, or deliberate acts that can be passed off as accidental or unauthorized.

One of the most significant facts of the war in the former Yugoslavia is the lack of centralized control over large numbers of military units and of huge stockpiles of weapons and ammunition. This by itself makes the question of incidents more difficult. For instance, an incident on Hungarian territory may indeed be unauthorized by higher officials, while being deliberate by local commanders. The fact that local commanders are not under firm central controls creates an ongoing security danger for Hungary. And of course Budapest cannot predict when the next violation of airspace or the border may occur.

There is a third major consequence for Hungary of the civil war in the former Yugoslavia. It has imposed substantial economic losses. Early in the war, an oil pipeline connecting Hungary to the Adriatic coast, through Yugoslavian territory, was damaged and then shut down. There is no other pipeline from Hungary to the Mediterranean, which meant that direct shipment of oil from the Middle East became impossible.

The greatest economic losses for Hungary have been caused by the United Nations' embargo on Serbia–Montenegro. The Hungarian government supported the UN decision and has done its best to help implement it. However, as a result of the UN embargo a number of Hungarian firms lost their markets, and thus their export earnings. In addition, Hungarian transporation companies who had been shipping large amounts of cargo through Hungary to Yugoslavia lost these earnings.[6] To the end of 1994, the total economic losses exceeded US $1.5 billion. This is a major loss for a small country that is in the midst of a profound economic transformation, which is proving more difficult than expected.

In spite of the costs, Hungary has supported the tightening of the UN embargo. In May 1993 Hungary signed an agreement with the Western European Union, to cooperate in controlling shipping on the Danube River. The WEU sent motor boats and customs officers to Hungary for enforcement. While continuing to support the embargo, Hungary has also applied to the United Nations for financial compensation for its losses. As of the beginning of 1995 there has been no positive reply.

In addition to this discussion of specific problems created for Hungary by the civil war in the former Yugoslavia, some more general observations should be made about Hungary's relationship to this war. The most basic concerns the perceptions of legitimacy. The general feeling of the Hungarian public has been that the different nationalities that previously were joined together in Yugoslavia have a right to self-determination, and that they may legitimately break away from the federal state. This also has been the official position of the Hungarian government. At the same time, Hungary has tried to be careful to take no sides in the conflict.[7]

The caution that Hungary has shown in Yugoslav affairs is demonstrated by the fact that Hungary gave official recognition to the new states of Croatia and Slovenia only after the European Community did so, in January 1992. Extreme caution has also been shown in military affairs. Hungary took the position that the violations of its airspace by the Yugoslav Federal military were unintentional. This also was the position taken when the bomb was dropped on the Hungarian town. Furthermore, a direct communications channel was established between the General Staffs of the two armies (Hungarian and Yugoslav Federal), and explanations from the Yugoslav side about border violations have been prompt. These things have been helped by the fact that good relations between the two militaries have been encouraged by their close links established in the past.

Hungary's posture toward the war raging beyond its southern border entered a new stage in January 1993. Hungary signed an agreement with NATO allowing NATO to fly its AWACS aircraft in Hungarian airspace. The AWACS planes control the NATO warplanes flying over Yugoslavia, which enforce a United Nations resolution that prohibits any flights by "Yugoslav" (that is, Serbian) Air Force planes over Bosnia. In Budapest, some Members of Parliament criticized this agreement as being a violation of Hungarian sovereignty. But most political leaders and most Hungarian specialists supported the agreement as one that would enhance Hungary's security. It strongly demonstrates Hungary's support of the United Nations, which besides being the right thing to do could also be beneficial to Hungary in the future. At least equally important, it strongly demonstrates Hungary's support of NATO and it creates a link to NATO.

Developments in Russia

The future of Russia is a question of fundamental importance for Hungary, as it is for all of Central Europe. The huge size and immense military power of a country so close to Hungary means that Russia's intentions must always be a basic factor in Budapest's thinking. Naturally, Hungary hopes for success for the reform efforts in Moscow aimed at developing a more democratic political system and a market economy. Any unfavorable internal developments in Russia would be sources of great security concern for Hungary. A failure of democratic transformation would unavoidably lead to the emergence of destructive, extremist political forces. A prolonged crisis and chaotic situation in Russia would also keep the Central European countries hostage by preventing important strategic decisions about their future status in Europe. Unfortunately, in late 1993 and 1994, trends in Moscow were disturbing for Hungarian specialists. In Budapest's view, elements in Russia that seek a more assertive foreign policy are gaining influence.

Examples of this trend are the publication in November 1993 of the Russian military doctrine and the Primakov Report, discussed in an earlier chapter. Hungarian specialists see these documents and their publication as signs of growing assertiveness by the Russian military and the Russian intelligence/security apparatus. Furthermore it seems clear that these institutions would play a larger rule in any future, less democratic regime in Moscow than they play in the current Russian government. Important questions are raised, therefore, about whether the current government can and wants to continue democratic reforms; about whether it can and wants to establish firm political control over these institutions and reform their ways of thinking; and about whether a pro-democratic government in Moscow can last. These basic uncertainties about developments in Moscow have potentially profound implications for security for all the Central European countries.

Anxieties in Hungary and the other Central European states have also been raised by Russian actions toward other states that formerly were republics of the USSR, and especially toward Ukraine. Most specialists and political leaders in Hungary would like to see Russia show more tolerance and flexibility toward Ukraine, a new state that is experiencing serious problems.

One of the chief tools that Russia has in influencing Ukraine is to reduce or cut off Russian oil and gas supplies to Ukraine. But any disruption could also disrupt the oil and gas that flow from Russia through Ukraine to Hungary and other Central European countries, on which they are heavily dependent. Other important Russian raw materials being traded to the Central European countries also pass through Ukraine.

For Hungary, Ukraine is an important new neighbor. Hungary recognized, and established full diplomatic relations with, Ukraine immediately following Ukraine's independence. Not long thereafter, the two countries signed a bilateral agreement, which has proven mutually satisfactory, regarding the conditions and rights of the Hungarian minority living in Ukraine. In this agreement the Ukrainian government took responsibility for protecting the collective rights of Hungarians in Ukraine, and Hungary committed itself to seek no changes in, and to respect the inviolability of, the Hungarian–Ukrainian border. This provision of the agreement was criticized by some extreme members of the Hungarian Parliament during the ratification process. But the vast majority of the deputies voted to ratify the agreement, which was also approved by a clear majority of the Hungarian public.

For Hungary, Russia poses both a potential danger, if a future Russia should prove aggressive, and also a potential opportunity. A stable, democratic Russia would not only be an important economic partner, but could also play a positive role in another important way. One of the most complicated and difficult problems in the eastern half of Europe is the problem of the national minorities in many countries. Hungary and Russia are similar in one important respect. Both face a situation in which large numbers of their ethnic group live outside the home country, as national minorities in neighboring lands. Hungary and Russia thus share a strong interest in finding good solutions for the protection of national minorities, presumably in the form of some sort of internationally accepted legal framework that would guarantee the preservation of a minority's national identity, cultural heritage, language and other rights.

In 1990, the first freely elected Hungarian government offered friendship and cooperation to the then Soviet Union, with the expectation that the full independence and sovereignty of Hungary would be restored. Since then it also has been Hungary's position that the Soviet Union, and later Russia, should not be excluded from the security order of Europe. In Budapest's view, no general security arrangements for Europe that exclude Russia are either desirable or possible.

In December 1991, when the USSR was dissolving, a new bilateral treaty was signed in Moscow by Hungarian Prime Minister Antall and Russian President Yeltsin. This agreement brought to an end the long and unpleasant episode in which Soviet diplomats tried to get Hungary and the other former WTO states to agree not to join any international organization that the *Soviets* considered to be hostile. The obviously one-sided nature of this demand, and its severe restriction on the Central Europeans' freedom of action, made it unacceptable to most of the Central European states. The new Russian government under Yeltsin dropped this demand, and a reasonable bilateral agreement, establishing normal relations, was quickly signed.

A further positive step with Russia was reached in June 1993, when Hungary decided to accept twenty-eight Russian Mig-29 fighter aircraft, as Russian payment of debts in international trade worth US $800 million. Russia also took on the obligation to provide spare parts for these aircraft, and to train Hungarian pilots to fly them. Discussions also began for a similar arrangement by which Hungary might accept Russian air-defense missiles as payment for some additional Russian debt. The aircraft agreement produced a mutually beneficial solution to the problem of Russian debt to Hungary which Russia was not otherwise in a position to pay. The aircraft agreement and possible air-defense missile agreement are also important to Hungary because air defense is the weakest point in Hungary's defense system. (Air defense in the WTO region had been controlled by the Warsaw Treaty Organization until it vanished, and much of the equipment was removed to the Soviet Union.)

Hungarian political leaders and policy specialists, and also the Hungarian public, genuinely wanted to make a fresh start with Russia, and continue to want good and normal relations with Russia, in spite of the decades of what was, in essence, Russian domination and occupation. With the pro-democratic Russia of Yeltsin, normal relations have proven successful. At the same time, fears naturally persist of Russia again becoming imperialist. The apparently growing influence of imperialist elements in Russia is deepening those fears.

Hungarian minorities abroad

Hungary faces the most difficult situation of any country in Europe, in terms of the proportion of the nationality that lives in the home country compared to the proportion that lives in other countries as minorities. Large numbers of Hungarians live across the southern, eastern and northern borders of Hungary: about 340,000 in the Vojvodina district of Serbia, some two million in Romania, about 600,000 in Slovakia, and about 150,000 in Ukraine.[8] The total of all the cross-border Hungarians comes to roughly one-third of the population of Hungary itself.

In the regions around Hungary, as elsewhere in the eastern half of Europe, there have been tragic episodes through the twentieth century of hostility, conflict and sometimes violence. The rise of nation-based states and, at times, accompanying nationalism, has sometimes created great difficulties, both for the Hungarian minorities in various countries and for other minority groups in the region. More than 10 percent of the population of the whole region is made up of minority groups scattered through most of the countries of the region. Furthermore, Central and Eastern European countries were on different sides in the two World Wars, and this can make the relationship difficult, not only among neighboring countries but also among majorities and ethnic minorities within individual countries.

In the period between the two World Wars, the League of Nations made unsuccessful efforts to give national minorities some protection. Largely due to disagreements and diverging interests among the large European powers, these efforts, like the League's efforts to preserve peace in Europe, were not successful. The rise of Nazi Germany produced an aggressively expansionistic power which was committed not only to extreme nationalism but also to extreme views on all ethnic issues. Resulting events compromised, for a long time, any ability to resolve (and often, even to discuss) ethnic problems. For complicated historical and geostrategic reasons,

Hungary was an ally of Germany in World War II, and this had the long-term effect of worsening the position of the Hungarian minorities in the neighboring countries.[9]

The Soviet Union always considered ethnic issues as potentially explosive, and hence as a potential basic threat to the security of the Soviet state and empire. In Soviet-controlled territories, ethnic questions were simply suppressed. No reasonable discussion of the rights or needs of national minorities was possible, either in the USSR proper or, in the Cold War years, in Soviet-controlled Eastern Europe. This led to an appearance of ethnic calm on the surface. In reality, minorities found it more and more difficult to preserve their heritage, language and identity under the forced and artificial unity of the communist regimes. For decades there was continual suppression of the need, not only of Hungarians but of many peoples living as minorities in various countries, for cultural and national identity. Needs long suppressed will come to the surface even more strongly when the ice finally melts, which is one reason why we see such ethnic turmoil in the eastern half of Europe today. After the Cold War, two multiethnic states, Czechoslovakia and the USSR itself, soon collapsed. A third, Yugoslavia, erupted into war.

The movement toward democracy in the region since 1989 *both* has allowed countries to express more freely the national feelings of their majority population, and *also* has allowed minorities in many countries to express their own needs and interests more freely. Of course these two trends directly clash with each other. This is why greater democracy does not produce more ethnic peace in the short term. In the short term it gives all parties freedom to express their own ethnic and national desires. Of course, in the longer term democracy is a necessary condition for working out reasonable accommodations and a general respect for the rights of all.

Hungary's case is complicated by the refugee problem mentioned above. The mistreatment of Hungarians in Romania by the Ceausescu dictatorship before 1989, and the civil war in the former Yugoslavia, have forced many Hungarians to come to Hungary as refugees. Any serious mistreatment of Hungarians in neighboring countries could lead to more mass displacement of populations, and perhaps to a crisis. It is the common interest of Hungary and of the Hungarians abroad that they continue living where they were born and where their ancestors lived. Historical experience shows that enforced mass migration of people causes great hardships and sufferings.

The democratic changes in Central Europe beginning in 1989 made it possible for the Hungarian minorities in the neighboring countries to set up their own political parties and various organizations designed to regain and preserve their Hungarian culture and identity. These efforts produced some disputes with central and regional governments in these countries that represented the national majority. The main disputes revolved around various forms of the language question. One was teaching Hungarian children the Hungarian language in the schools. Another centered on the desire of Hungarians to open universities that would teach in Hungarian. Another was the use of Hungarian in public administration in those districts where Hungarians were the majority. There were heated disputes about the names of the towns and streets in the Hungarian districts. Many streets and even whole towns had two names, a Hungarian name and a name in the language of the country's majority population (Romanian, Serbo-Croatian, Slovak, etc.).

Unfortunately it has proven difficult for people to take a pragmatic approach and reach reasonable accommodations in these matters, for three reasons. One is that the past keeps being recalled. In the tangled history of this region, there has often been conflict and sometimes violence. All parties can find cases, at one time or another over the centuries, of real injustices against themselves. Hence all parties can find ways of using history to feel aggrieved, and to press their claims now.

A second difficulty, already mentioned, is the widespread resurgence of nationalist feelings after such a long period of suppression. Many people understand intellectually that there is a difference between the legitimate need for a cultural and ethnic identity and an extreme nationalism that harms others, but some people find it hard to draw this line in practice.

The third barrier to reasonable agreements is that these issues are very convenient for ambitious politicians. Almost nothing is easier, for a politician who wants to attract attention and to gain more power, than to play on the keyboard of ethnic issues. There are innumerable ways that genuine, but not very serious, ethnic problems can be exaggerated and distorted by politicians to make them seem big threats, which in turn will naturally arouse heated feelings.

An especially dangerous, yet easy, step both for ambitious politicians and for extreme nationalists is to claim that Hungary wants to change – that is, to enlarge – its borders. This is a sinister step that is almost guaranteed to arouse hostile feelings against both Hungary and the Hungarian minorities in the neighboring lands. Once hostile feelings are aroused, they can be channeled into actions that restrict and violate the rights of the Hungarian minorities. In principle, this claim that someone else wants to change the borders is a game that can be played in many countries in the eastern half of Europe, and we do see it from time to time in various places. But this move is especially easy to make against Hungary and Hungarians, because the Hungarian minorities outside Hungary are so numerous, and also because the enormous reduction in the size of Hungary made by the Trianon Treaty in 1920 makes it easy for people to believe that Hungary might wish to regain old lands.

The enormously complex mosaic of the areas where different nationalities live, in the eastern half of Europe, should make everyone cautious about issues of nationalism. Much care is needed in deciding what is honest pride in one's own nation and what is excessive nationalism, and in deciding what demands by one's own group are really justified. Much care is also needed in making claims that some other national group, or home country, is behaving nationalistically or aggressively, or intends to. In this region the peoples are so intermingled that it is wholly impossible to draw political borders to coincide with the boundaries of ethnic groups. Over much of history, different nationalities lived together peacefully. One reason is that the great empires, especially the Austro-Hungarian and the Russian empires, were explicitly multinational empires, where it did not even occur to people to draw maps according to where different nations lived.

In this century, the rise of the *national* state played a role in the worsening of nationalist problems. In particular, any suggestion that the national state should be put above all other political ideas can make national and ethnic problems insoluble. If the concept of the sovereignty of the state is raised too far above the concept of self-determination and rights for nations, then the rights of national groups will inevitably suffer. The way out is for states, even ones in which one national group has a strong majority, to recognize fully the rights of the national minorities living within the state. And of course no borders should be changed.

Unless and until there is some European law or "regime" that can effectively and reliably protect the rights of national minorities, it is inevitable and necessary that the minorities will seek help from their "home country." Thus the Hungarian minorities in the neighboring countries, lacking any way to appeal to a European law and mechanisms for protecting their rights, will look to Budapest to help them. Naturally Budapest must and will try to do so. Of course this should be done without any improper interference in the affairs of the neighboring countries.

The new Hungarian government formed by the free elections in the spring of 1990 included, among its most important foreign policy objectives, the improvement of conditions of the Hungarian minorities abroad. Budapest tried first to do so in its bilateral relations with Ukraine, Romania, the Slovak part of the Czech and Slovak Federal Republic (CSFR) and the Serbian part of Yugoslavia. This effort was successful with Ukraine, as noted above. With the other three, the Hungarian government was not able to achieve its objectives. Subsequently Budapest turned increasingly to international forums such as the Council of Europe and the CSCE, while not abandoning bilateral efforts. There has been some progress through the international forums. But it also has become increasingly clear that there will be, at least for some time, limits to what can be accomplished through them. One reason is that the international forums do not have a clear, enforceable charter of national minority rights. Another is that other countries have different ideas about what constitute fair solutions and even different perceptions of what the problems are. At present, therefore,

Hungary is encountering difficulties in its effort to protect the Hungarians abroad.[10]

During 1993, opposition parties in Parliament criticized the governing coalition for not having done enough to improve relations with the governments of the neighboring countries. Many opposition parties and many specialists believe that good bilateral relations between governments can contribute to creating goodwill and better understanding of the problems in the neighboring countries, among both politicians and the public of the majority nationality. Some in Budapest also want the various Hungarian organizations and parties in those countries to enlarge their dialogue with the organizations and parties of the majority, again in a spirit of improving goodwill and understanding. In the long run, improved understanding among citizens of different ethnic groups is the only real solution for ensuring the rights of all groups.

Unfortunately, the center-right coalition led by the Hungarian Democratic Forum, which governed Hungary until the May 1994 elections, used a vague formula in expressing its attitude about the borders. In the formula, borrowed from the Helsinki Final Act, Hungary said that it "opposes any change of borders by violent means." This wording seems to leave open the possibility that Budapest might like to change the borders by non-violent means. This in turn allows a degree of reasonable ground for suspicion in the neighboring countries regarding Hungary's intentions.

In the May 1994 elections, a coalition of the Hungarian Socialist Party and the Alliance of Free Democrats received the majority of parliamentary seats and formed a new government. The new governing coalition soon made it clear that Hungary is not interested in any change of borders at all. The coalition also adopted a more cooperative and conciliatory policy toward the neighboring countries. Budapest now views the question of the Hungarian minority abroad in the context of good relations with the neighboring countries and their governments. This new stance is creating a momentum toward improved bilateral relations with the neighbors, especially with Slovakia and Romania.

It is clear that the public in Hungary does not wish to see the borders changed by any means, violent or non-violent.[11] Therefore it is politically "open" for the current Hungarian government or a future one to make a firm commitment not to seek any change of borders by any means. Such a commitment is not only desirable for the obvious general reasons; it also can have a specific benefit. As a result of this firm commitment, the neighboring countries should be able to, and should, relax their pressure on the Hungarian minorities. The reason for this is simple. If any neighbor fears that it may lose territory to Hungary in the future, a possible response now is forced assimilation of its Hungarians (making their language illegal, etc.). This response can be seen as a way of defending against future claims to territories where Hungarians are living. But if the neighbor knows that there is no possibility of losing any of its terrority to Hungary, it does not need to fear its own Hungarians, and can more readily respect their rights.

3 European security

Hungary, like other small countries of Central Europe, is able to have only limited means to protect its security. It is inevitable, therefore, that Hungary must place great emphasis on common or collective security and on the organizations that can embody and enforce it. A reliable international security system would be the best guarantee for the security of small countries like Hungary.

Here "security" is not limited to its narrower, military, meaning and the relevant "organizations" are not only military ones like NATO. Security has a number of meanings and a number of organizations might be relevant. The full integration of Hungary into all main Western European organizations has been the chief foreign policy priority for Hungary, but the country has experienced significant differences in the way various Western European organizations have responded. The most responsive was the Council of Europe. Even before the "revolutions" of 1989, Hungary was the first socialist country to be given a special Observer status in the Parliamentary Assembly, in June 1989. Hungary was also the first country of Central or Eastern Europe to receive full membership in the Council of Europe, in November 1990. For Hungary, an active role in the Council of Europe is highly important because the Council is the most active Western European organization in the protection of human rights, including the rights of minorities. For this reason it clearly is in the interest of all Hungarians that the neighboring countries be full members in the Council of Europe as soon as possible, as this can definitely assist in the resolution of minority problems.[12]

A second organization in which Hungary has also enjoyed a measure of success is the EU, formerly the EC. In December 1992 the EC signed Association Agreements with Hungary, Czechoslovakia and Poland, which came into full force in February 1994. The agreements call for these countries to become full members of the EU, although at a time not yet determined. In Hungary's view, the EU will be the most important organization in Europe in the long run, partly because its Maastricht Treaty includes provisions for extending the EU into the domain of security. The Association Agreements also provide a valuable framework in which Hungary can make plans for its economic development and its movement toward full EU membership.

Meanwhile Hungary has been actively seeking membership in NATO. This is a goal that Hungary adopted after an evolution in its security thinking, discussed earlier in this chapter. By July 1990, Hungary's prime minister, Jozsef Antall, declared that Hungary would seek close political and military cooperation with NATO, although full membership was not yet a goal.[13] By 1991, Hungarian political leaders were unofficially exploring, with their Western counterparts, the possibility of membership. Since then it has become generally understood that Hungary is seeking NATO membership, a goal that Budapest has asserted clearly and repeatedly.

The creation of NACC in late 1991 made possible some limited cooperative activities with NATO. And of course Hungary has applied to join the Partnership for Peace.[14] In the view of most Central European specialists, PfP is essentially an attempt to find a creative compromise between the Central Europeans' desire to join NATO and the strong objections of Russia to their doing so.

Hungarian specialists have been following carefully the debate within NATO about its extension into Central Europe, as well as the Russian objections to it. Many Hungarian specialists have been surprised by NATO's responsiveness to Russian objections. They do not understand why Russian fears of NATO's extension should be more respected than Central Europeans' fears of an aggressive Russia. This seems especially surprising because NATO is fundamentally a defensive organization, whereas expansionist and even imperial tendencies in Russia are growing. Also, NATO was expanded earlier, in the 1950s, in spite of vehement Soviet protests, to include Germany. Some Hungarian specialists feel that the NATO refusal to bring in the Central European countries is so unreasonable that these specialists even wonder if NATO has other, unstated, reasons for the continuing refusal.

Hungary much welcomed the change in NATO's position at its December 1994 foreign ministers' meeting in Brussels, where it was declared that the Alliance is open to new members joining and that it will not allow Russia to veto an extension to the East. Budapest hopes that this will continue to be NATO's policy in fact as well as in declaration, in spite of Boris Yeltsin's statement a few days later that a NATO extension could trigger a "cold peace" in Europe.

Opinion can also be found in Hungary that opposes Hungary's membership in NATO, chiefly because of fears that it might prove more expensive than an independent national defense. One party, the Socialist Party, has proposed a public referendum on Hungary joining NATO.

Two other European security organizations have significance for Hungary. Some cooperation has developed with the Western European Union (WEU). It has remained limited, partly because of uncertainties about what the WEU's role is and will be. But it may prove important that the Maastricht Treaty designates the WEU as the military arm of the EU. The WEU has also offered regular consultations on security to Hungary and the other Central European countries. It is worth noting that Russia seems to be less worried about contacts between its "former allies" and the WEU, apparently because Russia sees the WEU as less threatening than NATO.

In the 1970s and 1980s, Hungary was an enthusiastic supporter of the CSCE. The Helsinki Final Act of 1975, especially its "basket" on human rights, was quite helpful to democratic elements in Hungary thereafter, and thus helped lay groundwork for the peaceful revolutions of 1989. In the 1990s, CSCE lost momentum. In Hungary, many experts became disillusioned with the CSCE's complete failure to cope with the wars in the former Yugoslavia. Some felt that these were precisely the kinds of small wars that CSCE was supposed to deal with. Prior to the CSCE summit of December 1994, most Hungarian specialists had come to feel that CSCE was becoming almost irrelevant and unable to deal with Europe's problems, at least its security problems. Government officials also expressed criticism, while in general feeling more optimistic, stressing that CSCE remained the only organization that embraces all European countries and the United States and Canada, something that could give it future potential.

In the early 1990s Hungary was somewhat encouraged by another aspect of CSCE, namely the appointment of High Commissioner of National Minorities. If the High Commissioner's role grows, this office could become a very positive influence in the problems of national minorities. So far, however, efforts have failed to create a Charter for National Minorities. There are disagreements about what such a charter should say, and many governments give this problem only a low priority.

The CSCE, renamed the OSCE, received some new momentum at the December 1994 summit, held in Budapest. Some new expectations were created. The prime minister of Hungary, Mr Gyula Horn, reflected the somewhat more optimistic, if still cautious, mood in his opening statement at the Summit: "The past two years have been characterized by both security and insecurity, progress and sudden standstills, war and peace. I am afraid we will have to come to terms with the perspective that the European situation will continue to be marked by these contradictions for some time to come. It is also a fact, however, that the European states have never had such collective means at their disposal for limiting unfavorable tendencies and reinforcing positive changes."[15]

Different specialists in Hungary have differing views regarding the OSCE summit. The dominant view is that it was partly a success and partly a failure. On the success side, an agreement was reached on future peacekeeping operations in Nagorno-Karabakh. But no agreement could be reached even about a joint statement on the conflict in Bosnia. The atmosphere of the summit was also affected by a clear disagreement in the statements of President Clinton and Russian President Yeltsin. The change in name, on the other hand, may signal a new importance for the OSCE. The Hungarian government, which began a one-year term in the rotating chairmanship, expressed hope that the OSCE will now become more useful for crisis management and crisis prevention.

4   Concluding remarks

In Europe today we see two kinds of excess in national behavior. One, typical in Central and Eastern Europe, is an excessive, touchy and anxious sense of national position and rights. Relationships between different national groups within one country are tense, with each group feeling that the other is demanding too much for itself and is trampling on its own rights. The other excess is found in the behavior of states, and not only in Central and Eastern Europe. Partly for reasons of national pride, states assert themselves and their points of view, in ways that disturb the smooth flow of international relations and that slow down positive processes of integration. The first excess creates sources of potential conflicts and crises. The second impedes the prevention of conflicts and the peaceful management and resolution of crises.

The general impression in Central Europe, certainly including Hungary, is that the states of Western Europe have not committed themselves to the solution of the most fundamental security problems that have resulted from the historic revolutions of 1989. In Hungary there is a widespread feeling that the encouraging words of solidarity and support, received from the West at the beginning of those great changes, have not been followed by practical steps to solve concrete problems.

At present Hungary faces basic problems that are rendered worse by Western inaction. Several may be mentioned briefly. Today's democratic Hungary inherited enormous debts run up by the previous, communist regime. Hungary intends to pay these debts. But to do so, Hungary needs new foreign markets and thus export earnings. The market that was the Soviet Union has collapsed. Meanwhile Hungary's efforts to enter the Western European markets are being deliberately hindered by the EU, which maintains trade restrictions on Hungary and other Central European states.

NATO's continual refusal to admit Hungary and the other Central European states creates, in addition to other difficulties, a simple but basic planning problem for Budapest. Important decisions have to be made about Hungary's military forces. These decisions must consider a time horizon of ten to fifteen years ahead, partly because equipment must be purchased that will be used for that long. But planners do not have the most basic facts they need in order to plan. Will Hungary be integrated into an alliance during that time, or be obliged to rely entirely on itself for its defense? Almost all military decisions hinge on this question.

The Partnership for Peace program may have its own negative effects. Implicitly it creates a kind of competition, since it invites countries to make proposals that will be treated differently. Unless carefully managed, the program could create strong and unhealthy feelings of rivalry among the Central European countries, each trying to get as close to NATO as possible, as rapidly as possible, in the hope of being admitted to full membership soon. However, this danger can be sidestepped if NATO will treat the Visegrad countries as a group.

NATO not admitting Hungary and the other Central Europeans into membership also presents a much more fundamental problem. Those responsible for Hungary's future must ask themselves what it really means when NATO allows Russia's objections to determine NATO's policy. Might the West agree, in the end, to Central Europe returning again into Russia's sphere of influence? Or will the West finally decide to protect Central Europe if and when an expansionist Russia begins to move toward recapturing what it had not long ago? Or there is a third possibility. A continuing stalemate between the West and Russia could leave Central Europe perpetually stranded in limbo, a kind of buffer zone between two great power centers. Such a situation would, of course, leave Hungarians and other Central Europeans in a state of perpetual insecurity and anxiety.

Today one can find three viewpoints among Hungarian specialists on the basic issue of how Hungary can avoid these grim outcomes and find security with the West. One group of specialists believes that, through a series of gradual and practical steps, Hungary will eventually be admitted fully into NATO. Another group believes that sometime in the coming years, something dramatic will happen in Russia which will cause NATO to act quickly to bring in the Central Europeans. A third group does not place its hopes on NATO at all. This group believes that after 1996 the EU will begin to develop a strong security and defense dimension, as the Maastricht Treaty says is the intention. This may provide the best answer for Hungary's security, assuming that Hungary does become a member of the European Union in the next five to ten years.

Even under these optimistic scenarios, the next few years seem likely to be an insecure, perhaps anxious, time for Hungary. None of these three favorable outcomes is certain. The grim possibilities are also quite real; Hungary could be left in limbo between East and West, or even fall again under the Russian shadow. During the coming years, Hungarians will be caught between strong hopes and strong anxieties. The future will unfold through events that are almost entirely outside Hungary's control. And in the meantime, Hungary lives in a kind of vacuum, able to rely on nobody for its security.

Notes

1 Yugoslavia proper is often referred to as Serbia or Serbia-Montenegro. The Czech Republic is also a new state resulting from the split of Czechoslovakia, but the Czech Republic does not border on Hungary.

2 One must say "partial" exception because Hungary's freedom of action in the period immediately following the Treaty of Trianon was extremely limited. A country that had not been self-governing for centuries had to face, quite suddenly, the political, economic, moral and psychological consequences, not only of a disastrous defeat in a great war, but the loss of two-thirds of its territory and one-third of its population. Furthermore, several of the neighboring countries soon formed a hostile alliance, called the "Little Entente."

3 Professor Oleg Bogomolov, at that time Director of the Soviet Institute of Socialist World Economy, said in an interview in February 1989 that if Hungary were to leave the WTO the security of the Soviet Union would not be threatened. *Magyar Hirlap* (February 18, 1989).

4 Statement by Gyula Horn, Foreign Minister of Hungary, *Magyar Hirlap* (April 25, 1989).

5 Statement by Prime Minister Karoly Grosz, *Magyar Hirlap* (March 25, 1989).

6 The largest loser has been the Hungarian state railways.

7 However, an unfortunate incident caused tensions in the Hungarian–Serbian relationship in the autumn of 1990. Hungary sold 10,000 guns to the Croatian police forces, from the stocks of a dissolved Hungarian workers' guard. The Hungarian side considered this to be a normal business transaction, but Serbian politicians perceived it as support to the secessionist Croatian forces.

    Serbia's perception of Hungary has also been influenced by an important fact of history. Croatia and Hungary were parts of the same state – the Austrian empire – for 800 years. Croatia became part of "Yugoslavia" only at the end of World War I, when Yugoslavia was created. When the disintegration of Yugoslavia began in 1990, several Hungarian officials made unfortunate statements that put emphasis on the historical connection between Hungary and Croatia. In Belgrade this may have created an impression, which was not intended, that Hungary actively supported the separation and independence of Croatia. Since then, Budapest has been careful to demonstrate neutrality.

8 The number of ethnic Hungarians living in Vojvodina used to be somewhat larger; the number has declined as a result of people leaving the former Yugoslavia because of the wars.

9 One very readable brief history of Hungary in the English language is *The Corvina History of Hungary*, ed. Peter Hanak (Budapest: Corvina, 1991).

10 On May 1, 1994, Prime Ministers Peter Boross of Hungary and Joseph Moravcik of Slovakia met and reached agreement to make new efforts to improve the situation.

11 This has been reported, for example, by the public opinion research conducted by the Security for Europe Project. See chapter 3 here, or the *Final Report* of the Security for Europe Project.

12 Czechoslovakia as a united country became a member of the Council of Europe in February 1991. After its division, the Czech Republic and Slovakia applied

for membership individually, and each was accepted in June 1993. Romania became a member in October 1993.

13 This announcement was made during Prime Minister Antall's first visit to NATO headquarters in Brussels.

14 Hungary signed the "framework document," the basic first step toward joining PfP, in February 1994.

15 From the Hungarian Foreign Ministry press statement *Current Policy*, no. 1994/19.

Part IV

Ukraine: public attitudes and expert assessment

Public attiudes in Ukraine

Nikolay Churilov and Tatyana Koshechkina KYIV

Introduction

Ukraine is a new state on the map of Europe and also, in a sense, an ancient state. Its capital, Kyiv, was also the capital of the great land of Kyivan Rus in the Middle Ages. The realm of Kyivan Rus lasted for centuries. Kyiv was a glorious center of Slavic civilization and of Orthodox Christianity at a time when Moscow was a tiny unknown village. But then Kyivan Rus was overrun and conquered by the invading Mongols in the thirteenth century. Later, most of the regions around Kyiv were held by the Polish–Lithuanian empire.

As time passed, that empire was partly pushed back, and some regions gained independence and self-rule. Help was sought from Moscow, particularly an alliance signed in 1654 by the military hero Bohdan Khmelnytskyi. But Moscow, now rapidly rising, sought to expand its own rule southward as it helped push out the Poles and Lithuanians. Over the next century the czars consolidated their control and "the Ukraine" became part of the Russian empire. Thereafter, many people born throughout the empire were taught to believe that a Ukrainian was a kind of Russian.[1]

Ukrainians tried to create a Ukrainian state in 1917–1921, during the chaos surrounding the end of the empire and the birth of the Soviet Union. The effort was snuffed out by the Soviets.[2] With the end of the USSR came a more successful attempt. Three days after the aborted coup in Moscow in 1991, Ukraine declared its independence (on August 24).

For the people of Ukraine now, life in an independent, sovereign state is a new experience. It is a new experience in a profound sense that might not be easily understood by people who have lived in their own countries for a long time. It cannot be expected that the public in Ukraine as yet grasp deeply all the implications of living in a self-governing country that must make its own decisions. After so many centuries of having their affairs entirely controlled by others, people cannot shift quickly and completely into an emotional stance of self-confidently making their own independent decisions.

On many questions facing Ukraine today, large parts of the public do not necessarily have well-formed, firm attitudes. Of course there are various political parties and other political groupings that have sharply defined positions. But these groups are small compared to the whole of society, much of which has not yet fully made up its mind on many topics. Nonetheless, a number of public attitudes exist that can be identified and described. Although the main subject of this book is foreign affairs, the internal crisis in Ukraine today is so central for the public that we must begin with some brief remarks about it, before turning to the external topics.[3]

1   Internal insecurities

For the public, no other topic in Ukraine's affairs even remotely approaches in importance the country's internal crisis and in particular its economic crisis. Especially in 1993 and since, the economic crisis of Ukraine has been so deep, and public anxiety about it so enormous, that no other subject can compare.

Industrial production in Ukraine fell nearly 20 percent in 1993 and more than 30 percent further in 1994. Meanwhile the currency in people's pockets became rapidly more worthless. During 1994, inflation raged at about 400 percent annually; just before, in the second half of 1993, it skyrocketed to well over 100 percent *per month*. At this rate, any quantity of money loses more than half its value in a month. No brief reference to a few statistics such as these can adequately communicate the toll in human suffering caused by the ever-deepening economic collapse. The point need not be belabored here. What many call an economic disaster is *the* preoccupying issue for the public in Ukraine.

Under such conditions, it is not surprising that Ukrainians are fearful for the future and are deeply pessimistic. People are desperate for an improved, or at least a stabilized, economic situation; simultaneously they do not expect to see it, but rather expect things to continue to worsen.[4] There was an upsurge of hope when a new president was elected in July 1994, but thereafter the mood gradually returned to its previous pessimism, especially after unpopular price increases in November of that year. In an annual survey conducted at the end of 1994, 49 percent of the public expected that 1995 would be worse.[5] In addition to anxiety and pessimism, a mood of uncertainty pervades most social topics. For the public, the situation is so difficult, the government so paralyzed, and the issues so ill-defined, that many people find it hard to form a definite opinion or expectation on many questions.

In addition to the presidential election of July 1994, a new Parliament was elected in separate elections in March 1994. Nearly every party and candidate running in the parliamentary elections promised to address the country's economic plight, but in general the public did not believe that the parties or the state are actually able to do so. There are about thirty political parties registered in Ukraine, but none of them have solid, substantial popular support. None present a program that arouses enthusiasm among a much-abused public.[6]

Ukrainians are well aware that a desperate economic situation breeds other social disorders. People fear soaring crime. The extent of the fear can be judged by this: when asked by a public opinion research organization a standard social research question, "What appliances do you have in your home?" the number of people who refused to answer soared during 1993. They refused to answer because they did not want anyone to know that they have something in their home, such as a refrigerator, that might be worth stealing.[7]

Anxiety about organized crime – "mafias" – is another part of the public's worry and pessimism. Especially in urban areas, much of the public knows or assumes that mafia organizations are playing a powerful and central role in society.[8] While much of the organized crime is thought to be Ukrainian, people are becoming increasingly aware that mafias from Moscow are interlaced with, or perhaps sometimes controlling, the local mafias. There is also growing public concern about "foreign mafias," mainly from the Caucasus region.

The environment

In addition to the enormity of the economic decline, Ukrainians are anxious also about the environment. Perhaps the chief reason is Chernobyl. Chernobyl is in Ukraine, and the serious nuclear power plant accident there in April 1986 had its worst consequences in Ukraine. The crisis had an enormous emotional impact which is still felt today. Lives were lost; all people living in a large area around the plant had to be evacuated; livestock in the region had to be killed; considerable farmlands had to be abandoned. For Ukrainians, the disaster is not merely an event in the past. Cancers and other illnesses are appearing now, and will continue to appear, which both doctors and the public feel sure are consequences of Chernobyl. At the same time, Ukraine is so poor and so much in need of electrical energy that many people feel that the Ukrainian nuclear power plants must continue to run.[9] Since they are running but are accident-prone, another accident could happen at any time. The anxiety, also felt elsewhere in Europe, that there may be another nuclear disaster, is felt even more keenly in Ukraine.

Public anxiety about nuclear accidents and nuclear radiation also has another source. There have been reports in the media that nuclear waste products from Western Europe are being shipped to Ukraine for storage.

Ukrainians feel that they are being exposed to radiation risks that Western Europeans will not accept for themselves.

The public has also heard reports and rumors of chemical and other wastes being shipped from Western Europe to Ukraine. Exact and reliable information is not publicly available, so people are unsure how much waste is arriving. There is a general public feeling that Ukraine is being turned into Europe's rubbish dump.

The public also understand that Ukraine's own industries are environmentally unsafe. In Ukraine, as elsewhere in the Soviet Union and in Soviet-controlled Eastern Europe, planners of factories, mines, etc. sought mainly to maximize production and paid almost no attention to environmental consequences. The public know that by now large areas have been ecologically damaged – but how large, how seriously and with what consequences for human health is unclear. An example drawing increased attention is pollution from the Odessa oil terminal.[10] It is not unusual in Ukraine for even the drinking water to be questionable.[11] There was a cholera epidemic, primarily in southern Ukraine, during 1994, which was probably related to the drinking water. People have the feeling of being surrounded by unseen health hazards and that a major disaster could happen anytime. Yet the public understand that Ukraine also is so poor that not much can be done about it quickly.[12]

2   Russia

For the public in Ukraine, Russia is by far the most important factor in Ukraine's relationship with the external world. Nothing else in the country's external affairs commands nearly as much public attention. The subject is made still more important, as well as more complicated, by the fact that a large number of ethnic Russians live in Ukraine. Topics involving Russia and Ukraine's relations with Russia on the one hand, and the position of Russians (and Russian culture) within Ukraine on the other, are intertwined for the public. Various specific topics will be discussed here under several headings, but it must be kept in mind that for the public, these topics are intimately related.

Anxiety about Russia

Much of the public in Ukraine feels anxiety about Russia and its possible future actions toward Ukraine. Ukrainians are generally aware that many elements in the current and likely future governments in Moscow, as well as much of the population of Russia, do not accept the permanent existence of an independent Ukraine. Many people anticipate that Russia may be motivated at some point to bring Ukraine back under Moscow's control. This anxiety rose further after the December 1993 elections in Russia that brought the Russian ultra-nationalist Vladimir Zhirinovsky to prominence. Reabsorption of Ukraine is part of the Russian ultra-nationalists' program. Anxiety rose again after the Russian attack on Chechnya, beginning in December 1994.

Future Russian domination of Ukraine could also be a matter of degree. As much of the public in Ukraine understand, the question is not simply one of whether Ukraine will be fully independent or be completely reabsorbed by Russia. There also are various intermediate possibilities, in which Ukraine might have some elements of quasi-independence while Moscow dominates Ukraine in practice.

For some citizens of Ukraine who are ethnic Russians, Russia is not a source of anxiety but potentially of promise. To a greater or lesser degree, depending on the issue and the circumstances, some at least of these Russian Ukrainians may look to Moscow for support in meeting their needs and protecting their interests.

Ukraine's position vis-à-vis Russia

People in Ukraine, even including Ukrainian nationalists, understand that Ukraine is and will probably remain in a position in which it may not be easy to resist Moscow's embrace, for a number of reasons. Obvious ones include the more than three centuries of union, the exceedingly close cultural and ethnic links, Ukraine's economic weakness and the simple facts of Russia's huge size and great power. In addition, the economic situation in Russia is better. Another reason, well known to Ukrainians, deserves particular mention here. Ukraine is highly dependent upon Russia for energy. Ukraine has little oil or gas of its own, and little hard currency to buy oil or gas on the world market even if means of importing it could be developed. Russia has huge quantities of oil and gas and supplies the bulk of Ukraine's needs.

People in Ukraine understand well that in this situation, Russia need not take or threaten military steps against Ukraine. Moscow can simply switch off the energy. Ukraine has hardly any economic levers against Russia that it could use to retaliate, and hence no practical way to deter this kind of Russian action. The public thus feel that their country is already in a subordinate and dependent position vis-à-vis Russia in a basic way that little can be done about.

The general public in Ukraine are also vaguely aware, and educated people quite aware, that Ukraine's entire economy is interlinked with Russia's. For more than seventy years, both were simply republics of the Soviet Union, and the Soviets made and carried out all plans without reference to republic boundaries. The result is that many Ukrainian factories can obtain the supplies and parts they need to operate only from sources that are now located in Russia.

Who is the "minority" in Ukraine?

These material facts about Ukrainian dependence on Russia cannot be entirely separated from some basic social facts. From a purely statistical viewpoint, Russians are the minority (22 percent) and Ukrainians are the majority (73 percent) in Ukraine.[13] Of course the public in Ukraine are aware of these proportions. From an emotional viewpoint, however, many Ukrainians feel that their position is really the "minority" position in society.[14]

During the long Soviet era, the Ukrainian language was discouraged and few schools were allowed to teach in Ukrainian. Partly for this reason, many ethnic Ukrainians are more comfortable speaking in Russian and some speak Russian even in their own homes.[15] Needless to say the ethnic Russians do also. In rural areas, the language of daily use usually is Ukrainian, but in most cities, Russian is the language mostly used. Even government officials in the capital sometimes conduct their daily business in Russian.

The psychological significance of the Russian language for the public goes beyond even this. For generations, everyone in Ukraine has believed that to be "a well-educated person" means to speak fluent Russian. For centuries, all higher education in Ukraine has been in Russian, a situation that is only now beginning to change. When a certain language is so identified with the public's idea of what it means to be educated, that language has a kind of dominance.

In the short time since independence, the government of Ukraine has tried to increase the number of schools teaching the Ukrainian language, and to promote its use in other ways. Ukrainian has been made the official language of the country. But there are few economic resources for building new schools or training teachers of Ukrainian, so it will take a long time for the country's language to come into general use.

The sense that Ukrainian culture is really in a secondary position is increased by profound influences that pour in from Russia via the Russian language. For instance, about three-quarters of the Ukrainian population regularly watches the main television channel of Russia, called Ostankino, naturally including the news. Several leading Russian newspapers are among the most widely read newspapers in Ukraine. Ukrainians are presented on a daily basis with the Russian point of view on events.

For these and related reasons, there is a tendency for Ukrainians to feel that emotionally and socially, they are in the position, in their own country, that somewhat resembles the position generally occupied by a minority group, even though statistically Ukrainians are the majority. There is a common attitude among Ukrainians that if there is any "minority problem" in Ukraine, it is the problem of the Ukrainians' position. For some Ukrainians, this situation is one source of nationalist feelings. Other, less nationalist, Ukrainians feel that after centuries of being part of Russia, the situation is not so unnatural.

The level of nationalist feelings, and of national consciousness, in Ukraine is not constant. It can rise and fall. The extent to which Ukrainians feel a strong national identity is itself a question about which the public are divided. Some feel that national feelings are growing. A larger number of people feel that national feelings were at their height around the time, late in 1991, that Ukraine became independent, and have since declined. One possible reason for decrease could be a growing feeling of dependence on Russia. Social scientists might add that a fresh wave of national feelings could be triggered by certain dramatic events.

Relations between the groups

It might be easy for foreigners to misunderstand the relations between ethnic Ukrainians and ethnic Russians in Ukraine, and to have an exaggerated idea of tensions. At least until recently, most of the time in most places there has been hardly any tensions between the two groups. Citizenship in Ukraine does not distinguish between ethnic groups; both are Ukrainians in the citizenship sense. It is impossible to find any difference in the physical appearance of the two. In urban areas, the two groups are completely interspersed and are often speaking one language. Ukrainians and Russians work and live side by side, often not caring, and sometimes scarcely noticing, who is whom.

This thorough and warm intermingling, especially in urban areas, means that at least until recently, people practically could not imagine violent conflict between the two groups. Merely the idea of violent civil conflict inside Ukraine feels so unnatural that some people feel embarrassed if someone raises the idea. However, tensions rose noticeably in 1994 and some degree of ethnic conflict came to seem more plausible.[16] Even so, almost everyone wants to find non-violent solutions. Most people also find violence between Ukraine and Russia as states hard to imagine.

This set of attitudes exists side by side with Ukrainian resentments. The result is that many Ukrainians experience two sets of feelings. On the one hand, many genuinely feel, resentfully, that in various ways they are living in a subordinate position in Ukraine, and that Ukraine as a country is in a subordinate position vis-à-vis Russia, due to myriad forms of Russian domination that go back centuries. On the other hand, most Ukrainains also feel genuinely that the two peoples are so similar and so intimately bound together that violence must be avoided. Even those Ukrainians who are generally regarded as "strong Ukrainian nationalists," and who are most ready to struggle against "Russian domination," usually agree that the struggle should not descend to violence.

People from both groups also feel that to the extent ethnic conflict could arise in Ukraine, it would probably arise from political maneuvering. Various political leaders, groups and organizations could manipulate some question for their own advantage. Because there is a consensus that the "natural" relationship between Ukrainians and Russians is warm, friendly and not conflicted, people feel that if ethnic tensions do arise over some question, it is because certain forces are manipulating the situation.[17]

Something similar applies to Ukrainians' attitude toward Russia. On the one hand they feel some resentment about Russia's behavior. On the other, many citizens recognize that it might be very convenient for certain political leaders or groups in Ukraine to have an external threat that they can play upon. The complexity of these various public attitudes is amplified by regional differences and by some specific bones of contention.

Crimea and other regional differences

Crimea is attached directly to Ukraine, not to Russian territory, and was formally transferred to Ukraine by Soviet General Secretary Nikita Khrushchev in 1954. However, its population is two-thirds ethnic Russian. Earlier it was populated by Tatars, who were removed by Stalin and are now beginning to return. The complex claims and counter-claims of the Ukrainian, Russian and Tatar peoples to this especially desirable territory have a complicated impact on the feelings of the public of Ukraine as a whole. Ethnic Ukrainians have no doubt that Crimea should naturally belong to Ukraine.[18] But the stronger and deeper feeling across all ethnic groups is that it should be possible to find reasonable and intelligent compromises on any Crimean questions. Crimea is one of the topics that many citizens of Ukraine feel is being manipulated, and heated up, by politicians in various camps to suit their own purposes.

Other important parts of Ukraine also have concentrations of ethnic Russians. Odessa, an attractive coastal city on the Black Sea, is largely Russian. There are other areas in the southern part of the country where the proportion of Russians is somewhat higher than average. Ethnic Russians are especially concentrated in the eastern part of Ukraine, particularly the districts of Donetsk and Luhansk.

Conversely, the western part of the country contains very few ethnic Russians and a high concentration of ethnic Ukrainians. Nationalist Ukrainian groups enjoy their greatest support in this region. A historical factor is also important in understanding this region. A portion of western Ukraine was never part of the Russian empire and was joined to the Soviet Union only in 1939. Previously it had been part of Poland and Hungary, and earlier it had been inside the Austro-Hungarian empire. People in this area are naturally drawing on a different historical experience.

There are regional differences in political attitudes which often reflect differences in ethnic make-up. Speaking in the most general terms, ethnic Russians in the areas of Russian concentration tend to hold the "Russian viewpoint" on issues that are seen as dividing along a Russian/Ukrainian cleavage, while ethnic Ukrainians, especially in areas where they are concentrated, tend to hold the "Ukrainian viewpoint." However, these correlations are only rough; they are subject to variations depending on the issue and on changes over time; and there are many exceptions. People do not always hold attitudes according to their ethnicity. Furthermore, even when some people see a question as dividing along the "Ukrainian/Russian" cleavage, others may see the question in some different way. After the election of Leonid Kuchma as the new president in July 1994, ethnic Russians tended to hold less sharply divergent views, because they believe he is developing a more cooperative policy toward Russia.

Indeed, whether some political or social issue should be seen in ethnic terms is often ambiguous for policy analysts and other kinds of intellectuals, as well as for the public. However, on some current issues, public attitudes generally do divide, at least to a considerable extent, along ethnic lines. One such issue, already mentioned, is the status of Crimea. Another issue that divides this way to some extent, and that involves foreign and security affairs, is the Black Sea Fleet.

The Black Sea Fleet as an illustrative issue

Both Ukraine and Russia have claims on the Black Sea Fleet that formerly belonged to the Soviet Navy, and its disposition is one of the points of contention between the two countries. Public attitudes on this question illustrate well the nature of public attitudes in Ukraine on policy affairs generally.

The most important feature of the public attitude on the question of the Fleet is *not* that the public divides along ethnic lines. To some extent it does, but that division is a weaker feature. The stronger feeling, shared by both ethnic groups, is that a reasonable agreement should be reached. The strongest public attitude is that the issue is not worth a major struggle. Ethnic Ukrainians and ethnic Russians tend to agree that the future of the Fleet is not terribly important for Ukraine, for Russia or for anyone else.

Furthermore, people tend to feel that this issue, like others, is being manipulated and used by politicians on both sides. The Fleet, people feel, has become a "football" being used for the ambitions of various groups in Moscow and Kyiv. A rational and reasonable effort actually to solve the problem is not being tried, because the struggling political forces do not want it. Were such an effort made, people feel, it would probably succeed because the question is really one where a sensible compromise should be possible. This feeling is not only widespread; it is also typical of an attitude that applies also to the Crimean question and to many other possible issues between Russia and Ukraine (or between Russians and Ukrainians inside Ukraine). Few people think, about almost any of these questions, that a reasonable mutual accommodation is impossible or that something is so vital that a sharp conflict is warranted. Instead people normally feel that an acceptable compromise could be found if all parties would be reasonable.

Simultaneously, people have so little respect for most politicians that they regard them generally as not interested in finding reasonable solutions. Some people add that many politicians may be so incompetent that they do not know how to go about achieving a sensible compromise. Most people feel roughly the same lack of respect for politicians whether they be the politicians in Kyiv, Moscow, or regional politicians in Crimea or elsewhere.

It is typical of the ambiguous and contradictory quality of Ukrainian public opinion that a substantial part of the public *also* wants a "Ukrainian" solution to the question of the Black Sea Fleet. Many people want Ukraine to get the Fleet or most of it.[19] As mentioned, public opinion on this question, as on many others, does not always split along ethnic lines. Some people who are ethnic Russian also want a Ukrainian solution. For these people, their "patriotic" feelings or identity outweigh their "ethnic" feelings or identity, at least on this question and at least for the present. Although they happen to be ethnic Russian, these patriotic Ukrainians want their country, Ukraine, to win on the issue of the Fleet.

It is normal among the public in Ukraine for this attitude – the desire for a Ukrainian victory on some issue – to exist side by side with the other attitude: the belief that a reasonable compromise is possible and desirable. It is not abnormal to hear the same person say both things within a short time. Many citizens have not thought about policy issues enough to realize that there might be a conflict between these ideas.

3   Other topics

There are some half-dozen other areas involving foreign affairs and security where attitudes held by the public in Ukraine can be identified and briefly assessed. Those topics are taken up now.

Peacekeeping

Three ideas about peacekeeping are widely held in Ukraine. One is related to the previous subject as it also involves Russia.

A large number of people in Ukraine are aware of Moscow's claim that Russia should have the right to conduct peacekeeping operations throughout the territory of the former Soviet Union. This is not an area of public ignorance; people are aware of it. The majority of the public does not accept this claim as right. On the contrary, the majority feels that the claim is an unwanted intrusion on Ukrainian sovereignty, and that any actual peacekeeping actions by Russia on Ukrainian soil would definitely not be legitimate. People are inclined to feel that Moscow's claim is another expression of its old imperial attitudes.

Although this is the most widespread view, here too there are ambiguities. A few Ukrainians feel that the claim means that at least Moscow is willing to provide security. In an insecure and confusing situation that may be a comfort. However, other Ukrainians doubt that Russia could deliver the security that it apparently promises, because of Russia's own weaknesses and instability. In addition, ethnic Russians in some areas of Ukraine might hold a quite different attitude, at least in some circumstances. If these people came to feel sufficiently anxious in some future situation, they might welcome a "peacekeeping" action by Russia that had the result of making them feel secure.[20]

The violent Russian attack on Chechnya, beginning at the end of 1994, is having a pronounced effect on Ukrainian attitudes. Public opinion has reacted sharply against Russia, and many Ukrainians feel that they have received a preview of what Russian "peacekeeping" might be like. A long-term hardening of public attitudes against the legitimacy of Russian peacekeeping will probably result.

The second attitude about peacekeeping widely held by the public in Ukraine is related to the rejection of peacekeeping by Russia. Peacekeeping done by the whole world, for example by the United Nations, is seen as quite legitimate by the public. Many Ukrainians are aware that the UN undertakes peacekeeping in various places around the world, and say that UN peacekeeping in the former Soviet area would be entirely legitimate. More generally, the public (including people who are not familiar with UN activities) want normal international laws and procedures to be applied in the normal fashion in their own area. People explicitly reject the idea that Ukraine or areas nearby should be different for some reason, and they say this on the understanding that they are implying that Russia should not be able to treat the former Soviet territory as somehow different from the rest of the world. Again, some ethnic Russians in some parts of Ukraine may feel differently.

The third attitude held by the public in Ukraine is the same attitude held in every country discussed in this book. The soldiers who undertake peacekeeping duties must be volunteers. It is not legitimate to compel soldiers to risk their lives in some foreign land on peacekeeping duties. On this, the public in Ukraine is in agreement.

Nuclear weapons

Ukraine is one country in Europe where nuclear weapons are the subject of strong public attention. In no other European country are the public so interested in any nuclear weapons question. In 1992 and 1993, the public in Ukraine were quite interested, from two opposite and conflicting points of view. In 1994, public interest declined somewhat; but it has not vanished.

On the one hand, Ukrainians feel a "nuclear allergy" because of Chernobyl. People feel that they have been the victims of nuclear energy once already. They feel a distaste for all things nuclear and, from this viewpoint, would feel relieved if all nuclear weapons could be removed from their country. In the first months following Ukraine's independence, the public overwhelmingly favored getting rid of the weapons, which also was the announced position of the government. Some people feel also that the short-range (tactical) nuclear weapons might have been useful for Ukraine, but since these have already been turned over to Russia there is no major question left, because the long-range (strategic) weapons are not useful (and therefore might as well be disposed of).

On the other hand, Ukrainians increasingly came to feel during 1992 and 1993 that keeping the nuclear weapons, at least for a time, brings some important benefits. During these years, the public noticed more and more that the nuclear weapons seemed to be the only thing about Ukraine that the West (and especially the United States) was paying attention to. The West did not seem to be much interested in Ukraine for any other reason. But Ukrainians noticed that the United States seemed intensely interested in the nuclear weapons in Ukraine. Many people drew the conclusion that if these weapons were what it took to get the West's attention, perhaps Ukraine should keep them for a while longer.

Other reasons for keeping the weapons, at least for a time, also gathered some public support. Having these weapons demonstrates to the world that Ukraine is an independent country and an important country. Also, nationalist political leaders argue that having such weapons makes Ukraine a country that must be reckoned with, by Russia and by everyone else. Without the weapons, these leaders said, Ukraine would be seen as much weaker. In 1993, the public mood in Ukraine shifted substantially toward support for Ukraine retaining its nuclear weapons.[21]

However, to some extent the public also became aware of reasons to doubt these ideas and found more reasons to get rid of the weapons. Many Ukrainians learned that the weapons, though located in Ukraine, are actually in the hands of Russian troops. Many people feel that, in that case, perhaps the weapons do not add much to Ukraine's ability to cope with Russia. Many also learned that keeping the weapons is not free, but imposes costs on a country ill-equipped to afford them, whereas some money could be made from the West by selling the weapons. In addition, some people feel that Ukraine has already promised the world that it will give up the weapons, and if Ukraine wishes to be respected it should keep its word.

For a considerable time, these reasons for and against keeping the nuclear weapons were swirling around in the Ukrainian public mind. Contrasting arguments were kept in the public eye by the media. At times during 1993 the major newspapers printed articles on this subject every day. For example, the media reported speeches about the weapons made by Members of Parliament, and there was a fast tempo of speeches from both sides.

The significance of the public's attitudes, on both this topic and others, should be neither overestimated nor underestimated. Ukrainians understand that presently their country is democratic only in a limited sense, and there is no question but that the public will go along with the government's decision – on this topic and many others – whatever that decision may be. The public will go along even if a clear majority holds the contrary view. At the same time, the public's views have been used as a tool in the intense political struggles of the capital. Members of Parliament and other high officials in the government can and do cite public support as a reason why the policy they want should become the government's policy. This has been done both by those who want to keep, and those who want to sell, the nuclear weapons, since both sets of officials can find evidence of public support for their views. Both positions have had a certain amount of support among an ambivalent public.[22]

In January 1994, President Kravchuk signed a "Trilateral Agreement" with Russia and the United States, committing Ukraine to give up nuclear weapons. The next month the Parliament essentially endorsed this step, and in November 1994 Parliament voted that Ukraine should join the Nuclear Non-Proliferation Treaty.[23] The public observed these decisions and are largely ready to support them.[24] Perhaps ironically, after Russia's attack on Chechnya a few weeks later, there was again some public discussion of the desirability of having nuclear weapons, as a way of improving Ukraine's security vis-à-vis Russia.

Borders

The public in Ukraine are well aware that questions could arise in some way about Ukraine's borders, and they want the borders to remain as they are. The special problem of Crimea has been discussed already. Practically all the external borders of Ukraine could also be thrown into question and people do not want them to be.

People are aware that Russia could make claims on Ukrainian territory, and many people are aware that other countries such as Poland and Romania could do so also. The public are keenly aware that, for its part, Ukraine could make claims on some land presently held by Russia and land held by neighbors to the west. People do not want claims to be made, neither by others against Ukraine, nor by Ukraine against others. The public also want Ukraine to take the lead in ensuring that the borders are kept where they are. They want their country to take the initiative in saying to all neighbors that Ukraine will make no claim against them, naturally hoping that the neighbors will say the same regarding Ukraine.

The public in Ukraine are well aware that once a border dispute arises, a serious conflict could develop. People have no desire to expand Ukraine's territories and they want no conflicts. For people in Ukraine, there are enough insecurities already. The borders should not be allowed to become another.

Migration

In Ukraine the public feel two fears about migration: both into and out of the country. There is some concern about refugees coming into Ukraine from wars elsewhere in the former Soviet territories, such as the Caucasus region or Central Asia. People do not wish to be ungenerous, but they are worried that the impoverished Ukrainian economy could not provide housing and other support for newcomers. People arriving from elsewhere might also take jobs that Ukrainians could be holding. There appears also to be some concern about migrants bringing in diseases.[25] Concern is also rising that Ukraine could become, and perhaps is already, an avenue for people from further east and south to migrate illegally into Western Europe (and, closely related, an avenue for the drug trade into Western Europe).[26]

Worry about migration out of Ukraine may actually be the greater of the two anxieties. There is fear of a "brain drain." The public fear that talented individuals, particularly people in highly skilled professions, may be able to and may choose to leave Ukraine. Such people may find jobs in the West, with vastly higher salaries and much better living conditions. As a result the loss to Ukraine might be great, because it is these people especially who are needed to build a modern economy in Ukraine.

US forces in Europe

The fact that some US military forces remain in Europe does not receive attention from the public in Ukraine. Many people assume that those forces have now left. Asked about whether US forces should be in Europe now, a consensus of the public responds "no."

This attitude has at least two sources. One is that it was a standard political stance during Soviet times, repeated constantly for decades by the Soviet authorities, that troops should not be stationed on foreign soil in peacetime. People in Ukraine have deeply absorbed the idea that in normal times troops are never stationed on another country's territory, and if they are, it is abnormal. The other source is, of course, a general belief that the

US forces were positioned in Europe in the first place because of the Cold War, and since the Cold War is over they should go home.

These feelings exist side by side with a vague but fairly widespread awareness that Ukraine itself is interested in developing some kind of connection with "Western military structures" (as people often put it).[27] The coexistence of both feelings is not unusual, even if there might be some inconsistency between them. People do not have enough information, and have not focused on this topic sufficiently, to grasp that a reason why "Western military structures" might have some importance for Ukraine could be connected to the presence of US forces in those structures. A chief reason why few people make such a connection is that almost no one is really interested in this topic. Hardly anyone among the public in Ukraine imagines that the distant US would ever use its forces to help Ukraine anyway. Therefore those forces, and this topic, are emotionally irrelevant.

There also is a vague feeling among the public in Ukraine that "Europe" should create its own military forces – *not* including Americans – at which point Ukraine, as an important European country, would naturally contribute its share. This idea carries a strongly positive feeling for the public.[28]

Information

The public in Ukraine are immensely sceptical about the information received about Ukraine's external affairs and security questions (and indeed, about all political affairs). The newspapers, television and radio are seen as enormously influenced by the government and by various parliamentary and other political leaders and groups.[29] Distrust of the government is so deep that an official source is by itself sufficient to make information questionable. Of course there have been few other sources of information about foreign or security affairs within Ukraine, although the quantity of information on these topics is slowly increasing. From long experience, people feel that information from Moscow is no better, not to mention the fact that information from that source will be shaped by a Russian viewpoint.

Among well-educated elements of society, there is some access to news from Western and world sources. But this is limited in significance, partly for financial reasons (for instance, newspapers are priced far above what almost anyone can pay), and partly because Western and world sources are not interested enough in Ukraine to include much about it in their news.

4 Concluding remarks

We return in conclusion to emphasize something said at the outset. Because Ukraine is so new a country, it cannot be expected that the public has yet developed clearly defined views on many topics. Ukraine has not existed as a separate country for many centuries. It is impossible that after so long a time, the public could quickly form well-defined attitudes about a separate, independent Ukraine.

Because many ideas and feelings in the public mind are only beginning to form, it is natural that some partly-formed feelings are in conflict with others. Inconsistencies arise easily when ideas have not yet been thought about much. A couple of examples have been mentioned already. One more example may be provided that is especially striking. This one involves attitudes about government censorship and about freedom of speech. A public opinion survey in July 1993 asked respondents to agree or disagree with two statements. One was "Before making something public, specialists should decide whether people need it or not." The other was "Everyone has a right to make his or her views public even if the majority of people holds the opposite view." The statements were worded in such a way as to avoid making it blatantly obvious that they are in conflict with each other. Strikingly, 79 percent agreed with the first statement and 82 percent agreed with the second.[30] We conclude that for the great majority, an example of a conflict between state control of information and individual freedom is something not yet noticed. In other words, two conflicting viewpoints coexist side by side.

This kind of coexistence of conflicting ideas in the public mind is fairly common in Ukraine at present. A natural result is some public confusion. At times people feel torn and conflicted between competing points of view. Another natural result is public uncertainty. It is common for citizens spontaneously to express their uncertainty about political issues. They do so partly because they do not receive much information and they mistrust the information they do receive. They also express uncertainty because to some extent they recognize that they are feeling conflicting ideas. Naturally, people also feel uncertainty at times, such as now, of high political and economic instability.

This state of public attitudes, especially on difficult issues, is surely not unusual in a brand new country. Some time may be needed for attitudes in Ukraine to mature and for society to develop greater clarity about questions facing the country. The achievement of Ukraine's independence was the decisive first step on this road.

Notes

1   The region was a frontier for both Moscow and the Polish–Lithuanian empire, and during these centuries became known as the *ukraina*, a Russian word that means frontier or borderlands. The name of the country is pronounced oo-kra-yeen-a in Ukrainian and oo-kra-een-a in Russian. The spelling of the capital city, Kiev, most often seen in the West, is the transliteration of the Russian

spelling. One major transliteration (there are several possible) of the Ukrainian spelling is Kyiv. The Russian pronunciation, usually also used in the West, is kee-yev. The Ukrainian pronunciation is kuh-yeev.

2 Ukrainian insurgents also made efforts to create a Ukrainian state during and after World War II. These attempts, which never succeeded in establishing a fully functioning government, were crushed by the Nazis and then by the Soviets.

3 The assessment presented in this chapter is drawn partly from a series of eleven focus groups held in Ukraine during 1993 by the Security for Europe Project, and partly from other research done then and later by the SOCIS Company, and earlier by the Institute of Sociology of the Academy of Sciences of Ukraine. Revision of this chapter was completed in the first days of 1995. Although we can expect most public attitudes to change slowly thereafter, major events could change some of the conclusions reported here.

4 For example, in a SOCIS omnibus survey conducted in December 1993 for the Gallup International "End of the Year Poll 1993," 58 percent of the public expected that 1994 would be worse.

5 From a SOCIS survey conducted in December 1994 for the Gallup International "End of the Year Poll 1994."

6 A SOCIS survey in June 1994 asked respondents "which political party offers the best solutions to the problems of Ukraine?" All the parties were then listed. Not one party was endorsed by more than 7 percent of the respondents. *Ukrainian Political and Economic Index* (Kyiv: SOCIS, June 1994).

7 People in the former Soviet countries may also have more suspicion than people in the West of poll-takers asking questions from a questionnaire. But Ukrainians were not so closed-mouthed in former years.

8 Respondents in a survey conducted by the "Democratic Initiative" Research Center in June 1993 were asked which of fifteen named social groups played a prominent role in the process of building the Ukrainian state. The mafia or criminal world was the group selected by the largest proportion of respondents (68 percent). Yevgen Golovakha, *Politichnii portret Ukraini,* Bulletin No. 1 of the "Democratic Initiative" Research Center (1993).

9 A survey in December 1993 asked about whether Chernobyl should continue in operation. Only 27 percent said it should be shut down immediately; 37 percent said it should be phased out gradually; and 23 percent said it should stay in operation indefinitely. *Ukrainian Political and Economic Index* (Kyiv: SOCIS, December 1993).

10 An environmental campaign against this pollution, organized partly by Greenpeace and emphasizing damage to the local region, began in 1994 and is likely to grow in 1995. Yet the need of the whole country for energy means that there also is strong support nationwide for continued regular use of the Odessa oil facilities.

11 At one point during 1993, the drinking water in Kyiv was officially declared unsafe due to an industrial accident. Only a few weeks later it was declared safe again. It is a sign of the depth of people's distrust of the authorities that many wondered whether the water could really have been made safe again so quickly.

12 The Ukrainian government is supposed to have a program for improving the environment but people doubt whether it has much effect. The government is

so universally believed to be corrupt that people assume that high officials are paid off to allow polluting industries to continue operation, and that they are bribed by hard currency from Western Europe to allow shipping in of wastes from Europe.

13　The other 5 percent represent other nationalities and ethnic groups, of which there are more than 100 in Ukraine.

14　For an extensive analysis of the situation of Russians in Ukraine and the relative positions of Ukrainians and Russians by various measures, see Evgenii Golovakha, Natalia Panina, and Nikolay Churilov, "Russians in Ukraine," in *The New Russian Diaspora: Russian Minorities in the Former Soviet Republics*, ed. Vladimir Shlapentokh, Munir Sendich and Emil Payin (Armonk, NY: M. E. Sharpe Publishing Co., 1994).

15　According to one survey, 52 percent of the whole population of Ukraine speaks Russian in their own homes. *Ukrainian Political and Economic Index* (Kyiv: SOCIS, January 1994). The political and cultural significance of this number is larger than it might appear because many who speak Ukrainian at home are living in rural areas.

16　A SOCIS survey asked this question in June 1994: "How probable is civil war in Ukraine?" Of the respondents willing to answer, 22 percent said "very" or "somewhat" probable, while 47 percent said "somewhat" or "completely" improbable. Another 19 percent judged it to be "equally likely/unlikely." *Ukrainian Political and Economic Index* (Kyiv: SOCIS, June 1994). The question does not specify ethnic conflict and some respondents may have interpreted the question in a non-ethnic way.

17　People, especially ethnic Ukrainians, also acknowledge that ethnic tension could rise if a noticeable difference appears over time in the rate of economic development of different ethnic groups.

18　In a public opinion survey on Ukrainian–Russian relations conducted in March 1993 by the Institute of Sociology of the Academy of Sciences of Ukraine, 18 percent of ethnic Russians but only 5 percent of ethnic Ukrainians agreed that Russia's territorial claim on Crimea has sufficient historical and legal justification. More striking is the high proportion of respondents of both ethnic groups – 42 percent of Russians and 36 percent of Ukrainians – who felt unable to express any judgement on this issue. This finding is relevant to our point, expressed at the beginning of this chapter, that many public attitudes are as yet relatively undeveloped in Ukraine. Kyiv: Institute of Sociology of the Academy of Sciences of Ukraine, 1993, "Informatsiino-analitichna dovidka pro rezultati sotsiologichnogo doslidzhennya 'Ukrainsko-rosiiski vidnosini i ikh vpliv na politchnu situatsiy v Ukraini' " (table 2.4).

　　According to a USIA survey conducted in Ukraine in October 1994, 66 percent of the public in Ukraine favor Crimea remaining a part of Ukraine, 20 percent support the idea of an independent Crimea, and only 4 percent want Crimea to become a part of Russia. USIA Office of Research and Media Reaction, *Briefing Paper* (November 17, 1994). Notice that it is easier for the public to express a view about what should be done with Crimea than to express a view about whether somebody's historical and legal justification is sufficient. The USIA survey did not break down respondents by their ethnicity.

19　In a December 1993 SOCIS survey, respondents were asked this question:

"Should Ukraine step by step give up to Russia the Black Sea Fleet in exchange for continuing deliveries of gas and oil?" Half of the respondents said "No, under no circumstances"; only 8 percent agreed unconditionally. (The remainder felt it might be done only under some circumstances or had no opinion.) *Ukrainian Political and Economic Index* (Kyiv: SOCIS, December 1993.)

A USIA-commissioned survey of October 1994 showed 78 percent wanting a division of the Fleet between Ukraine and Russia. Only 6 percent said that Russia should have the whole Fleet. USIA Office of Research and Media Reaction, Briefing Paper (November 17, 1994).

20 The contradictory attitudes held by the public in Ukraine on these problems are revealed by a March 1993 survey. While 61 percent of respondents agreed with a statement that Russia should "act as guarantor of peace and stability" on the territory of the former USSR, only 5 percent agreed that Russia "should have special rights" on that territory. Institute of Sociology of the Academy of Sciences of Ukraine, "Informatsiino-analitichna dovidka . . ." (table 2.9).

21 In a January 1992 poll, 13 percent of respondents expressed themselves in favor of Ukraine keeping nuclear weapons; in a March 1993 survey, 36 percent of respondents took this view: survey by the Research Center of the Ukrainian Sociological Survey for the USIA (January 1992); survey by the Institute of Sociology of the Academy of Sciences of Ukraine (March 1993).

22 On this question and others, polling data in Ukraine may be only partially useful and can even be misleading. People may give contradictory answers to separate questions on the same topic. Much depends on how the question is worded, and also on the timing of the poll. Opinion among part of the public is volatile, and a poll taken shortly after a widely reported speech by a major politician may give a different result from a poll taken before. At the same time, there are "hard cores" among the public of those who definitely want to keep the weapons, and of those who definitely want to give them up. Incidentally, almost everyone agrees that Ukraine can and should give up its nuclear weapons if the whole world does so also. If Russia, the US and all other nuclear states abolish their weapons, then certainly Ukraine should also.

23 Particulars are discussed in the next chapter.

24 A USIA-commissioned survey in October 1994 found that two-thirds of the public supported a non-nuclear status for Ukraine. USIA Office of Research and Media Reaction, *Briefing Paper* (November 17, 1994).

25 During 1993, there were some articles published in the Ukrainian press about immigrants in Kyiv having contagious diseases. People know that the health system in Ukraine is already extremely weak, and therefore are more concerned about the potential spread of diseases than people in some other countries might be.

26 These public anxieties mirror anxieties that have been felt for several years by the public in Poland, the Czech Republic, Slovakia and Hungary.

27 Public interest in Ukraine making connections with "Western military structures" increased in the period just following the Russian military intervention in Chechnya.

28 In December 1993, a SOCIS poll showed that 51 percent of Ukrainians believe Ukraine should seek membership in NATO, with only 20 percent saying definitely it should not. *Ukrainian Political and Economic Index* (Kyiv: SOCIS,

December 1993). These results should not necessarily be interpreted in the
context of Ukrainians' feelings about US troops in Europe. Many people in
Ukraine do not know that the US is a member of NATO; or they do not think
that NATO needs US forces to be stationed in Europe; or they simply have not
made any connection in their minds between Ukraine's interest in NATO and
the question of US forces in Europe.

29 A SOCIS survey in June 1994 asked people how much they trust the Ukrainian
media. Only 19 percent responded "trust completely"; 56 percent responded
"trust somewhat." *Ukrainian Political and Economic Index* (Kyiv: SOCIS, June
1994).

30 SOCIS Omnibus survey (July 1993).

14

Ukraine: policy analysis and options

Leonid Kistersky and Serhii Pirozhkov KYIV

1 Introduction

Ukraine has reemerged as a sovereign country after declaring its independence on August 24, 1991, three days after the aborted coup in Moscow. Ukraine's independence was convincingly ratified by a national referendum on December 1 of that year, in which more than 90 percent of the voters supported its separation from the Soviet Union.[1] On the same day, a president of Ukraine, Leonid Kravchuk, was elected on a democratic basis from among several candidates. On December 9, the presidents of Russia, Ukraine and Belarus jointly announced the dissolution of the Soviet Union by declaring null and void the Union Treaty of 1922.

Ukraine is a major European country, approximately equal to France in size of both territory and population (51.9 million). Of all the countries that formerly were republics of the Soviet Union, Ukraine has by far the largest economy after Russia. When it was a Union republic, Ukraine produced almost a quarter of the Soviet Union's Net Material Product. Ukraine also has, after Russia, by far the largest army and the largest and best scientific and industrial establishments of the former Soviet republics.[2]

Ukraine's size and its geographical location in the center of Europe make the country especially important in the overall security of Europe. Along with Belarus, Ukraine occupies a unique position between Russia on one side and much of the rest of Europe on the other. Ukraine's position of being an immediate neighbor to the huge country of Russia, plus other factors to be discussed later, make the relationship with Russia extraordinarily important to Ukraine. This chapter attempts to provide a comprehensive picture of Ukraine's security position and the main lines of Ukraine's thinking about security.

2   Security for Ukraine

General overview

Ukraine, as a new country, faces an extraordinary situation. It must begin
its assessment of how to achieve security absolutely from a blank sheet of
paper. There is no prior policy that one can refer to, not even much tradition
of thought about the subject. For centuries, virtually all decisions about
Ukraine's security, and all thinking about the rationales for decisions, have
been done in Moscow. (The brief attempt during the World War I years to
create an independent Ukraine did not provide enough opportunity to form
any developed set of ideas about Ukrainian security.)

After regaining independence, Ukraine faces major difficulties from the
necessity to create the structures and processes of the state, beginning from
zero. Or in some ways it may be said that Ukraine must begin from less than
zero, since it must struggle with many negative legacies from the Soviet era.
Ukraine must create a new constitution, a normal professional Parliament,
professional and competent state organs, an immense body of law and many
other necessities including a concept and policy for national security. As of
this writing, a general security policy for Ukraine has not yet been approved
by Parliament, although certain parts of it have been, as discussed later.[3]

Specialists on national security and foreign policy for Ukraine, inside and
outside the government, are presently in the process of developing a comprehensive assessment of what security for the country means. They need to
think broadly about every aspect of security to determine what is needed for
the state and society. A general view of security is now evolving among
specialists in Kyiv. Our interpretation of this developing thinking may be
briefly presented as follows.

National security

Broadly speaking, Ukraine's national security is a way of self-preservation
for the people of Ukraine. National security is required for the existence of
the state and the free development of society. Security must include reliable
defense from both external and internal threats. In a broad sense, the
national security of Ukraine represents a system of state and social guarantees that secure the permanent viability and development of Ukraine and its
people.[4]

Security for Ukraine may be seen as comprising four major dimensions,
which may be called (1) state-political, (2) social-economic, (3) national-
cultural and (4) ecological. State-political security means the security, in its
political and military sense, of the state and the country. Social-economic
security means securing the preservation and development of people's economic well-being and the security of society. National-cultural security
means securing the preservation and development of the country's culture,

and of the various national cultures and social units within the country. The meaning of ecological security is obvious. We will use these categories in the first part of this chapter as a way of organizing both concepts and some current developments and issues. The order of the four is not always their order of importance. After this overall survey of Ukrainian security, we will turn to the predominant foreign policy and security problem: the relationship with Russia.

The state-political dimension of security

Ukraine as a state and a political entity must provide for the territorial integrity of Ukraine and of its frontiers, to defend against any unconstitutional attempts to alter the arrangements of power, and to guarantee the rights of the people. Firm independent statehood is the highest and most essential form of national self-consciousness and identity.

This dimension of security requires the smooth functioning of the constitution and the legal order of the state. It requires the smooth and proper operation of the organs of government. The constitution, legal order and organs of the government must also be protected so they may operate normally. The relevant institutions of government must determine and implement measures to counter any possible threats and to prevent any conflicts that might jeopardize Ukraine's development as a sovereign state.

Protection of Ukraine's national security in its state-political sense requires the following institutions at a minimum:

- military forces, to guarantee against any invasion from another state;
- intelligence and counter-intelligence organizations;
- internal security forces (which may include some military units and/or national guard);
- organs of state to determine and implement the foreign policy and external economic affairs of Ukraine;
- organs of state to control, in the proper constitutional manner, the military, intelligence and internal security institutions.

It is of the utmost importance for Ukraine to identify the proper place and mode of activity for each of these institutions. This can only be done, in turn, if both current and potential sources of threat to Ukraine's security, and the degree and form of danger they pose, are identified with the greatest possible precision. This work can only be properly done in the framework of a general security doctrine for Ukraine, as well as various specialized doctrines such as military, foreign policy, intelligence and internal security doctrines. These matters are now under study in Kyiv. Of course many of the institutions just listed were inherited, in their Soviet forms, from the USSR.

Two important components of security doctrine have been adopted by Ukraine's Parliament. In July 1993, Parliament approved a document entitled "The Main Directions of Ukraine's External Policy." Strengthening national security was identified as one of the priorities for Ukraine's external policy and major emphasis was placed on this strengthening. According to this document, Ukraine's foreign policy will focus on developing reliable international mechanisms for protecting security on several levels: bilaterally with individual foreign countries; in the local region; in the larger region comprising Europe; and globally. The document also states the goal of developing cooperative relations with foreign countries, in particular the neighboring ones.

Ukraine's developing foreign policy places emphasis on the improvement of security in Europe. Ukraine perceives a general lack of security in Central and Eastern Europe, a kind of security vacuum in the region. This perception was part of the background for President Kravchuk's initiative which he put forward in February 1993, to create a zone of stability and security in Central and Eastern Europe. His initiative suggested a zone of cooperation for security affairs, comprising the Central and Eastern European countries west of Russia from the Black Sea to the Baltic Sea. Within this zone a system of joint consultations would be created, based on the CSCE principles. Unfortunately, this initiative has not yet received a firm positive response from the states in the region.

Presidential elections were held in July 1994 and Leonid Kuchma was elected the new president of Ukraine. He indicated that he intended to make some corrections in Ukrainian foreign policy. Later that year, he specified that policy must be more economically oriented, and in particular must obtain greater economic advantages in Ukraine's dealing with foreign countries.

The second component of Ukraine's security doctrine is a military doctrine, adopted by Parliament in October 1993. This document defines the country's military objectives and doctrine as strictly defensive. Ukraine's chief military goals are to secure Ukraine's sovereignty, its political independence, its territorial integrity and the inviolability of its borders. The document states that Ukraine is not a potential enemy to any country and does not see any country as an enemy to itself. However, in the future Ukraine may perceive any country as an enemy that poses a military threat to Ukraine or encroaches on Ukraine's territorial integrity. The military doctrine rejects war as a means of furthering any state policy, and limits the use of the armed forces to defense against any hypothetical aggression.

The doctrine on Ukraine's military policy also established some major principles for policy. Ukraine makes no territorial claims on any other country. Ukraine will observe the inviolability of existing borders. Ukraine will honor the sovereignty and political independence of other countries. Ukraine will seek to resolve all disputes with other countries only by political means and according to the norms of international law. The use of Ukraine's armed forces to resolve any political problems on Ukraine's own territory is expressly prohibited.

Other important features of the military doctrine involve deployment of troops. According to the document, Ukraine shall not deploy its troops on the territory of any other state without its consent, and Ukraine opposes the deployment of any foreign troops on its own territory. The latter could pose additional difficulties in resolving the questions of the Black Sea Fleet (discussed below).

Ukraine has worked out a three-stage plan for restructuring the armed forces. In the spirit of the military doctrine's defensive character, the plan envisages a reduction in the 726,000 troops, inherited at the time the Soviet Union collapsed, down to 400,000 or 450,000 by the autumn of 1995.

Social-economic security

This sphere of security is intended to secure the socio-economic system, protecting it against internal and external threats. In the current period, it is necessary to overcome the severe crisis in the economy and the resulting crisis of society. Social-economic security requires above all the structural transformation of the economy. The full range of changes needed would require a long analysis but a few points may be made here.[5]

Ukraine's economy is heavily and dangerously interdependent with the economies of the other former Soviet republics, especially Russia. The enormous planning establishment of the Soviet era created a single economic plan for the Soviet Union as one entity. The natural result was that every part of the Union became highly dependent on every other part. For example, it was common for a single factory, somewhere in the Union, to be the only producer of some machine in the entire Soviet Union. Naturally in many cases that factory was not located in Ukraine. Unfortunately, Ukraine's *political* declaration of independence and sovereignty in 1991 could not immediately change these basic economic facts.

Hence it has been clear from the outset that the high economic interdependence with the other republics, and mainly with Russia, would keep all the former republics in a very vulnerable position. Ukraine inherited one of the world's most vulnerable economic systems, and consequently, very low security in this sense. In particular, Ukraine has a strong concentration of high energy-consuming industries, such as metallurgy, but has only modest energy resources, notably little oil. No less than 92 percent of the country's oil is imported from Russia. Russia's decision in 1993 to charge the world market price for oil has been one of the causes of the sharp decline in Ukraine's industrial production. Furthermore, where trade links with the other republics *have* been reduced or severed, alternative trading arrangements have not been created quickly. The inevitable result has been a sharp decline in Ukraine's trade, and this is another of the causes of the current economic crisis.

The industrial structure of Ukraine is warped. Ukraine inherited from the Soviet Union a dangerously high proportion of its total production in one sector, the military-industrial complex. Here also is located most of the skilled manpower. Ukraine needs a consistent and well-coordinated plan of conversion from military to civilian production, combined with a well-calculated social policy aimed at retraining and shifting the workers. Furthermore, in certain critical respects Ukraine's military-industrial complex is, again, dependent upon supplies from Russian producers. Economic security requires that these products be manufactured internally as quickly as possible.

Ukraine enjoys a favorable geographic position, in the heart of Europe and on the Black Sea, and also enjoys a favorable climate. The country has a great deal of very rich farmland. In spite of this, Ukraine has found it impossible to achieve self-sufficiency in food, which is another central component of economic security, on the basis of a state-run agricultural system. Although a formal legal basis now exists for private ownership of farms, they are largely discouraged by the powerful bureaucrats and by some Members of Parliament who are part of the state farm system. Economic security in agriculture requires the development of private-sector farming and the defense, in practice, of farmers' rights.

Something similar applies throughout the economy. Much still remains to be done to secure property rights of all kinds and on all levels. Although some property laws exist, a lack of enforcement plus the general collective psychology that pervades all spheres of government create difficult conditions for anyone who would like to develop a business. Numerous, essentially political, hurdles still limit the entrepreneurial possibilities for Ukrainian citizens, for those private enterprises and farms that exist, and for foreign investors.

Economic security in Ukraine also urgently demands the development of market financial systems. The lack of them has contributed to the huge government deficits and enormous inflation of the first years of independence. A new investment policy is also being worked out, which may be more conducive to implementing modern management and new technologies.

On October 11, 1994, President Kuchma presented to the Parliament a well-designed plan for the economic transformation of the country, a plan clearly prepared by competent economists. Indeed, the plan contains all the essential steps for the transformation of Ukraine into a market economy. However, its implementation was assigned to officials who have the old Soviet mentality. In practical terms, the successes achieved by the end of the new president's first half-year in office leave much to be desired, to say the least.

Some people in high places still count on economic salvation arriving from the West. More realistic observers know that, fundamentally, the country must solve its own problems, and that help from the West can be useful but never more than supplementary. Especially helpful would be intellectual and technical assistance in developing market reforms, and a limited amount of such assistance is being received.[6]

National-cultural security

This sphere of security aims to coordinate the interests of Ukraine's citizens of different nationalities, to prevent ethnic conflicts and to determine policies for migration. Ethnic Ukrainians constitute 73 percent of the country's population; 22 percent are ethnic Russians; the other 5 percent include more than 100 other nationalities and ethnic groups.[7] Ukraine's security in this sphere depends to a large extent on the self-respect and morality of its citizens. Policies of state are also needed to ensure equal treatment of all, and there is a Ministry of Nationalities to further this goal.

National-cultural security has both internal and external aspects. Internally, Ukraine seeks to improve this sphere of life through the development of democratic social norms and ridding society of totalitarian stereotypes. Equally important is the development of national consciousness, through a revitalization of Ukrainian language and culture, and a deeper appreciation of Ukraine's unique history.

Ukraine's security problems in this sphere are exacerbated by growing cultural discrepancies between its eastern and western regions, which are partly caused by the country's deteriorating economy. Eastern Ukraine, where ethnic Russians are relatively numerous, is heavily over-industrialized, and therefore heavily dependent on economic links with enterprises in Russia. After the collapse of the Soviet Union, these links deteriorated dramatically, and the eastern (and also southern) regions are pressuring the government hard to restore close economic and other links with Russia.[8] Western Ukraine, which is mostly ethnic Ukrainian, is also mostly rural, and part of it entered the Soviet Union only in 1939, having previously lived under much softer Polish, and earlier, Austrian, rule. It is chiefly in the west where traditional Ukrainian culture has been retained, and after 1939 this region always resisted the Soviet policy of Russification. This region still retains high distrust of everything related to Russia. As a matter of economic necessity, however, Ukraine will have to have close economic ties with Russia for many years ahead. Kyiv is making cautious steps toward the CIS in an effort to repair the damage caused by the economic disintegration of the Soviet Union.

External factors in this sphere include factors that are conducive to, and others that hinder, the spiritual and intellectual renaissance of the Ukrainian people. The former includes steps by various countries, and by foreign scholars and foreign political and cultural personalities, to help the rebirth of Ukrainian culture. The Ukrainian diaspora has already undertaken helpful actions and could undertake very positive ones in the future. Factors that hinder include externally generated disinformation for the world community about Ukraine and events inside Ukraine. Other possibilities include incitement and artificial inflation of regional and ethnic conflicts from external sources, or external support for imperialist and non-Ukrainian nationalistic groups.

Ecological security

Ecological security should provide mechanisms to prevent further degradation of Ukraine's environment, its improvement and regeneration. It should also include legal and other ways to prevent any ecological damage to Ukraine by businesses or people, or by other countries. Ecological security deserves priority among the national security values of Ukraine because modern technology includes the possibility for very widespread, even global, impact on the environment.[9]

The Chernobyl nuclear reactor explosion of 1986 was the greatest nuclear disaster ever experienced by humanity. Tons of radioactive material were sent into the atmosphere and were disseminated throughout northern and central Europe. More than 50,000 people had to be moved away from the most heavily contaminated zone, a thirty-kilometer zone around Chernobyl. Scientists calculate that the most contaminated area will remain uninhabitable for 26,000 years because of the long half-life of plutonium. Meanwhile Ukraine's territory is dotted with other nuclear power stations of the Chernobyl type. Almost 40 percent of Ukraine's power comes from nuclear power stations. Some steps are being taken to improve the safety of these reactors, and some degree of international aid has been provided, but much more is needed before they will be secure.

In 1991, Parliament decided to shut down the Chernobyl power station within two years, but in 1993 Parliament reversed this decision because of the country's acute need for energy. The shortage of energy is so serious that, for example, many factories were shut down for a period during the winter of 1993–94 due to lack of heat. Meanwhile, Ukraine's severe economic crisis makes it impossible to find enough resources to cope with all the consequences of Chernobyl. For example, many of the 50,000 displaced people still do not have permanent living quarters.

3   The relationship with Russia

Ukraine's relationship with Russia is by far the most important subject on the foreign policy and security agenda. This follows not only from the elementary facts of geography and centuries of history, but also from Ukraine's economic dependence on Russia, already discussed. The basic fact also should not be forgotten that when Ukraine declared its independence in 1991, it declared independence from the regime in Moscow, although that regime was the Soviet government, not the Russian government.

Unfortunately, even now many Russian policy-makers, along with many people in the Russian intelligentsia and among Russian people generally, do not respect Ukraine's independence. They see a sovereign, separate Ukraine as a temporary aberration of history, and look forward to what seems natural and inevitable to them: a reincorporation of Ukraine into Russia.[10]

Formally, the Yeltsin government acknowledges Ukraine's sovereignty, but there is much in Russia that Yeltsin's government controls only partly or hardly at all. The widespread expectation in Russia that Ukraine's independence is only temporary is a background against which Ukraine must contend every day in some way or other. At the time of this writing, two issues in Ukraine's relations with Russia are particularly difficult, and even dangerous. One is Crimea; the other is the Black Sea Fleet.

Crimea

Presently the problem of Crimea is the most explosive issue in Ukrainian–Russian relations. In earlier centuries, the Crimean peninsula was populated mainly by Tatars; at times it was a protectorate of the Ottoman empire; and at times it was independent. Crimea was conquered by the Russian empire at the end of the eighteenth century, and thereafter Slavic people began to settle there. In May 1944, Stalin forcibly moved the Crimean Tatars, more than half a million people, to distant Central Asia and it became Soviet policy to make the peninsula entirely Slav. In 1954, Nikita Khrushchev, then the leader of the Soviet Union, formally transferred Crimea from Russia to Ukraine; at the time both were merely constituent republics of the Soviet Union and the step was only a gesture with no real political significance. The gesture was meant as a gift to Ukraine in celebration of the 300th anniversary of the important 1654 alliance, initially military, between Ukrainians and the Moscovite state. The ethnic composition in Crimea is predominantly Russian, although recently some Tatars have begun to return. About 67 percent of the people in Crimea consider themselves Russian and more than 80 percent say that Russian is their native language.

Since the break-up of the Soviet Union, living standards in Ukraine have declined even more rapidly than in Russia. Originally, Ukrainians, including Crimeans, hoped that Ukrainian independence would lead to a better standard of living. In 1991, almost 60 percent of the Crimean population voted for Ukraine's independence. But by now, living standards in Ukraine are so much worse than in Russia that people are starting to view Russia, even with all its problems, as a kind of promised land by comparison.

Some political mistakes by extreme nationalists in the Ukrainian Parliament provoked the Parliament of Crimea to declare independence from Ukraine in May 1992. At first, the Parliament in Kyiv strongly objected. But driven by economic hardship and lack of political experience, it made a crucial mistake. Crimea was granted a special position as an "autonomous republic" within Ukraine. In Crimea, this move was seen as a sign of weakness and further separatist moves followed. In May 1993 the Parliament in Moscow acted. Driven by its own nationalists and by the Russian nationalists in Crimea, the Russian Parliament declared Sevastopol, which is the headquarters of the disputed Black Sea Fleet, to be a Russian city. This step forced Ukraine to appeal to the United Nations, whose Security Council issued a statement in support of Ukraine's legitimate rights to Sevastopol and Ukraine's territorial integrity.

The situation grew more complicated in January 1994, when Yuri Meshkov, an ardent Russian nationalist, was elected president of the Crimean autonomous republic. Since then, he and the Crimean Parliament have been taking various steps – small ones so far – to distance Crimea from Ukraine. Logically their next steps, if not blocked jointly by Ukraine and Russia, may lead to decisive moves to establish an independent status for Crimea, to secede from Ukraine and, possibly, to join Russia.[11]

One step leading to direct confrontation with Kyiv has nearly been taken by Crimea's Parliament. It plans to consider a separation. In response, the president and Parliament of Ukraine issued a formal statement on May 19, 1994 that all necessary steps would be taken to secure the territorial integrity of Ukraine. The statement also made note of interference by some politicians and public figures in Russia in the internal affairs of Ukraine.

The Crimean situation is rendered more complicated, yet also more favorable for Ukraine, by the returning Tatars. They distrust Moscow and feel safer under the rule of Ukraine, which has a long history of tolerance and support for ethnic minority groups of all kinds. In addition, the Kyiv government has been allocating scarce funds to assist the Tatars' return to their homeland.

The Black Sea Fleet

The Black Sea Fleet is another major source of tension between Ukraine and Russia, intimately related to Crimea and directly involved with military affairs. The Black Sea Fleet was one of the large naval fleets of the former Soviet Union. It has some 300 combat and support ships, with its headquarters, as well as its main base and infrastructure, in Sevastopol in Crimea. Since the collapse of the Soviet Union, Ukraine and Russia have been disputing ownership of the Fleet.

The Fleet is far larger than either Ukraine or Russia needs in order to protect the Black Sea. It has no real military value, and as a defense force it never did.[12] It poses a great burden on the budgets of both Russia and Ukraine, especially Ukraine. The cost and the value of the Fleet can be assessed in various ways, as representatives of both countries have done. Unquestionably, the value of the infrastructure on land exceeds the value of the ships by several times. Russia could have relocated the Fleet to one of the ports on Russia's Black Sea coast, such as Novorossiysk, but Russia does not want to lose Sevastopol. The valuable infrastructure there mostly cannot be moved. And Sevastopol has long been one of the great naval cities of Russia, carrying a tradition of Russian glory at sea, so its symbolic value for Russia is high.

In intermittent negotiations, a number of attempts have been made to reach some agreement about a division of the Fleet between the two countries. In spite of personal negotiations between the presidents of the two countries, very little progress has been made so far. In September 1993, the two presidents met at Massandra, a resort town, and reached a personal agreement whereby Ukraine would sell part of its share of the Fleet to Russia and rent Sevastopol to Russia. Russia's payment would come in the form of writing off Ukraine's debt for past energy supplies (some $2.5 billion) plus further oil and gas supplies in the future from Russia. This was a good bargain for Ukraine, but the deal was killed by the Parliament in Kyiv.

The best solution for Ukraine would be to sell to Russia, as soon as possible, its share of Russia's very expensive "naval glory," and to rent to Russia bases in Crimea on market terms. Another valuable part of the deal could be a ban on introducing any new vessels into the Fleet. As the existing vessels are slowly rusting into junk the Fleet, and hence the issue, would become steadily less significant. Following the elections of a new Parliament in April 1994, Ukraine indicated its willingness to make a deal along these lines. But it appears that renting the Crimean infrastructure at world market rates is unacceptable to Moscow.

Prospects for these issues

On a number of occasions the presidents of Ukraine and Russia have met in Crimea to discuss the complex problems of Crimea and the Fleet. Important delegations from the two countries have held negotiations in Kyiv and Moscow, including at the level of the prime ministers. During 1994, negotiations were intensified and some significant progress was made. However, the Russian intervention in Chechnya at the end of the year, in which Russia used very tough military measures to prevent Chechnya from leaving the Russian Federation, caused concern in Ukraine. Some Ukrainian politicians had a strong reaction. But many foreign policy specialists counseled the Ukrainian government to take a cautious position.

So far, therefore, the major issues of Crimea and the Fleet have not been resolved. It seems likely that these complicated questions may remain unresolved for some time. Unfortunately, these extremely important security problems have not received much international attention, perhaps because they do not threaten European, American or world security directly.

The Ukrainian–Russian disputes over Crimea, the Black Sea Fleet and other issues will not disappear by themselves. Both sides need to moderate their more extreme patriotic feelings, and to demonstrate a high level of flexibility and reasonableness, to achieve some mutually acceptable compromises. Mediation from abroad might facilitate this effort.

Despite the collapse of the Soviet Union, Russia still retains a good deal of the old imperial mentality. For those people in high places in Russia who would like to reconstruct an empire, Ukraine may become a major test for the new democracy in Russia and for Moscow's real willingness to put the Soviet past behind it. Ukraine's development of truly normal relations with Russia will depend to a great extent on the developing balance of political forces within Russia itself.

Meanwhile, Ukraine has taken steps to improve its position with the CIS. On April 15, 1994, Ukraine signed an accord that will give it representation, as an associate member, in all structures of the recently established CIS Economic Union. Ukraine's involvement is only partial. Ukraine will provide a share of financial support only for those activities it takes part in. Ukraine will have a vote on those matters that are governed by the particular documents it has signed; otherwise Ukraine need only be consulted.

Ukraine is unhappily aware that the West in general and the United States in particular lacks any interest or political will to provide any real security guarantee or military deterrence on Ukraine's behalf, or in Eastern Europe in general. The West will not be willing to halt an expansion of Russia's influence in Eastern Europe, which might mean a confrontation. Nowadays the West cannot even deal effectively with the former Yugoslavia.

4 Nuclear weapons

At the time of the dissolution of the Soviet Union, the republics agreed that Russia would be the sole successor state for the Soviet nuclear weapons. At the time, Soviet nuclear weapons were deployed in four republics: Russia, Ukraine, Belarus and Kazakhstan. The other three agreed that the nuclear weapons on their soil would be transferred to Russia.

Ukraine formally declared its intention to be a nuclear weapons-free state. This decision included both a commitment to rid itself of all nuclear weapons already on its soil, and not to build any new ones. Ukraine agreed to adhere to the Nuclear Non-Proliferation Treaty (NPT) as a non-nuclear state. In May 1992 Ukraine, together with Belarus, Kazakhstan and Russia, signed the Lisbon Protocol to the START I Treaty.[13] The Protocol, signed also by the United States, is a formal addition to the START I Treaty, signed earlier by the Soviet Union and the United States.

Meanwhile, a substantial number of the weapons actually existed on Ukrainian territory through no decision of Ukraine's. In fact, the largest number of formerly Soviet nuclear weapons outside Russia were to be found in Ukraine. All the tactical nuclear weapons, which are easy to move, were taken back to Russia quickly following the break-up of the Soviet Union. The long-range strategic weapons, many of which are more difficult to move, remained. Ukraine inherited 1,760 strategic nuclear weapons, more than the whole strategic arsenals of Britain, France or China. Thus Ukraine found itself to be the third greatest nuclear weapons power on earth, after Russia and the United States. It is worth emphasizing that this remarkable situation existed through no decision or action that Ukraine had ever taken, and that Ukraine was not responsible for the presence of the weapons on its territory. However, upon achieving independence Ukraine did take responsibility for them, by committing itself to give them up.

From Ukraine's point of view, there were several ironies in this situation. One was that Ukraine suddenly had so many weapons, even though it was Ukraine that had suffered the tragedy of Chernobyl and knew better than anyone how dangerous nuclear material can be. Another irony was that Ukraine now had to pay the bills for maintaining the weapons in a safe condition, even though Ukraine had played no part in the original decision to put the weapons on its territory. A third irony concerned the military significance of the weapons. The tactical nuclear weapons that were so promptly removed to Russia might have had some military value for Ukraine had they remained, but the strategic weapons that did remain have no military value for Ukraine. The strategic missiles were aimed at the United States, which is certainly no enemy of Ukraine's, and these missiles cannot be retargeted to short-range distances. They have never been tested over any short range, and for technical reasons it would be extremely difficult or impossible to try to reconfigure them for short distances. The missiles, therefore, are almost perfectly useless in any military sense.[14]

Although Kyiv announced in June 1992 that it was taking "administrative control" of the strategic weapons in Ukraine, this had a purely formal significance. The weapons are entirely under the control of Moscow in not one but two respects. They have electronic locks which prevent their detonation and the keys are only in Moscow. In addition, the bases where the weapons are kept or deployed are manned and guarded by Russian forces.[15]

The strategic weapons inherited by Ukraine included two types of ballistic missiles and one type of cruise missile. There were forty-six ICBMs, of the type called SS-24 in the West; each of these carries ten MIRV warheads. There were 130 of an older ICBM, of the type called SS-19 in the West; each of these carries 6 MIRV warheads. In addition, Ukraine inherited approximately 520 cruise missiles that can be launched from bomber aircraft, a missile called AS-15 in the West. Some bomber aircraft for carrying these missiles were also inherited.[16]

During 1992 and 1993, opinion about the weapons diverged among security specialists in Ukraine. Several points of view developed. One group of specialists continued to believe that Ukraine should give up the weapons quickly and without conditions. These specialists argued that the weapons actually detract from Ukraine's security, for several reasons. They pose an ecological threat if they are inadequately maintained. They lead other nuclear powers to continue targeting the nuclear weapons in Ukraine. They cause tensions in Ukraine's relations with the US and other Western countries, and they give Russia a pretext for a hostile relationship with Ukraine. And the weapons drain funds that are badly needed for other national needs.

In this period, the majority of specialists in Kyiv agreed that Ukraine should give up the weapons but argued that Ukraine, in return, should be given security guarantees and financial compensation. Different specialists took somewhat different views on just what guarantees Ukraine should require and how much compensation should be sufficient.

Finally, a small group of specialists argued that Ukraine should keep at least a certain number of weapons for a period of time. Ukraine should not give up all nuclear weapons, this group argued, until the country is more secure.

During 1993 the Parliament in Kyiv increasingly adopted the viewpoint of the specialists who wanted Ukraine to be given guarantees and financial compensation for the weapons. Increasingly, the Parliament and government came to see the weapons as a bargaining chip in international negotiations, and chose to play a somewhat dangerous game. During 1993, various Members of Parliament made statements, intended partly for ears abroad, that Ukraine might keep the weapons. Then, in November 1993, the Parliament made a formal decision in a closed session. It overwhemingly ratified the main START I Treaty, resolving to destroy 36 percent of the arsenal promptly. But it also passed thirteen reservations to the ratification, one of them being an explicit rejection of Article 5 of the Lisbon Protocol, which commits Ukraine to adhere to the NPT. In return for lifting its reservations, the Parliament demanded international (that is, Western) security guarantees, and financial aid from the West ranging from $2.5 billion to $5 billion. The US had earlier promised $175 million to help pay the costs of dismantling the weapons.

This parliamentary decision provoked a sharp response from both Russia and the United States. Russia reacted angrily to this partial and very vague and conditional ratification. And the parliamentary decision was a severe embarrassment for the Clinton administration, which had been consistently saying that it anticipated that Ukraine would carry out its original commitments to rid itself of the weapons.

However, the decision also galvanized a trilateral diplomacy that had been stalled for months. Two weeks later, Washington offered its services to mediate various security disputes between Ukraine and Russia. The US also made a new offer to Ukraine. In exchange for full nuclear disarmament, the US now offered increased financial assistance for the nuclear dismantling plus some security guarantees for Ukraine. The US also offered Russia compensation for the enriched uranium that would be destroyed when the weapons were dismantled (naturally on Russian territory). This is significant because Russia had wanted the economic benefit of this uranium to pay for the rather expensive costs of dismantling.

The result of this offer was a new agreement, signed in Moscow on January 14, 1994 by the three heads of state. President Kravchuk flew to Moscow to join President Clinton, who was there for a summit, and President Yeltsin, to sign the Trilateral Statement. Ukraine now recommitted itself to giving up the weapons, as its national interests had been taken into account. Under the agreement, Ukraine receives international security guarantees of its territorial integrity. American financial aid for the costs of the dismantlement will be doubled. And Ukraine will receive fair remuneration in the form of uranium components to be used at Ukraine's nuclear power stations.

On this basis, the Parliament in Kyiv voted, on February 3, 1994, to lift its earlier reservations to the Lisbon Protocol. In the spring of 1994, some of the ICBMs began to be dismantled. However, the parliamentary resolution omitted an explicit approval of Ukraine joining the NPT. Only late that year, and under heavy pressure from the major nuclear powers, did the Parliament put aside its reservations. On November 16, 1994, the Parliament ratified the NPT, thus removing an obstacle in the way of carrying out two major arms control treaties. The delay was largely due to an effort to use the nuclear warheads as a bargaining chip for international security guarantees and aid. The Clinton administration offered $200 million in additional economic aid to Ukraine, thus raising total American aid to $900 million for 1994 and 1995. For this period Ukraine is the fourth largest recipient of US aid, after Israel, Egypt and Russia. On December 5, 1994, in Budapest, the presidents of the United States, Russia and Ukraine, together with the prime minister of Great Britain, signed a memorandum providing Ukraine with security assurances in return for its nuclear-free status.[17]

5 Concluding remarks

The foreign policy of Ukraine is, and will continue to be, aimed toward two fundamental goals. In the eastern and northern direction, Ukraine will seek to avoid any conflict with its huge, powerful and ideologically aggressive neighbor. In the western direction, Ukraine will seek to establish as many and as strong links as possible.

Geography and history predestine Ukraine in certain respects regarding Russia. Ukraine will for ever be an immediate neighbor of Russia, with a very long mutual border. For as far into the future as we can imagine, many people among the large Russian minority in Ukraine will feel that their Russian identity is important to them. For these reasons at a minimum, Ukraine will always want to have good and peaceful relations with Russia, and Russia will always have a very large place in Ukraine's security and foreign affairs.

In the westward direction, Ukraine has somewhat more choice. The choice of a free and independent Ukraine is to deepen its links as much as possible with Central and Western Europe and with the West as a whole. Ukraine, unlike Russia, does not have any territory extending beyond the Urals into Asia. Ukraine, unlike Russia, is an exclusively European country. The Ukrainian people are a European people. Even the fact that for more than three centuries Ukraine was part of a huge Eurasian empire has evidently not changed the fundamentally European nature of the Ukrainian people, culture and identity. After finally achieving its independence, Ukraine desires to link its destiny more and more with Europe and the West.

In the coming years, Ukraine needs to build its relationships with European and Western security structures, as well as political, economic and cultural structures. As interrelationships increase, the interests of Ukraine and the West will become more linked. Both Ukraine and the West should work to make some treaties that Ukraine has recently signed increasingly effective and significant. These include a new agreement with the European Union,[18] and the Partnership for Peace program with NATO. Both Ukraine and the West should also develop the many bilateral links, and the role of the OSCE.

The OSCE deserves more attention than it is receiving. Ukraine should promote, and take a larger role in, the OSCE. The organization played a valuable role in the later years of the Cold War in promoting respect for human rights and promoting democratic thinking, in many of the Soviet republics. That positive legacy can be built upon now. Ukraine should insist that the OSCE play a greater role in preventing and resolving conflicts within and between the former Soviet republics. Improved political and military security in Europe can best be achieved by enhancing the OSCE, giving it more authority and power.

It is most important for an effective European security regime that it be preventative rather than punitive. Almost alone among Western security structures, the OSCE has this preventative nature. Developing this approach to security in the region is a crucial challenge facing the United States and Western Europe.

In the years immediately following the collapse of the Soviet Union, the Western democracies believed that the democratization and market transformation of the former Soviet republics could develop with only slight Western technical and other guidance and very modest financial assistance. By now it is clear that this meager and superficial policy is facing rising opposition in Russia, and producing deepening pessimism in Ukraine. Western countries in general and the United States especially have a much greater role to play in encouraging the democratization of political life and the transformation to market economies throughout the former Soviet area, and especially in the two largest states, Russia and Ukraine.

A general interlocking of Ukraine's security with the overall European security framework should be timed to be completed about the time that the last nuclear weapons leave Ukraine. Thus over the coming years, Ukraine's security would rest more and more on the European framework and less and less on the nuclear arsenal. During this period, Ukraine needs to receive firmer support of its territorial integrity (especially in the context of possible challenges to Crimea) from the OSCE, from Europe in general and especially from the United States.

Kyiv understands that naturally, the United States has important strategic interests vis-à-vis Russia, including such matters as nuclear non-proliferation and peacekeeping in the framework of the United Nations. Kyiv understands that the magnitude of American interests vis-à-vis Ukraine cannot be comparable to American interests vis-à-vis Russia.

On the other hand, Ukraine's sovereignty and territorial integrity is vital for the United States from many viewpoints. Above all, an independent Ukraine is a guarantee of the irreversibility of the democratic process throughout the former Soviet states, and the main guarantee that there will be no new empire and no revival of the Cold War. In the security vacuum left by the collapse of the USSR, the great question is the nature of relations between Russia and its neighbors, especially Ukraine. Friendly relations between the two independent states are crucial for European security. Hostile relations between them or the end of Ukraine's independence would create a completely different, and much less favorable, situation in Europe.

We must conclude, therefore, by pointing out that the current dangerous level of insecurity in Ukrainian–Russian relations is the most important threat on the continent to European security, and thus to the basic security of the West. If by any chance, relations between the two countries should degenerate into force, it may mean the ruin of security for all of Europe, and perhaps even for the whole world. Therefore it is truly vital for the West's own interests that the West play a much larger role in assisting these two powerful countries, both to maintain the peace between them, and to make greater progress along the path toward democracy, upon which peace will depend in the end.

Notes

1 In the referendum, 84 percent of eligible citizens voted. Ukraine has *re*emerged as a sovereign country because a sovereign Ukraine existed for several months in 1918. At that time, Ukraine had a constitution, a functioning government and was recognized as a sovereign country by some forty other countries.

2 Leonid Kistersky, *Trade Related Issues of the Systemic Changes in the C.I.S. Region: the Case of Ukraine* (Geneva: UNCTAD, 1992).

3 Serhii Pirozhkov, "Natsionalni Interesi Ukraini," *Viche*, no. 11 (November 1992).

4 S. Pirozhkov and V. Selivanov, "Natsionala Bezpeka Ukraini: Suchasne Rozuminnia," *Visnik Akademii Nauk Ukraini* (September 1992).

5 For a longer analysis, see Leonid Kistersky, "Economic reasons for the political crisis in Ukraine," *The Brown Journal of Foreign Affairs* (Providence) 1 (1) (Winter 1993–4).

6 L. Kistersky and S. Shenfield, "Security of Ukraine: situation and prospects," *The Brown Journal of Foreign Affairs* (Providence) 1 (2) (Spring 1994).

7 In decreasing order, the most numerous ethnic groups are Jewish, Belorussian, Moldovan, Bulgarian, Polish, Hungarian and Romanian, each of which is represented by more than 100,000 people.

There are approximately eleven million ethnic Ukrainians living in other countries. The largest group abroad is the five million Ukrainians living in the Russian Federation. About two million live in other former republics of the Soviet Union. About five million ethnic Ukrainians live in the diaspora in North and South America, Europe and Australia.

8 L. Kistersky, C. M. Soussan and D. L. Cruise (eds.), *Security in Eastern Europe: the Case of Ukraine* (Providence: Brown University, 1994).

9 A. Kachinsky, "Kontseptsia Riziku u Svitli Ekologichnoi Bezpeki Ukraini," Kyiv: National Institute of Strategic Studies, Working Paper no. 14 (1993).

10 W. Kincade and N. Melnyczuk, "Eurasia letter: unneighborly neighbors," *Foreign Policy*, 94 (Spring 1994).

11 "Ukraine: the birth and possible death of a country," *The Economist* (London) (May 7, 1994).

12 The Soviet Union built such a large fleet with the intention of eventually challenging the US Navy's control of the Mediterranean, something that neither Ukraine nor Russia has any intention or need to do.

13 One of the authors, Leonid Kistersky, was a member of the Ukrainian delegation to the Lisbon talks.

14 There may be some question whether the small number of cruise missiles, for carrying by bomber aircraft, could have some military significance.

15 C. Gasteyger (ed.), *The Commonwealth of Independent States: a First Balance Sheet*, Geneva, Switzerland: Graduate Institute of International Studies: Program for Strategic and International Security Studies (PBIS), Occasional Paper no. 1 (1994).

16 These numbers are derived from Western sources. For an interesting, rather technical, analysis of the nuclear weapons in Ukraine, see Martin J. Dewing, "The Ukrainian nuclear arsenal: problems of command, control and mainten-

ance," Working Paper no. 3, Program for Nonproliferation Studies, Monterey Institute of International Studies (October 1993).

17   *Uriadoviy Kurier* (Kyiv) (8 December 1994).

18   The EU has a class of agreements with the former Soviet states, called New Generation Agreements (NGA). Ukraine was the first of these states to sign an NGA with the EU. Impetus toward preparing the NGA came initially from the first high-ranking Ukrainian governmental delegation to visit Brussels, in September 1992. One of the authors, Leonid Kistersky, was a member of this delegation. Nearly two years of complicated negotiations were then required before the NGA could be signed.

Part V

Russia: public attitudes and expert assessment

15

Public attitudes in Russia

Andrei Melville MOSCOW

1 Introduction

Before describing any of the substance of public attitudes in Russia today, it is necessary to explain in a book meant mainly for Western readers some basic aspects of the situation of the Russian people. It is not possible in the current period that the state of the Russian mind could resemble what is found in the West.[1]

In the first place, one must remember that Russia has practically no tradition of public involvement in matters of foreign and security affairs. In both Soviet and czarist times, such matters were the business of the state. Even until fairly recently, even the educated strata of the public were given no reason to have views on such matters and any views they had were not listened to. Beginning with the 1960s, some elite elements began to develop their own opinions. But only with the arrival of Gorbachev and *perestroika* in the 1980s did the idea begin to develop in Russian society that multiple points of view in this sphere were possible and perhaps legitimate. Even now the idea of a "public opinion" on foreign and security matters is a somewhat novel one in Russian culture.

As public opinion begins to form in any culture, its first stage is the development of stereotypes. From various sources, first of all the media, people in Russia have absorbed stereotypes about other countries, about the basic relationship of those countries to Russia, and about Russia's place in the world. When asked their opinions, in polls or by other methods, to a considerable extent they simply repeat the stereotypes they have absorbed. The result is "public opinion" in a sense, but the largely stereotypic nature of this opinion must be kept in mind. Some stereotypes may be held in a deep and lasting way, and thus become "attitudes" of a kind. Only as a culture develops do people, beginning with the better-educated strata, gradually evolve beyond stereotypes into more thoughtful kinds of opinions and attitudes. The Russian public today is only at an early stage in this evolution.[2]

There is another reason why public views in this area are not much developed in Russia. In the particular circumstances of the 1990s, Russians are primarily inward-looking ("introverted"). As discussed shortly, the internal problems of Russia are so enormous, and the specific external threats are so few, that it is only natural that Russians are giving little thought to the outside world. At the same time, certain recent events have generated several fixed ideas and almost obsessive anxieties, which are discussed below.

A third fundamental feature of the Russian public mood is confusion. Even elites feel considerable confusion; the feelings of the general public are practically chaotic in important respects. It is not unusual for the same individual to express contradictory viewpoints within the span of a few minutes. In the short time since 1989, people have lived through the loss of the European allies, the sudden switch of traditional foes to the status of friends, the August 1991 coup, the sudden break-up of the Soviet Union, the emergence of new threats from places that previously were safely inside the Union, several elections, a military attack on Parliament ordered by President Yeltsin in October 1993 and the bloody and extremely ineffective use of military force by federal troops in Chechnya. After so many drastic events in such a short time, it is not surprising that people should feel confused. And all this does not count the disastrous decline in the economy.

Of all these changes, perhaps the most deeply confusing is the matter of what "our country" is. Throughout the lifetime of everyone, until just a few years ago, "our country" was the Soviet Union. It is difficult for people to keep in mind that "our country" is now Russia. Of course nearly everyone understands that when they think about it. But when they are not thinking about it, the previous deeper feeling of what "our country" is naturally returns. Today it is still common for even well-educated people to think spontaneously of the Soviet territory when they think of "my country," and then perhaps to correct themselves. The term "near abroad," meaning the former Soviet territories outside Russia has come quickly into general use precisely because people find the term helpful to overcome the confusion.[3]

However the very term "near abroad" also signals that this region has a special emotional status for Russians. The term "far abroad" means all lands outside the former Soviet territory, in other words everything that was "abroad" in the Soviet era. Emotionally still, "far abroad" really means for Russians what other people on earth mean by "abroad." The so-called "near abroad" has an intermediate status, special and ambiguous. Emotionally it is not foreign territory, even when people can remember that legally it is.

2 Major anxieties of the Russian public

Two anxieties are fundamental in the viewpoint of the Russian public today. One is the primacy of the internal crisis, which is inseparably intertwined with the immense fall in the country's international position. The other is the near abroad and the problems it presents. In the absence of any great enemy someplace on Earth, no other question or topic that could be related to external affairs carries much force for the public at present. This chapter will take up various more concrete topics later, but they can only be properly understood in the context of these fundamentals of the Russian public's viewpoint.

The internal crisis of Russia is so overwhelming and has so many aspects that by itself it leaves many citizens bewildered and confused. What has been presented as a process of democratization has produced a series of political crises, with a nearly universal expectation of more to come. The fabric of society is deformed and disconnected, in some spheres still authoritarian and top-down, in other spheres freewheeling and hyper-individualistic. Organized crime, especially in urban areas, now surpasses anything found nearly anywhere else. Meanwhile Russia's economy is lurching, generally downward, although with certain pockets of prosperity (sometimes crime-connected). No quick description can communicate how the political, social and economic dimensions of current life add up, especially in urban regions, to an experience of practically permanent crisis and, at times, near-chaos.[4]

Another chapter of this book emphasizes that the public in Central European countries feel that internal insecurities are much more important than any external danger. Yet Russians would say that the internal crises of those countries are mild compared to Russia's crisis. To report that the chief insecurities felt by Russians involve internal, not external, matters would be an understatement. Asked about what threatens Russia, citizens respond spontaneously by speaking about economic collapse, soaring crime, ethnic troubles, the general spread of chaos and fear of the outright disintegration of Russia itself. They rarely mention the far abroad.[5]

So severe and lasting an internal crisis would hardly be possible in a country that was a true superpower. People feel this, and in this way at least, the collapse of the superpower of which people used to be proud is linked to their feelings about their daily situation now. Whatever their opinions (which may often be critical) about various specific actions taken by the old USSR, it is hard for Russians to forget that, not long ago, words spoken in the Kremlin could make the world tremble, while now Russia is receiving handouts that almost seem like charity. In today's public attitudes, feelings of loss of position in the world mingle with feelings of loss of a stable, functioning society at home. For many, the old Soviet way of life may not have been the best they could imagine, but it also was far from the worst, and it was *their* way of life. It was familiar and, for many Soviet citizens, not so uncomfortable. In many ways it is now crumbling or gone.[6]

Among the public in Russia, it is not uncommon to find an attitude of outright hopelessness about Russia's situation. Of course this feeling is far from universal. Many people feel that positive possibilities remain, and there are even some optimists. But hopeless feelings are widespread. Focus group and other research reveals relatively common feelings that Russia is in a state of complete collapse and degradation, and that no path to a better future is clearly visible.[7]

The one subject involving the world outside Russia to which Russians give great attention is the near abroad. As noted, this is a matter of "external" relations only in a rather unreal sense. The Russian public is all too well aware that a number of dangers or possible dangers, some of them complicated, are arising in the near abroad. It is worth emphasizing that for the public, the fact that this is possible *at all* is already a disaster. Only a few years ago, and throughout all the time that anyone can remember, the whole of these regions was totally and unquestionably under Moscow's control. Any internal threat from within the Soviet Union was simply not a possibility. The mere fact that one must now think about a dozen actual and potential risks from the near abroad is therefore a shock in itself. For citizens this is one of the basic realities that shows how much has been lost.

For the public in Russia, by far the greatest question involving the near abroad is the threat to Russians living there. Even something as important as large-scale fighting between non-Russians, for example recently in Tajikistan, is not nearly as important to the public in Russia. Threats to the human rights and sometimes outright violations of human rights of the Russians living in various countries of the near abroad are reported almost daily in the media in Russia and are a common topic of conversation. About 25 million Russians live in these countries. So most people in Russia have friends or relatives, or know people who have friends or relatives, living there. The difficulties facing the Russians living there now, and the difficulties and dangers they may face in the future, are not only a "political" problem "for society," but for many people are matters of immediate and personal concern.

It is essential to keep in mind the viewpoint of Russians on what happened at the end of 1991, when the Soviet Union collapsed. Previously those 25 million Russians had simply been living, like all Russians, in their own country, which naturally was the Soviet Union. Then suddenly these Russians found themselves living "in a foreign country" through no action of their own, and indeed *against their will*. No one had consulted them about whether the Soviet Union should be ended and they were not responsible for it. Suddenly they discovered they were now "foreigners" living in new countries that were not their own. The problems created thereby can be profound, both for these Russians and also, to be sure, for the dominant national groups in the new countries.

The concern for these Russians felt by the public in Russia is strong enough for it to be one area where a substantial part of the public would support strong action – force – by Moscow if it seemed necessary to protect the Russians in the near abroad, particularly to protect them from any physical threat. It is important to notice that from the viewpoint of the public in Russia, any such action would be defensive, not offensive. Public support for forceful action by Moscow to protect these Russians would apply, of course, to action taken within the territory of the former Soviet Union, not beyond it.

One more point should be made about public attitudes in Russia about the near abroad. To a considerable degree, the public realizes that the problems of the Russians in the new countries are complicated. Particularly in urban areas, much of the public does not have an overly simplistic view of this question. Rather, much of the public understands that the dominant national groups in the new countries also have rights, and that good solutions to these problems will be complicated and not easy to find. The public in Russia would much prefer negotiated, peaceful solutions.[8]

3 Specific attitudes and perceptions

Against the background now sketched of the public's strongest anxieties, we may now turn to some more concrete topics. The topics discussed below are limited to security and foreign affairs, plus several topics directly linked to them.

External threats

A basic and simple paradox exists in Russian public attitudes. On the one hand, people realize that there is no outside great power to be feared, at least for the present. On the other, people feel that the country of Russia is in so precarious a state that it might be in a weak position vis-à-vis any new threat that might appear.

Russians are very glad that the Cold War, and the sense of threat that it brought, is over. After their immense sufferings and losses of World War II, Russians feel that they love and want peace as much or more than any people. One of the positive features of today's situation for Russians is that there is no specific enemy and no immediate threat from anywhere in the world.

People also feel that their country should be strong, and is not. With vast territories to protect and hardly any natural barriers such as oceans or

mountain ranges, Russians feel today (as they have for centuries) a vulner-
ability to attack from the outside. A Russia that is strong in military and
other ways could protect itself. But people today fear that economic collapse, political paralysis and the general internal crisis must surely mean
that Russia is weak. The result is a generalized, non-specific anxiety about
the outside world and threats that could appear from some direction. This
anxiety about Russia's insecure place in the world and about what the
future might bring naturally adds one more element to people's overall
fears.[9]

The United States and the West

In one important way, Russians have traditionally been interested in no
foreign country more than the USA (it is very often referred to by the
equivalent Russian initials, not by words). In psychologists' language, the
USA has high "salience" for Russians, whether the content of their feelings
is favorable or unfavorable. Russians inhabit the largest country on earth
and one that, for decades, was one of only two superpowers on earth. For
these and other reasons, Russians wish to compare their country to the
greatest other power on earth, which at present is the USA. Thus the USA,
more than any country, is Russians' point of reference when thinking about
other countries in general.

The content of public views of the USA in Russia is still somewhat
polarized. On the one hand, there are a considerable number of Russians
who continue to see the USA as a model for Russia. Some even see the USA
as an ally. Several attitudes are apparent here. Those who hold democratic
values feel that the USA is the greatest proponent of those values; the same
applies to people who like Western values and perspectives generally. Other
people who may hold different values may merely like the idea of Russia
and the USA as partners. Here we see a residue of an old idea, once rather
popular, that these two powers should together control the world.

On the other hand, there are many Russians who feel suspicious and even
adversarial about the USA. Few now would put their feelings in ideological
terms. Also, not many people, except some with links to the military, think
of the USA as a probable future enemy. The most common suspicion is of
American domination, especially economic domination. Drawing partly on
the Marxist idea, on which they were raised, that economic struggle is by far
the most important part of international life, these people fear American
economic power and fear that the USA may use it to dominate and exploit
Russia. There is also some anxiety about cultural domination, as American
television shows and commercials penetrate increasingly.

The fear of economic domination by the USA (or by the West in general)
appears in one particular form with considerable frequency. Russians fear

that their country is going to be reduced to Third World status, as a more or less deliberate act by the USA and the West. Some Russian intelligentsia speak of a Western policy to "deindustrialize" Russia. Among the general public, it is not uncommon to hear anxieties voiced that Russia will become an American economic colony. Everyone knows that Russia is both enormously rich in natural resources and at present is industrially backward by Western standards (not counting the military sector). Many people fear that the real goals of the West are to get the raw materials for itself, while taking steps to make sure that Russian industry will not be any competition.[10]

Once people are thinking this way, it is not hard to find "evidence" supporting this view. For example, the International Monetary Fund (IMF) sets conditions for loans. The IMF says that its conditions are determined merely by objective economic factors. But proud Russians may see it differently. Believing that the IMF is dominated by the West, and by the USA primarily, people complain that the IMF is "dictating preconditions" for its loans, preconditions that surely suit its sponsors. Here again, as so frequently, we find Russian attitudes taking shape against the background of keen awareness of how great the country was for so long. Why should a country that until recently was a global superpower now find that some Western organization is dictating preconditions to it?

Part of the negative feeling about the USA now is an unconscious reaction to a collapse of earlier illusions that huge American aid would miraculously solve Russia's domestic problems. In a much broader way too, there was a kind of "Russian–Western honeymoon" for a time in Russian public attitudes. Large numbers of people who grasped that Western aid could bring, at best, only limited benefits also shared in this feeling, which partly was just a normal, very human reaction and relief after many years of tense hostility. The honeymoon period has now faded, as Russia's situation grows no better and the realization sinks in that the Western world has only limited interest in Russia.

The media and information

The Russian public holds a deeply sceptical attitude toward the media and toward the information received from the government and the media about foreign and security affairs, and about public affairs generally. Chapter 3 discussed dissatisfaction with information and the media among the public in Central Europe. The public attitude in Russia is much stronger than dissatisfaction. Almost unanimously, Russians believe that the information they receive is unprofessional, insufficient and, indeed, untrustworthy. People not only doubt what they are told, they commonly believe that it is misinformation, perhaps even deliberate disinformation. There is a wide-

spread cynical feeling that the whole of Russian media, including its relationship with the state, is an organized system for feeding the people what
those in power want them to hear.[11] However, the public were very pleased,
in the weeks following the Chechnya intervention, to see the frank and open
treatment of that war in the newspapers and on the independent (not state-
controlled) television channels.

To a considerable extent, Russians' deep scepticism is a continuation of a
similar public attitude during the Soviet era. During that era not only was
it generally understood that the media transmitted whatever the authorities
wished, but further, society developed an art of gleaning the truth by
"reading between the lines" in Soviet media and by passing along information from foreign sources. Since this stance was already deeply ingrained,
it is only natural that it largely continues now, when people also mistrust the
state (if for somewhat different reasons). Although some newspapers are
less mistrusted than others, and certain writers and television programs may
gain some reputation for honesty for a while, the public does not believe it
has any lasting source of trustworthy information about foreign affairs or
any public affairs. The public's cynicism about information from official
sources and about the media was only deepened, first after the destruction
of the White House in the autumn of 1993, and especially after the official
propaganda, including lies, about the bloodshed in Chechnya.

Ukraine

The public in Russia hold extremely diverse views about the independence
of Ukraine. There also is considerable confusion, in part simply as a product
of public feelings that could hardly be more sharply conflicting. Some
people fully respect Ukraine's sovereignty and independence. Others
feel that historically and culturally, Ukraine is simply part of Russia and
that any "independent" Ukraine is a senseless idea that should quickly come
to an end. Every degree of opinion between these extremes can also be
found.

Perceptions of Ukraine provide a good example of the confused and
jumbled state of the public mind generally. This enormous diversity of views
is found in one political "layer" of attitudes. Right next to it, in an emotional layer of feelings, the near abroad including Ukraine is felt to be not
really abroad, as discussed earlier. Emotionally, most Russians simply cannot comprehend that Russia and Ukraine have become two independent
countries. Thus it is common, even for individuals who say that politically
they respect Ukrainian independence, to make some remark in the same
conversation that, for instance, refers to Kiev as one of "our" cities. Similar
disconnections among attitudes are found across many topics.

The fact that Ukraine is not emotionally separated from Russia in
the Russian mind is not only a source of difficulties; it also has positive

implications. Most Russians do not accept that there is even a slight chance that political confrontations between the two could lead to military conflict. Here is an attitude strikingly different from the public's view in Central Europe and Germany, where a military clash is one of the possibilities the public takes seriously. Not surprisingly, the public in Ukraine tend to share the attitude of the public in Russia (as discussed in chapter 13). The Russian and Ukrainian peoples have shared the same country and the same culture for so long that war is almost unthinkable.

Simultaneously, and perhaps paradoxically, the Russian public can be outraged and even a bit frightened by actions of the Ukrainian government. Russians commonly feel that the ambitions of the authorities in Kiev are excessive and even dangerous. On this topic as on many others, Russians' feelings are much influenced by Moscow's official rhetoric and confrontation at the state level easily translates into popular mistrust and fears. People generally assume, however, that Kiev's excesses can be handled by means well short of war.

Slavic unity

An attitude appears to be growing among the public in Russia that a "Slavic unity" exists and has always existed among Russia, Belarus and Ukraine, and that it inevitably will reassert itself again. In 1992, just after the sudden and frustrating collapse of the Soviet Union and the emergence of these three as independent countries, this idea could be encountered only sometimes. In 1993 and since, it has become more widespread.[12] Of course Russia, Belarus and Ukraine are the only Slavic states of the former Soviet Union.

This "Slavic unity" is understood primarily as a deep blood relationship, and a historical, cultural, psychological and emotional affinity among Russians, Ukrainians and Belorussians who are felt to be practically the same nation. Among some people this feeling of unity has an almost metaphysical overtone. The Russian people have great difficulty accepting – and ultimately perhaps cannot accept – the separation of the three, and want to believe that sooner or later their natural unity will triumph again.

Here is another reason why there is no place in today's Russian mentality for any idea of a "Ukrainian threat." This also may be why there is almost no interest among the Russian public in the question of the nuclear weapons in Ukraine. Except for some among the educated elite who are concerned about the global proliferation of nuclear weapons, Russians are paying little attention to the Ukrainian weapons or to any matter involving nuclear weapons.

Interestingly, the sense of Slavic unity among Russia, Belarus and Ukraine, which is more a feeling than a thought-through idea, seems to be distinctly different from traditional pan-Slav ideology. For centuries, various intellectuals in Russia and other Slavic countries put forward pan-Slavism as an intellectual doctrine and a political program. But traditional pan-Slavism usually embraced all Slavs, including the South Slavs who live in the Balkans and the West Slavs – Poles, Czechs and Slovaks. Today's attitude in Russia seems not to include these peoples and certainly does not contain a wish for any assertive attempt to create some kind of political bond among them all. Part of the reason for this is doubtless the vividness of the distinction between the near abroad and the far abroad.

The new form of feelings of Slavic unity may help explain why most of the *public* in Russia did not become greatly interested in the civil war in the former Yugoslavia for a long time. In spite of a traditional sympathy for the Serbs, and in spite of many statements by certain political figures, events in Yugoslavia did not deeply engage most of the public for years. This must also be seen in the context of several wars occurring during the same period *within* the near abroad. However, pro-Serbian feelings among the Russian public grew during 1994.[13]

Nationalism and political ambitions

Russians' attitude about the ambitions of the Kiev government is typical of public attitudes about nationalistic ambitions and striving for independence in all the new states in the near abroad and, for that matter, about similar ambitions and strivings in the autonomous regions within the Russian Federation controlled by non-Russian ethnic groups. (Chechnya is only one such region, of many.) The Russian public are inclined to feel that these nationalistic ambitions are inflamed and manipulated by local politicians.

Most Russians, certainly most living in urban areas and having some education, accept that other nationalities have a right to their own identity.[14] The Soviet Union, and the czarist empire before it, were always multiethnic states and in many significant ways Russians accept and respect the needs of other nationalities for their own identity and culture. Russians feel that these needs, in their moderate and "natural" form, should present little problem. The ambitions of local politicians are blamed for inflating nationalistic feelings out of all proportion, and thereby creating political and social problems which otherwise would not exist. The strong similarities should be noticed between this attitude held by Russians and similar attitudes felt by Ukrainians and Central Europeans (discussed elsewhere in this book). Throughout Eastern and Central Europe this is a point of public consensus. Of course, Russians disagree about whether and how much *Russian* nationalism may be a problem, and may be inflamed by Russian politicians. Obviously a considerable number of Russians are now finding Russian nationalist leaders appealing.

Borders

The public in Russia are generally aware that nearly all of Russia's borders, and nearly all borders within the territory of the former Soviet Union, were drawn arbitrarily and thus are not very legitimate. This is not an area of public ignorance. The public are generally aware that many borders are simply lines drawn on maps by communist bureaucrats.

Beyond this, the public are rather confused and unsure what practical conclusions should be drawn. There are conflicting impulses. Some people feel that since the lines are artificial and do not mean much to begin with, it should be possible and reasonable to change them. These people are not interested in increasing Russian territory for its own sake, but rather in adjusting borders where the current ones split some nationality into two countries, or to redress clear injustices. On the other hand, many people feel that it could be dangerous to start making changes. Since nearly all borders are questionable, changing some could be potentially explosive. The net result of these two contrary impulses is a sense of confusion. The public hear demands from various sources for border changes and do not know how to respond.[15]

In 1992, in the months following the collapse of the USSR, the public were worried about the shrinking territory of the former superpower. This concern has diminished as time has passed and borders have apparently stabilized.

Peacekeeping

The Russian public have relatively complicated attitudes about peace-keeping, including who should do it and where. For Russians there is a decisive difference between peacekeeping outside and peacekeeping inside the territory of the former Soviet Union. Again we see how central it is in Russian attitudes that the far abroad is really abroad, and the near abroad is not.

For the world outside the former USSR, Russian attitudes about peace-keeping differ only somewhat from the attitudes of other Europeans. Most Russians support the legitimacy of peacekeeping by the United Nations in the world outside. However, Russians may be somewhat more sceptical than other Europeans that international peacekeeping can be effective in many situations. There is a strong tendency for Russians to think that "outside interference" in local conflicts may aggravate them, and certainly that there is no universal formula for success in peacekeeping.

Another difference in Russian attitudes is that Russians are not enthusiastic about "sending Russian boys" to some far-off place as peacekeepers. In part this feeling results from a suspicion that there may be all too many situations, in coming years, where Russian boys will be needed to manage conflicts much closer to home. In part this feeling is simply a product of the introversion mentioned earlier. Russia itself is vast, and the near abroad is vaster. Anything beyond that feels far away.

The public in Russia feels emphatically that Russian soldiers who are called upon to risk their lives in peacekeeping anywhere must be volunteers. Here is a point where a consensus within Russia is in full agreement with the consensus in other countries, reported in other chapters.

Attitudes about peacekeeping in the near abroad are strikingly different from those about peacekeeping elsewhere around the world. A consensus of the Russian public feels that *only Russian troops* may be used for peace-keeping in the near abroad. "Foreign" involvement, by the United Nations or anyone else, on the territory of the former Soviet Union is absolutely unacceptable to the great majority of Russians.[16]

Clearly this is a topic on which Russians strongly disagree with the attitudes of Central Europeans, and perhaps more significantly, the attitudes of Ukrainians. The emotional quality of the difference in attitudes can be described in even stronger terms. Russians do not merely hold a different position. The public in Russia *take it for granted* that only Russian forces and no others may act as peacekeepers on formerly Soviet territory. For most Russians this is so clear that the matter is not worth discussing.

Here is one topic where the current policy of the Moscow government is fully rooted in public attitudes. In 1993 and since, Moscow has officially and repeatedly appealed to the world community and the United Nations to give the Russian Federation a mandate to conduct peacekeeping on the former Soviet territory. This appeal, which so far has received little positive response from the world,[17] is not merely a "position" worked out by policy specialists in Moscow; it genuinely reflects an attitude strongly held by the Russian people. (Notice that this means that a more democratic regime in Moscow would not only seek the same goal but might seek it even more vigorously.)

East Central Europe

In general, the public in Russia are not very interested in Hungary, Poland and the Czech and Slovak Republics. People feel that these countries neither present any threat nor have much of importance to offer, and that Russia has dozens of more pressing concerns. Beyond this, two specific attitudes are widely held. From the Western viewpoint these attitudes appear to be in conflict with each other; from the Russian viewpoint they are consistent.

The public in Russia, especially people with some education living in urban areas, generally approve of the fact that these countries now find their own way in the world. Their past control from Moscow is seen as some-thing that was enforced by communism. People feel that these countries today are properly returning to their own identities. At the same time the public in Russia oppose any idea that these countries should join Western structures, such as the European Union or NATO, if Russia does not also join simultaneously. People simply do not accept that these countries should, or should want to, join Western institutions before or without Russia.

From the Western viewpoint, these attitudes seem to be in conflict. If the East Central European countries are really free, they should be free to join whatever institutions they choose. Russians see it differently. For them the central feature of this question is the inclusion of Russia. If Western institutions are going to expand eastward, then their expansion must include Russia. In particular, Russia must not be deliberately excluded.

Here is one manifestation of a feeling that has run very deep in Russia for centuries. Ever since the time of Peter the Great, there has been a recurrent anxiety in the Russian mind that Russia might somehow discover that it is not being included in Europe. Russians have feared that in some fashion they might be pushed away, "defined out," defined as "not European." Down the centuries, making sure that this does not occur has been a recurrent need and often a source of policy. In different periods of history this anxiety has naturally taken different specific forms. In the current period, one form is a Russian belief that any eastward expansion of Western institutions must include Russia if it is to occur at all. In particular, there must be no new "line" drawn – say on Poland's eastern border – that makes it possible for the world to say that "Europe" lies on one side and the other side is "not Europe." The depth of this concern, which is felt by the general public as well as by policy-makers and politicians, must not be underestimated.

Russia as a source of threat?

The public in Russia today hold a mixture of ideas about the possibility of Russia being a threat to others. Naturally, in this country like any other, most people do not see their homeland as a potential military threat to others. However, views in Russia are so very diverse that even that idea can sometimes be found.

There is a widespread acceptance among Russians of a quite different idea of "a Russian threat," namely that Russia's instability can pose a danger to others. Many people readily agree that a collapse of the country into chaos would endanger the outside world and especially Europe. Some are ready to accept comparisons between what Russia could become and the situation of the Balkans today.

Definite disagreements arise over whether a strongly authoritarian regime would be a greater or lesser threat to the outside world. People who wish for such a regime see chaos as the greater danger, for Europe as well as for

Russia. Many other people, especially in urban areas, feel that a new authoritarian regime could create a new danger for Europe and the world. Despite all the things said outside Russia (and sometimes inside) about the so-called authoritarian instincts of Russians, more than half the public is opposed to the imposition of a new dictatorship in Russia on *any* grounds (54 percent against, 28 percent in favor).[18]

There has been much speculation since the December 1993 elections about the extent of public support for the extreme views of Zhirinovsky. A certain number of people voting for his party does not mean that the same number agree with his views. Some people were voting "no" against an almost unbearable status quo. There appears to be no great swing of public opinion back to outright neo-imperial and neo-interventionist ambitions. It seems, rather, that the public are learning to accept today's Russia as it is, without wishing to restore the USSR and without imperial ambitions.[19]

Both focus group and quantitative research show that a majority of people do want Russia to be strong, and to be a great power even if that might mean some deterioration of relations with other countries.[20] This is not at all the same as wanting to embark on a new wave of expansionism. Unquestionably, broad public support has been building since at least sometime in 1993 for a more definite, independent and assertive foreign policy. Previously, people felt that foreign policy seemed to consist too much of agreeing with and following Washington. People want Russia to define its own needs and interests.

However, it is important to observe that people also feel that such a policy is merely normal. It is normal even for ordinary states, and certainly for a great power such as Russia. Some of the mood that to outside observers may seem like assertiveness is really just a desire that Russia be subservient to no foreign power, and that Russia make its own decisions about what is right for itself, as any country does. Many Russians who feel this desire for strength, independence and pride would not make any connection from this to expansionism; indeed many would say expansionism is not at all in Russia's interests and could be dangerous for Russia. Here "expansionism" refers to Russia's stance toward the outer world; the near abroad is a more ambiguous topic.[21]

Other feelings of threat

An earlier chapter mentioned the strong public concern in some other countries about crime, about ecological dangers and about the migration of peoples. These worries are felt also by Russians, in specifically Russian forms. To a large extent these matters are not seen as external.

The huge presence of crime in Russia's cities today has been mentioned already. Ordinary people living in cities must consider the possibility of danger to themselves on a daily basis.[22] The public also are aware in a general way that "mafia" organizations now pervade enormous areas of society and the economy. For many, such things are among the most visible of Russia's illnesses.

There is also awareness of the dangers of "another Chernobyl" or other environmental disasters. Nuclear power stations, as people know, are scattered around various places in the near abroad and Russia. Environmental concerns would be relatively keen, were it not that they tend to be pushed to one side by even more urgent worries. For many people, the feeling that an ecological disaster could occur at any time is just one more ingredient in the more general feeling that society is constantly on the brink of disaster.

Russians see an important movement of peoples already, namely the many Russians who are returning, or who may be returning soon, from various places in the near abroad. The feeling that fellow-Russians are being forced out of places where they have long lived (in some cases for generations) is a natural source of resentment. At the same time, people feel that Russia itself is so poor and so burdened with problems that there is no way that even fellow-Russians can be received. Here is another reason why sentiment is growing that Moscow should take steps to ensure just and reasonable living conditions for the Russians of the near abroad, both for their sake and so that they will not have to move.

There are clear signs that animosities are now growing among the Russian public, especially in cities, toward darker-skinned people – often called "blacks" – from the south. Azerbaijanis and other peoples from the Caucasus area, often seen now in kiosks and market-places in the cities, are widely viewed as profiteering at the expense of ordinary Russians and as occupying jobs that Russians used to hold. Popular resentment has been reinforced by some official actions, for instance some forced deportations of Azerbaijanis ordered by the Moscow mayor's office in 1993. (This sort of official action may be taken partly to create scapegoats, and to deflect public attention from widespread corruption and the huge inability of the bureaucracy to solve real problems.)[23]

4 Concluding remarks

In the early 1990s the Russian people find themselves living in a confusing and extremely difficult time. For decades, nearly all aspects of the life of society and of the country were definite and sure. The life of individuals was secure and, for many, not so unsatisfactory. More recently Russians have experienced a great series of profound shocks and upheavals, which taken together have added up to nothing short of a cataclysm. For most of the public, the huge losses in territories controlled by Moscow, disastrous as those are, are less profound than the stunning decline of the country internally. A previously firm political order has been replaced by a freer but badly disorganized politics punctuated by crises in Moscow. Society presents people with a bewildering combination of greater freedoms and more opportunities in some respects, combined with severely degraded, even collapsing, services and structures in many other respects. The economy, despite pockets of growth, is falling visibly overall with no upturn in sight. Taken together, these things give many Russians a feeling of living inside a disaster, with worse possibly to come and with outright chaos feeling uncomfortably close. Hopelessness about the future is common.

Against this background, it is not surprising that Russians are fixated on Russia's situation and care little about the outer world. Russians know, with relief, that no great enemy elsewhere threatens attack, and they have hardly any other reason to be interested in the world beyond the near abroad. The near abroad does receive people's selective attention. In particular, current and likely future dangers to the many millions of Russians living there produce anxiety and resentment. The legitimacy of intervention by Moscow to "keep the peace" and protect Russians against any physical threat is taken for granted. Thus all necessary attitudes are already in place in the public mind to produce public support for Moscow's use of force in the near abroad, should circumstances seem to warrant it.

People want Russia to be strong, in military and other ways, and see anxiously that Russia is not. They also feel that their desire for a strong, secure Russia is only normal. The majority of Russians, at least at present, do not equate "strength" with any policy of expanding beyond the near abroad. Most Russians do not want their country to seek world leadership again anytime soon. People do expect Russia to be treated by others as the great power that, in basic ways, it is. They do not want their country to fall into line behind somebody else. They expect Moscow to define reasonable national interests for the country and then to pursue them, as every country does. Most Russians are also ready to see reasonable accommodations made with other major powers in the interest of preserving peace, as also is normal. To live in peace with the world is greatly desired. If the West and everyone will treat Russia with the respect due to any great power, most Russians will be generally satisfied with their relations with the outer world, and will focus their attention on improving the grim situation at home.

Notes

1   This chapter is based on research conducted by the Center for International Projects for the Security for Europe Project, and on other research by the Center for International Projects. See also note 11.

In the Russian language, the name of the country is pronounced "Ross-ee-ya." The word "Moscow" is the English-language name for the capital city. In Russian its name is pronounced as if it were spelled "Mosk-va" in English.

2 Examples of stereotype and cliché words in common use at present include "totalitarianism," "empire," "partocracy," "democracy" and "market."

3 A further ambiguity is created by the fact that some people use the term "near abroad" to include the three Baltic countries, whereas other people exclude the Baltics from what they mean by the "near abroad."

4 According to a VTSIOM poll in November 1993, 42 percent of those polled said they fear the loss of order and an increase in anarchy in the country. Reported in *Moscow News* (December 5, 1993). VTSIOM are the initials for the organization whose name in translation is "All-Russian Central Public Opinion Research Institute."

In a VTSIOM poll of January 1993, 86 percent of respondents feel insecure and unprotected from crime and criminals. Reported in *Moscow News* (February 14, 1993).

5 These conclusions are drawn primarily from the research sources mentioned in note 1. Quantitative research data agrees. In June 1994, the Russian Independent Institute on Social and National Problems conducted a survey that asked "What is the major danger for Russia today?" No respondent referred to external matters; all mentioned internal ones only. The internal dangers were assessed by respondents as follows. In the political sphere, 45 percent mentioned the danger of civil war and 36 percent mentioned the activity of mafias. In the economic sphere, 42 percent mentioned the fall in the standards of living, 36 percent mentioned the fall in production, 28 percent mentioned hyper-inflation, and 28 percent mentioned unemployment. In the social sphere, 49 percent mentioned the rise in crime, 27 percent mentioned an inability to provide good education for children, and 25 percent mentioned precarious old age: Vladimir Petoukhov and Andrei Riabov, "How are you doing, Russia?" *Moskva* (magazine) (September 1994), pp. 114–21.

In a poll conducted for the US Information Agency by the ROMIR survey research firm in November and December 1993, the greatest threat to Russia's security was identified by 75 percent of respondents as coming from problems inside Russia, by 6 percent as coming from the near abroad, and by 4 percent as coming from the far abroad. *USIA Opinion Research Memorandum* (January 3, 1994).

As early as February 1993, 46 percent of public opinion leaders judged the likelihood of Russia breaking up as "high" or "very high." Four hundred opinion leaders were polled by "Vox Populi." *Mir mnenii i mneniya o mire*, 2 (13), Moscow: Vox Populi Service for the Study of Public Opinion (March 1993).

6 The Eurobarometer surveys show how the public in the European part of Russia have become disillusioned with the transformation of society. In the autumn of 1991, only 34 percent of Russians agreed with the statement that "the creation of a free market economy is a bad thing for Russia's future." By December 1993 the proportion taking this view had risen to 58 percent. European Commission, *Central and Eastern Eurobarometer*, 4 (March 1994), p. 33.

7 This public pessimism is aggravated by a widespread perception of a fundamental gap between the government (which claims to be democratic) and the people. One poll of late 1994 revealed only negative public feelings toward the

government: distrust and fear (73 percent), resentment and protest (63 percent), disrespect (60 percent), indifference (50 percent) and pessimism (49 percent). From a survey conducted by the Institute of the Sociology of Parliamentarianism. Nougzar Betanely, "One would awfully much like to live without fear," *Obshaya Gazeta*, (weekly) (December 2–8, 1994), no. 48/73. Notice that these results date from before the intervention in Chechnya.

The gap between government and people was further reinforced by the government's mishandling of the crisis in Chechnya. Even at the beginning of the intervention, 63 percent of the public disapproved of Moscow's use of military force, and a full quarter of the public said that they believe the military conflict in Chechnya means the end of democracy in Russia. From a poll conducted by the Public Opinion Foundation. Lef Aleinik, "Engagement of troops in Chechnya reduced President Yeltsin's rating," *Segodnia* (December 27, 1994).

It is also worth noting that the public reaction, in the first weeks, to the intervention in Chechnya revealed the confusion felt by many Russians between what is "domestic" and what is "international," and what are the appropriate means of domestic and international politics.

8   These conclusions emerge from the focus group research conducted by the Security for Europe Project. It is also true that some among the public have simpler feelings. It would not be easy to determine with any accuracy, by polling, what proportions of the public in Russia hold what view, because much would depend on how questions were worded, and on the context in which they were asked.

9   The uncertain and indeterminate nature of the feeling of potential external danger is suggested by the results of a survey conducted by the "Vox Populi" Service for the Study of Public Opinion in August and September 1993. Asked which country they considered Russia's "enemy number one," only 16 percent replied that Russia has no enemies and only 26 percent named a specific country, while 20 percent said that Russia has "many enemies" and 38 percent were unable to answer at all. *Mir mnenii i mneniya o mire*, 1 (85). Moscow: "Vox Populi" Service for the Study of Public Opinion (November 1993).

10 An example sometimes mentioned in the summer and autumn of 1993 was the demand by the US government that Russia halt the sale of a cryogenic rocket to India. Although Washington claimed that its motive was to slow down the proliferation of rocket technology to the Third World, many Russians saw this step as an American blow against Russian industry in one of the areas, rocket technology, where it is competitive with the West.

"Vox Populi" asked 400 public opinion leaders in July 1993 this question: "What lies behind the West's current interest in Russia – a striving to revive Russia, or on the contrary, to weaken it?" The "revive" response was chosen by 20 percent and the "weaken" response by 35 percent, while 40 percent rejected both. *Mir mnenii i mneniya o mire*, 2 (60). Moscow: "Vox Populi" Service for the Study of Public Opinion (August 1993).

11 According to a VTSIOM poll of January 1993, 50 percent of Russians polled do not trust "at all" any of the branches of authority in Moscow. Reported in *Moscow News* (January 31, 1993).

The Center for International Projects conducted another extensive series of focus groups in the autumn of 1993; groups were held in eleven regions around Russia. The findings of these regional focus groups confirmed and reiterated the findings of the groups held specifically for the Security for Europe Project.

One of the main findings in all regions was a deep alienation of the people from all central authorities. The public have an undifferentiated perception of the executive and legislative branches in Moscow as simply "the authorities," who are basically in opposition to the people. The public's strong disillusionment with the so-called "democrats" *in power*, which is part of the public's alienation from all forces in power, may help explain the democrats' defeat in the December 1993 parliamentary elections in Russia. At the same time, no strong inclinations toward neocommunist and/or strong nationalist opposition forces were visible.

12 In 1992, one or two individuals in focus groups held by the Security for Europe Project would typically express this idea. In groups held in 1993, this attitude was typically endorsed by a majority. Since then this attitude certainly has not declined among the public, and political and economic events may be reinforcing it.

13 Violence on a large scale took place during the early 1990s in Tajikistan, in Georgia, and elsewhere in the Caucasus area, as well as between Armenia and Azerbaijan. In the focus group research conducted by the Security for Europe Project in 1992 and 1993, very few participants even mentioned Serbs or Yugoslavia spontaneously. Even after the groups were asked about this topic explicitly, the typical group reaction was passive and uninterested. Interest grew in 1994, however, and it also must be kept in mind that future events in the former Yugoslavia could arouse Russian feelings.

Polls conducted in Russia for the US Information Agency by the ROMIR survey research firm showed an increase in the proportion of the public who feel that Russia should support the Serb side from 13 percent in September 1993 to 39 percent in April 1994. *USIA Opinion Research Memorandum* (April 19, 1994).

14 Whether certain groups, such as Ukrainians, are really "another nationality" is a separate question.

15 According to a poll conducted for the US Information Agency by the ROMIR survey research firm in June 1992, 54 percent of Russians thought that Crimea should be part of Russia; 27 percent disagreed. In the same poll, 43 percent thought that the areas of Kazakhstan where Russians are in the majority should *not* be part of Russia; 33 percent thought that they should. *USIA Opinion Research Memorandum* (August 6, 1992).

16 This conclusion emerged clearly from the research conducted by the Security for Europe Project. See also the article on this topic in the *Moscow News* (July 26, 1993). The consensus in support of using "only Russian troops" naturally includes allied CIS troops, such as Kazakh, Uzbek or Kyrgyz troops, who may be deployed alongside Russian forces.

17 In July 1994 the United Nations Security Council gave its approval to Russian peacekeeping activities in Georgia, and only in Georgia. The Budapest Summit of the CSCE, held in December 1994, declined a Russian request that Russia take the predominant role in peacekeeping in Nagorno-Karabakh, and approved a different plan in which Russia would have a smaller role.

18   Data from a poll conducted by the Public Opinion Foundation. Reported in
     Izvestia (January 6, 1995).
19   Only 18 percent of Russians support the idea of a restoration of the USSR.
     Moskva (September 1994).
20   In a VTSIOM poll in the summer of 1993, 69 percent of Russians agreed with
     the statement that Russia should preserve itself as a great nation even if it led
     to a deterioration of relations with the outside world. Reported in *Moscow
     News* (July 26, 1993). Note that the popular desire that Russia be, and be seen
     as, a great power is not necessarily the same as Russia being a "Great Power"
     as specialists use the term.
21   A VTSIOM poll of December 1992 showed that only 4 percent of Russians rely
     on a restoration of military power as a means to return to superpower status.
     Meanwhile 66 percent rely on economic reforms, while 30 percent think that
     superpower status does not mean anything today and what is important is
     being "a country where people have a good life." Reported in *Izvestia* (January
     23, 1993).
22   According to a survey conducted in late 1994, 71 percent of Russians believe
     that crime has increased in the place where they live, 59 percent have fears
     about their personal security, and 56 percent of adult Russians are afraid to
     walk outdoors in the dark. *Obshaya Gazeta* (December 2–8, 1994).
23   Western readers may wish to note that the word "Caucasian" is used in Russia
     and throughout the countries of the former Soviet Union in exactly the opposite
     sense that it is used in the West. In the West this word is the formal word for
     "white" people. In the former Soviet countries, it is a not entirely polite word,
     commonly used, that means "black" people. The Caucasian peoples are not, of
     course, "black" in the sense of African, but their much darker skin is sometimes
     colloquially called "black."

16

Russia: policy analysis and options

Yuri Davydov MOSCOW

1   Introduction

Russia has experienced changes of staggering magnitude in recent years, and this has produced much confusion among Russian specialists on questions of security. Until late in 1991, the country that all specialists in Moscow were thinking about was, of course, not Russia but the Soviet Union. This should be emphasized at the outset, because many Western experts do not entirely appreciate the depth of the shock that policy specialists in Moscow have lived through, nor how emotionally difficult it has been, and still is, to adapt to the new realities. Feelings of confusion about what "our country" is still continue today.

The shock of the sudden end of the USSR was made even more difficult psychologically, because it came so quickly after Moscow had lost the alliance of six important countries in East Central Europe. So far as security on the European side of the USSR was concerned, the Warsaw Treaty Organization was the pillar of Soviet policy and Soviet ideas. All thinking about security in the Western direction revolved around the WTO. Then at the end of the 1980s, the WTO became quickly undermined as an effective military alliance. East Germany was allowed to unify with West Germany on terms extremely favorable to the West. Moscow proposed that the WTO be converted into a political organization, but the European allies rejected that also. Thus specialists in Moscow found themselves in a situation where the bedrock alliance on the Western side was dissolving completely. The impact was comparable to what specialists and officials in Washington or London might feel, if NATO dissolved, completely and in a short time, in spite of every effort by Washington to prevent it.

Before the implications of the loss of the alliance could fully sink in emotionally, or be entirely understood intellectually, experts in Moscow were overwhelmed by the still greater catastrophe of the end of the Soviet Union itself. It is perhaps understandable that, for some time then, experts and officials in Moscow were hardly able to think creatively or develop much new policy about Europe and about security on the westward side.

The new and democratically oriented government of Russia, headed by Boris Yeltsin, understood that the United States and NATO did not really represent a threat, and rejected the previous Soviet perception that they did. For political as well as psychological stability in Moscow, this was important. It meant that in the months and years following the disasters, at least Moscow did not need to worry about a military threat from the West. The great double shock was not followed by a military emergency. Specialists and the government were thus allowed some time, which they badly needed, to begin to comprehend the shape of the new landscape.

Several features of the new situation clearly were fundamental. Most basic of all, of course, was that a foreign policy and a security policy had to be constructed for *Russia*. Another basic feature was that for the first time in decades, there was no definite enemy. There was no great foreign power that was able to, and might want to, invade or destroy the country. Indeed, the traditional adversaries, the United States and the Western European countries, were now partners. A third basic feature was that the danger of a global nuclear war, which only recently had seemed an enormous danger, was now insignificant. The second and third of these were, of course, highly positive for security. Nonetheless, these changes in combination represented a complete upheaval and required wholly fresh thinking.

As the old landscape vanished and specialists were obliged to rethink everything completely, some main trends and ideas began to appear. The next section surveys viewpoints that began emerging and the bases for them. Incidentally this chapter will use "Russia" to mean the Russian Federation.

2   Trends in Russian thinking in the first half of the 1990s

Introduction

The need to think in a completely new way about foreign and security affairs for the new, and very old, country of Russia created a special intellectual atmosphere in Moscow in the first half of the 1990s. Not only was the situation completely new; it also did not present clear and obvious features from which knowledgeable people could draw conclusions that would find general agreement. The uncertainty and ambiguity permitted a flowering of a broad spectrum of opinions. Almost any idea, over a vast range of viewpoints, could now be expressed and explored. Incidentally, in one way this debate was delightful for a community of experts who had spent much of their lives thinking along well-defined tracks.

In the Soviet era, the basic approach to national security was ideological. Security was seen as an external problem. The prevailing view was that the

USSR was surrounded by a hostile, capitalist, world that threatened to destroy the chief socialist state. This vision of the world satisfied the interests of the ruling elite (the "nomenklatura") who needed external hostility to justify the lack of freedoms in society.[1] Full security for the USSR could be achieved only if socialism prevailed around the world, and most directly, security required that socialism prevail in all neighboring countries. This was the rationale for the "Brezhnev Doctrine," which justified the use of force if necessary to maintain socialism in Eastern Europe. In principle, and to a large extent in reality, the Soviet people shared this vision (they were allowed hardly any exposure to any other) and were ready to sacrifice prosperity and freedoms for the sake of their country's security. They supported the Soviet military build-up and all of Moscow's actions to expand the zone of socialism beyond Soviet frontiers.

The government of the new Russia has rid itself of the ideological approach to security. The sphere of values, which had been the main source of confrontation in the past, now became a basis for cooperation, now that Russia shares the values of democracy and market economics. In the new circumstances, the majority of specialists feel almost no security threat from the West. For these specialists, the greatest security threats are internal: political instabilities; the difficulties of economic reforms; inflation; the danger of widespread social impoverishment; the collapse of the medical system; difficulties and worsening conditions in social welfare supports, in education, in the transportation and communication systems and in infrastructure generally; the startling growth in crime and the influence of mafias; the declining birth rate; separatist movements within the Russian Federation, both nationalist and regionalist; and the fact that many millions of Russians now find themselves living outside the country.

At the same time, there are many experts who continue to insist on the reality of an external military threat. These specialists are associated mainly with the military and intelligence establishments, and with pro-communist or extreme nationalist groups, but sometimes also with liberals who are trying to work out a liberal conception of Russian national identity.[2] This viewpoint emphasizes that NATO did not dissolve when the WTO did but continues in existence, that NATO retains an immense offensive military potential, that NATO is trying to expand eastward, that US forces remain in Europe, and that since the Cold War the United States has reduced its military budget only a little. The victory of Republican hardliners in the Congressional elections in the US in November 1994 has supported their anxiety. Looking in another direction, some of these specialists also point out the overpopulation of China, which shares a long border with Russia and which may have territorial claims on Russian land. Beyond the question of whether internal or external dangers are emphasized, there are innumerable issues facing the country and there is a welter of conflicting opinions, ideas and points of view.

In the West, and to a degree in Russia, the contending viewpoints on Russia's place in the world were often organized into two broad categories, the "Atlanticists" and the "Eurasians." These categories correspond to a traditional debate in Russian thought for centuries: the debate between "Westernizers" who would like to see Russia become a country approximately resembling other European countries, and "Slavophiles" who see Russia as a unique land, both European and Asian, that must find and create its own special character that is not Western. However, to organize the new debate about foreign and security affairs into the two categories of "Atlanticists" and "Eurasians" is only partly helpful. Experts disagree on larger and deeper issues. The watersheds between different viewpoints really reflect basic disagreements in the ways different thinkers see the past, present and future of Russia, their conflicting views of what path will lead to economic stability and prosperity, their differing views of where to find allies, their differing views of what destructive forces (abroad and at home) must be neutralized, as well as differences about how they intend to accomplish their goals. Specialists' views about security and foreign affairs depend in the last analysis on their views of a changing Russia. Before describing these differences, a few fundamental facts of the new situation must be reviewed.

Basic elements of the new situation

Russia is not the same thing as the Soviet Union was. To be sure, Russia makes up about 80 percent of the former USSR's territory. But Russia has only about 50 percent of its population. Russia's economy, too, is not huge. Russian GDP (gross domestic product) is only about half that of Germany's, and is less than the GDP of Britain, France or even Italy.[3] Russian resources to support any foreign and security policy are more limited than Soviet resources were.

For that matter, the Soviet resources were not, in reality, as great as they were portrayed to be, and certainly not great enough to sustain indefinitely a superpower policy that tried to operate all around the world. The insupportable burden of that effort is one of the reasons why the Soviet economy declined during the 1980s. The main real source of Soviet influence in the world was not economic, but military, power. That form of power was most useful in a situation of global confrontation, the Cold War. Military power is not very useful when there is no confrontation and no military enemy. Russia has no other basic sources (industrial, financial, technological, etc.) to influence events on the global scale. The political instability, difficulties in economic reform, and ethno-political crises that have shaken the country have undermined its global position. Together these things mean that Russia is not a superpower.

At the same time, Russia remains a country of enormous significance in important ways. It has a huge territory, by far the largest of any country on earth. It has enormous natural resources, again by far the most of any country. (So far these have been poorly used.) Russia is a country with an important and long history; it has made great contributions to European and world civilization; and it continues to have a large reservoir of well-educated and articulate intellectuals. It has a large scientific research establishment. And, of course, it has an immense number of nuclear weapons.

These assets, together with its tremendous current economic and other problems, create a unique combination of strengths and weaknesses. It is not easy for anyone, inside Russia or outside, to understand what possibilities this combination allows and what possibilities it does not. This includes what possibilities there may be in foreign affairs, as well as in other spheres. Russia also has inherited the legacy of a superpower, including many international agreements, the debts and many of the assets of the USSR, and the Soviet habit of imperial thinking and global ambitions.

The geopolitical situation

Russia now finds itself in a geopolitical situation worse than any it has experienced, other than in wartime, for centuries. On this point experts in Moscow are in general agreement. Russia's geopolitical situation has no real parallel since the Middle Ages.

Now as then, Russia has no natural frontiers. It is surrounded by almost a dozen unfriendly states and the borders with almost all of them are, in some degree, artificial, open to challenge or otherwise not entirely certain. In no direction, save the frozen Arctic, can Russians feel that the borders of their land are definite and secure.

Also as in the Middle Ages, Russia finds itself now removed from Europe. Not one but two belts of states separate Russia from Western Europe, the first belt consisting of Belarus, Ukraine and the Baltic states, and the second one consisting of the former WTO allies of Eastern Central Europe. The "window to Europe" opened by Peter the Great two centuries ago has been, in a sense, closed again.

Furthermore, except for Belarus none of the countries in these two belts is friendly to Russia. All of the others fear Russia and its predominant military power and some of them are ready to associate themselves with any potential rival of Russia's. Various tensions and potential conflicts among them also might be exploited by outside great powers, for their own interests and against Russia's interests. Moscow's new bureaucracy continues to see the former Soviet republics, now independent states, and even the countries of East Central Europe, as "junior brothers," and this arrogant habit does not improve the relationships.

In addition to this, some important harbors to the sea, air defense radars and anti-ballistic missile (ABM) radars are now located in these newly independent states.[4] Military experts in Moscow fear "holes" in the air and missile defense system, through which an enemy could fly right into Russia. The loss of some harbors, of which the Soviet Union already had too few, further restricts both the navy and shipping.

Russia faces hostility along the perimeter of its frontiers, separatist tendencies inside the country and threats to its territorial integrity. Many policy analysts are concerned that these geopolitical shifts make Russia dangerously vulnerable. In addition, these shifts have aroused two basic anxieties which are traditional anxieties in the Russian psyche. One is a fear that Russia will be cut off from Europe and Western civilization; the other is a fear that Russia will find itself alone in the world, surrounded by hostile lands.

Russia's insecurity

The things just described are now operating in combination to produce in Russia a deep feeling of insecurity. To recapitulate briefly, the sudden collapse, first of the alliance system in Eastern Central Europe, and then of the USSR itself, were staggering blows. Russia by itself is necessarily much weaker than was the USSR. The geopolitical shifts are entirely negative. And these factors are operating in a domestic environment of great political uncertainty and immense economic problems, including not merely "no growth" but serious economic decline. At the same time, in certain other ways Russia's security situation is much more favorable than before. As mentioned earlier, the end of the Cold War means that Russia has no great enemies anywhere in the world. There is no direct threat of attack from any direction. And the previously grave threat of a global nuclear holocaust has practically vanished.

These new elements of insecurity and security intermingled in the thinking of policy specialists in Moscow in 1992 and succeeding years. Experts felt themselves grappling with a new and strange situation, in which things that had been dangers were either gone or, like the relationship with the United States, had turned normal, while other things that had been secure, like well-guarded frontiers far away, had turned negative.

As perceptions and thinking took shape in the new situation, a paradox emerged. At the very moment that Russia is less *directly* threatened than at any time for decades, Russia actually feels *more* insecure. As the new realities sank in, many specialists found themselves nostalgic for the old days of the Cold War, when Russia was strong and in many ways was really rather secure. Any understanding of current thinking in Moscow about security and foreign affairs must begin from this basic fact: today Russia feels much less secure than it has felt, in peacetime, for a long time. This fundamental insecurity is the starting point for almost all of the many lines of thought that can be found today in Moscow about Russia's position in the world.

Larger questions

Everyone in Russia understands that the country is in some kind of transitional period in its history. But transition to what? Toward what destinations should we move, and how should we go about getting there? Here there are vast uncertainties and intense disagreements. The great uncertainties and disagreements themselves produce a political situation, and also an intellectual atmosphere, that present difficulties of their own. All perceptions of, and analysis of, Russian security and Russia's interests are complicated by these larger questions and by the difficulties they create.

What kind of Russia should policy analysts be discussing? A democratic Russia or an authoritarian one? A national or an imperial power? A "Russia" that is only today's Russian Federation, or something more? (Or conceivably, something less?) Is Russia one country among others in the CIS and equal to the others, or is it to a degree the leader of the CIS, or is it the master of the CIS? Different answers to these questions generate different concepts of Russia's "national interests" and different proposals for its security arrangements.

The present situation in Russia is so unstable and so uncertain that practically all imaginable scenarios are quite possible. This conclusion is reinforced by the concessions that have been made by the Yeltsin government to hardliners on both domestic and foreign policy issues, and by the dubious intervention in Chechnya. In 1992 and the years following, all efforts by government bodies such as the Ministry of Foreign Affairs or the Security Council to develop a defined doctrine of Russia's national interests and security imperatives lagged behind the pace of events. Under these chaotic conditions, almost every expert has his or her own interpretation of Russia's role and place in the world, and of what Russia's foreign policy and security policy should be. It is difficult even to know how to evaluate the conflicting ideas, because who can say what the standards of judgement should be?

Even so, any debate, however disorganized, tends to take some kind of shape. Four general lines of thinking can be distinguished. These are not precise categories. Some experts occupy intermediate positions, and some propound ideas taken from more than one approach. But four general trends are nonetheless perceptible.

One begins from a starting point of world development and the development of Western civilization. This starting point is a broad one, and the viewpoint that develops from it is often stated somewhat vaguely. The basic interest of Russia, as these thinkers see it, is for Russia to become an integral part of the overall democratic system evolving in the Northern Hemisphere.

Russia must become a fourth, equal, partner along with the USA, Western Europe and Japan. Russia must not become marginalized, must not be rejected by the others, and must not allow itself to become a backwater in world progress. It must be fully incorporated into the evolving and increasingly integrated "West" (including Japan). This school of thought, generally called "Atlanticist," basically identifies Russia's interests (especially in the long term) with Western interests. Andrei Kozyrev, the Minister of Foreign Affairs, has advocated approximately this viewpoint in the past, and has been widely criticized for it, and specifically for ignoring Russia's specialness. More recently, Kozyrev has retreated somewhat from this viewpoint, but there are still many political leaders and experts who advocate it.[5]

A second line is propounded by the thinkers and politicians called "Eurasians." They oppose any rapid Westernization of Russia, arguing that Russia should develop its own identity. They contend that Russia has never been closely part of Western political and cultural traditions, and that today Russia faces problems similar to many of the developing countries. Therefore Russia should strengthen, not abandon, its ties to Central Asia and the developing world. This school maintains that Russia's traditional and natural allies are in the South rather than in the West.[6] Russia should not accept the Western perception, but develop its own view, of the Muslim world, India and China. The failure of Yeltsin's economic reforms, and the relatively painless and far more successful Chinese path of economic and political modernization, have increased the appeal of this viewpoint.

A third line takes geopolitics as its point of departure. These thinkers argue that, despite the loss of Eastern Central Europe and the disintegration of the USSR, Russia continues to control the "heartland" of the great Eurasian continent. As geopolitical specialists have suggested for a long time, compared to that great continent all other parts of the world are appendages or islands. Whoever controls the heartland of the world's great continent is automatically in a central position. From this idea, this school goes on to suggest that Russia, being in the central position, should act as the mediator, the translator and the shock-absorber between the civilizations of the West and of the East. Russia can mitigate and manage the pressures that the East and West (seen as civilizations, not just geographical places) put on each other. To some extent, this viewpoint is a revival of one of the great old ideas in the Russian intellectual tradition, namely that it is Russia's destiny to act as a buffer between, to mediate between, and ultimately to synthesize, the worlds of West and East. From this viewpoint, for instance, Kievan Rus acted in this role in the Middle Ages, when it acted as a buffer, and thus saved Europe and the Western Enlightenment from the Mongol hordes.[7] In short, Russia's geographical position makes the country unique, and makes it impossible for Russia to belong either to Europe or to Asia.[8]

The fourth line gives preeminence to the internal development of Russia, and defines external affairs in terms of providing a favorable environment for internal development.[9] Thus the task of Russia's foreign policy is to ensure that the outside world remains friendly, or at worst, not threatening. Aside from that, Russia's resources should be focused not on external affairs but on the rebuilding of the country. A friendly environment will mean that resources need not be diverted for defense, and at best, Russia may gain some help from the outside world to accelerate the country's modernization. Having good relations with the "near abroad" is not an exception, but part of, this approach. For instance, some argue that for Russia, having good relations with Ukraine is more important than having good relations with the United States.

These four general trends do not exhaust the whole spectrum of the current security debate in Russia. There are also pro-communists, who continue to dream about a restoration of the "socialist center" of a world-wide socialist revolution, and see this dream as Russia's main national interest. There are ultra-nationalists like Zhirinovsky and his supporters, who want not only the restoration of the empire of the czars, but also a new "drive to the south" (the title of his recent book) and to warm seas. There is the military-industrial complex, which does not necessarily have a defined security strategy but wants a return to its previously privileged position in the Russian economy, and therefore has an interest in there being some international tension. (Only if there is tension and a potential for conflict will large funds be diverted to "the defense of the motherland.")

Currently none of the viewpoints just described has achieved any commanding position. Different parts of the ministries of state, the president's offices and of the Parliament hold different ideas, and hold various mixtures of the ideas summarized here. If, in the future, any of these viewpoints should come to predominate among the ruling elite, the official vision of Russia's goals and national interests would change accordingly. This could have serious implications for European security and even for world security. The reader will have noticed that the possibilities are extremely varied – from embracing the West, to imperialism, to isolationism. At the same time, there is an overall tendency to orient Russia's foreign and security policy to its genuine national interests, however vague they may seem.

3   Issues and problems in Russia's external affairs

While experts on foreign and security affairs have many conflicting viewpoints, most of them share a common agenda of the issues and problems presently facing Russia. The principal ones relevant for this book are discussed in this section.[10]

Russia's borders and Russians beyond them

There is a "gray area" surrounding much of Russia that is generating new threats to Russia's security. This area is the "near abroad," the countries that were formerly Soviet republics. What are the sources of potential security challenges here?

Every state begins with a territory. But in Russia's case, 75 percent of the borders are not formally defined. There are numerous, conflicting territorial claims between Russia and neighboring lands: Ukraine, Kazakhstan, Georgia and the three Baltic states. The conflicting claims and the uncertainties about the borders are presently being heated by nationalistic feelings. In many of the new states there is also lack of experience in conflict resolution. The result can be an apparently permament tension between Russia and some states of the near abroad.

At the time the USSR disintegrated, 25 million Russians were living within the Soviet Union but outside Russia. Naturally, nearly all of them had no choice but to stay where they were at that time, even though they now found themselves "foreigners" in newly created countries. Neither these people, nor Russia, nor for that matter the new countries, were prepared for this situation.

By now, the new national governments of those countries and their societies have generally come to see the Russians in their midst as an alien element. Russians are seen both as "the former masters" and now as the potential or active agents of Moscow. The natural desire is to get rid of them. Sometimes, for instance in the Baltic states, Russians' human rights may be violated. To many Russians living in Russia, this seems similar to the "ethnic cleansing" we have seen in the former Yugoslavia. The view in Russia is that the Central Asian states are also trying to get rid of their Russians, although they do it more cautiously since there the majority of the sophisticated professional people are Russians.

Meanwhile the leadership in Moscow has no idea what to do with these millions of fellow Russians living in the near abroad. It cannot encourage them to leave the new countries. The immigration of millions of people into Russia would be a disaster for Russia, which does not remotely have the resources to resettle them.[11] At the same time, Moscow cannot overlook gross violations of the human rights of the Russians in the near abroad, including violations of their ethnic rights to their Russian nationality. Thus Moscow tends to vacillate back and forth between doing nothing and taking sudden steps that may not be fully thought through.

All this is merely, as it were, the first part of the problem. Moscow's controversial steps are then seized upon and used by extreme nationalists on both sides of all the borders. Extreme Russian nationalists say that Moscow has done too little and call for much more. Extreme nationalists in the other countries say they are alarmed by what Moscow is doing already. In any case, all parties discredit the Moscow authorities for having done the wrong thing.

Some specialists in Moscow emphasize that the problem of the Russians of the near abroad is the most sensitive and the most difficult security problem facing Russia today. For Russia itself, it continually raises possibilities, perhaps demands and needs, for perpetual involvements. For the newly independent countries, it continually raises possibilities of Russian intervention.

There is yet another angle to this perplexing issue, namely the Russian military presence in the new states. When the USSR collapsed, many Soviet (in many cases, mostly Russian) military units naturally remained where they were, even though "where they were" might now be a new country. When the ethnic Russians in these countries are treated unjustly, and receive no relief from the local authorities, they naturally appeal to Russian military units in the area to intervene. At times, those units do. Sometimes their intervention is justified; sometimes it is not.

The mere presence of Russian military units can be a trigger for a conflict, or their intervention may trigger wider conflict. At the same time, the units may feel themselves to be practically hostages, surrounded and vastly outnumbered in a foreign land.[12] Russian military units, who so recently were heroes of the (Soviet) state, now feel disoriented. There is great concern that in a crisis situation, the uncertain and disoriented Russian armies may begin to act independently, outside Moscow's control.[13]

The many national and ethnic rivalries, inside the Russian Federation and across the former Soviet territory generally, are enormously complex. In a great many ways they can threaten the territorial integrity of Russia and spoil relations with the neighboring countries. Many specialists emphasize the great complexity of these questions, and their roots in factors that are beyond Moscow's control. There are deep historical prejudices resulting from events in the past, both the communist and the czarist past. The Soviet regime suppressed national cultures and languages. Both the Soviets and the czars moved peoples, drew boundary lines and did other things that disrupted previous ethnic equilibriums. Other factors outside Moscow's control include deep differences among groups in economic development and in political culture. There are religious incompatibilities, and in many places an absence of a culture of tolerance and mutual cohabitation. There are clan rivalries, seen today even in Georgia, to say nothing of Central Asia. It is easy for all sorts of groups to define their identify first of all by their opposition to Moscow, which can always be labeled the old imperial center. And indeed, for many extreme nationalists the only way to free their people from a condition that is both subservience and dependency is to be hostile to Russia. Finally, and perhaps worst, practically all political leaders and political groupings of all kinds can use nationality and ethnic issues as a tool in their own ambitions to gain power.

The brutal war against Chechnya was a manifestation of the dangers inherent in the problem of separatism. There is no doubt that Chechnya is a part of the Russian Federation. Yet the Chechen leaders declared independence from Russia and began to ignore all Russian laws. In fact this small republic in the Caucasus was turning itself into a bulwark for criminal elements that were undermining the economic and financial security of the country, not to mention the personal security of citizens. Unfortunately, Moscow could not find a political solution to the problem and chose a military route to restoring its authority in Chechnya. That led to tragedy. There was much loss of life, the capital of the republic was ruined and its industrial base was destroyed. In Russia itself, the war has resulted in undermining a fragile democracy and the economic reforms, not to mention the country's image around the world.

Nuclear weapons issues

Because nuclear weapons issues, far more than any other issue in Russian security affairs, are widely written about in the West, the discussion here can be brief.

Unquestionably, the uncertain status of the weapons in Ukraine and Kazakhstan poses some security problems for Russia. Moscow considers these (and all former Soviet) nuclear weapons to be its own property, while leaders of the two countries, especially Ukraine, see those weapons as theirs. It might be added that specialists in Moscow also believe that the West ought to see Russian control of all these weapons as being in the West's interests; again leaders in Kazakhstan and especially Ukraine feel differently.

Disagreement on the nuclear weapons issue between Moscow and the two countries is not only a problem in itself; it also breeds suspicion and tensions between Russia and the two neighbors. Furthermore, in the case of the weapons in Ukraine the nuclear dilemma is exploited by nationalistic elements on both the Russian and Ukrainian sides. Some nationalist elements in Ukraine argue that Ukraine should keep the nuclear weapons located there now, explicitly as a way to "deter" Russia, and as insurance against the possibility of Russia seeking hegemony in the near abroad. Ideas like this, in turn, inflame nationalist elements in Russia. Meanwhile, specialists in Russia have genuine concerns about those nuclear weapons. These specialists are sincere in arguing that Ukraine lacks the technical capacities and experts to keep the weapons safe indefinitely, and that unsafe weapons could result in an ecological disaster similar to Chernobyl.

More recently the situation has improved, thanks to three things. First, in January 1994 President Yeltsin, US President Clinton and President Kravchuk of Ukraine signed a "trilateral" agreement on the withdrawal of all Ukrainian nuclear weapons to Russia for dismantling. In spite of some technical difficulties, the implementation of this agreement is under way. Second, a new president of Ukraine, Leonid Kuchma, was elected in July 1994, and he is more oriented toward cooperation with Russia than was his predecessor. Third, in December 1994 Ukraine joined the Non-Proliferation Treaty (NPT) in exchange for a security guarantee. In spite of these favorable developments, the general political instability in Russia, and also in Ukraine, means that one cannot exclude the possibility of further problems in Russian–Ukrainian relations involving nuclear weapons.

Russia's relation to the CIS

From Moscow's viewpoint, how and why did the Commonwealth of Independent States come into existence? If one puts aside personal motives (Yeltsin's desire to get rid of Gorbachev), three reasons have been advanced by specialists as to why Moscow consented to the disintegration of the Soviet Union and the creation of the CIS. First, Moscow yielded to pressure from other republics, above all Ukraine, for sovereignty. Second, Moscow's political elite viewed the other republics as a burden on Russia, while believing that in a new, post-Soviet structure Russia would easily hold the leading position. And third, there was fear of "another Yugoslavia" on a far vaster scale and a need to find a new form of integration that would be generally acceptable.

These calculations turned out to be largely futile. For many of the new states, the road to real independence and competent self-government proved to be much harder than expected. The new leaders there, not willing to acknowledge their own mistakes, put all blame on outside forces, chiefly Russia. Meanwhile Russia was too burdened by its own profound economic, social and other problems to be attractive to the others for building genuine cooperation. Not much real cooperation has been built. At the same time, Moscow leaders were not always wise enough to recognize reasonable limits to their power, and sometimes flexed their muscles. The net outcome is that now Russia finds itself in an insecure, disorganized and in some ways hostile environment.

The main security achievement for the CIS was supposed to be the Tashkent Treaty, signed by Russia, four Central Asian states and Armenia in June 1992. Later it was enlarged, and it now embraces nine states.[14] But in fact this Treaty amounted not to a real collective security arrangement but only a set of bilateral agreements. Each of the other states was interested not in genuine collective security but in its own security interests and in getting Russia engaged in defending those interests.

In the time since, the CIS has failed, not suprisingly, to prevent the wave of ethnic and other conflict in the former Soviet area. It has not and probably cannot divert the real threats its members face, and thus the CIS is becoming less and less significant. Actually no member of the CIS,

Russia included, is ready to place its security into the hands of the Commonwealth.

Imperial thinking

Many specialists in Moscow are aware that almost no question involving Russia excites more concern, in neighboring countries and in the West, than whether imperial thinking will come to dominate Russian policy. For experts in Moscow this question is not simple. Of course there are basic disagreements, described above, between several conflicting points of view about what Russia's goals should be. Several additional observations should be made on this complicated question.

In the first place, it must be reiterated that the majority of people in Russia today feel themselves less secure than they felt under communist rule. That is not an argument for communism, simply a social fact. It also does not mean that most people want to restore a communist regime. It does mean that there is a deep dissatisfaction in society with the Moscow leadership's inability to provide security from internal and external dangers. For many Russians it is not a disappointment in democracy, it is a disappointment in the democrats in power. Of course, this mood is exploited by extremists of both right and left, to discredit both the democrats and democracy, and to discredit the overall reform process. The president and the government are accused regularly of a failure of will to use their influence to guarantee the human rights of the Russians living in the near abroad, to stop armed clashes between various rival groups of nationalities in various places and, more basically, to impose on the near abroad Moscow's vision of how to solve problems.

Psychologically, there is a nostalgia for the "iron hand" that has so often been a part of Russian political culture. Not only the Soviets, but also often the czars, ruled with an iron hand. In Russian culture it is familiar, and in that sense comfortable. There is only one step from authoritarian rule at home to imperial thinking in foreign affairs.

What might be encompassed by a new imperial mood? Here is a point of ambiguity. For some it means the near abroad; for others, more. There is some tendency to equate what should naturally be under Russian influence with the whole sphere of influence of the former USSR. Of course that sphere was much larger than the USSR itself. It included East Central Europe, and indeed the whole communist world including Cuba and some countries in Africa. Exactly what the proper sphere for Russian control should be in the future is not only a question about which specialists disagree, it also is an ambiguous question even among those who might be considered "pro-imperial."

There is no simple dividing line between those who are pro-imperial and those who are not. Some democrats are infected with the virus as well.

Andrei Kozyrev, the Minister of Foreign Affairs, has been seen in the West as the most liberal of the democrats, but even he has become stricter in his approach to the Baltic states. And in a speech delivered in Peking he referred to China as part of the "near abroad," to the confusion of his hosts.[15]

It is sometimes overlooked in the West that there can be more than one basis for apparently "imperial" thinking. It does not have to be highly nationalistic. There are radical democrats who hold what they consider a pragmatic view. Adronik Migranyan, a member of Yeltsin's presidential council, believes that Russia should declare its own "Monroe Doctrine."[16] If the United States could declare, early in the nineteenth century, that the entire Western Hemisphere would be "under its protection" and be closed to all outside great powers, why can Russia not declare, on the eve of the twenty-first century, that the near abroad has a similar status?

What might "imperial thinking" mean for the near abroad, in practical terms? Is it a simple restoration of the Soviet empire, or merely some adaptation to new circumstances? Both ideas are present in, for instance, debates about Russia and the CIS. Some nationalists want a restoration of the 1913 borders of Russia. In liberal "imperial" thinking, on the other hand, the near abroad could have a status similar to the status of East Central Europe in the Soviet era. And in this thinking, the countries of East Central Europe in the future should have a status similar to Finland in the Soviet era.

Imperial thinking in Moscow today is not a coherent doctrine or set of ideas. Different specialists emphasize different views. The most important ideas advanced by various experts might be gathered together and summarized as follows:

1 Russia will have supreme responsibility for the former Soviet space, including crisis management and crisis resolution. Since international law is vague in this area and nobody knows exactly what this "responsibility" means, it would be up to Moscow to interpret it.
2 Russia has the right to expect that countries within its sphere of vital interests will have friendly regimes. Naturally only Moscow can determine the size of that sphere and what "friendly" means.
3 A Russian military presence in the near abroad must be maintained. It can be legitimated in separate bilateral treaties with each country.
4 The countries of the near abroad must not be allowed to make any alliance that Russia regards as hostile.
5 Each country in the near abroad must consult with Moscow in advance about any forthcoming decision that might touch on the security or foreign policy interests of Russia.
6 In the near abroad, and in all countries in Russia's sphere of influence, no anti-Russian propaganda can be permitted, nor any activities by anti-Russian ultra-nationalist groups.

Scepticism about imperial thinking

Almost all specialists in Moscow see Russia as the natural center of gravity in the post-Soviet space. But liberal groups are sceptical about the stronger forms of imperial thinking, for several reasons.

First, imperial thinking and attempts to carry it out in almost any form will inevitably lead to at least a halt, and perhaps a reversal, of Russia's movement toward democracy. Any new imperial elite needs loyalty in society but not freedom. That elite will never take the risks involved in playing by the democratic rules in the game of politics.

Second, a new empire would be an unbearable burden for Russia. Inevitably it would plunge the country into yet another disaster. The price involved in imposing a new loyalty on the former Soviet vassals could be so high that Moscow would once again be, as it was in the Soviet era, the only empire in world history in which the capital was poorer than the vassals.

Third, Russia does not have the necessary legitimacy, and hence genuine authority, to rule the former Soviet space. In much of that space Moscow is not trusted. This means that Russia could impose its rule only by force, and ultimately by military force. This is difficult, and in the long run perhaps impossible. Furthermore, going down this road could lead to another Cold War.

Finally, some liberal specialists have concluded that the imperial idea is another of the illusions and fantasies of which there is no shortage in Moscow these days. It is an idea held by people who are out of touch with reality. In anything like Russia's current circumstances of weakness, to revive the empire would be no less difficult than to fully achieve democracy.

However, while a successful new empire may be an illusion, a shift toward an authoritarian regime in Moscow is seen by many specialists as probable. Even many politicians who consider themselves pro-democrats want something of the kind. Radical democrats whose schemes of economic and political reform have encountered difficulties can easily come to the conclusion that they failed mainly because the reformers did not have enough power to implement their plans. Power, previously diffused, must be concentrated in one iron hand to push the reforms through. To justify their retreat from democratic methods, these thinkers refer to the Russian tradition of, and familiarity with, autocracy. They also point to successful experiences abroad, in Pinochet's Chile and the "tigers" of the Far East. In addition they argue that the West, especially Western Europe, would tolerate an "enlightened" authoritarian regime in Moscow whose ultimate aim was democracy. If obliged to choose between an unstable democratic regime and a stable undemocratic one in Moscow, the West will prefer the latter. This is shown, they say, by the West's approval of Yeltsin's disbanding of

Parliament and subsequently his military attack on the Parliament building (the White House) in autumn 1993.

Other experts agree that Russia is moving toward authoritarian rule but are sceptical that it will really be "enlightened." As early as the beginning of 1994 they say that Russia was already living under such a rule in some ways. The first evidence was the removal of some reformers from the government and the growing influence of both the state bureaucracy and the military establishment, neither of which are under Yeltsin's control. On the contrary, evidence is mounting that he is under their control. The sceptics forecast that an authoritarian Moscow may change its priority from internal to external issues and follow a more assertive, if not actually aggressive, foreign policy. To control the country, the government may feel a need for an external threat. Such a threat can be "discovered" in the near abroad, in East Central Europe, or of course in the West.

Military doctrine

A military doctrine for Russia was approved by the president and by the Security Council on November 2, 1993.[17] In one of its central principles, it defines the purpose of the Russian armed forces as being only the defense of the country. Since its publication, the doctrine has been widely criticized by specialists and also in the media.[18] Among the chief criticisms are these:

1 The doctrine says nothing about the country's role in regional security systems; this absence can be interpreted as an intention to ensure Russia's security by unilateral, purely national efforts.
2 The doctrine asserts the possibility of a Russian military presence beyond Russia's borders. Although it says any such presence must be codified by agreements, the possibility is left open that such agreements could be imposed by Russia on weaker states.
3 The doctrine does not identify any specific enemy. While positive in some respects, this also allows a future possibility to define enemies broadly and consider any state as such.
4 The doctrine reverses what many considered to be one of the positive features of previous Soviet doctrine, namely the principle of "no first use" of nuclear weapons. This principle is explicitly renounced.
5 The doctrine contemplates the use of the armed forces if necessary in internal (ethnic) conflict. This element in the doctrine was implemented in Chechnya.

For these and other reasons, the doctrine has not resolved issues but, among civilian specialists, has itself become another topic of contention. As several of these criticisms suggest, the doctrine also tends either to be silent or vague on key questions.

Foreign policy-making

This discussion of trends in Russian thinking should not conclude without briefly mentioning problems in the making of foreign and security policy. In the last several years the process of democratization in domestic affairs has not been significantly carried over into foreign and security policy. In that realm democratic process is hardly found. And public opinion, with rare exceptions, is not taken into account in policy-making.

The vast majority of specialists, except those who represent the official line, are dissatisfied with governmental policy-making processes and institutions for security affairs. For example, the leadership decided to imitate some Western institutions and processes, but never defined the allocation of responsibilities between these new institutions and the old ones. Hence all of these bodies interfere in each other's spheres of activity, and their decisions often contradict each other. Many specialists in Moscow believe that the important decisions on security issues are actually being made now by an even smaller group of people than in the Soviet years.

4   Security in Europe

Presently Europe is not one of the leading security concerns for specialists in Russia, and it is not expected to be. The security issues that take up the majority of specialists' time and attention are issues involving the near abroad. With the exception of one important question – the possible expansion of NATO – there does not appear to be any significant security problem that specialists can foresee, originating to Russia's west in the coming years. Basic perceptions of Europe, involving security, can be reviewed in a few pages in this section.[19]

East Central Europe and Russia

The countries of East Central Europe, the former WTO allies, are usually not considered as any potential threat to Russia. They are too small and too weak. At the same time, some specialists are worried by the current state of relations between these countries and Russia. The withdrawal of Soviet troops from those countries (often seen there as Russian troops, as in many cases they were) closed the old era of relations between the "elder brother" and the "younger brothers," as the relationship was generally seen in Russia. At the time, Moscow naturally believed that its support of the "Velvet Revolutions" in the East Central European countries would ensure a friendly relationship with these countries in all spheres, no doubt including security.

But this did not happen. The old era closed but no new one has opened. Instead, a feeling of alienation has grown up in Russian–East Central

European relations. Specialists point out that both sides, whatever their excuses, share the blame. Neither side hurried to make a fresh start. What are the reasons for this?

One element was a revival of prejudices dating from the (pre-1945) past, which were only worsened by the enforced "socialist friendship" of recent decades. There also is a basic difference in the perceptions of the public on the two sides. Many people in the East Central European countries believe that the former Soviet Union pitilessly exploited them (and undoubtedly they find evidence for that). At the same time, the Russian public believe the opposite, as they have for decades. Russians believe that, during the Soviet era, the East Central Europeans lived much better than Russians (and Soviets generally) did, and did so because the Soviet Union subsidized East Central Europe. Since 1989–90, therefore, *both* sides have had no intention of perpetuating the old situation. Instead both sides have wanted to put a distance between them. Greater distance, created almost deliberately, has in turn led to some mutual suspicions.

Furthermore, both sides concluded after 1989–90 that they did not need each other much. The democratic leaders of the new Russia tied their hopes for the rebuilding of the country to the West, and not to the former allies, from whom they could receive neither capital, nor new technology, nor experience in building a modern economy. The East Central Europeans also looked to the West, not to Russia, for the help they wanted. Thus both sides concluded that they needed the West, but not each other, to reform their countries.

On top of this, the universal and simultaneous turn of all parties to the West gave rise to a certain rivalry for the West's goodwill, aid, credits and preferences. For objective reasons, the West paid more attention to Russia than to East Central Europe, and directed to Russia the bulk of its aid and credits. The more Russia got, the less was left for the East Central European countries. Some of the leaders of those countries reacted painfully. Addressing the West, they started speaking in anti-Russian tones. They said that Russia could hardly become a truly European country in the foreseeable future, that it embodied a different civilization and that Russia's current friendship with the West was merely tactical in nature. The East Central Europeans also found it easy to shift from anti-communist attitudes to anti-Russian ones.[20]

Moscow made the situation worse for itself, not for the first time in history. Russian leaders, trying to be democrats but raised of course in the old system, sometimes behaved toward the East Central Europeans in their habitual ways. They acted, if not in the imperial style, at least with the condescending arrogance of those who have (once again!) discovered a "new bright future."

For all these reasons, relations between Russia and the East Central Europeans cooled after 1989–90 and both sides came to feel alienated from each other. Meanwhile Russia found itself with other pressing concerns. Step by step, East Central Europe fell to one of the last rungs on Russia's scale of foreign policy priorities. There is no sign yet of this changing for the better.

The alienation between the former allies is not confrontational in nature. But some experts in Moscow feel that it has created an unfavorable environment for Russia's security in Europe. The alienation can be used by forces hostile to Russia to influence the East Central Europeans toward anti-Russian behavior of various sorts. Some in Moscow see regional cooperation among the East Central Europeans as something that can isolate Russia from Europe, and perhaps even set the stage for an anti-Russian coalition that might include one or more countries of the near abroad. This is the reason why Moscow is suspicious of all contacts between the latter and the East Central European countries. Some experts fear that the lack of harmony between Moscow and the East Central Europeans suggests that the latter may be ignoring the evident reality that the near abroad is a sphere of vital interests and of natural influence for Russia. Such an attitude could lead to misunderstandings. Furthermore, all these things can be exploited by the extreme nationalist and pro-communist forces in Russia, to accuse the pro-democrats now in power of ignoring the national interests of Russia.

In any case, many analysts in Moscow now emphasize the importance of preventing East Central Europe from becoming any source of threat to the territorial or economic security of Russia. The best way to prevent it, they say, is to make sure that Russia itself is involved in security arrangements for East Central Europe.

The issue of the expansion of NATO

Some specialists in Moscow recognize that Russia, despite its process of democratization and accompanying new political attitudes, is still often perceived in East Central Europe as a potential threat. In one way this is almost unavoidable. Even if Moscow reduced its armed forces all the way down to 1.5 million men, an intention declared by the Minister of Defense,[21] it would still have the largest army of any country in Europe by far, an army much superior to the armies of all the East Central European countries taken together. But it is not raw numbers that are the main source of the East Central Europeans' anxiety. Rather it is the great uncertainty about Russia's political future. Moscow's military intervention in Chechnya and the brutality of the war have aggravated their fears. The combination of this uncertainty and the existence of a security vacuum in East Central Europe means that the leaders of those countries cannot help but be disturbed. Under these circumstances, their turn toward NATO and their wish to join is understandable and may be justifiable.

In Moscow this wish is highly controversial to say the least. Russia cannot object in principle to the desire of sovereign states to conduct their own foreign policy, including joining an alliance. But for Moscow two questions are extremely important. First, will these countries join NATO together with Russia or without Russia? Second, would their membership in NATO make the Eastern Central part of Europe, which is on Russia's very doorstep, a region more hostile to Russia, or less hostile? One might also ask whether their joining would make NATO itself more or less hostile to Russia.

The majority of Russian analysts are agreed that at its present stage of development, a Russia that is politically unstable and overloaded with its own internal problems is not ready to join NATO. Russian specialists also recognize that NATO is not about to take Russia's many troubles on to its shoulders. But there are deep concerns about the East Central Europeans joining NATO without Russia. Should a "threat" that supposedly originates in Russia be tackled not in cooperation with Russia, but on the contrary, by isolating Russia? In that case, leaders in Moscow could only conclude that Russia's security is being separated from Europe's security. This grim conclusion could lead to serious consequences for Russia. Moscow would be forced to decide that, once again, Russia's security will have to be ensured by Russia's own efforts.

The arguments against expanding NATO into East Central Europe were elaborated in a report released late in 1993 ("Perspectives on NATO expanding and Russia's interests") prepared by the external intelligence service.[22] The report concludes that this expansion is contrary to Russia's national interests, so long as NATO remains what it is. The report emphasizes that NATO has not transformed itself from a military alliance into something different for the post-Cold War world, such as a political organization. And NATO does not seem to have a clear understanding of its place and role in the post-Cold War world. Should NATO transform itself suitably, either in advance of any geographical expansion or in parallel with it, then many of Russia's concerns about an expansion would be removed or diminished. What is needed is a new security structure for all of Europe including Russia. The report points out that NATO's offer of "partnership" arrangements for Russia and others (the Partnership for Peace) is nowhere near this and will not lead to this.

According to the report, there would be several costs and risks to Russia, should NATO expand eastward. First, the approach of the world's largest and most powerful military grouping, practically to Russia's very borders, would make it necessary for Russia to reconsider all its security and defense concepts, to carry out structural reorganizations of the armed forces, to redeploy troops, and to change operational plans, training and other things. Second, carrying out these measures will naturally strain the military budget. To pay for it other important programs will have to be cut, thus weakening the country's security. Third, all these changes will threaten the military reforms presently under way, including the difficult transition from a mass army to a smaller, professional army. Fourth, Russian society, which for forty years has seen NATO as an enemy, may perceive NATO's expansion toward Russia's frontiers as a direct threat. Conservative and ultra-nationalist elements will, in turn, surely play on that. Fifth, this expansion in NATO's scope would render nonsensical the important CFE Treaty, currently the main arms control agreement that limits conventional armies in Europe and thus restrains the arms race. At best, the CFE Treaty would have to be renegotiated, and whether it successfully can be is questionable.

Supporters of the view that an eastward expansion of NATO would be dangerous for Russia can marshall additional arguments. Once the East Central European countries were in NATO, they might feel free to allow anti-Russian feelings to develop that currently are muted. Once inside, these countries could also animate a more anti-Russian mood throughout NATO. The military elite of that alliance are suspicious enough already of the successor state of the former enemy superpower.

Another group of specialists in Moscow sees no serious problems in NATO's expansion to incorporate the East Central European countries. These specialists are interested in finding more ways to cooperate with NATO, and with the EU and other Western organizations. These specialists point out that Russia has a common border already with NATO, in the far north-west, where there is a border with Norway on the Kola peninsula. Furthermore, for forty years the USSR had a common border with a NATO country, Turkey. These common borders created no problems. Why, then, should there be any problem if Poland enters NATO and thus has a common border with the Kaliningrad part of Russia?

These specialists argue that including into NATO some countries that view Russia with anxiety can diminish their fears, especially since the alliance itself is interested in cooperation with Moscow. Once in NATO, the countries of East Central Europe will feel more confident, and more ready to cooperate with Russia themselves. Indeed, say these specialists, it would be better for Russia to have on its frontier one large and friendly NATO than a multitude of countries all feeling distrust toward their huge neighbor. However, many specialists in this group also feel, for tactical reasons, that it would be better to delay NATO's expansion until conditions in Russia are more favorable.

There is a consensus among Russian specialists on the undesirability of the East Central European countries joining NATO at the present time. This does not mean that these countries should not or cannot be brought under NATO's wing in some way later. But NATO needs to couple any prospect of bringing those states into the alliance with a simultaneous effort to address Russia's concerns about the future of security in Europe. Not to do that would contradict a declared principle of all Western security policy, namely that Russia is a security "partner" in Europe. If that means anything, it means that major decisions affecting Russia's security should not be made without taking Russia's needs, as Russia sees them, into account, which naturally would include detailed consultations with Moscow. If Russia is really the West's security "partner," then the two should also work to reach a common understanding and agreement about arrangements in Europe that will protect the security of *all* parties, including Russia.

It was supposed that NATO's Partnership for Peace (PfP) program could help close the gap between the security interests of Russia, of the East Central European countries and of the West, because (according to the Western viewpoint) it gave equal opportunities to all participants from the East. However, this did not satisfy Moscow, which hoped for some special status with NATO. This goal, in turn, was opposed by both the Western and the East Central European countries. The Russian military pressured the government not to sign PfP, partly because they feared that any joining with NATO might lead to a democratization of the army and to increased civilian control over it. But the fear of Russia being isolated proved decisive in government circles, and Russia officially joined PfP on June 22, 1994. In addition to other considerations, there was a hope that this step would delay the expansion of NATO into East Central Europe.

This hope was illusory and soon Moscow began to understand the reality of the situation. For the East Central European countries, PfP is really a classroom preparing them to join NATO. For Russia, there is a great risk that PfP will hold them in class forever. During a visit to NATO headquarters in Brussels in December 1994, Foreign Minister Kozyrev refused to sign a protocol on PfP cooperation, an action generally interpreted in the West as Russia reversing its decision to join PfP. In Moscow this step was understood as a signal that Russia will now do its best to prevent the East Central European countries from joining NATO.

Some liberal security specialists in Moscow see this gesture as one of fighting windmills. They argue that the best choice for Russia does not involve a question of PfP or of joining NATO. Instead, Russia should seek a new treaty on partnership and cooperation in the security field between itself and NATO, seen as two equal bodies. The new treaty must not be conceived as "sixteen plus one" but as "one plus one." The two sides must be equal partners. This approach, they argue, can lead to the development of a security space from the Atlantic to the Pacific Oceans.

Peacekeeping in eastern Europe

Peacekeeping in the eastern half of Europe in general, and in the former Soviet space in particular, is a tangled and complicated topic.[23] Russian specialists point out that there are great differences in the sources, content and forms of ethno-political conflicts in these regions. Among other consequences, this makes it difficult to develop any consensus about the right role (if any) for various parties, such as Russia or the UN, to play in peacekeeping in various conflicts. There also are basic differences among specialists in their views of peacekeeping, and of the prevention and resolution of conflicts in general.

Many experts in Moscow who specialize on ethno-political conflicts emphasize that real peacekeeping should aim to accomplish two main tasks: to be objective and refrain from taking sides in a conflict, and to close all alternatives to the belligerents except negotiation. Most of these specialists believe that any attempt from the outside to impose a resolution to a conflict ("peacemaking") is unlikely to succeed.

There is great disagreement among security and foreign affairs specialists in Moscow on Russia's proper role in peacekeeping and conflict resolution in the post-Soviet space. Some experts doubt the necessity for Russia to intervene in conflicts outside the territory of the Russian Federation proper. They cite, as major reasons, Russia's overall political and economic weakness, and questionable moral right to intervene. Moreover, these specialists doubt that Moscow can really refrain from taking sides in conflicts. Some of them point out that this is precisely why many of the fighting parties in various places in the former Soviet space would prefer "foreigners" such as the UN to be the peacekeeper; the foreigners can be more neutral and unprejudiced than Russia can be.

Many other specialists in Moscow hold an opposite view. They believe that Russia is destined to bear the burden of being the leader in the post-Soviet space and to bear the chief peacekeeping responsibility. They argue that the UN is already overburdened and does not really wish to take on the numerous complicated conflicts in the post-Soviet region, in addition to what it is doing already. These specialists argue that, even now, the Russian Army's role in conflicts in the near abroad is mainly positive, because it "quarantines" regional violence and isolates local instabilities. These specialists believe that conflicts in the region could be aggravated by foreign interference. The West has little knowledge or understanding of the complicated historical and local causes behind ethno-political clashes in the former Soviet region. Typically the West also perceives all conflicts in the framework of "pro-democrats" versus "totalitarians," a simplistic viewpoint that often fails to comprehend the real nature of these conflicts.

Another aspect of the complicated question of Russia's peacekeeping role in the former Soviet space involves legitimacy. To be effective, the legitimacy of Russia's leading role and special responsibility for peace in the region must be recognized by the neighboring countries and by the world at large. Yet only a few states of the near abroad will agree. Paradoxically, the West probably is willing to agree in fact, but finds it politically impossible to say so.[24]

At the same time, Moscow's recent behavior in some parts of the post-Soviet space (for instance Georgia-Abkhazia and Chechnya) undermines the legitimacy of Russia's intention to conduct peacekeeping in such a way that Russia acts both on its own and on behalf of the international community.

5 Concluding remarks

Russia, perhaps even more than most countries, feels keenly the inadequacy of all the old arrangements and ways of thinking for security in Europe. Their inadequacy is felt so keenly because Russia feels less secure now than previously, as emphasized earlier. And Russia, more than most countries now, discovers that the tools it traditionally relied upon for security are no longer very applicable. Moscow cannot use its nuclear weapons or strategic missiles to cope with local conflicts among nationalities and ethnic groups. Moscow's fleet of nuclear submarines cannot solve the problem of the persecuted Russian minority in nearby countries. Moscow's tank armadas cannot restore the poisoned land and polluted rivers.

The new character of security problems goes far beyond Russia's borders. The wars in the former Yugoslavia, and the complete inability of current European security arrangements to cope with it, prove that amply. The new dangers to security extend beyond even Europe; they are a worldwide question.

In Moscow, as in other capitals, there is a long-running conflict between two fundamentally different ways of seeing security in today's world. One viewpoint believes that security can and should be built on widely agreed norms for international behavior, such as the norms of the UN Charter, the Helsinki Final Act and the Paris Charter of 1990. This approach necessarily leads to advocacy of collective security systems based on cooperation.

Currently the chief collective organization for Europe is the OSCE. On the eve of this organization's Budapest summit in December 1994, some Russian experts tried to put forward some new ideas for increasing the OSCE's role in security and peacekeeping. The core of their approach was an intention to convert OSCE into the main organization responsible for security in Europe. OSCE could become the political umbrella for all military arrangements on the continent – NATO, the WEU and the CIS collective security organization. It could monitor the military balances and relationships in Europe and could issue mandates for peacekeeping actions. OSCE could create a new body, a Security Council, modeled on the UN Security Council. This new body could cope adequately with all emerging threats to security in Europe, and even prevent their emergence. Unfortunately, the evident weakness of OSCE and the obsession with the issue of expanding NATO prevented these ideas from being discussed fruitfully at the Budapest summit. The old name of the organization was changed, but of course this does not change its essence. Thus security in Europe continues to be disunited.[25]

The other approach sees all this as essentially wishful thinking. From the second viewpoint, sometimes called "realistic," a balance of military power will be the only reliable way to ensure security for Russia and for Europe for the foreseeable future. More fundamentally, specialists holding this viewpoint argue that at this historical stage, Russia cannot transfer its basic security to some international organization. Russia faces real hazards, which an organization made up of many countries might not recognize or might not actually deal with.

We may hope that, during this transitional era in European affairs, both these points of view may coexist and may even help sustain each other. If norms of behavior are really to be respected and implemented, they need to be backed by force under some circumstances. At the same time, the use of force in international conflicts is in need of codification. And in our time, force increasingly must be legitimized by some form of international approval; otherwise it incurs too heavy costs for the international position of the state using it. The challenge facing Russia, and Europe also, is increasingly to synthesize these approaches in ways that can produce genuine security.

Notes

1 For a more detailed analysis, see Yuri Davydov, "The USA and Western Europe in a changing world," *Nauka* (Moscow, 1991), pp. 76–86.

2 See, for example, I. Serebyakov, "Russia's military doctrine," *Nezavisimaya Gazeta* (February 8, 1994); and A. Eremeev, "We will defend ourselves even with kitchen utensils," in *Pravda* (Moscow) (April 29, 1994).

3 "Report for 1993" (Moscow: Goskomstat, 1994), p. 3; also *International Financial Statistics* (Washington: The International Monetary Fund, March 1994), p. 250.

4 Five of the eight main ABM radars are located outside Russia, in new states that formerly were republics of the USSR. See, for example, *Krasnaya zvezda* (Moscow) (January 10, 1994), p. 3.

5 On Kozyrev's views, see for instance, Andrei Kozyrev, "Russia looks West," *Moscow News*, no. 39 (1991); and Andrei Kozyrev, "Russia: a chance for survival," in *Foreign Affairs* (spring 1992), pp. 1–16. For commentaries, see for example the following: A. Zagorski et al., "After the disintegration of the USSR: Russia in the New World" (Moscow: MGIMO, February 1992); and A. Zagorski and M. Lukas, "Russia and the European challenge," *Mezhdurarodniye Otnosheniya* (Moscow, 1993), pp. 64–107.

6 A. Bogaturov and M. Kozhokin, "Russia's Oriental question," *Nezavisimaya Gazeta* (Moscow) (March 26, 1992); S. Goncharov, "The special interests of Russia – what are they?" *Izvestia* (Moscow) (February 25, 1992); N. Simoniya,

"North–South: is conflict inevitable?" *Moscow News*, no. 12 (March 22, 1992); V. Tsimburski, "Russia's metamorphosis," *Nezavisimaya Gazeta* (March 1994).

7 This viewpoint of seeing the world in terms of clashing "civilizations" helps explain the support most Russians feel for the Serbs in the former Yugoslavia, and particularly in the current war in Bosnia. While conceding that the Serbs, like all other parties, are guilty of brutalities, this viewpoint holds that it is Russia's duty to side with the Christian Serbs against the Moslems, who represent another civilization.

8 S. Steankevich, "A power in search of self-identification," *Nezavisimaya Gazeta* (March 28, 1992); E. Pozdnyakov, "The problem of returning the Soviet Union to European civilization," *Paradigm*, 1–2 (1991), pp. 45–49; B. Kapustin, "European and Russian civilizations," *World Economy and International Relations* (Moscow), no. 4 (1992), pp. 48–49.

9 "Summary of the report prepared by the Institute of International Economic and Political Studies," *Rossiya* weekly, no. 16 (1993); V. Dashichev, "Freaks of Russia's foreign policy thinking," *Nezavisimaya Gazeta* (April 23, 1994).

10 For purposes of a book on European security, this agenda of issues and problems deemphasizes questions, such as the role of the CIS, that concern the whole former Soviet territory, in order to emphasize European topics.

11 The official figures for Russian refugees, 0.5 million people, are not adequate. According to the evaluation of independent sources, there are about 2 million Russians who have left the countries of the near abroad since 1991. About 6 million Russians are considered potential refugees. See V. Terekhov, "Refugees and immigrants, how to prevent a disaster?" *Nezavisimaya Gazeta* (January 12, 1994).

12 The treaty between Moscow and Tbilisi that legalized the Russian military presence in Georgia has been strongly criticized in the Duma and in the mass media for this reason. See A. Arbatov, "Grand politics or petty game," *Moscow News*, no. 6 (1994); and "The statement of the state Duma Committee on the CIS – On the treaty between Russia and Georgia," *Nezavisimaya Gazeta* (February 24, 1994).

13 In January 1994, local authorities in Riga, Latvia provocatively arrested two Russian generals. Immediately the Commander-in-Chief of the military district put all his (Russian) troops on alert. Other examples could be cited, and specialists fear that more may come in the future.

14 See the interview with General Leonid Ivashov, Secretary of the Defense Ministers' Council of the CIS, *Nezavisimaya Gazeta* (May 17, 1994).

15 "Moscow has no intention of following the West's advice," *Segodnya* (Moscow) (February 1, 1994).

16 A. Migranyan, "Russia and the near abroad," *Nezavisimaya Gazeta* (January 12, 1994).

17 "The basic principles of Russia's military doctrine," *Izvestia* (November 18, 1993).

18 See, for example, I. Serebyakov, "Russia's military doctrine," and V. Tsygichko, "What kind of army do we need?" *Nezavisimaya Gazeta* (April 13, 1994).

19 Here and throughout this chapter, I refer to "Europe" meaning the portion of

Europe that lies to the west of the former Soviet territory. Of course, an important part of Russia also lies within Europe. The majority of the Russian population lives to the west of the Urals, and that region also is the "ancient Russia," the original homeland of the Russian people. Western readers must keep in mind that no Russian will accept the idea that "Europe," in the general sense of the word, is something that does not include Russia.

20 In this context it might be added that the Russian public as well as the Russian intelligentsia tends to resent any implication from other countries that Russia is to blame for all the ills of communism and the Soviet era. On the contrary, Russians typically believe that their country suffered worst of all from the evils of communism.

21 Pavel Grachev, "Military doctrine and the security of Russia," *Nezavisimaya Gazeta* (June 9, 1994). See also the interview with M. Kolesnikov, Head of the General Staff, Ministry of Defense: "Real reduction of the army is carried out ahead of schedule," *Segodnya* (December 25, 1993).

22 "Perspectives on NATO expanding and Russia's interests," Summary of the Report Prepared by the External Intelligence Service, *Nezavisimaya Gazeta* (November 26, 1993). This report is often referred to in the West as the Primakov Report, after the head of the External Intelligence Service, Evgeny Primakov.

23 As the term is normally used, "peacekeeping" does not refer to actions, such as the military intervention in Chechnya, where the central government aims to restore its authority inside the territory of its country. This section is not intended to discuss the intervention in Chechnya.

24 As Moscow sees it, the general attitude in Western capitals is that no Western country and no Western organization wants to get entangled in the messy and distant conflicts in the former Soviet territory. At the same time, the West cannot declare openly that it is willing to turn responsibility for the region over to Moscow. The awkward result is that in general the West simply says and does nothing, which among other things denies Moscow the legitimacy it needs to act effectively. There is one recent exception to the foregoing. On July 21, 1994, the United Nations Security Council endorsed one Russian peacekeeping operation, already under way, in Georgia, and assigned UN monitors to observe.

25 Mikhail Karpov, "The triumph that never happened," *Nezavisimaya Gazeta* (December 3, 1994).

Part VI

Concluding observations

17

Concluding observations

Mark Kramer and Richard Smoke

The preceding chapters have offered assessments of security in Central and Eastern Europe as seen by the public and by policy experts in six countries. What overall picture emerges of security in the eastern half of Europe? What observations and generalizations might now be made, as one steps back from these individual chapters to survey the region as a whole? Naturally it is not our purpose in this final chapter to pass judgements where the preceding authors have presented conflicting viewpoints; in this book each chapter is allowed to speak for itself. As mentioned earlier, it is also not a goal of this book for any American authors to put forward prescriptions for policy, either for these countries or for the United States or the West. Instead this final chapter offers, by way of conclusion, analytical observations about the overall pattern and dynamics of security in the region. (In this chapter, as throughout the book, the observations apply to Central and Eastern Europe generally but not to the special problems of the Balkans or Caucasus.) Let us begin by observing three paradoxes.

Insecurity amidst few threats

One paradox lies in the fact that people feel so insecure in a situation that contains so few external threats. In all six countries surveyed here, insecurities are high. Yet with several minor exceptions discussed in a moment, in all six there is no sense of imminent threat from another country.

This paradox is evident both among the public and among policy specialists. The public in all six countries feel deeply insecure. In not one of these countries does the population in general feel secure about its country's situation. Yet in most of them, people do not believe that any country is threatening them. Meanwhile policy specialists in Central Europe say that their region is now a dangerous "security vacuum"; and specialists in Moscow believe that Russia is insecure. Yet in none of these countries do specialists identify any threat from another country. For both public and experts, today's Central and Eastern Europe presents a paradox of insecurity among few external threats.

The paradox is more vivid if one thinks back to the past – indeed to almost any period in the past. The Cold War included immense standing threats by two great blocs against each other. The great wars of th' _entury were preceded by periods of threat and threatening maneuvers. These periods, as well as the centuries past, were filled with threats by some country or alliance against another, threats that inspired the feelings of insecurity one would expect. In this historical light, today's Europe is extraordinary for its *absence* of threats. Indeed, it is hard to think of any other period in the last 300 years when there were almost no threats by any of the major countries of Europe against others. Even so, in today's Central and Eastern Europe, insecurities are remarkably high.

It is true that there are several minor exceptions to the general absence of threats. Some Hungarians feel a degree of threat from Serbia, or at least from the possibility that Hungary may somehow be dragged into a Balkans war.[1] Europeans in general feel a vague anxiety that the current fighting in the former Yugoslavia could escalate into a larger war. Almost everyone outside Russia feels a potential threat from imperialist and ultra-nationalist forces in Moscow, and these misgivings have increased as a result of Russia's violent intervention in Chechnya.[2] Even so, there is no sense that an expansionist threat to Central Europe from Russia is likely in the near term. The outlook among specialists in Ukraine is slightly more pessimistic, and indeed, the closest thing to a serious external threat in Central and Eastern Europe may be the danger of spillover from trouble in Ukraine, perhaps from an explosion in the Crimea. The various national groups in Crimea do feel threatened, each by the other and by the great outside forces that might intervene. But even this threat, though quite real, is localized. The possibility of a large war between Ukraine and Moscow is almost entirely dismissed on both sides, at least for now. Thus the general paradox in Central and Eastern Europe remains. Most countries and peoples in the region see no imminent threat from any neighbor, yet insecurity is strikingly high.

Of course the paradox has its explanation, which has been offered at various points in these chapters. The insecurity stems from the fact that these countries are all now genuinely independent, fully sovereign, and compelled to cope with a very unfamiliar situation. In particular, all these countries have abandoned a social system that they found to be unworkable and intolerable, and all of them, with the partial exception of Ukraine, now find themselves in the throes of a great transition toward something very different, with which they have almost no experience. Thus the insecurity, as many authors here have said, is chiefly internal. In the early 1990s these countries have put behind them a system that they were accustomed to operating, but did not want, and are trying painfully to create something they want, but are not at all accustomed to operating.

Even as we understand this, we nonetheless may remark at the paradox of insecurity in the midst of almost no external threats or enemies. It is well worth noticing if only for one reason: supposing threats do appear? If the level of insecurity is already so high, even in so pacific an environment, how high might it rise if threats do emerge? How high might it rise if events in Moscow take a disastrous turn for the worse?

Central Europe and NATO

A second paradox concerns the chief point of contention between the Central Europeans and the Russians, namely, whether the Central European states will be admitted into NATO. The chief security goal of all the Visegrad countries is membership in NATO, but that goal has been strongly opposed by the Russians. The paradox lies in the fact that the Central Europeans' and Russians' desires are deeply at odds, yet the issue does not need to be resolved by any specific time.

The Russian government has done all it can to prevent NATO from moving its borders further eastward, that is, nearer to Russia. Russian leaders have spoken often against any enlargement of NATO "at Russia's expense," meaning an enlargement that does not include Russia also.[3] Again in December 1994, Russian President Boris Yeltsin warned that supporters of NATO's expansion were "sowing the seeds of mistrust" and "threatening to plunge Europe into a cold peace." Rightly or wrongly, most NATO governments have been deeply concerned about the impact in Russia of admitting the Visegrad countries into NATO. In particular, Western leaders want to avoid giving ammunition to the virulently anti-democratic forces in Russia, who are the elements most hostile to NATO.[4]

Moscow's stance, and the implicit endorsement of it by most NATO governments, create a basic conflict with the goals of the Visegrad countries. The Central European states are determined to join the Western alliance as soon as possible, while the Russian government is just as determined to prevent them from doing so. Barring a drastic change in the position of one side or the other, which at present seems remote, the stalemate is bound to continue.

The paradox is that, although the conflict appears fundamental, there is no particular time by which it must be resolved. There is no deadline for the Central European states to become, or fail to become, members of NATO.[5] Hence, there is no urgency for the issue to be confronted by the West (unless there is a disastrous turn of events in Moscow). Europe finds itself in an odd situation in which, on the one hand, the goals of the Visegrad countries clash with the position of Russia, but on the other hand, the clash does not have to be faced at any specific moment.

In these circumstances, the natural course of action, at least for the West, has been delay. No one wants a crisis and a crisis might well erupt if the issue were to be forced. The natural result has been that in any particular year, the West judges that *this* year is not the time to press the question. Of course the same is also true the following year, and so on.

As the issue is put off, the West predictably has sought other devices to mollify Central European concerns. Most specialists judge the Partnership for Peace (PfP) to be, at root, a NATO device to placate the Central Europeans for a time. Although NATO decided, at its December 1994 meeting, to create within one year a plan to expand the alliance, the "plan" does not need to include any specific dates for action. The core issue may continue to be postponed, either until there is a change in Moscow's attitudes favorable for the Central Europeans, or until some unpredictable set of events forces the issue.

The security vacuum

There is a third paradox worth noting in the security constellation of Central and Eastern Europe. This one is related to both of the previous paradoxes. It concerns the "security vacuum" in the region.

There may be no pronouncement about security in the eastern half of Europe made more frequently in the 1990s than the statement that there is a "security vacuum" there. References to the security vacuum recur constantly among policy analysts and even in many official statements in most of the countries located between NATO and Russia. Certainly the security vacuum is a staple, nearly a cliché, in commentaries from all four of the Central European countries discussed in this book and also in Ukrainian commentaries.

To some extent, of course, a security vacuum does exist. For decades, all these countries were either members of the Warsaw Treaty Organization or constituent republics of the Soviet Union. Those highly organized structures have vanished and have been replaced with nothing. In that sense the vacuum is real. Nonetheless there is a paradox in the security vacuum idea.

The paradox lies, again, in the fact that all the states in the region face no imminent threats or enemies, aside from the minor exceptions mentioned earlier. No country perceives any enemies nearby and no country regards itself as the enemy of some other country. Thus a basic paradox of today's Europe is that many countries say they are living in a "security vacuum" at the same moment that in fact they are threatened by nobody and do not even anticipate any near-term threats.

This observation must not be misinterpreted as implying that the security vacuum is an illusion or that the status quo should be seen as satisfactory. That is not the implication. Rather, two truths need to be kept in mind at once here, for this is a true paradox. The security vacuum is real and worrisome; and yet simultaneously there are no serious external threats, at least for the present.

Because there are no threats at present, the security vacuum may continue for some time. In spite of how intolerable or impossible the security vacuum might sometimes be described, it has endured for some years now and it may endure for some years further. Only if serious threats or hostilities emerge will the security vacuum really become intolerable.

A secondary reason that the security vacuum is not intolerable is that some nascent elements of security, which might be likened to a partial and "phantom" structure, do exist. NACC and the Partnership for Peace create relationships with NATO that to some extent shape expectations, and may constrain some countries' behavior. The same applies to the "associate partnership" status in the Western European Union given to the Visegrad countries, Romania, Bulgaria and the three Baltic states, in May 1994. Moreover, nobody wishes to be provocative toward Moscow, which surely constrains behavior. In addition, the Central European countries are all applicants to become members of the EU, and this ambition greatly constrains and shapes their behavior, just as their behavior has already been affected by their successful efforts to join the Council of Europe. These factors do not add up to an adequate security system and do not fill the vacuum, but they do provide some forces for stability. Without such factors the situation in the eastern half of Europe might be much more unstable than it is.

The determining role of Moscow's policy

Nearly all of the observations made here require a major precondition to be met, namely, relative moderation in the behavior of Moscow. During the first half of the 1990s, Russia has posed only an indirect threat to Ukraine and no threat at all to the other countries discussed in this book. That posture may continue or it may change.

Every chapter in this book written by policy specialists has pointed out the critical place of Russia in the affairs of Central and Eastern Europe. The public throughout the region also is deeply aware of it. It is obvious that Russia by itself can go far toward generating security or insecurity in Central and Eastern Europe. Through the time period embraced by this book, the relatively democratic government of Boris Yeltsin has generally played a constructive and peaceful role in Europe.

A different government, perhaps adopting quite different policies, may emerge in Moscow in the future. It is also possible that a government still headed by Boris Yeltsin could adopt quite different policies, as the intervention in Chechnya suggests. Of course many degrees of greater assertiveness are possible. A sharply aggressive policy is, unfortunately, one of the real possibilities. Especially since the strong showing of Zhirinovsky in the December 1993 elections, a turn toward a far more aggressive Russian policy in the future has seemed all too possible. Such a course could alter the security situation in Europe completely. It also would explode all three of the paradoxes discussed above.

Naturally such a course would create real threats. Instead of a paradox of insecurity amidst little threat, we would see much heightened insecurity resulting from definite threats. A sense of insecurity and threat would certainly not be limited to Ukraine. The Central European states would surely feel threatened as well by an aggressive Moscow, even if specific Russian demands or actions against them did not appear immediately.

A shift by Moscow toward a considerably more aggressive posture would very probably bring to the surface the underlying clash of goals regarding the Central Europeans' membership in NATO. On the one hand, a more aggressive Russia would be even more sharply opposed. On the other, the Central Europeans' sense of heightened threat would, from their viewpoint, make NATO membership even more urgent. Thus the present luxury of being able to postpone the issue might vanish. The combination of the Central Europeans' anxious need for prompt acceptance and Moscow's sharper insistence on definite rejection could force the issue. Depending on the circumstances, it conceivably could force the issue to the point of a European crisis.

As this suggests, a considerably more aggressive posture by Moscow would also accentuate the existing security vacuum. It would be accentuated not only for the Central European countries discussed here, but also for other countries in the region that presently feel they are living in a security vacuum, and perhaps most of all for Ukraine. Instead of being worrisome but tolerable, the security vacuum would become genuinely unbearable.

Thus the various paradoxes of security in the region that can be observed today all require that Russian policy continue along the lines it did in the first half of the 1990s. A sharply more aggressive Russian policy would demolish them, and would create a new, more dangerous situation in Central and Eastern Europe.

The critical place of Ukraine

If Moscow should turn toward a more aggressive course, what would be its aims? Russia could seek to regain control in one or more of the Baltic states and/or the Transcaucasus republics. Sooner or later, more aggressive Russian leaders would undoubtedly try to regain control of Ukraine. An independent Ukraine is already seen by the assertive, imperial-minded elements in Moscow as barely tolerable, and also as nonsensical. These elements believe that recovering control of Ukraine would be nothing more than restoring the natural and inevitable territory of historic Russia.

For Ukraine to lose its effective independence and become a satrapy of Moscow would have enormous significance. Such an outcome would not simply mean that one country had come under Moscow's control. For this particular country to do so would greatly change the whole constellation of security and power in the eastern half of Europe. As Leonid Kistersky points out in his chapter, it would create a different Europe. The meaning would be so great for two sets of reasons.

One set of reasons involves the direct consequences, particularly for the neighboring Central European countries. Poland, Slovakia and Hungary border on Ukraine directly (as does Romania). Russian power would march up to their very frontiers. Even if Russian military forces were not assembled there immediately, they could be at any moment thereafter, thus creating an enormous threat. The general absence of threat in these countries is attributable to the fact that they border on a country, Ukraine, which is both a friendly state with no expansionist impulses, and a state that separates them from Russia. That reality, and the unthreatened feeling that accompanies it, would be lost.

The other set of reasons involves the relationship between "restoring the empire" and democracy in Russia itself. The two are almost surely incompatible. A Russia that is bent on regaining control of most or all of the territories of the former Soviet Union, or has successfully done so, would be a Russia that had fallen far from its democratic aspirations of the early 1990s. (Conversely, a Russia that continues to make progress toward real democracy is unlikely to make a serious bid to restore its empire.) The reason is not that it is impossible for Russians to want democracy sincerely and also to wish to regain control of the former Soviet territory. As goals, both can be entertained by the same person. The reason, rather, is that there are many peoples across the former Soviet territory, including many Ukrainians, who do not want to be ruled from Moscow. If *these* people are to have democracy, they will choose to be ruled by governments of their own creation, as Ukrainians did for example in 1991. Any reimposition of imperial control from Moscow would contradict and nullify democracy for Ukrainians, and for various other peoples in the former Soviet territory. A regime that is nullifying democracy in the "near abroad" cannot simultaneously be very democratic in Russia itself.[6]

Thus the independence, or not, of Ukraine is of special importance for European security, both because of what it means for Central Europe directly and for what it tells Europe and the world about Russia. Ukraine will remain independent only as long as Russia holds its imperial impulses in check, and only a democratic Russia is likely to do so.[7]

This assessment of the significance of Ukrainian independence, in its most basic respects, may be complicated by two factors. One is that "imperial" control from Moscow is not something that will either exist or not. Russian control of Ukraine can be a matter of degree. For instance, Ukraine might not be formally stripped of its flag and other symbols of its statehood. For Moscow's purposes it might suffice for the country to assume a status resembling the status that Tajikistan has now, namely, a land that formally is an independent country but in fact is wholly dependent on Moscow and does its bidding. Ukraine in the future may have an ambiguous status, which in turn could have more ambiguous implications for European security.

Another potential complication is that Ukraine could split. A substantial portion of it, doubtless including the Crimea and eastern Ukraine, and perhaps other parts, might come under Russian control. Western Ukraine might retain considerable independence. Since anti-Russian feeling is strongest in western Ukraine, Moscow might accept some arrangement in which that region enjoyed considerable autonomy (conceivably, even independent statehood), so long as Russia enjoyed control of the Crimea and eastern Ukraine. Such an outcome would also have ambiguous implications for European security.

Mutual security between Europe and Russia

No matter what kind of regime and what character of foreign policy Russia may have in the coming years, Russia will inevitably remain one of the greatest factors shaping the security situation of all other countries in the eastern half of Europe. The sheer size and the actual and potential military power of Russia ensure its central role in the calculations of all others. This will remain true even if Moscow has a peaceful and non-imperial policy over the coming years, because a change in regime and policy could come later. It will be a long time before Europe can count on a stable and mature democracy in Russia, the way Europe has come to count on a stable and mature democracy in Germany. Until democracy is firmly entrenched in Russia, all states in the region must take into account the possibility of a shift to a much more assertive and perhaps imperial policy.

No matter what direction events take in Moscow, Russia's security relationship with Europe as a whole will continue to play a leading role on Western Europe's security agenda as well. The idea of some kind of "partnership" with a democratic Russia has been voiced in Western Europe (and by extension, the United States) ever since the end of the Soviet Union. One aspect of it materialized in June 1994 when Russia tentatively agreed to join the NATO Partnership for Peace program (a decision that was reversed, at least temporarily, in December 1994). But both Russia and the West have had continuing difficulty defining their overall relationship fully or firmly, again partly because of uncertainties about the future complexion of the Russian government. In addition, the West is still busy deciding how to structure its own security affairs. For example, the relationship between NATO, the EU and the WEU have also been evolving. This has been another factor complicating the development of a firm, well-defined relationship with Russia. For several reasons, then, considerable ambiguity and perhaps some confusion are likely to characterize the relationship between Europe and Russia for some time to come. The ambiguity and confusion will be increased by the fact that the Central European states would like to be part of "Europe" immediately, before the new relationship between Europe and Russia is forged. Precisely that is opposed by strong forces in Russia.

One area where the relationship between Europe and Russia needs particularly to be clarified and developed is their mutual security vis-à-vis each other. Here there is an important principle to be observed. If the security of either vis-à-vis the other is to be enhanced, each needs to pay considerable attention to the legitimate security needs of the other. In his chapter on Poland's policy, Janusz Stefanowicz raises this theme. His remarks, presented mainly in terms of policy for Poland and for Central Europe, apply also to the larger terms of European–Russian relations. Professor Stefanowicz emphasizes that Poland does not seek a security arrangement that works against Russia, but one in which Central Europe and Russia enjoy a relationship of mutual security, with neither threatened by the other.

This theme applies with equal validity to the relationship between Europe as a whole and Russia, especially insofar as Moscow is genuinely seeking security and not aggrandizement in its relationship with Europe. In a situation where both Europe and Russia are greatly interested in finding security for *themselves* vis-à-vis one another, they will make the most progress toward it by developing, in cooperation with each other, a relationship that creates security for *both*.[8]

Barring the emergence of a severe Russian threat to Europe, this theme will be applicable across a wide spectrum of situations that may appear in the coming years in European–Russian affairs. The exact form that arrangements and understandings for mutual security take will depend considerably on the character and intentions of the Russian government. With a democratic, peaceful regime it may take one form; with a moderately assertive regime it will need to take another. But the search for mutual security would be rendered difficult or irrelevant only if the most aggressive kind of Russian regime appears, one with sharply expansionist ambitions in Europe.

Ambiguous situations like this one, in which powerful states or alliances are uncertain about their relationship and the mere existence and power of each can be seen as a threat by the other, have arisen before in history. (A recent example is provided by the last years of the Cold War.) In such situations, policy-makers on either side usually have a range of options. They can emphasize what may be called a "unilateral" approach to security, or a mutual approach as recommended here.[9] A unilateral approach by one side stresses the measures that it can take, by itself, to improve its own security, paying little attention to the effects on other states. To mention one example among many possibilities, one side may choose to enlarge its military forces and to modernize its weapons. A "mutual security" approach stresses the arrangements and understandings that the two sides can create together to improve the security of both. One example among other possibilities might be that they agree to deploy only small forces in the geographical areas near each other, and to deploy those forces in a way that emphasizes defensive capabilities over offensive capabilities. In practice, policy-makers rarely adopt either the unilateral or the mutual approach to the complete exclusion of the other.[10] But they do have a range of choice of where to place their emphases.

Both Europe and Russia are likely to find, in the mid-1990s and beyond, that each can improve its security by working with the other to improve the mutual security of both. Such an effort will not produce perfect security, but it is likely to produce greater security than the unilateral approach. Even a Russia that is asserting itself strongly *inside* the former Soviet territory may have hardly any expansionist desires further west, and may be seeking chiefly *security*, not aggrandizement, in its relationship with Central and Western Europe. Even in this case, Central and Western Europe (as well as Russia) are likely to have the most to gain by seeking a relationship of mutual security. Only an extremist of the Zhirinovsky type, with strong ambitions of westward expansion, would make such a relationship impossible, and would compel Europe and the West to look (unilaterally) to their own defense.

Concluding remarks

Security in Central and Eastern Europe is a troubled subject. By 1995 it also has become a difficult and complex subject, in ways no one had imagined or could have imagined in the late 1980s. The eastern half of Europe has become a region in which the security and geopolitical relationships of many countries intersect in complicated ways. The numerous nationalities and ethnic groups overlap in many places, yielding a maze of interstate as well as intrastate nationality relations. Throughout the region, current leaders and would-be leaders are operating in a political environment far more fluid than anything known for decades. Often they try to manipulate the uncertain and shifting "rules of the game" for their own advantage, and sometimes in ways that intentionally or unintentionally reduce someone else's security. Security problems are more difficult because whole societies are in the midst of changing their character in basic ways.

In Central Europe, the "triple transformation" is difficult and painful, but progress is being made that offers promise for the future. In Russia the democratic and market transformation is at an earlier stage, and in Ukraine it has barely begun. The Russian economy is still deeply troubled and the Ukrainian economy was practically in free-fall between 1991 and 1994, due to lack of any meaningful reform. In such a situation there is a real question of how much these societies will want, or be able, to pursue genuine democratic and market reforms. In the next few years, the Visegrad countries and the former Soviet republics of Eastern Europe may increasingly come to seem two distinct regions.

A shift in course in Russia toward more authoritarian policies at home and abroad could easily have the result that in the mid-1990s and beyond, security in the region may become an even more troubled subject. In 1993 and 1994, demands for a more assertive role for Russia were voiced with increasing frequency in some quarters in Moscow. Even some of the more liberal Russian politicans seemed to agree that Russia should be more assertive in the "near abroad" at least, and perhaps also beyond. The bloody conflict in Chechnya, though confined to the Russian Federation, showed what the consequence of such a trend could be. If the trend in Russian policy takes an even more ominous turn, the landscape will darken. Ukraine's independence will be gravely threatened and the security of the Central Europeans may be rendered more precarious.

This more threatening future will also go far to revive the idea, among ordinary citizens in Europe as well as among specialists and governments, that security in Europe must again be thought of in terms of an "East" and a "West." After the dramatic changes of 1989, and after the replacement of the Soviet Union with democratically minded new countries, this way of thinking was consigned to the past. Europeans in all parts of Europe, as well as Americans, hoped and believed that Europe could now be thought of as one whole, and would only become more so with the passing of years. But if Russia acts in ways that everyone else considers aggressive, that optimistic vision will have to be put aside, at least for some time. Security affairs in Europe will tend to become defined once more in terms of an axis with two poles, eastern and western. It will be the greatest paradox of all, and certainly an unhappy paradox, if so soon after Europe seemed whole, its affairs once again are divided, and the security of many countries again revolves around a dominating East–West axis.

Notes

1 Some Hungarians also perceive a threat from Romania. In an interview with the Budapest daily *Uj Demokrata* (December 15, 1994, pp. 8–9), Erno Raffay, a former top official in the Hungarian defense ministry, warned that Serbia, Romania and Slovakia might form a military alliance against Hungary.
2 See, for example, Jiri Doubrava, "Postsovetska dvanactka ma propletenez koreny," *Mlada fronta dnes* (Prague) (December 31, 1994), p. 10.
3 Although President Yeltsin seemed to drop his objections to the Visegrad states' membership in NATO when he visited Poland in August 1993, he quickly reversed himself.

It is difficult to tell how deep-rooted Russia's opposition to the expansion of NATO really is. An example from the past may be instructive here. From the mid-1950s until the late 1980s, Western analysts assumed that the Soviet Union would never permit Germany to be reunified as a non-communist state. But soon after the East German communist regime collapsed in late 1989, Soviet leaders realized they could no longer forestall eventual German reunification, and the main question was whether Moscow would permit a united Germany to be a member of NATO. Many Western observers, once again, predicted that no such thing would ever be tolerable for the Soviet leadership. Those predictions corresponded with Moscow's own position in the first half of 1990. Soviet officials spoke vehemently against the prospect of a reunified Germany within NATO, warning that such a development would be "unacceptable to the Soviet people" and would inspire a hardline backlash. But in July 1990, Gorbachev agreed that Germany could remain a member of NATO after reunification, and the thing that had long seemed inconceivable was suddenly regarded as perfectly routine. The public in the Soviet Union took hardly any notice of the outcome, and no hardline backlash resulted. It is conceivable that Russia's opposition to the entry of the Visegrad states into NATO could prove equally ephemeral. No doubt, the admission of the Central European states would be accompanied by vigorous protests from the Russian government, but the whole matter might then quickly fade. This would be more likely if NATO accompanied the Visegrad countries' entry with a "mutual security" approach (discussed below) to Russia.

4   This is not to say that concerns about Moscow's reaction are the only reason that NATO has refused to grant full membership to the Central European countries, but they clearly are the dominant reason, irrespective of what may be said for public consumption.

5   It should be noted, however, that advocates of expanding NATO have argued that the alliance must act as soon as possible because further delay is likely to have a highly adverse effect on the policy debate in Moscow. Delay may allow hardline opponents of NATO to consolidate their influence by undercutting moderate officials who would be willing to accept NATO's expansion under certain conditions. See, for example, Zbigniew Brzezinski, "A plan for Europe," *Foreign Affairs*, 74 (1) (January–February 1995).

6   It would be possible for a future regime in Moscow that controlled most or all of the former Soviet territory to retain some of the trappings and forms of democracy, such as an elected Parliament. This would not mean that the regime was really democratic, nor trying to become so. It might also be possible for such a Russia to include some other, quite limited, elements of democracy in certain respects.

7   This is not to imply that democracy in Russia requires that all groups within the Russian Federation who want to secede be permitted to do so. The claim here applies only to countries that once were constituent republics of the Soviet Union. What the limits of national self-determination will be in a democratic Russia is a topic for a different essay.

8   To advance the theme, this paragraph and the next three put to one side the question what exactly "Europe" may prove to mean in this context.

9   The topic of the mutual and unilateral approaches to security is a vast subject in its own right, one that cannot be explored and developed in this book. In the late Cold War years, a large body of literature grew up on mutual or, as it was

often called then, "common" security. Naturally at that time the specific subject was mutual security between the Cold War adversaries. But the general conceptual approach, and even some of the specific policy ideas, developed then may turn out to have relevance between Russia and Europe in the mid-1990s and later.

For a book-length analysis of theory and policy for mutual security, from the viewpoint of the last Cold War years, see Richard Smoke and Andrei Kortunov, eds., *Mutual Security* (New York: St Martin's Press, 1991). Mutual security, which in the sense used here involves a certain kind of bipolar relationship, should not be confused with collective security, which is multilateral.

10 One must reach to extremes to find a historical example of a leader who did pursue unilateral security to the complete exclusion of mutual security. One example is the policy of Hitler in the late 1930s and early 1940s.

Appendices

Appendix 1

Public attitudes in Eastern and Western Germany

Helmut Jung and Roland Silberreiss   FRANKFURT AND DRESDEN

Introduction

Germany is a country quite different from all the others discussed in this book. It is a Western country. It has a highly developed market economy. For decades it has been a stable, mature democracy. Germany's position in Europe and the world is also radically different from that of all other countries discussed in this book. Germany is one of the leaders of the European Union, and Germany's security has been guaranteed for decades by NATO. Germany is one of the wealthiest countries on earth, and in many respects one of the most influential. The overall situation of Germany is so different from the situation of all other countries discussed here that few direct comparisons are appropriate.

In spite of these things, there are two reasons why attention to attitudes held by the public in Germany have a useful place in this book. One is that German public attitudes on certain specific questions could be of relevance to the Central and Eastern European countries discussed here. The other is that until quite recently, an important part of Germany was itself part of "Eastern Europe." The German Democratic Republic, one of the countries of the Warsaw Treaty Organization, came to an end, and its constituent states joined the Federal Republic of Germany, only in 1990 at the end of the Cold War. Cultures change slowly, and many political and other attitudes found in the eastern part of Germany today are greatly shaped by the fact that the people living there have lived most of their lives in the former "East Germany."

For these reasons, we offer in this appendix a brief assessment of current public attitudes in Germany. Naturally we emphasize attitudes involving external and especially security affairs, with special attention to differences between eastern and western Germans. We begin with some differences that have developed gradually, at a basic level, over the decades.

Basic viewpoints in western and eastern Germany

Western Germany, with some initial help from the United States, Britain and France, recovered relatively quickly from the devastation of World War II. With its democratic system and its free, liberal and social economy, the Federal Republic of Germany soon prospered. The *Wirtschaftswunder* (economic miracle) of the immediate postwar decades was admired by the whole world. Since then, most political, social and economic developments in the Federal Republic have been quite similar to those of other Western industrial societies.

In international affairs, however, Western Germany found itself in a specific geographical position and heir to a specific history. On the one hand, Western Germany responded by joining NATO in the 1950s and by developing substantial military forces (the *Bundeswehr*) committed to the Alliance. Germany also took a leading role, along with France, in the development of the European Community. In most other respects, the West German people and their political leaders tried to stay away from international and world affairs, especially politico-military affairs. The combination of this reticence and the ever-growing prosperity had definite results. The West German self-consciousness focused on economic affairs, the sciences, culture and sports. In security and politico-military affairs, the Federal Republic fundamentally followed the lead of NATO and was careful to take few independent initiatives. In some ways, West Germany lived in a kind of "splendid isolation" for more than forty years.

In East Germany the development was very different. After the war, the USSR was not able and also not willing to help East Germany to recover. War devastation remained for a long time and the economy, which became thoroughly integrated into the planned Soviet system, grew only slowly. Any impulse toward democracy or toward any independent economic system was cut off immediately. Riots in 1953 were put down forcibly. Year after year East Germans left for the West, and finally to stop them the regime had to put up the Wall in Berlin in 1961. East Germany lived in another kind of isolation, certainly not splendid, for decades. For the people, life under centralized control led to a psychology of dependence on authority, and to a lack of autonomy and initiative in work and in other spheres of life. East Germans were able to watch West German television, and they became very aware of the tangible differences between the two Germanies. However, on television they saw the wealth of West Germany but not the hard work that generated it. After the fall of the iron curtain and the reunification of the country, they hoped quickly to become just as prosperous, with the help of their brothers and sisters in the West.

After a short honeymoon period, frustration began growing rapidly in both parts of the country. The western Germans grew frustrated because they felt the eastern Germans wanted too much, too quickly, without working for it. The eastern Germans grew frustrated because they suddenly discovered disadvantages of the new political and economic system that they had not expected, and because they did not immediately become as prosperous as the westerners. They also felt the "wessies" (westerners) to be arrogant and dominating. The western Germans felt the "ossies" (easterners) to be lazy and demanding. The recession, which grew serious in Germany in 1993, made things more difficult for both.

In spite of many cultural similarities between eastern and western Germans, which were not eradicated by the four decades living in different systems, many cultural and psychological differences developed in that time also. It now is clear to everyone that these differences will not quickly vanish. The eastern and western parts of the country will remain distinctly different for some time to come. We turn now to more specific attitudes in both parts of the country.[1]

Insecurities about internal matters

In both eastern and western Germany, the public's main feelings of insecurity involve domestic, not international affairs.[2] Although this is true of all the other countries discussed in this book also, the domestic insecurities in Germany are naturally somewhat different. Germany is in an entirely different political and economic position. The country as a whole is not in the process of becoming a democracy, but already is one. And while the country experienced economic difficulties, mainly during 1993 due to the recession, its overall economic situation is, of course, greatly different. In the spring of 1994, Germany reemerged from recession and its economic prospects improved.

Even so there have been, and still are, feelings of economic insecurity in eastern Germany which are not completely different from the economic insecurities that people feel in the neighboring lands to the east and southeast. Eastern Germany is also going through the transition from a socialist to a market economy, and some of the pains involved, such as high unemployment, are similar. However, the economic anxieties of eastern Germans are not as deep as among the neighbors. Eastern Germany is receiving an immense flow of funds from western Germany; there is not remotely any analogy for the neighbors. And people in the eastern part of the country know that they are now part of a strong and much larger economy, that of the whole Germany, in which they feel some confidence.

There is a substantial difference in the economic concerns between eastern and western Germans, which is easy to understand. Western Germans fear mainly that they may have to give up some of the wealth already gained. Eastern Germans fear that they will not soon gain the economic status they want. For the one, there is a risk of losing some of a happy status quo; for the other, the status quo is completely unsatisfactory and there is a risk of failing to rise out of it.

Germans feel some other insecurities in their internal affairs that are roughly similar in the two parts of the country, and also are roughly similar to certain insecurities felt among the eastern neighbors. One is anxiety about a rising rate of crime. In Germany, concern about crime includes concern about the use of drugs. In the public's view, the growing crime is partly the work of mafias from Eastern Europe, previously unknown.

A second anxiety is that social disorder, already visible to some degree, may increase. In both parts of Germany, one symptom of social disorder often mentioned by the public is skinheads. Skinheads exist also in the neighboring countries and are likewise mentioned there as a worrisome symptom. In eastern Germany, the anxiety about possible social disorder is considerably stronger than in western Germany. Eastern Germans worry about a possibility of mass public riots; few western Germans do. Eastern Germans feel that this danger is most likely if high unemployment lasts a long time.

Insecurities about external non-military dangers

Germans in both parts of the country also feel certain insecurities about dangers from the east that are similar to insecurities felt in the neighboring countries. Germans feel concern about possible ecological dangers, especially from the nuclear power plants in the eastern countries. There is widespread awareness in both parts of Germany that many nuclear power plants, built in the Soviet era in the eastern countries, are unsafe. People feel that the quality of maintenance and security for these plants also has decreased, due to the bad economic situation in these countries. In addition, the public in western Germany has become aware that some plants of the Chernobyl type are located in eastern Germany, so emotionally, "Chernobyl got closer." People also do not dismiss entirely the possibility that in some future war on the territory of the former Soviet Union, nuclear weapons might possibly be used. The radiation from this could affect Germany in ways similar to radiation from a nuclear power plant disaster.

Anxieties about environmental dangers other than nuclear ones are also significant. In the last several years, the media in Germany have published more and more details about environmental problems and damage in the countries to the east. Concerns in Germany have been sharpened because of some major accidents that occurred in the chemical industry in Germany itself around the same time.

In both parts of Germany, the predominant external threat that people fear is the arrival of refugees and migrants. This has been the leading anxiety among Germans, regarding external risks, for years. In the early 1990s, Germany was receiving more asylum-seekers than any other Western

European country. A change in the asylum law in 1993 reduced the inflow of asylum-seekers, which in turn has led to some reduction in the salience of this issue for the public. However, the public in both parts of Germany think a problem of excessive asylum-seekers still exists and that the politicians could do more. A more basic change in the asylum law would require a major amendment to the constitution, which would require a two-thirds majority in the Bundestag and thus the agreement of both major political parties.

Underneath the concern about the present situation involving migrants and environmental dangers lies an anxiety about the future. In both parts of Germany, people have a sense that Eastern Europe, especially the countries of the former Soviet Union, may be sliding into chaos. Growing chaos in the east could take forms of political, social, economic, environmental and probably also military chaos. A chaotic situation in the east in the future could generate new problems involving migrants and environmental hazards, and also other problems. There is a not very specific, but continuing and broad, anxiety that future chaos in the east would probably have negative consequences for Germany.

Since growing crime is seen partly as an international problem, we have mentioned four areas in which Germans in both parts of the country feel some external threat: the inflow of migrants, nuclear power plants, other environmental dangers and crime. All four are non-military in character.

In both eastern and western Germany, the public feels practically no military threat to Germany at all. Certainly people see none at present, and most do not anticipate any military threat in the future.

The rise in nationalist feelings

Because of its unique history, attitudes in Germany toward the rise of nationalist feelings in Europe are complex, and differ by generation. The strongest attitude is a feeling, which is shared across generations and in all parts of the country, that the rise of nationalism is something to be observed carefully. Eastern as well as western Germans regard this phenomenon as one of the most dangerous in contemporary Europe.

In both parts of Germany, the public generally feel that rising nationalism is something found elsewhere in Europe, and that there is little nationalist feeling to be found among the German population as a whole. Most people also say they themselves do not feel it.

In elections held in 1992 at the state (*lander*) level, right-wing parties gained somewhat. Afterwards the public felt that most of their increased support represented only a protest vote and was not really motivated by racism or nationalism. In the next couple of years, the public felt that the modest support for these parties (in total 5 percent to 10 percent of the electorate) to be a normal pathology of modern industrialized countries undergoing rapid social change.³ In the Federal elections held in October 1994, support for the rightist parties fell. None achieved a single seat in the Federal Parliament.⁴

The public in Germany are much more concerned about the violence committed by right-wing extremists, including skinheads, who may also use nationalist slogans. But people generally feel that this violence is a specific phenomenon limited to a fringe of society; people feel it is not the same as the rising nationalism to be found among large parts of the public in some other countries. Germans, like Poles, Hungarians and other Central Europeans, believe that the rising nationalism in Central and Eastern Europe is largely a product of maneuvers by politicians.

The dominant attitude in Germany remains, as it long has been, that nationalist feelings among Germans would be inappropriate due to the history of the 1930s and 1940s, and also that this is so universally recognized among Germans that in fact nationalism is impossible. Of course Germans are proud of their economic success and social achievements, but they always try to avoid any statements or behavior that, from the viewpoint of other nations, could be regarded as nationalistic.

Underneath this attitude a second one is growing. Mainly it is felt by the increasing number of Germans who were not yet born in 1945. Many of them feel that there is nothing to be ashamed of *now*. These people feel that Germany is a good country and that by this time there is no longer reason to suppress one's natural pride in one's country.

Borders

The general public in both parts of Germany has no interest at all in any change in Germany's borders, to the point that the public regards this topic as not even worth discussing. Contrary to some anxieties sometimes expressed elsewhere, the German public is not interested in Germany regaining Kaliningrad.

In Germany there are some relatively small social clubs made up of German families who lost their lands in the east when the German–Polish border was moved westward at the end of World War II. These clubs talk about "regaining the lost lands." The general public dismisses this idea as quite irrelevant, even when people know about these clubs (many do not).

German military forces

After the catastrophe of World War II, the public in western Germany were trained for four decades to believe that there was only one possible legitimate reason for Germany to have any military forces. That reason was to defend Germany, with the NATO allies, against an attack by the Warsaw

Pact. This meant that the end of the Warsaw Pact caused a crisis in legitimacy for the *Bundeswehr*. For many western Germans, the end of any military threat meant automatically that Germany no longer needs any military forces. Some people feel that the *Bundeswehr* could be made into an emergency-response force, for coping with floods, big fires and other civil emergencies.

The possibility of Germany participating in United Nations blue-helmet missions introduced a new dimension into this question. At first, only a minority of the public accepted that blue-helmet missions could also be a legitimate role for the *Bundeswehr*. The majority rejected this role too. Attitudes are now shifting. In 1993, Germany sent a small force for a period of time to join the UN operation in Somalia. The German force did not fight and engaged only in humanitarian work. Since then, the former majority that considered blue-helmet missions illegitimate has been shrinking and those who consider such missions legitimate for German forces has been growing. Some people are also prepared to give consideration to German forces taking part in other missions. Of course the defense of Germany would still be regarded as legitimate, but since people see no military threat this is felt to be not relevant.[5]

Meanwhile, eastern Germans have a quite different viewpoint on the whole topic. Most eastern Germans regard it as only natural and normal that any country has a military force. Hence eastern Germans often take it for granted that Germany should have its *Bundeswehr*.

The net result of all these factors is that attitudes in Germany about German military forces are unstable as well as complicated. Attitudes are in transition, and it seems unlikely that a consensus will form for some years.

Perceptions of the east and southeast

The public in Germany feel a mixture of fatalism and anxiety about the two big countries of the former Soviet Union, Russia and Ukraine. People feel both that there may be much to be concerned about, and that there is not a great deal that Germany or Europe can do. The general sense that these countries are sliding into chaos has already been discussed.

Russia is seen as a giant country, full of many cultures and ethnic groups. As Germans see it, Russia has huge, nearly unresolvable economic problems, but has many technological capacities also. There is public anxiety that the disorder in Russia could deepen into riots, violent struggles, perhaps some kind of disintegration of the country, and possibly outright civil war.[6] After the December 1993 elections which brought Zhirinovsky to prominence, the public in Germany also grew concerned about the possibility of a hyper-nationalist and aggressive government in power in Moscow. In the period following the elections, Zhirinovsky's threats against

Germany were widely mentioned in German televison and newspapers, and therefore much of the public became aware of them. However, a Russia ruled by Zhirinovsky or someone like him is only a hypothetical possibility for the future, which may not occur, and Germans generally continue to feel that there is no actual military threat from Russia.

Germans know much less about Ukraine than about Russia. Ukraine is generally thought of as the granary of the former Soviet Union. The public does know that there has been conflict between Russia and Ukraine, and are concerned that there may be more.

It is noteworthy in this book to mention that the public in Germany generally are not greatly interested in Poland, Hungary and the Czech and Slovak Republics. Although some German businesses are active in these countries, the public as a whole pay little attention to them. The public feel that their main path in the future, toward democracy, market economies and links with Western Europe, seems clear. The German public have no particular concerns about these countries.

There is a strong difference between eastern and western Germans, not in their judgements about Russia, Poland and these other countries, but in how much people feel they know about them. Eastern Germans feel that they are far more familiar with these lands (except perhaps Ukraine) than western Germans are. This sense of familiarity is based on the reality that during the long Soviet era, many eastern Germans traveled in these countries, both on business and on their holidays.

The public in both parts of Germany feel a degree of fatalism about the Balkan area. Especially the poorest countries (sometimes called "alms house" countries) such as Albania, Bulgaria and Romania are seen as places where wars could arise in the future that probably cannot be prevented.

The public feel a strong frustration that apparently no mechanisms seem to be available to stop the war in the former Yugoslavia. People feel that the efforts of individual countries, of the EU, of NATO and of the UN have all failed. Interestingly, the OSCE as a potential tool has been almost entirely forgotten by the public.

For obvious historical reasons, the public in Germany strongly oppose including German troops as peacekeepers anywhere in the Balkans (or any place else that Nazi forces occupied during World War II). Incidentally, the public in both parts of Germany feel with absolute clarity that only the United Nations can legitimately authorize peacekeeping missions, in any part of the world. Once the UN has approved (that is, legitimized) an international action, the public are not much interested in whether the action is carried out by UN forces directly or by another entity (for instance, NATO aircraft in the former Yugoslav area) acting under the authority of the UN.[7]

NATO and the US troops in Germany

There is no topic involving external affairs where the attitudes of eastern and western Germans are more different than in their attitudes toward NATO and the presence of US military forces in Germany.

In eastern Germany, a considerable part of the public perceives both NATO and the US troops in terms of the role they played during the Cold War. Most eastern Germans acknowledge that NATO and the US forces helped preserve peace and security in Europe at that time. But with the Cold War's end, many eastern Germans feel that arrangements that were based on the Cold War should naturally be terminated. They see NATO as an institution parallel to the Warsaw Treaty Organization, and since the WTO has been dissolved, of course NATO should be also. The American troops should depart from Germany and Europe, which should manage security affairs without any non-European participants. Some people suggest that perhaps NATO could be turned into some kind of non-military, strictly political, organization.

Although these attitudes are widely prevalent in eastern Germany, they are held in many cases without much emotional heat. There are no US military bases or forces in the eastern part of the country, so eastern Germans do not often encounter American military people. There are many other issues, almost entirely domestic ones, that arouse stronger feelings among most eastern Germans than anything involving NATO or US troops.

In eastern Germany, a portion of the public also believes that the real reason for the presence of US troops in Europe is to protect and advance American capitalist interests. Of course this idea was taught by the East German state for decades.

Attitudes in western Germany are quite different, and also are ambivalent and complicated. At the outset it should be said that in western Germany also, this topic is not a politically "hot" one. The public in western Germany feel that the country is quite secure militarily. People feel so partly because they see no enemies on the horizon. But they also feel so because in the back of their minds they are still relying on NATO. It is noteworthy that for many, this source of the general feeling of security is partly unconscious. Others explicitly name NATO as one reason why military threats to Germany scarcely exist. Since there is no threat, there is general agreement that the number of American troops can be significantly reduced. Whether they should be reduced to zero is another question.

A part of the western German public would prefer to substitute a strictly European security system for the alliance with the United States. As such a system forms, the American troops would naturally go home. However, there is doubt whether such a system could be effective without the nuclear protection of the United States (in which case, some American forces in

Europe might be needed after all). As a further complication, there is a vague feeling among western Germans that in any case, the US may lose interest in Europe and withdraw all its forces, for financial reasons and to concentrate on internal American troubles.

Another part of the public in western Germany would prefer that a modest number of American troops remain in Germany for a while yet, from anxiety about possible authoritarian developments in the east. Some people would like a few troops to stay indefinitely, as a symbol of close Euro-American bonds and also of the long-term trend toward global integration.

There are also other, mixed feelings in western Germany. Some people feel that the presence of any foreign troops is abnormal and that they should leave. Others believe that the departure of the American troops would mean a loss in jobs held by Germans (in shops and restaurants in the areas of the US bases, for example). Some people see the Americans simply as a familiar, friendly presence that will be missed if the troops leave.

Concluding remarks: a basic German attitude in this period

Since 1990, Germans in both the western and eastern parts of the country have been greatly preoccupied with the enormous challenges of reunifying the country, which effectively means rebuilding and transforming eastern Germany in a number of ways simultaneously. Furthermore, in 1993 and early 1994 the German economy found itself in one of the two worst recessions that the country has experienced since 1945. The recession meant that rebuilding eastern Germany, plus meeting other social needs, created more strain than otherwise would have been felt. The net result, from an international viewpoint, has been that Germans have been deeply preoccupied with their internal affairs. Of course Germans remain profoundly involved in innumerable ways with the European Union. But in nearly all other respects, German society at present does not wish to give much attention to the outside world.

A metaphor can capture this basic feeling. In the early 1990s, the western and eastern Germans have been like a honeymoon couple in the world hotel. The honeymoon may have turned sour fairly soon, but the couple have remained preoccupied with each other. They have wanted to stay in their room, and they have kept a "do not disturb" sign on the door.

Notes

1   The conclusions reported here are based partly on focus group reseach conducted by BASIS Research for the Security for Europe Project in 1992 and 1993, and partly on other ongoing research by BASIS Research, including a monthly sociopolitical survey, the *Trendmonitor*. National elections were held in

Germany in October 1994, as mentioned again later. Foreign and security issues did not play a significant role in those elections.

2   BASIS Research publishes a monthly survey, the *Trendmonitor*, that asks the public, among other things, what the most important political problems in Germany are. Throughout the first half of the 1990s, the list of problems identified by the public has been strongly dominated by internal issues.

3   This evaluation by the German public emerged clearly from focus groups held by the Security for Europe Project.

4   The vote for the Republican Party, the principal party of the extreme right, fell to 1.9 percent. Chancellor Helmut Kohl and the coalition of parties that had formed the previous government were reelected by the extremely thin majority of four parliamentary seats. A primary factor in their reelection was the strong recovery of the economy during 1994. As noted, issues of foreign and security policy did not play a significant role in the October 1994 elections.

 During 1994 the public's perception of economic recovery was striking. During January, February and March, less than 20 percent of the public evaluated Germany's economic situation as "good or very good." From August through the rest of the year, the proportion evaluating the economic situation so varied between 32 percent and 36 percent – that is, nearly double. From the *Trendmonitor* (BASIS Research), monthly.

5   For the period discussed in this book, there also was a constitutional question whether Germany may legally send troops abroad. In July 1994, the Constitutional Court ruled that Germany may legally do so with the approval of a simple majority of the Parliament.

6   The German public felt this anxiety long before the December 1994 Russian military intervention in Chechnya and subsequent events. This anxiety emerged clearly, for instance, in focus groups held by the Security for Europe Project as early as 1992.

7   These attitudes are very similar to ones held in the Central European countries. In Ukraine there is a broadly similar feeling, less clearly defined and less deeply felt.

Appendix 2

Synopsis of arms control agreements

This appendix briefly surveys the most significant East–West arms control agreements applying to Europe, reached in the late 1980s and 1990 as part of the Cold War's end, and reached in the early 1990s in its aftermath. A short summary is also provided of the START Agreements, which are significant for Ukraine and Russia.

East–West agreements in Europe in the late 1980s

As part of their goal to end the Cold War, Mikhail Gorbachev and Eduard Shevardnadze reached a series of arms control agreements with the West in the late 1980s. A long-stalled negotiation about nuclear weapons in Europe was resumed and completed. The Intermediate Nuclear Forces (INF) Treaty of late 1987 removed one entire class of these weapons from European territory (although many other nuclear weapons remained there). The weapons removed were ballistic or cruise missiles of ranges between 1,000 and 5,500 kilometers, and also other missiles with a range between 500 and 1,000 kilometers. A total of 1,846 Soviet and 846 American missiles were eliminated. British and French nuclear forces were not affected by the INF Treaty, and neither were nuclear weapons carried on American aircraft stationed in Europe.

Fresh negotiations were also begun about conventional forces, which had been a topic of desultory and fruitless talks for a long time. The new talks on Conventional Forces in Europe opened in Vienna in March 1989. In these CFE negotiations (as in the INF talks) the Soviet Union made concessions that no Soviet government before Gorbachev would have considered. By late the following year the two sides had agreed on ceilings for numbers of conventional weapons in five categories: tanks, artillery, armored combat vehicles, combat aircraft and attack helicopters. Overall ceilings applied to NATO and the WTO states and to the whole territory from the Atlantic to the Urals; sub-ceilings applied to various smaller geographic zones in Europe. Although both sides retained huge forces even afterwards, the CFE did achieve real reductions (mainly on the Soviet side). It also helped to create momentum toward reductions and withdrawals, which continued later as Soviet forces withdrew from Central Europe and the United States reduced its forces in Western Europe.

In the late 1980s, progress was also made in other spheres of arms control, at a pace that was very rapid by Cold War standards. Back in 1975, all the countries of Europe, including the neutral states as well as all countries in the two alliances (including the United States and Canada) had created the Conference on Security and Cooperation in Europe, or CSCE. The Conference was held in Helsinki, Finland, and the main resulting document was called the Helsinki Final Act. It was agreed to hold a second, "review conference" later, which turned into a regular series of conferences. The Helsinki Final Act also included a "basket" of human rights provisions, which became a principal basis in the following years for human rights appeals by dissidents in the communist countries. In addition, the Final Act included the first of what later would become many "confidence- and security-building measures."

These measures, generally called "csbm's" by specialists, potentially can include a wide variety of steps by which a country or alliance can gain confidence that a potentially hostile neighbor is not preparing any threatening actions. For example, csbm's can place limits on the number of troops that can participate in one country's military exercises, require notification in advance of when and where military exercises will be held, and allow the other side to send observers to watch them. Other csbm's can provide other ways that each side can observe and verify the other's military activities, and thus gain confidence that it knows what the other side is doing with its military forces. The ability of each side to observe the other's military behavior is called "transparency."

In 1984, CSCE launched a new set of negotiations, often called "the Stockholm talks," to try to establish further csbm's. After difficult negotiations, an agreement was successfully reached in September 1986, after Gorbachev had come to power in Moscow. For the first time, the USSR agreed to a continuing obligation to allow foreign observers to observe large military maneuvers inside Soviet territory. (Previously the Soviets had allowed observers on a few occasions at their own choice.) The new agreement also strengthened the csbm "regime" in other ways.

As the Cold War in Europe continued to wind down thereafter, new negotiations were opened, in March 1989 in Vienna, on a new and more extensive set of csbm's. An agreement, called the "Vienna Document 1990" was reached by the autumn of that year.

The Paris Conference

In November 1990, a grand summit conference was held in Paris, attended by the heads of state of all the CSCE countries. Several items were on the agenda, which collectively resolved various arms control questions and attempted to set the stage for new and more peaceful relations in Europe. The Paris Conference is sometimes considered the symbolic end of the East–West confrontation in Europe, although for practical purposes the confrontation had ended already.

The Paris Conference proclaimed a "Charter of Paris for a New Europe," promising further development of peace and security in Europe and greater cooperation among the CSCE states on a wide range of matters.

In addition, the CFE Treaty was formally signed during the conference, and the new csbm agreement was formally endorsed. It was also agreed that the CSCE would be strengthened by giving it a permanent secretariat (to be located in Prague), a Conflict Prevention Center (to be located in Vienna) and an Office on Free Elections (to be located in Warsaw). Over the next several years, however, the secretariat and these centers were not very active. The Warsaw office has since been renamed the "CSCE Office for Democratic Institutions and Human Rights," and the secretariat is now located in Vienna as well as Prague.

Further agreements of the early 1990s

In 1992, a further csbm agreement was reached, amplifying the 1990 csbm regime. The "Vienna Document 1992" was completed at the end of February of that year.

The collapse of the Soviet Union at the end of 1991 and the appearance of new states on its territory made it necessary to make a modification in the CFE Treaty, which had specified limits for various categories of *Soviet* conventional weapons. Accordingly, a new agreement was prepared, to distribute the former limits among eight of the successor states of the USSR lying west of the Urals. (The Baltic states were not included.)

In addition, by this time negotiators were able to agree on limiting personnel as well as weapons. An agreement, called "CFE 1A," was reached that set ceilings on military personnel in Europe for all the countries that were part of CFE. Forces that were limited included those of the European NATO countries, the American and Canadian forces in Europe, the national forces of the former WTO countries of Central Europe, and the forces of the same eight Soviet successor states. Naturally American and Canadian forces in North America or elsewhere, and Russian forces east of the Urals, were not included, just as the original CFE had not included military equipment outside Europe.

In 1993, after the division of Czechoslovakia, a further minor modification to the CFE agreements endorsed the division of Czechoslovakia's military forces and assets that the Czechs and Slovaks had agreed upon, namely a two-to-one ratio transferred to the Czech and Slovak Republics respectively.

The Helsinki and Budapest CSCE summits

The Paris CSCE summit had decided that another CSCE summit would be held every two years. The heads of state of all the CSCE countries met in Helsinki in July 1992.

This new summit had several purposes. The csbm agreement just reached in Vienna was endorsed by the heads of state. All the CSCE states who were also part of CFE also met in an "extraordinary" CFE session to formally approve and sign the CFE 1A agreement, and the agreement distributing the formerly Soviet military equipment.

In addition, the Helsinki summit created a new office, the CSCE High Commissioner for National Minorities. The main task of the High Commissioner is to engage in informal mediation on minorities issues. In addition, if an issue is found to be "of grave concern," the High Commissioner may issue an "early warning" of a threat to peace and security. The High Commissioner may not become involved in cases where armed conflict has already broken out.

The Helsinki summit also created a new institution, the CSCE Forum for Security Cooperation, which began meeting in Vienna in September 1992. It has two main "tracks," a security dialogue for informal and wide-ranging discussions, and a negotiation forum for more formal negotiation of specific issues. A basic purpose behind the new Forum was to establish a generally agreed principle that henceforward, all European arms control would be conducted under the aegis of CSCE.

The next summit of CSCE was held in Budapest in December 1994. It was agreed that CSCE would conduct a peacekeeping operation in Nagorno-Karabakh, where Armenia and Azerbaijan had been fighting for years. This represented the first time that CSCE had authorized or conducted any specific peacekeeping operation, although the principle of peacekeeping under CSCE authority had been agreed before. It was also at the Budapest summit that the name of CSCE was changed to the Organization for Security and Cooperation in Europe (OSCE).

START and strategic weapons

Although the Strategic Arms Reduction Talks (START) and resulting agreements involve intercontinental weapons, they also are relevant to

European affairs because Russia and Ukraine are directly involved. These and related strategic developments may be very briefly summarized as follows.

Almost ten years after the first START negotiations were begun, a START I agreement was finally signed, on July 31, 1991 in Moscow. START I was a highly complex agreement; a full description is not possible here. In essence, START I reduced the strategic, long-range nuclear forces that the United States and USSR kept aimed at each other, to between half and two-thirds of their previous size. Various ceilings were placed on intercontinental ballistic missiles (ICBMs), on submarine-launched ballistic missiles (SLBMs), and on cruise missiles and other nuclear warheads carried by bomber aircraft. START I was signed between the United States and the *Soviet Union*; the view of it subsequently taken in Ukraine is discussed in chapter 14.

In September 1991, the United States took some additional steps unilaterally, the most important being that strategic weapons would be taken off "alert" status and short-range nuclear weapons abroad would be returned to US territory. Washington hoped that Moscow would respond quickly with similar measures, by-passing any time-consuming formal negotiations, and Gorbachev quickly did.

In the sphere of strategic weapons, as in the sphere of European conventional weapons, the collapse of the USSR necessitated some modification of the START I agreement. Strategic nuclear weapons, formerly Soviet, now were located on the territories of four post-Soviet countries, Russia, Belarus, Ukraine and Kazakhstan. In principle at least, the position of the last three of these at the time was that the weapons on their territories would be turned over to Russia. Negotiators from all four countries met with American negotiators in May 1992 in Lisbon, Portugal, and agreed upon a so-called "Lisbon Protocol" to the START I agreement. The main purposes of the Lisbon Protocol were two. All four of the former Soviet countries formally agreed to assume the obligations of the START I agreement that previously had applied to the USSR. Secondly, Ukraine, Belarus and Kazakhstan committed themselves to joining the Nuclear Non-Proliferation Treaty (NPT) "as soon as possible" as non-nuclear states. This provision, in Article 5 of the Protocol, meant not only that all nuclear weapons would be removed from the territories of these three countries, but also that they committed themselves not to manufacture nuclear weapons themselves in the future.

Subsequently, the Lisbon Protocol was ratified reasonably promptly by the United States and by all of the formerly Soviet countries except Ukraine. The Parliament of Ukraine postponed ratification, then "ratified" it with many conditions attached in November 1993, as described in chapter 14. On February 3, 1994, the Ukrainian Parliament fully ratified START I and lifted its reservations to the Lisbon Protocol. On November 16, 1994, the Ukrainian Parliament fully ratified the NPT, as also described in chapter 14.

On January 2, 1993, a START II agreement was signed between the United States and Russia. START II like START I was a complicated agreement. In essence, START II considerably lowers the ceiling on the numbers of ICBM and SLBM warheads, and of cruise missiles carried by bombers, that the US and Russia will be permitted to keep in their arsenals in the future. The START II reductions are to be carried out in two phases, with the second completed by January 1, 2003. In September 1994, Presidents Bill Clinton and Boris Yeltsin agreed at a summit meeting to speed the pace of dismantling and complete it sooner. However, dismantling cannot begin until the START II agreement is ratified by both sides, which cannot occur until START I comes into effect. It is widely believed that whether the START II agreement is fully carried out will depend upon the complete removal (or not) of the nuclear missiles in Ukraine (as well as Belarus and Kazakhstan), and of course upon whether all parties have carried out the START I provisions fully.

Appendix 3

The Security for Europe Project and acknowledgements

This book is based substantially on the Security for Europe Project, as mentioned in the preface, and also on additional research done by the individual authors. The Security for Europe Project was conducted in 1992 and 1993 by a partnership of fifteen research organizations. The additional research and writing by the chapter authors was done during 1994.

The Project was led by the Center for Foreign Policy Development (CFPD), a unit of the Thomas J. Watson Jr. Institute of International Studies at Brown University in the United States. Fourteen research organizations in Central and Eastern Europe participated in the project. The overall framework and goals of the project were established by the CFPD; the agenda of research questions was determined collectively by all the collaborating organizations.

The fourteen European organizations comprised two research organizations from each of seven countries. One research organization was a leading research institute on foreign and security policy affairs. (In Hungary, two such institutes participated at different times.) The other research organization was a leading institute or firm specializing in research and analysis of public opinion. The seven countries and the partner research organizations (both listed alphabetically) were as follows:

Czech Republic: AISA
Institute of International Relations

Germany: BASIS Research
Stiftung Wissenschaft und Politik

Hungary: Hungarian Institute for International Affairs (1992)
Institute for Strategic and Defense Studies (1993)
Median Opinion and Market Research

Poland:	Centrum Badania Opinii Spoleczney (CBOS) Institute of Political Studies, Polish Academy of Sciences
Russia:	Center for European Studies of the Institute of the USA and Canada, Russian Academy of Sciences Center for International Projects
Slovakia:	AISA Institute for International Studies
Ukraine:	Ukrainian Center for International Security Studies Institute of Sociology of the Academy of Sciences of Ukraine

The CFPD expresses its cordial thanks to the European partners for their participation in the project.

In 1992, the project conducted research in a united Czechoslovakia and not in Ukraine. In 1993, Ukraine was added as a subject country and the two Ukrainian partners joined the project. Meanwhile the split of Czechoslovakia meant that research was conducted during 1993 in both the Czech and Slovak Republics. In this way, the total number of European partner organizations reached fourteen for the second year of the project.

In addition to these fourteen, three more organizations assisted in the Security for Europe Project in various ways. The CFPD gratefully acknowledges the following assistance. For more than two years, the Centre for Defence Studies at Kings College, London graciously supplied a European office and other support for the Americans involved in the project. The Institute for East–West Studies, headquartered in New York, supported several conferences at its European Studies Centre at Stirin, near Prague. In Ukraine, the International Institute on Global and Regional Security contributed analyses and seminars to the project during 1993.

The CFPD expresses its gratitude to four American funding organizations that generously supported the Security for Europe Project: the W. Alton Jones Foundation, the Joyce Mertz-Gilmore Foundation, the US Institute of Peace, and the Rockefeller Family and Associates. Additional support was provided by the European partners in the project from their own resources. Further support was provided by the Watson Institute at Brown University.

Six major conferences or meetings were held by the Security for Europe Project, as follows:

1 *July 1991*: Preliminary planning meeting. Stirin, Czechoslovakia. (Hosted by the Institute of East–West Studies.)
2 *January 1992*: Methodological workshop on public attitude assessment. Providence, RI, United States.

3   *March 1992*: Research planning meeting: development of first-year research agenda. Stirin, Czechoslovakia. (Hosted by the Institute of East–West Studies.)
4   *October 1992*: Mid-Project conference: Review of research results to date and development of second-year research agenda. Budapest, Hungary. (Hosted by the Hungarian Institute of International Affairs.)
5   *July 1993*: Policy conference: Analysis of policy issues (with selected additional guests). Moscow, Russia. (Hosted by the Center for International Projects.)
6   *December 1993*: Final conference: Announcement and assessment of project results (with selected additional guests). Warsaw, Poland. (Hosted by the Institute of Political Studies, Polish Academy of Sciences.)

During 1994, research and writing of the chapters of this book was carried out by the authors, in close consultation with the book editor.

The Security for Europe Project released an *Interim Report* in December 1992 and a *Final Report* in December 1993. Both, and especially the *Final Report*, were distributed widely to various offices of governments, to research institutes, to academic organizations, to independent specialists and to the press in Europe and North America. In December 1993, press conferences were held in the capitals of all six of the Central and Eastern European countries discussed in this book to announce and disseminate the Project's *Final Report* to the media. Some press conferences were also held in these countries in December 1992 to disseminate the *Interim Report*.

The CFPD expresses special gratitude to the W. Alton Jones Foundation for an extraordinary supplemental grant that made possible the translation and publication of the *Final Report* in five languages: Czech, Hungarian, Polish, Russian and Ukrainian. Translations were prepared under the supervision of the Project partner organizations, who also disseminated the translated editions in all six participating countries. (The Czech edition was disseminated in Slovakia by the Slovak partners.) The translated editions were disseminated during the spring of 1994.

The Security for Europe Project was codirected at the CFPD by Richard Smoke and Jan Kalicki. The deputy Project director was Mark Kramer; Stephen Shenfield participated substantially in Project research. At one time or another three individuals served as Project coordinators at CFPD: Michael Song, Kathleen Walsh and Leslie Baxter.

Grateful acknowledgement is made to Stephen Shenfield for his preparation of the notes in this book that give public opinion data from Western sources, and for his similar contribution to both Project reports. The assistance of P. Terrence Hopmann in the preparation of appendix 2 is also acknowledged gratefully.

An Advisory Committee provided assistance in planning the project. Grateful appreciation is extended to its members: Lawrence Freedman, Alexander George, James Goodby, William Luers, Andrew Pierre and John Steinbruner. Helpful advice was also received at other times from Michael Clarke.

All the European authors of chapters in this book are senior members of the research staffs (and in many cases, the directors) of the Project partner organizations listed above, with the exception of the authors of chapter 14. Leonid Kistersky and Serhii Pirozhkov are senior members, not of the Project partner institute, but of the National Institute of Strategic Studies in Ukraine. During the academic year 1993–94, Leonid Kistersky was the E. L. Wiegand Distinguished Visiting Professor at the Watson Institute at Brown University.

Final editing of this volume was completed while the editor was a Fellow at the Center for Advanced Study in the Behavioral Sciences (Stanford, California). His work at that time was partially supported by National Science Foundation grant no. SBR-9022192.

Contributors

RICHARD SMOKE was Research Director of the Center for Foreign Policy Development, a unit of the Thomas J. Watson Jr. Institute of International Studies at Brown University in the United States, from 1984 to 1995. He was also Professor of Political Science at Brown University. He was codirector of the Security for Europe Project which formed the principal basis for this book. He was author or editor of numerous books and articles on topics in international relations, international peace and security, and American foreign and security policy.

MAGDA BOGUSZAKOVA is Director of Qualitative Research at AISA in the Czech Republic; IVAN GABAL was one of the founders of AISA. AISA is the leading public opinion research firm in the Czech Republic. Dr Boguszakova received her PhD from Charles University in Prague in 1984. Dr Gabal, a well-known authority on Czech and Central European public opinion, has been an advisor to President Vaclav Havel.

SVETOSLAV BOMBIK was the Director and principal founder of the Slovak Institute for International Studies. He died in a tragic automobile accident in January 1995. Prior to the creation of the Institute, Dr Bombik was a member of the diplomatic corps of the Foreign Ministry of Slovakia. Mr IVO SAMSON is a Research Associate of the same Institute. He has also been a member of the research staff at the Institute of Political Sciences of the Slovak Academy of Sciences; he is presently completing his doctoral degree.

YURI DAVYDOV has for many years been Head of the Center for European Studies of the Institute of the USA and Canada (ISKAN), an institute of the Russian Academy of Sciences. A leading Russian authority on European affairs and on Russian and Soviet policy toward Europe, he is the author of numerous books and articles in these fields.

MILOSLAV HAD and VLADIMIR HANDL are both senior researchers at the Institute of International Relations in Prague. Dr Had, who specializes in European security affairs and European integration, holds a PhD in History from the Czechoslovak Academy of Sciences. Dr Handl, who specializes in German and Czech foreign and security policy, holds his PhD in International Affairs from the Moscow State Institute of International Relations.

ENDRE HANN is founder and Managing Director of Median Opinion and Market Research, one of the leading public opinion research firms in Hungary. Dr Hann received his PhD in psychology from the Hungarian Academy of Sciences.

HELMUT JUNG was Managing Director of BASIS Research Gmbh, and ROLAND SILBERREISS was a Senior Researcher at BASIS, throughout the period of the Security for Europe Project. BASIS Research is a public opinion research firm with headquarters in Frankfurt and Dresden. Recently Dr Jung became Managing Director of the Sample Institut Gmbh, a similar firm with headquarters near Hamburg.

JAN KALICKI is Counselor and US–Russian Ombudsman in the Commerce Department of the United States Government. He writes in this volume in his private capacity; his chapter does not represent any official statement. Dr Kalicki was codirector of the Security for Europe Project. From 1991 through 1993, the principal period of project research, he was a Senior Vice-President at Lehman Brothers in New York, and Senior Advisor to the Center for Foreign Policy Development at Brown University.

LEONID KISTERSKY is a Leading Researcher, and SERHII PIROZHKOV is Director, of the National Institute for Strategic Studies in Kyiv, Ukraine. Dr Kistersky has held ministerial rank in the Ukrainian government, and was E. L. Wiegand Distinguished Visiting Professor at Brown University during the 1993–94 academic year. Dr Pirozhkov, an internationally recognized scholar in demography, is a Corresponding Member of the National Ukrainian Academy of Sciences.

TANYA KOSHECHKINA is Managing Director, and NIKOLAY CHURILOV is President, of SOCIS-GALLUP, a leading public opinion research firm in Ukraine. Previously both were members of the research staff of the Institute of Sociology of the Academy of Sciences of Ukraine.

MARK KRAMER is a Research Fellow of the Center for Foreign Policy Development at Brown University, and also a Fellow of the Russian Research Center at Harvard University. He holds a DPhil in International Relations from Balliol College, Oxford. He is the author of numerous articles on Soviet and Russian military and foreign policy, on US foreign policy, and on Soviet–East European relations.

JANOS MATUS was a senior research fellow at the Institute for Strategic and Defense Studies of the Hungarian Ministry of Defense during the time that he wrote his contribution to this book. Recently he became head of the office of international analysis and planning at the Ministry. From 1986 to 1993 he was a senior research fellow of the Hungarian Institute of International Affairs.

ANDREI MELVILLE is Director of the Center for International Projects, a research and consulting institute in Moscow which does public opinion research and analysis in addition to other work. Dr Melville is also Professor of Political Science and Chair of the Political Science Department at Moscow State Institute of International Relations.

PIOTR STARZYNSKI is Senior Researcher at CBOS, the Centrum Badania Opinii Spolecznej, one of the principal public opinion research firms in Poland. Mr Starzynski, who specializes in qualitative research and in public opinion on political affairs, received a masters degree in psychology from Warsaw University in 1986.

JANUSZ STEFANOWICZ is Professor in the Institute of Political Studies of the Polish Academy of Sciences. He specializes on Polish foreign and security policy, particularly for Europe. He was Poland's Ambassador to France from 1984 to 1989, and is author of some twenty books.

EVA TARACOVA is Manager, and STANISLAVA CHMELIKOVA is Director, of AISA Slovakia, the leading market and opinion research firm in Slovakia. Ms Taracova, who previously worked in international and public relations, became a partner in AISA in 1990, specializing in qualitative research. Ms Chmelikova has a degree in foreign trade from the Economics University in Bratislava and worked in foreign trade until she helped establish AISA in 1990.

Index

Note: 'n.' after a page reference indicates the number of a note on that page.